THE CLEANING OF PAINTINGS

A. National Gallery No. 1674, Rembrandt, 'Portrait of Jacob Trip', 130·5 × 95 cm. Detail during cleaning. The area in the centre is cleaned. The one on the left shows the dark varnish left untouched; on the right of the painting an uncleaned perpendicular strip shows the cloudiness of the varnish.

The
Cleaning of Paintings

Problems and Potentialities

by

HELMUT RUHEMANN

with bibliography and supplementary material
by
Joyce Plesters

and foreword by
Sir Philip Hendy

FREDERICK A. PRAEGER, *Publishers*

NEW YORK · WASHINGTON

BOOKS THAT MATTER

Published in the United States of America in 1968
by Frederick A. Praeger, Inc., Publishers
111 Fourth Avenue, New York, N.Y. 10003

© *1968 in London, England, by Helmut Ruhemann*

Library of Congress Catalog Card Number: 68–17958

Printed in Great Britain

To
the memory of my great teacher
M. J. FRIEDLÄNDER

'if it come to prohibiting, there is not aught more likely to be prohibited than truth itself, whose first appearance to our eyes bleared and dimmed with prejudice and custom is more unsightly and unplausible than many errors.'

MILTON: *Areopagitica*, 1644

Acknowledgements

To Sir Philip Hendy, the late Director of the National Gallery, and to Lord Robbins, the Chairman of its Board of Trustees, I owe a great debt of gratitude for the encouragement they have given me. Both have greatly improved my manuscript by their constructive criticism; and I am particularly grateful to them for their generous permission to reproduce numerous photographs (and texts) from the dossiers of the National Gallery.

Also for kindly allowing me to reproduce photographs of paintings in their Galleries I have to thank the Curators of the Glasgow Corporation Art Gallery (Colour Plate B), the National Gallery of Art, Washington (Plate 1), the Boston Museum of Fine Arts (Plate 2), the Alte Pinakothek, Munich (Plate 50), the Barber Institute, Birmingham (Plate 53), the City Art Gallery, York (Plates 80–83) and the Greater London Council as Trustee of the Iveagh Bequest, Kenwood (Plate 85).

The Editor of *Studies in Conservation*, Garry Thomson, and its printers, the Aberdeen University Press, have very kindly lent their blocks for Plates 55, 56, 59–64, 67 and 68. The blocks for the colour plate of the Glasgow Giorgione were generously lent by the publishers of the *Scottish Art Review*.

A special word of thanks is due to George Stout and his publishers, who have most generously permitted me to reprint long passages from his book *The Care of Pictures* (pages 99–103). For similar permission to include copyright material, I am indebted to the editor and publishers of *Studies in Conservation* (for extracts from various articles I originally wrote for that journal, here reprinted in the text and in Appendix D; and for the outline of the Murray Pease Report, also in Appendix D); to the author, Norman Brommelle, and the editor and publishers of *The Museums Journal* (for 'Controversy in 1846' reprinted in my Appendix D); and to Elizabeth Jones and her publishers (for the extract from *On Picture Varnishes and their Solvents* on page 205).

Mrs Vera Wilson, head of the Photographic Department of the National Gallery, and her able staff have earned my particular gratitude for the excellent photographs that form the greater part of my illustrations. Acknowledgements to other colleagues of mine figure in the text and bibliography.

Acknowledgements

I further wish to thank the friends who have provided useful criticism and information on the draft of my manuscript, particularly Guy Reed; and finally the publishers, especially Mr Richard de la Mare, for their helpfulness and patience, Mr David Bland for the typography and Mr Berthold Wolpe for the jacket design. I should also like to thank Mrs Herrmann for her very kind help in editing and arranging the text and the illustrations.

In a category on her own belongs my co-author, Joyce Plesters (Mrs N. S. Brommelle), who has organized and compiled the footnotes and the extensive bibliography, and written the greater part of it. And if there are in this book fewer errors than there might have been concerning scientific matters, it is largely due to Joyce Plesters' work.

Contents

CONTENTS

Illustrations

(N. G. = NATIONAL GALLERY)

COLOUR PLATES

MONOCHROME PLATES

Illustrations

Illustrations

Illustrations

Illustrations

LINE DIAGRAMS IN THE TEXT

Foreword

by SIR PHILIP HENDY

I can remember very well the summer, some forty years ago, when it was borne in upon me, with disturbing suddenness, that all the old pictures which I knew, in public collections or in private, would look more or less different if they were cleaned; that they would shed a common denominator which made them, whatever their differences in age or in temperament, 'old masters', that they would cease to appear to be the products of persons with a remote tranquillity unknown today who had used processes equally mysterious. I was perhaps unusually naïf, for I had been raised in the Wallace Collection and had not often been further than the National Gallery, where also the pictures were all decently covered with a glass. But my condition was then a common one, especially in England, where nothing was taught anywhere about the technique of earlier days unless it was in the studios of private restorers, where the secrets of a more or less hereditary craft were guarded jealously. There were the restorer-craftsmen in the British Museum and the Victoria and Albert, even at the Wallace Collection, where D. S. MacColl, to the discomfiture of many, initiated the restoration of French eighteenth-century furniture to its pristine brilliance; but what would now be called a conservation department for pictures did not exist in any of the English institutions.

In these picture-'restoring' was very largely a matter either of the tactful revival of old varnishes without much altering their colour or of 'blister-laying'. This is a process which needs explanation. Especially when their canvases have been lined or relined with aqueous adhesives or their panels submitted to the restraint of wooden 'cradles' and when their varnishes, which grow brittle with time, have a considerable admixture of oil — and these were regular practices — the paint-film on old pictures tends to detach itself in blisters as the supporting material expands and contracts with every change in the atmosphere. At certain seasons private restorers were kept almost continuously employed in public and private collections, making in these blisters constellations of punctures through which they could squirt (often unsuitable) adhesives under the paint-film, before they proceeded to iron it down. Fortunately blisters tend to come in the darker areas of a picture, where the paint is usually thinner and consequently less resistant to the drag of the embrittled varnish. The holes thus made could therefore be disguised — more easily under a reflecting glass — by painting them over with dark paint.

That summer I saw in quick succession the 'Madonna in Gloria' by Pietro Lorenzetti in the Uffizi Gallery in Florence and 'The Nativity' by Duccio (p. 35) in the Kaiser Friedrich Museum in Berlin (now in Washington), which had recently been completely cleaned and finished with a colourless varnish, a thing which had scarcely happened in any public gallery for a very long time. I did not know then that I owed half of this revelation to Helmut Ruhemann. I learned this a year or two later, when I became Curator of Paintings in the Boston Museum and wanted to rescue from obscurity in its depot Rogier van der Weyden's altarpiece from the Guild of St. Luke in Brussels. Enquiries among American colleagues concerning the best man to undertake work needing particular care and patience on a historic picture led again and again to Ruhemann, official restorer in Berlin. From the time that I caught up with the picture and introduced myself to Mr. Ruhemann in the studio of the Kaiser Friedrich Museum in 1930 or 1931 I began to learn things from him, and I am learning still. In 1933, returned to England, I invited him to stay with me; and, when he came, I successfully urged him to remain.

The England to which he came then was a quite different place from the England of today with regard to technical knowledge concerning old pictures and their conservation. The larger world, in this interval, has taken enormous strides forward, not merely in techniques, because technique is only the means to an end, but in consciousness of the whole vast field of conservation and the will to face the responsibilities and the problems of it. In this world the United Kingdom, which used to be well in the rear, has moved up into the van. It has been a general advance, led by art-historians at least in the case of paintings. But it was Helmut Ruhemann whom W. G. Constable brought in to lecture on technique in the newly founded Courtauld Institute, Helmut Ruhemann whom Kenneth Clark employed to clean pictures in a new campaign at the National Gallery.

He was a new kind of restorer, for he had no secrets and he had instead a longing to share his knowledge with everyone else who was interested. Before the war he was the leading light on picture-restoration in that pioneering body the International Museums Office. After the war he was one of the founding members of the International Institute for Conservation (I.C.C.). He loves to impart his skills, and is not happy without pupils. A goodly proportion of the finest restorers in this country have undergone the discipline of his studio and

Foreword

many of them have come to posts of public responsibility: Hans Schubart, Director of the Bristol Art Gallery; Norman Brommelle, Keeper of the Department of Conservation, Victoria and Albert Museum; Stefan Slabczynski, Chief Restorer at the Tate Gallery; Arthur Lucas, Chief Restorer at the National Gallery.

The principles which he will make plain in this book have always included the removal of all accretions which have come to obscure the original work of the artist and their replacement by clear and colourless varnishes which do not conceal the force and character of the artist's intentions. He is consequently not *persona grata* with those who are shocked by such revelations. But even these, if they knew of all the methods by which physical damage used to be done to pictures, would not withhold their gratitude for what he has accomplished in putting an end to them. An example is the electrically heated spatula by which wax-resin adhesives can often be pressed through the craquelure of the paint without any necessity of puncturing blisters. Patented, his invention might have brought him a steady income. Characteristically, he allowed the National Gallery to hand over a working model to the British Restorers Association. In the nearly twenty years that have ensued countless pictures must have been spared from the indignities which would otherwise have been their lot.

This is a small example of a great devotion, which has carried the author of the book which follows through experiences which might have embittered another man and has brought him into the haven of a fully earned international reputation. I have been an admiring witness of some of the tempests calmly surmounted, and count myself lucky to be associated with the book.

PHILIP HENDY
May, 1965

Introduction

This book relates how I began to clean and restore pictures, what came of it and what it has taught me, not only about restoring, but also about related matters of more general interest.

When I tried to clean a picture for the first time, I realized that I was literally groping in the dark, in accumulations of dark varnishes, and that I knew far too little of how and of what old paintings were made. So I set about exploring in order to learn how to clean. I soon found that cleaning and understanding are interdependent. On the one hand you must understand the construction of the different layers of a picture before you can clean it safely, while on the other hand it is impossible to study these properly without first removing the dirty, blind and darkened varnishes and the retouchings which so often hide too much of the original.

'Cleaning to explore' and 'exploring to clean' has had at least two positive results: it has made many pictures more enjoyable and it has made varnish removal safer than it used to be. It has also taught me a great deal about the way in which the old masters painted. In a later book I hope to go into further detail on ancient and modern painting methods, on questions concerning forgery and on the lessons a contemporary painter can learn from the great masters.

Of the picture restorer's many pursuits, cleaning is without doubt the most interesting and intriguing.

That is why I have chosen the word 'cleaning' for the title of this book, rather than 'restoring'. Another reason is that I have more to say about cleaning than about conserving and mending pictures. In this country, as it happens, the term 'picture cleaner' is almost synonymous with 'picture restorer' and this is well justified, for the less spectacular yet no less important part of restoration, the securing of flaking layers, the lining of canvases, the treatment of deteriorated panels and the retouching of gaps in the paint are closely bound up with the cleaning.

The word 'painting' in my title also needs explaining. I confine myself to *European easel painting* because I have too little practical experience of either

Introduction

Oriental paintings or murals, or for that matter of water-colour paintings or pastels.

I might have included these and other kindred fields by referring to existing books, adding here and there some points from my own experience. This would have resulted in a fuller treatise but I would have incurred the risk of taking over not only my predecessors' valid contributions but also any errors which they may have published. As it is, my mistakes will at least be entirely my own. I would rather give some picture of the kind of work I do than try to offer more than I can properly contribute. Nor shall I always pretend to be quite objective in my opinions. This is impossible, even in professional matters. Despite its slightly derogatory ring, I like the Spanish proverb, 'Each man's report upon the fair, Is coloured by his fortune there.' ('Cada uno cuenta de la feria segun le ha ido en ella.')[1] Others, moreover, may know more than I do of the facts, but cannot have of them quite my views and experience, whatever they may be worth.

All these reasons or pretexts for a partial book, partial in both senses of the word, apply of course only to my impressions and opinions. For the report on the work itself, cool impartiality is, naturally, imperative, and this I shall do my best to achieve in the technical chapters. I feel it must be left to the younger generation, bred to the scientific approach, to write the new orthodox text books on the restoration of pictures. There are several older publications on the subject in existence, some of them of high merit. Moreover, even the best and the most up-to-date processes are debatable and their value is extremely difficult to compare scientifically. Different methods may give just as good results or better than mine in different hands, and improved techniques or materials may exist still unknown to me. New ones are being developed continuously and published in the technical journals. And above all, the method is in the long run less decisive for the success of an operation than the experience, the skill and the principles of the person who is using it. The best tool is of little use in the wrong hands.

However, apart from the technical I shall also discuss aesthetic and ethical aspects of cleaning pictures. What I am attempting is not much more than an elaboration in book form of what the Exhibition of Cleaned Pictures at the National Gallery in 1947 and its Catalogue have set out to do: to allay certain misgivings by giving a straightforward account of the cleaner's work, of his problems and of the safeguards he applies to protect the pictures from any possible harm during their treatment.

That exhibition was an outcome of the controversies over the cleaning of pictures which have been going on in the press at intervals since 1936. The main issues involved have been lucidly and authoritatively dealt with by Philip Hendy

[1] Translation by Guy Reed.

in the Catalogue of that exhibition, as well as in his National Gallery reports of 1954, 1956 and 1962, and in scholarly papers on the literary sources concerning this subject by Denis Mahon and Joyce Plesters in *The Burlington Magazine*.[1]

Thus I need here only briefly recall the principal facts and add little comment of my own.

At the same time I have tried to answer some questions which many people interested in painting must have on the tips of their tongues. Among other problems I have discussed are: empirical and scientific data in methods of cleaning and restoration; thorough versus superficial cleaning; deceptive versus visible retouching, and other moral issues concerning the restorer's activities.

I have had the good fortune to spend the major part of my life in museums in the closest contact with the works of the great painters; and some of the most distinguished men in my own and related fields have been my teachers and friends. I should like it to be regarded as a tribute to them if I publish some of the countless notes that have accumulated in my drawers for these last forty-five years. Should they, in this form, prove at all useful the credit would be largely due to the illustrations, which the Trustees and the Director of the National Gallery have so generously allowed me to choose from the dossiers of the Restoration Department.

However I should like to make it quite clear that I am throughout writing, not on behalf of the National Gallery, but as a private person.

[1] Vol. CIV, November 1962, pp. 452–60 and 460–70 incl. See Bibliography, *Section 7* (26) and (28).

Part I

BACKGROUND

CHAPTER 1

Autobiographical and Historical Notes

In Chapter 2 I shall describe the orthodox way of becoming a picture restorer. The story of how I became one myself, through various hazards, can hardly serve as a model, but it may have some interest just because it was not the normal course.

At the turn of the century not many people had heard of picture restoring. In Germany, where I was born, there were few restorers; most of them still guarded their secrets carefully and taught them only to their sons. A number of important books on the subject existed (see Bibliography), but I did not know of them. My family had nothing to do with pictures, let alone their restoration. But as far back as I can remember, everybody at home and at school seemed to take it for granted that I was to become a painter.

When I was thirteen — much too early I now think — I was given regular painting lessons and at fourteen I had hardly any spontaneity left. At fifteen I began to earn money by painting portraits.

On the advice of Max Liebermann, who was in those days the almost undisputed leader of German Impressionist painters, I concentrated on drawing as soon as I left school.

At sixteen, I spent a long holiday in London, the London of horse-drawn buses and of elegant carriages parading up and down Park Lane. I naturally spent many hours at the National Gallery. The pictures which made the greatest impression on me were the 'Nativity' and the 'Baptism' by Piero della Francesca and the 'Woman Bathing' by Rembrandt. Little did I know then that one day I was to clean two of these masterpieces and would have the privilege of living in close contact with them for months on end.

After four years of assiduous drawing and painting at the Academies of Art at Karlsruhe and Munich, I went for two years to Paris, where I worked under Maurice Denis. I have never forgotten two excellent pieces of advice he gave me. One was: before starting a painting always make a rapid note, no bigger than a postcard, of the composition and the main colour scheme and never depart from this first fresh impression. The other was: always develop your drawing or painting evenly all over, so that if you had to stop for some reason, it would at any moment be balanced and in a way 'finished'.

I became intensely interested in the Impressionists, and later in Renoir, van Gogh and Cézanne.[1] Their daring and varied contributions seemed at that time all the more revolutionary, as most of the works of the great old masters in the museums were still covered with yellowed varnishes which obscured their colours and individuality and gave them all the same drab appearance.

After some years of painting landscapes, portraits and still life, I went in the early summer of 1914 to the South of France 'to follow in the footsteps of Cézanne and van Gogh', together with my friend Martin Bloch, now, alas, dead but celebrated by posthumous exhibitions as well as represented in a number of public galleries. I owe more to him than to any of my teachers. On an excursion to Spain, Martin and I were caught by the outbreak of the 1914–18 World War. Our efforts to get home failed and we were forced to stay in Spain throughout the war. At first I received a bursary from Germany — I was then still a promising young artist. When this lapsed I made my living by giving lessons in German and, after much travelling about, we settled in Madrid. It was a cold winter. We could not afford an expensive hotel or club, but found that the Prado Museum was beautifully heated. There we made ourselves comfortable from morning till dusk, painting copies, mostly from Tintoretto and El Greco. This proved, though I did not suspect it at the time, the first step towards my eventual profession.

I soon discovered how hopeless it was to attempt merely to imitate the surface of the painting and to try to match each tone directly, in one solid layer, with modern pigments. It gradually dawned on me that the old masters built up their works from within, while the average modern artist — from about the early nineteenth century onwards — rendered in one solid layer only the surface impression of what he saw.

I dimly guessed that there was more to the painting than just the top layer that was actually seen — or only half seen through the veil of dark varnish which then still covered nearly all the masterpieces in the museums. In 1916, like everybody else, including some of the great art historians, I was taken in by the discoloured varnish and copied it, assuming it to be part of the master's work and intention. The first copy I made was of a portrait by El Greco. It now forms a dark, flat patch on my wall. The brown varnish I used, to imitate the 'golden glow' on the original, has gone still darker in the meantime; and something else contributed to the darkening of my copy, namely that I painted directly on the

[1] H. Ruhemann, 'Methods of the Masters' (in 3 parts), *The Studio*, CXLV (1953).

dark ground, having failed to copy the light underpainting which I did not realize was below the top layer of the original. I did not then know of these subtleties.

So I began to read treatises by old masters on technique, in particular those of Pacheco and Cennino Cennini, and made friends with the restorers of the Prado, in order to learn from their practical experience more about the methods of the great painters.

In 1918, directly after the war, a boyhood friend of mine who had become an art dealer came to Madrid and saw my copies; from that moment he never ceased to pester and press me to become a restorer. For a long time I resisted, but in the end he succeeded in persuading me. When I eventually went home to Germany in 1919, the money I had earned in Spain by painting portraits soon melted away; inflation had already set in and by 1920 was in full swing.

One morning in 1921, a sum which the day before would have bought a grand piano just sufficed for a taxi ride. We became paupers overnight. I could not draw or paint as fast as my pictures sold — even they were of more lasting value than money. I did not learn how to raise my prices to keep pace with the devaluation of the currency. Fortunately we had a large flat and were able to let rooms to all sorts of foreigners with hard currency, and this kept our heads above water.

Among the things that maintained their value in the wild economic chaos of 1921 were Old Master paintings, just as they do in the present — so much slighter — inflation. My art dealer friend saw his opportunity — and incidentally my own — and practically forced me to deputize for his restorer, who had fallen ill. He brought me a picture, my first restoring job: nothing less than a Rubens. The job worried me so much that I went on restoring even in my dreams. When the work was finished the owners were satisfied and I was handsomely rewarded; but I was a nervous wreck and had to spend most of my fee at a sanatorium where I was sent in a hurry to recover!

As soon as I was again well enough I went back to restoring. There was no turning back now. Like almost everyone taking up restoration I had at first hoped to continue painting in my spare time, but soon I had none, and I realized that it was futile to hope to rise above the average as a restorer and as a painter at the same time. Either is a full life's work.

Now that, through a combination of circumstances, I had drifted into restoring, my main worry was that I had never had any specialized training for this profession. The little I had picked up at the Prado and from books did not count for much. At that time there were no schools for my new calling.

I can count myself extremely lucky that in my nerve-racking beginnings I had generous help from the very restorer whom I had tried to replace during his illness — William Suhr. He gave unselfish advice to his budding competitor. I mention his name here to record the debt of gratitude I owe him, since I can never repay it. In the 1920's he was called to the Detroit Museum in the U.S.A., where he soon made an international reputation.

My first patrons were pleased even with my earliest efforts, and soon I got plenty to do. For about ten years I worked for art dealers and private collectors.

Soon I had to train assistants. My large studio was crowded with more canvases and panels than I could cope with. Naturally I read all the books on the subject I could obtain, but I realized that they could not replace training and experience, and that only methods and recipes that one had tried oneself and tested for many years could be relied upon. It was a curious feeling to find myself teaching what I was still learning and, for that matter, I am still learning today.

I had not hoped that I would ever be able to catch up with, let alone outdo, the well-established restorers in Berlin. Hauser, the official restorer at the Kaiser Friedrich Museum, who had inherited a great reputation from his father, was ill; Suhr had gone and all the others do not seem to have offered much competition. Soon I was dealing not only with some of the finest pictures, but also with many of the worst preserved which were changing hands on the busy Berlin market. It was, I fear, not so much because I was particularly clever at curing and preserving them, as that I was able to make them look their best. I confess this with a mixture of pride and shame. With the same naive lack of inhibition I accepted all kinds of work thrust upon me. I mended small holes in the paintings, and large ones, and at times reconstructed sizeable missing parts of the composition. There was no time to ponder and hesitate. In those days I never seriously questioned the right of collectors and dealers to do what they liked with their pictures, and there was always the easy answer to any objection to extensive retouching: 'Put the picture under ultra-violet light and all the retouchings will show as dark spots.' Where I did draw the line was at signatures. I never retouched one, however genuine, but I must admit that I never removed a false one, except after special consultation with the owner. Only many years later did I learn by experience that the proper decision is sometimes rewarded by the reappearance of the genuine signature from under the false one.

I made several vows right at the beginning of my career: never to restore a fake, never to get involved in buying and selling pictures, never to write certificates of attribution and never to accept commissions on sales, though this is a legitimate and common practice among restorers.[1]

[1] In *Studies in Conservation*, IX, No. 3 (August 1964) *The Murray Pease Report* on Professional Standards and Procedures, p. 117. See also Appendix D, pp. 321–7.

1. Duccio, triptych 'Nativity', 43 × 43 cm., and 'The Prophets Josiah and Ezekiel', each 43 × 16 cm. Formerly at the Kaiser Friedrich Museum, Berlin, now in the National Gallery of Art, Washington, Andrew Mellon Collection. Under the Hitler regime the picture was exchanged for a Holbein. See p. 41.

2. Rogier van der Weyden, 'S. Luke drawing the Virgin', 54 × 43·5 cm. Museum of Fine Arts, Boston, Massachusetts. The cleaning of this picture led to its definite attribution to van der Weyden. See pp. 43–44.

3. National Gallery No. 654, Rogier van der Weyden, 'The Magdalen Reading', 61·5 × 54·5 cm. Before cleaning. A fragment had been turned into a complete picture by overpainting the background.

4. X-ray photograph of a detail, left of the Magdalen's head, taken before the cleaning carried out in 1956 by Norman Brommelle. It shows that drapery and a window exist beneath the overpainting.

5. The fragment after cleaning and restoring.

6. National Gallery No. 651, Bronzino, 'An Allegory', 146 × 116 cm. Ordinary photograph taken before the cleaning in 1958. For modesty's sake the veil on Venus' body and the sprig on Cupid's buttock had been added, probably between fifty and two hundred years after the original painting. See *The National Gallery 1659–1958*, pp. 70–71; and pp. 137–8 of this book.

7. The same picture, after cleaning, removal of the additions and restoring.

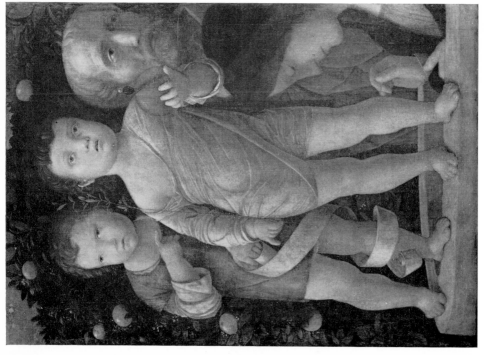

9. The same picture after restoration in 1946. The removal of the varnish and retouchings has restored some of the depth to the dark areas, the sewing hand with the proper forefinger, and the more subtle original folds. See p. 53.

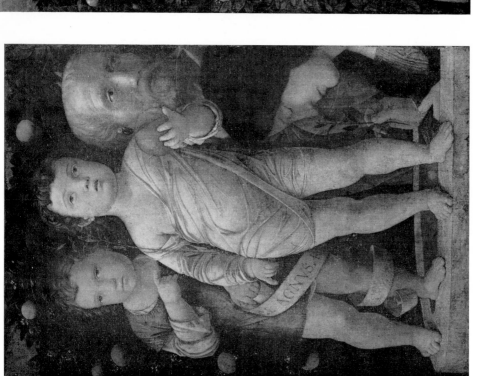

8. National Gallery No. 5641, Mantegna, 'The Holy Family with S. John', 71 × 50·5 cm. Before the cleaning in 1946, showing a typical nineteenth-century restoration: slightly darkened and cloudy varnish, a sprig added to the Virgin's hand and a joint too many to her forefinger. The abraded original lettering on the scroll and many of the folds had been reinforced by retouching. See p. 53.

Autobiographical and Historical Notes

Apart from the few self-imposed laws I mentioned, I did not have many qualms during the beginning of my free-lance work. A fuller sense of responsibility and reverence developed only later when I came to deal with the supreme master-pieces in the museums.

It has always been my dream to be able to dictate my own terms, particularly never to be hurried or to have to promise a definite date, and to be free to leave pictures as little 'finished' as I thought right. These dreams came true when, in 1929, I was made Chief Restorer of the Berlin State Galleries. It was actually Dr. Wilhelm von Bode, at that time Director of the Kaiser Friedrich Museum, who appointed me to this post on the very morning of the day he died.

Bode's successor was Dr. M. J. Friedländer. He was a most understanding and generous superior. In this, my first appointment, I had more liberty to do what I deemed right than as a free-lance. I was at last able to work without pressure and to begin a thorough study of the masters. It was only then that I realized the enormous difference in the responsibilities of a free-lance on the one hand, and a museum restorer on the other.

On one of the first pictures I restored at the Gallery I introduced *visible re-touchings* to satisfy the demands of scholars who regarded the closely matched, or so-called 'deceptive' retouchings as arrogant interference with the master's creation. The result of this new step was not welcomed by everybody. Four years later, when Hitler came to power, and Friedländer was succeeded by a Nazi director, the picture came up for review. Because I had purposely not entirely concealed the damage of past ages I was accused of having caused it. The new director exchanged this, the only Duccio Berlin possessed, for an average Holbein which had the advantage of being German. The very eminent art dealer who made the deal sold the Duccio to the National Gallery in Washington, where I saw it again in 1952 together with three other paintings I had restored very sparingly years before. Now they were all highly 'finished' with 'invisible' re-touchings (Plate 1).

It was perhaps just as well that not all the pictures I had to deal with in my first years as a private restorer lived up to the magnificent and optimistic names given to them, and that many of those on which I made my first attempts were not of great value. From the outset I had, of course, made a habit of always trying out on a little corner everything I was to use on the picture, such as adhesives and cleaning agents, so that no noticeable harm was done. A restorer who has never made a mistake, or thinks he has not, is in constant danger of erring. One who like myself has made mistakes, and knows it, is less likely to repeat them.

In those days the Kaiser Friedrich Museum was a very lively place. Berlin was the world's turnover market for old masters' pictures, partly because three or four of the best known art historians gave written certificates or attributions to any picture-owner who asked for one. As these 'expertises' could raise enormously the value of the paintings to which they were attached, and as they were to be had without charge, one can imagine the throng in the antechambers of these experts, most of whom were museum directors. As is well known the practice of selling pictures with certificates of authenticity frequently developed into abuse, but the authorities raised no objection, as the scholars, who were Civil Servants, did not take any fee for their opinion. On the contrary, the ensuing contact between museums and art dealers was considered beneficial to both sides. In this way many more fine works of art were offered to the galleries than they would otherwise have had the chance of seeing, and the experience of the staff was greatly widened by this practice.

My four years at the Kaiser Friedrich Museum were an ideal opportunity for working on first-rate paintings and, above all, of being trained in real connoisseurship by Friedländer, the finest teacher imaginable.[1] However carefully you read his beautifully written books, mostly on the early Flemish masters, you cannot learn nearly as much from them as by personal contact in the presence of actual pictures. My studio was next door to Friedländer's office, and every now and then he would bring in some particularly interesting case, a rare masterpiece, a fake or a titivated painting. In a second book dealing with both, methods of the masters and forgeries, I hope to describe a few of these uniquely instructive experiences.

My early impressions at the Kaiser Friedrich Museum were dramatic curtain-raisers to my career as a museum restorer and were decisive for my future attitude. On my first day at the K.F.M. I found in the restorers' studio a box, about one foot long, full of a brown powder. To my amazement the assistant restorer explained that it was the umber pigment with which the varnishes were normally tinted.

I must explain that in those days the art historians and directors of galleries did not work nearly so closely together with the restorers and technical staff as they do in many museums today, so that Dr. Bode could have had little cognizance of the practices in the conservation studios and workshops of the Kaiser Friedrich Museum. Also he might not have disapproved so strongly as one does today of the traditional application of tinted varnishes and of comparatively lavish oil retouchings which in his time were customary in the majority of picture galleries everywhere (and still are in some). It was only under Dr. Friedländer's regime — he was of a younger generation — that clear, untinted varnishes and more

[1] See Max J. Friedländer, *On Art and Connoisseurship* (Oxford, 1942). Bibliography, *Section* 7(5). Unfortunately his distinguished style does not come out well in the English translation.

sparing retouchings (done in tempera paint instead of oil) were introduced, and a closer contact between director and technical departments established.

My criticism is levelled not at the restorers of the Kaiser Friedrich Museum, who were among the foremost of their time, but at the general approach to matters of picture restoration at their period. It was sheer good fortune on my part that I began my career when a more scientific outlook was gaining ground.

But in the 1920's, for instance, the flaking of paint on pictures was still treated in a rough and primitive way; and (for the drawbacks of oil retouchings were then only just becoming known) I found that the copious retouching on many Kaiser Friedrich Museum pictures had been done with ordinary oil paint and had turned into dark blotches, often encroaching on original paint. They were not obvious to the layman because they were concealed by the useful brown umber veil of tinted varnish.

These impressions strengthened my determination to introduce a scheme of proper apprenticeship and teaching, to develop methods of scrupulous and thorough cleaning (including removal of unnecessary retouching); of colourless varnishing; of sparse, non-darkening and well-matched retouchings; and to improve methods for securing loose paint.[1] It goes without saying that I was, like many other restorers at that period, continuously seeking safer ways of cleaning and restoring paintings.

Mainly in Italy, Germany and Holland, a number of distinguished picture restorers had been busy for some time raising the standards of the profession and in the United States an institute for advanced research and training in our field had been founded as far back as 1925. The next chapter gives more details of these developments.

As soon as it was possible, I introduced the use of scientific aids for my work. I had always longed to have a scientist at hand to whom I could put my many questions. At that period in Berlin (where the scientific department of the Museum was hardly concerned with paintings) I did not expect that one day I would have some of the finest specialists next door to my studio, still less that I would myself one day become head of a laboratory for research on paintings.

In 1930 Philip Hendy, who was then Curator of Paintings at the Boston Museum of Fine Arts, brought to Berlin one of its most important pictures, 'S. Luke drawing the Virgin' by Rogier van der Weyden[2] (Plate 2) the attribution of which was at that time not generally accepted. Friedländer wanted to see the

[1] H. Ruhemann, 'La technique de la conservation des tableaux', *Mouseion*, XV (1931), No. 3, pp. 14–23. Bibliography *Section 4* (27), (28).

[2] H. Ruhemann, 'A Record of Restoration', *Technical Studies in the Field of the Fine Arts* (Cambridge, Mass.) III (1934–5), pp. 3–15. Bibliography *Section 9* (3).

painting freed from dark varnish and retouchings before giving his verdict, and welcomed the suggestion that I should clean it.

This was my first meeting with Hendy, with whom and under whom I have since worked so happily to this day.

In 1933, when Hitler came to power and things became unpleasant in Germany, Philip Hendy asked me to stay with him in Buckinghamshire so that I could use these few weeks for visiting my acquaintances in London and for sounding out possibilities of coming to live and work in this country. I decided to emigrate as soon as possible to England. The decision was easy to make. Three people of our acquaintance had already been 'liquidated'. My best clients had been for years the leading London art dealers, Duveens, Agnews, Colnaghis and Sabins, and I had many good friends in London.

W. G. Constable, then Director of the newly founded Courtauld Institute of Art, and Harold Plenderleith, then head of the Research Laboratory of the British Museum, were with me on the Editing Committee of the International Museums Office, and A. P. Laurie, a pioneer in research on paintings and Professor of Painting Technique at the Royal Academy, was another friend of long standing. Together with my London art dealer friends these people were particularly kind and helpful in paving the way for me in England and in getting me the necessary Home Office permit to work over here.

I must mention two more personalities to whom not only I but the English art world owe a great deal — Lord Lee of Fareham, in whose fine gallery in his Gloucestershire mansion I worked on National Gallery pictures which he had housed during part of the war, and Mr. Samuel Courtauld, the great collector of French nineteenth-century paintings, who bequeathed his beautiful house, most of his superb pictures and an ample fund to the Institute named after him. The wholesale transfer of the Warburg Institute from Hamburg to London is also mostly due to the extraordinary enthusiasm and generosity of these two men.

Fortunately I had been allowed to take just enough money out of Germany to tide me over the year I had to wait for a working permit. When it came I had twenty pounds left.

The greatest help in my fresh start in London was that early on W. G. Constable asked me to give regular lectures on 'The Methods of the Old Masters' at the Courtauld Institute. It was a rare privilege to work in the exquisite surroundings of the famous Adam house in Portman Square under the first Director of this now famous Institute, and to witness how in a comparatively short time he laid the foundations, how he engaged the best available art scholars, both British and foreign, and how he got the whole thing working in his gentle and slightly unorthodox manner. It was wonderful also to see the most gifted of the undergraduates soon work their way up to lecturer and curator posts.

The first commissions for restoring paintings soon began to come in. I found a suitable little studio with a good skylight, built for wool merchants, in Golden Square, Soho, and again before long I had to take apprentices to help cope with the work.

In 1934 Sir Kenneth Clark called me to the National Gallery (of which he was Director), where I have ever since spent half of each working week. When I retired as Consultant Restorer, one of my former pupils was made Chief Restorer of the newly-established Conservation Department, but I have continued to work happily beside him in restoration and in the training of the younger generation of restorers.

The years of work under Sir Kenneth and in collaboration with the keen and able staff, Martin Davies, Philip Pouncey, Neil MacLaren and later William Gibson, were extremely pleasant and fruitful. They were all very interested in the restoration and cleaning of the pictures, and the Director envisaged as the first aim to have at least one work of every great master properly cleaned. He had an ideal little studio built for me at the National Gallery, in which I am still working today.

At the beginning of the war, the Trustees decided to evacuate the pictures, and with them two restorers who were too old for active war service, and who could therefore go on working on the paintings. I was very happy to be engaged as one of them for the duration of the war at a modest retaining fee. This was the first case to my knowledge of a restorer being employed full time by the National Gallery.

We were moved about several times, and so we got to know various parts of England, Wales and Scotland well. My family and I lived and worked in turn in a delightful little old dower house in the Cotswolds; in a flat in Bangor overlooking the beautiful Straits of Anglesey; in the excellent little studio built at The Quarry in Manod, high up in the Welsh mountains; in a simple farmhouse in the foothills of the Trossachs near Glasgow; for short periods in great country houses and then again in a tiny gardener's cottage in Gloucestershire. It was not easy to find accommodation both safe enough for the pictures, and with good light for working on them. Much of the time I used as my studio greenhouses which, despite the fuel shortage, one was allowed to heat because they were full of tomatoes. Everywhere we were received in the most friendly way and we experienced several instances of exceptional kindness and extraordinary generosity. A typical and touching example: when I telephoned the Justice of the Peace of our village to ask if I could call on him with my naturalization papers, he insisted that he should come to our house for the signing; he was eighty years old.

I also enjoyed working from time to time in country houses in Scotland, Ireland and England. It was gratifying to discover at Lowther Castle, apart from minor works, a group of Hogarths unknown to the art world; at Clandeboye a cluster of excellent Lawrences; at Holkham Hall a splendid Rubens and at Kinnaird Castle two Cranachs, all nearly forgotten in dark corners of the vast houses.

In Glasgow, apart from restoring some of the more important pictures and training a young apprentice, I had the pleasant task of evacuating the pictures to the country. After a preliminary correspondence we visited — in a Rolls Royce provided by the Corporation — all the suitable country houses in the lovely surroundings of Glasgow, the owners of which had agreed to house pictures during the war. Having given those kind hosts as much latitude as possible in the choice of pictures, I was finally left with the famous 'Slaughter-House' by Rembrandt which nobody wanted. My wife and I were delighted to have it on our bare walls in the farmhouse. We had no objection to the subject matter, the flayed ox, but after a few weeks we took the Rembrandt down because, with its heavy black frame, the dark picture made the room still gloomier than it already was; a very enlightening experience which we could never have foreseen. It shows how instructive some practical experience in living with pictures may be for anyone called upon to judge or choose them. The nicest and most amusing part of it all was that we replaced the Rembrandt by van Gogh's 'Sunflowers', not a reproduction but the real thing, which had been sent to me by the Tate Gallery for lining and safe keeping, together with van Gogh's 'Yellow Chair', a wonderful late Turner and Whistler's 'Waterloo Bridge'; not a bad little collection to brighten up our wartime exile!

On returning to London after the war I again took up my official and private work. In 1946 I was appointed on a part-time basis as Lecturer-in-Charge of the Technology Department of the Courtauld Institute of Art, London University. Later in the same year I was made Consultant Restorer to the National Gallery. As half my time was already engaged by work at the Courtauld Institute, it was not possible for me to be appointed Chief Restorer, which officially is a full-time post. Therefore that post was left vacant until my retirement in 1953.

In spite of these official alterations in title, there has to this day been no change in my actual work at the Gallery.

In 1956 I went to Guatemala on behalf of UNESCO for three months, to train three artist-craftsmen in picture restoration. The many religious paintings in the charming baroque churches badly needed attention, though few were of high value. Hardly any had ever been restored or cleaned, but when it came to removing the darkened varnishes from some of the sacred pictures I hesitated. It

B. Glasgow City Art Gallery, Giorgione, 'The Adulteress brought before Christ', 139·2 × 181·7 cm. Before and after cleaning. Note that before the cleaning Christ's knee (which was damaged and badly retouched) was far too high.

occurred to me that the population, the great majority of whom are *Indios*, descendants of the Maya in fact, might be appalled if they suddenly saw their Saints, whom they had always known with skin as brown as their own, emerge as white Europeans.

The object of my mission was to choose suitable young artists, one of whom, after this trial period, could go to the United States, Italy or England on a UNESCO scholarship to complete his training. Unfortunately nothing has come of this; apparently the Guatemala art authorities were unable to reach agreement on a suitable candidate.

One unexpected and agreeable experience in Guatemala was that my Spanish, which I had not spoken for thirty-seven years, all came back to me in about a week. I firmly believe that I would never have assimilated and retained foreign languages so easily had not my parents given me the opportunity of speaking — not learning — English and French when I was a toddler. Without this my life would have been so much less rich. I believe that the introduction of at least two foreign languages in all kindergartens would do more than anything else to promote world peace. One does not easily misunderstand or hate a country whose language one knows well.

I was particularly fortunate in living and working during a period when progress in my field was at its greatest, and to find myself for the major part of the time in the English-speaking world, where this advance was least affected by the war.

HISTORICAL NOTES

The history of the restoration of paintings has not yet been written.[1] It would make a rewarding topic, but would in itself require a separate book and considerable research. There has been a great deal of writing on this subject, but for a long time its value was much limited by the traditional secrecy of restorers, the general lack of an objective approach and the absence of properly recorded case histories.

With the waning of secrecy, with the frankness of modern methods of recording and the sharing of data a History of Restoration can now be visualized.

The end of the nineteenth and the beginning of the twentieth century saw the publication of several authoritative books on picture restoration — for instance, by Forni and Secco-Suardo in Italy, Lucanus in Germany and Déon in France (see Bibliography) — and long chapters on restoration in books on painting in

[1] The nearest thing to it that I know are Th. v. Frimmel's *Gemäldekunde* (not translated from German), (Leipzig, 1920, 1st ed.), Bibliography *Section 4* (5); an article by Norman Brommelle, 'Material for a History of Conservation', *Studies in Conservation*, II, 4 (October, 1956), Bibliography *Section 2* (16), dealing mostly with nineteenth-century documents; and H. H. Pars, *Pictures in Peril* (Faber, London, 1957), Bibliography *Section 2* (18).

general, among others those by Bouvier, Mérimée and Montabert. Of indirect influence on restoration were the classic works on the technique of the masters by Ludwig, Berger, Eastlake, Merrifield, etc.

By the standards of their time, the restorers among these authors all knew their work thoroughly, and must have carried out some excellent restorations. I have seen many relinings of this period which are still in good condition today. But these restorers were hampered by the fact that in their lifetime few old masters' paintings could be properly seen and this prevented a clear grasp of the masters' techniques and intentions. For the darkened old varnish layers (and with them many a tinted one put on by eighteenth- and nineteenth-century restorers) were either taken for part of the artist's work, or the romantic 'golden glow' was so admired that more of it, in the form of pigmented varnishes, was applied. This propagation of the 'golden glow' or 'gallery tone' was the first step in a vicious circle of varnishing (see p. 236) which in turn has led to many of the criticisms levelled against restorers in recent years (see Chapter 3).

The veil which forty years ago obscured the great majority of pictures in public and private collections was like a curtain drawn between the art of the past and contemporary painting. It cut off the natural transition from the one to the other.

My young painter friends had become tired of the galleries where all the pictures were of a similar brown shade, all flat and smooth and gloomy.[1] There was no exciting colour or contrast, no expressive personal handling, no sparkling technique, no brilliant craftsmanship to be seen from which they could learn. In fact the tradition of fine, ingenious and sound craftsmanship in painting, built up by the masters in two thousand years of patient trial and error, in careful handing down of tradition and in revolutionary contributions, was gradually dropped. It had been obliterated by grime and varnish and was thrown away as the dirty old thing it appeared to be.

On the other hand, this may have been a good thing in one respect. Had the masterpieces been the shining examples they are now again becoming, would the revolt of Turner, Constable and the Impressionists and all the exciting subsequent developments have happened, and would there have been enough 'explosive stuff', as Marx called it, to set off a revolution?

Without the gloom, boredom and stuffiness accumulated in the galleries and consequently in Royal Academies and Salons, we might not have had the liberating and refreshing reaction of the Impressionists, who created their own necessary and revolutionary techniques, and provided the 'tesserae' of pure colour with which the Post Impressionists composed their great works.

[1] Horsin Déon, *De la conservation et de la restauration des tableaux* (Paris, 1851), p. 56. Bibliography *Section 3* (43).

Even Turner and Constable, those pioneers of colour and light, might have freed themselves sooner from the heavy brown that lingered on in their own pictures for many years, had they seen clean masterpieces in the galleries.

That dirt and darkening varnish were a menace to their own message had already been discovered by the Impressionists; Pissarro speaks in letters to his son of a marvellous man who can clean his paintings.[1] This may have only been surface cleaning; but Gauguin had clearly realized that the varnish was also at fault (see p. 229).

When in the 1920's I cleaned my first Impressionists they had naturally darkened considerably during the fifty years or so of their existence, and I was surprised by their dazzling brilliance that came to light on removing the varnish. Since we had all accepted the accumulations of dirt and darkened varnish as an intrinsic part of the pictures, it is not surprising that it has taken many curators in charge of these canvases so long to realize how much of their original brightness could be recovered at comparatively small risk. Luckily most of the Impressionist pictures were painted in pure oil paint and could, after about thirty years of hardening, be cleaned as safely as any old master's painting. This is not true of some works by Renoir and a great number of early twentieth-century pictures painted with excessive admixture of resin (see pp. 236–7).

One of the last important painters who did not lose interest in the old masters' methods was Delacroix. He admired Rubens immensely and tried to rival him in luminosity and richness of colour and in brilliance of technique. The fact that despite his acute observation and intelligence he lagged in these respects so far behind his idol makes one believe that he was able to see only works by Rubens which were distorted by yellowed varnish. It is difficult to understand why Delacroix should speak of green shadows unless he had seen Rubens' bluish flesh tints turned green by the effect of the yellow varnish that still covered them.

This hunch of mine seems to be largely confirmed by the following letter by Delacroix to which Veronica Wedgwood very kindly drew my attention.[2]

8th August 1858

'You very kindly ask my opinion on the restoration of the Rubens: On the whole I find the operation good; it is even extraordinary considering the varnish removals usually carried out on pictures. Here is my impression; the varnish removed entirely [à fond], specially in the lights, has revealed [découvert] a

---

[1] Camille Pissarro, *Letters to his Son Lucien* (Pantheon Books Inc., New York, 1943), p. 212: '. . . He (Portier) cleaned up the painting of Esther G., View of Louveciennes, it is a resurrection, Georges had brought it to Durand-Ruel before it was cleaned, what naiveté! George expected to sell it; not only did Durand reject it, he even denied that it was my work. I laugh to myself. . . .' See also p. 219, ibid.

[2] Eugène Delacroix to Dutillieux, *Lettres IV*, pp. 42–43.

freshness of tones which one had to expect. The freshmen in painting [*les jeunes nourrissons de la peinture*], who imagine it suffices to paint with fat oil and to give to their canvases with the help of bitumen what they call "warm tones" must have been disappointed. One will know from now on that one can be a very warm artist and yet render nature with her true tones. The only inconvenience of this (restoring) work results without doubt from the manner in which these pictures have been executed. It is probable that Rubens contented himself with simple scumbles [*frottis*] for the shadows. These scumbles or glazes were done with transparent tones which have turned darker. The yellow colouring of the varnishes accumulated with time and which extended also over the lights established a kind of unison between those lights and those shadows [*mettaient une sorte de liaison*]. Today the proportion is disturbed, that is to say the shadows are dark and the lights have such a vivid brightness — that which the painter had wanted — so that the appearance of the pictures has something metallic and monotone, due to the uniformly sombre effect of the shadow parts. This is, in fact, the effect continuously occurring in all varnish removals. It would be desirable never to varnish; then our descendants would, no doubt, get a more accurate idea of our pictures; but how to resist the desire to give to your contemporaries the best possible opinion [*sic* — impression?] of oneself and one's works?'

This letter shows that Delacroix saw cleaned Rubens only at the age of 59, in 1858, five years before his death; and even those cleaned Rubens appear to have been cleaned '*à fond*' — thoroughly — 'especially in the lights' only and not completely in the shadows.

This seems all the more likely as completely and evenly cleaned Rubens do not very well correspond with the description Delacroix gives here of the pictures in question: 'metallic and monotone'.

He must have seen that there was an interplay of warm and cool shades in that most luminous and shimmering flesh ever painted; but did it escape his observation that these elusive nuances were conjured up by a systematic device which produced the famous mother-of-pearl effects almost automatically, and always in the right place, where they belonged, in the transitions between light and shade?[1] Or did Delacroix perhaps despise it as too mechanical a trick?

In seeing at the big 1963 Delacroix exhibition in the Louvre a great number of his works well cleaned I wondered how he could ever have believed that he was nearing or attaining Rubens' luminosity unless he never saw a clean Rubens. At any rate he was surrounded by pictures covered with brownish accretions and perhaps, by comparison, his own fresh paintings looked colourful and bright.

[1] H. Ruhemann and E. M. Kemp, *The Artist at Work* (Penguin Books, 1951), p. 31.

Autobiographical and Historical Notes

Those seemingly 'green shadows' resulting from the effect of yellow varnish on uncleaned flesh paint should not be confused with the deliberate use of green in shadows, or rather half-shadows, of flesh elsewhere in painting. In many trecento and quattrocento Italian pictures the flesh tones are underpainted with green which was intended to show slightly through the overlying pink to produce, without the admixture of black or brown, a reasonably realistic half-shadow. This green is now often more prominent than was originally intended[1] because of wearing or increased transparency of the flesh paint on top.

Whereas the original bluish shade can be restored to Rubens' flesh paint by removing the yellow varnish, the now excessive green in the half tones of the Italian Primitive paintings is irreversible. The only remedy would be to repaint the flesh tints, but it would probably be generally agreed that this ought not to be done, at least not in museums.

We must not fall back into the less inhibited retouching practices of the nineteenth century and we must keep in mind that inevitably the style of most of the larger reconstructions does not seem to stand up to twentieth-century criticism, not even those of perhaps the most famous of nineteenth-century restorers, Cavenaghi. Neither the knowledge of style nor the respect for the great masters' works were then as developed as they are today, and often pictures were arbitrarily altered to fit the fashion of the time. Not only were draperies or fig leaves painted on nude figures, but entire unwanted parts of compositions were painted out (see plates 3–4), or changed, like Mantegna's Virgin in his 'Holy Family' (see plates 8 to 9) and so on.

Those retouchings of the time which do not strike us as technically unsuccessful must either have been executed in water-colour or egg tempera or are still concealed under the 'golden glow'.

Before they were aided by scientific observation or had mastered the art of distinguishing later additions from original paint, earlier restorers must often, in fits of uncertainty and guilty conscience, have overpainted large original areas under the impression that they had 'overcleaned' them.[2] This is one explanation which I can suggest for the extensive overpainting found on perfectly preserved dark areas on such pictures as the 'Old Man in an Armchair' by Rembrandt (National Gallery No. 6274) which I cleaned in 1962. This kind of very frequent overpainting is fortunately nearly always carried out in soft resin-oil paint and is easily removed. It is readily spotted by one of the many criteria mentioned on

[1] See for example the small Duccio 'Virgin and Child' at the National Gallery (No. 566).

[2] In fact, though, much of the 'wearing' found on canvas paintings is due not to over-cleaning but to injudicious ironing during lining (see p. 150). Occasionally, too, one finds irregular textural effects, obviously produced by the master himself, but often taken for damage inflicted at a later period (see plate 53, p. 173).

pp. 181–9, such as texture, craquelure or level differing from the original.

Eventually, with the spread of enlightenment, such malpractices ceased, at least in most public galleries. But the nineteenth century left behind it a legacy of undesirable accretions that are still with us today. Thus, to preservation and simple cleaning must be added the removal of old overpaintings and pigmented varnishes. Obviously this is an exacting task. In the last forty years it has been made safer and easier by the contribution of science to the work of picture restoration. Arthur van Schendel, director of the Rijksmuseum, Amsterdam, in his presidential address to the Rome Conference 1961, published in *I.I.C. News* Vol. II, No. 1, p. 3, gave an excellent summary of these developments.

Science and Restoration

At the end of the nineteenth century, physics and chemistry began to be systematically harnessed to the treatment of pictures. At first isolated restorers made use of scientific inventions, such as X-rays and a little later ultra-violet rays, for diagnosis. In 1915 the Vienna Kunsthistorische Museum had already begun to use X-ray photography (see also p. 127) but as early as 1888 the Berlin State Museum had founded its own science laboratories; the British Museum followed in 1921, the Museum of Fine Arts, Boston, Mass., U.S.A. and the Louvre in 1930. The laboratories of the Institut Royal du Patrimoine Artistique in Brussels and the Technology Department of the Courtauld Institute of Art, London University, were founded in 1935. Professors Scott and Laurie in London must be mentioned as pioneers. The Scientific Department at the National Gallery, now a leading centre of research, goes back to 1934 when Ian Rawlins, who improved methods of examining paintings by X-rays[1] was appointed as part-time Scientific Adviser to the Trustees.

Not only Museums but also colleges of art established laboratories for research into painting materials, and thus contributed indirectly to the progress in picture restoration. To name a few, the Doerner Institute in Munich and the Laboratory of the Staatliche Kunst-Akademie in Berlin under Professor Täuber; the laboratories of the leading artists' colour firms, particularly Winsor and Newton in England, Neisch in Germany and Lefranc in France, must also be named here.

Harvard (U.S.A.) was probably the first University to start a Research Department devoted almost entirely to putting picture restoration on a scientific basis. Founded in 1925 as a Department of the Fogg Art Museum, its pioneers were Edward Forbes, George Stout and John Gettens.

[1] F. I. G. Rawlins, *From the National Gallery Laboratory* (London, 1940). Published for the Trustees of the National Gallery. Bibliography, *Section 27* (27).

Autobiographical and Historical Notes

International Collaboration

One event, more than any other, promoted international collaboration which during the 1920's was still negligible in the field of conservation: the first international congress of picture restorers held in Rome in 1930 under the auspices of The League of Nations: the *International Conference for the Study of Scientific Methods for Examination and Preservation of Works of Art.*

Leading curators and restorers from all over the world met, many of them for the first time, in an environment of palaces and museums, lavishly entertained by Mussolini's government. A great number of important papers were read, followed by fascinating discussions, and many lasting friendships were founded. (It was here, for instance, that I met George Stout, the outstanding American restorer whose name appears so often in this book, and who is now Director of the Stewart Gardner Museum in Boston. By now a friend for years, he extended generous help to me when I had to leave my country and also whenever I visited the States.) There were two important tangible results of the Conference. One was the publication of the *Manuel de la Conservation et Restauration des Tableaux*[1] written by an international panel of experts. It fell to me to compose together with Harold Plenderleith the greater part of the chapter on restoration. Foundoukidis produced under the German occupation at great risk an excellent English edition of the Manual. Both versions have unfortunately long been out of print. The other outcome was the resolution of the committee on varnishes which sat under the able and amiable chairmanship of W. G. Constable (another of the lasting friendships founded on that occasion). The committee published[2] a method of varnishing which seemed at the time to be the best compromise known. This conference and the publications issuing from it probably dealt the death blow to secrecy in our profession. From that date onwards, a restorer who pretended to have secret cures patently relegated himself to the class of charlatan. I give more details of the Conference's achievements in the Bibliography.

The war of 1939–45 did not stop developments in the field of picture restoration but, on the contrary, gave them indirectly a great impulse. Here follows a brief enumeration of the main events which form a continuous sequence of causes and effects.

Thanks to Sir Kenneth Clark's initiative, about sixty evacuated National Gallery pictures by great masters were cleaned and restored in the country

---

[1] I must record here the gratitude owed by our profession to Harold Plenderleith for the devotion and competence of his collaboration in editing this first official handbook of its kind. (Bibliography, *Section 4* (28)). To him too a lasting friendship and admiration bind me since 1930.

[2] In *Les Dossiers de l'Office International des Musées*, No. 2 (Paris, 1933), pp. 34–6. The same number contains the resolutions adopted by the Conference. Bibliography, *Section 4* (22).

during the war. In October 1946 the cleaned pictures were rehung, together with the other pictures returned from the country. For over a year letters of criticism and approval of the cleaning appeared in the columns of *The Times* and *Daily Telegraph*.[1] The Trustees of the Gallery referred the essential points in the controversy to the Scientific Advisory Committee, and as a result of the advice given, the Weaver Committee was set up. Their deliberations were presented to the Trustees as the Weaver Report immediately before the opening in October 1947 at the National Gallery of the Exhibition of Cleaned Pictures with its important catalogue. Fundamental consequences of the Weaver Report were the expansion of the Conservation Department (established in 1946) and of the Scientific Department.

Among international repercussions of the report was the formation of the Commission for the Care of Paintings by the International Council of Museums (I.C.O.M.), composed of the Directors of the world's major art galleries and later a Committee for Museum Laboratories. The logical development was achieved this year by the fusion of these two groups so that in the future conservation problems will be considered by directors, restorers and scientists working together.

The International Institute for Conservation of Historic and Artistic Works, I.I.C. for short, with its headquarters in London, was founded in 1950 'to provide a permanent organization to co-ordinate and improve the knowledge, methods and working standards needed to protect and preserve precious materials of all kinds'. The many references to the I.I.C. in this book are some indication of how successful it has been.[2]

Periodicals

The first American periodical devoted exclusively to questions concerning the preservation and restoration of museum objects and paintings was *Technical Studies in the Field of the Fine Arts*. It was first published in 1933 by the Fogg Art Museum, Harvard University; its managing editor, George Stout, together with John Gettens, made it an exemplary publication, which kept the restorers and curators of the world abreast of the advances in their profession. Again the

[1] The earlier controversies from 1846 on have been described by Philip Hendy in the *Catalogue of the Cleaned Pictures Exhibition 1947* (Bibliography, *Section 6*, under 'London'), on pages xii and xvii to xx and by Norman Brommelle in an article in *Museums Journal*, LVI (1957), pp.257–62, Bibliography, *Section 2* (17).

[2] In Appendix A are given more details about the foundation of the I.C.O.M., the I.I.C. and other institutions of interest to restorers; and also further data about the periodicals mentioned in this chapter. For details of periodicals see also Bibliography, *Section 1*.

frequent reference to it in footnotes and in the Bibliography gives an idea of the importance of this periodical. 'It marks the beginning of the modern period of conservation . . .' as van Schendel puts it. Unfortunately, it lapsed in 1941; but it was succeeded in 1950 by *Studies in Conservation*, journal of the I.I.C., published in London. The first editor of this, Ian Rawlins, launched and kept it with untiring enthusiasm on the same high level as the original journal. The leading editors and contributors of *Technical Studies* carried on for *Conservation*. A new departure was the publication of summaries in languages other than the original article. Other innovations were *I.I.C. Abstracts* and *I.I.C. News* which are both invaluable for restorers.

Mouseion was the journal of the Office International des Musées from 1910 to 1945. It was admirably run by its editor, Monsieur Foundoukidis. Its successor is *Museum*, a magnificent quarterly published by UNESCO under the editorship of a distinguished international committee.

Many museums and institutions issue *Bulletins* which have also made contributions to progress in our profession, especially those published by the Istituto Centrale del Restauro in Rome; the Institut Royal du Patrimoine Artistique, Brussels; the Louvre; Metropolitan Museum, New York and the National Gallery, London (*Annual Reports*).

Other contributions of historical importance, for instance the publications by the pioneers Eastlake, Berger and Eibner, are mentioned in the Bibliography; details and dates of technical improvements and discoveries are given in the chapters dealing with the corresponding methods. The late Paul Coremans' epoch-making research into Dieric Bouts' technique will be described in the book on the Masters' methods.

Two truly historical achievements in our field remain to be mentioned; both of them connected with Rome. In 1959, the *International Centre for the Study of the Preservation and Restoration of Cultural Property* was founded to strengthen relations between all who are interested in the preservation of their cultural traditions. It does not at present carry out research work itself, but it does the important and necessary coordination of the work of others all over the world. Its director is the former head of the Research Laboratory of the British Museum, Harold Plenderleith.

Secondly, the *Congress* held in Rome in September 1961 on *Recent Advances in Conservation of Historic and Artistic Works*. This was organized by the I.I.C., and was modelled on the conference of restorers already mentioned, which had met in Rome thirty years earlier and was the first of its kind. The second can also claim pioneer title in so far as it included restorers and scientists concerned not only with paintings, but also with objets d'art and other museum objects. Specialists from twenty-five countries took part; altogether there were 195 delegates, among them eleven from Communist countries. All the lectures given at this Congress, some of them highly important, were duplicated and circulated in advance to every participant (see Bibliography, p. 408).[1] But perhaps the contacts made during the enjoyable outings and gatherings between people of so many different countries, age groups and convictions will be still more fruitful.

Thus during the past century, ignorance and secrecy have given way to detailed scientific knowledge and international collaboration, and restorers have become 'a knowledgeable as well as a skilled body of men and women'.[2]

[1] *Recent Advances in Conservation* (Butterworth, London, 1963), Bibliography, *Section 4* (69).
[2] *The National Gallery, January 1960–May 1962* (London, 1962), p. 79.

CHAPTER 2

The Restorer and his Training

The Restorer's Growing Task

The last chapter will have given the reader some idea of the restorer's role in maintaining our artistic heritage and of the ever-widening scope of his work.

The paintings in museums and galleries are ageing and decaying progressively, but unlike some in private possession hardly any of them have been thrown away or destroyed. More and more are crowding the public galleries and private collections; many of them, already ailing at an early age, are in greater need of the restorer's attention than some of the old masters' paintings which after hundreds of years are still in splendid condition. Outside the museums the value of works of art is steadily rising and, with it, concern for their preservation. They now form a considerable part of trade and investment, and the restorer's importance grows accordingly. The existing workshops, laboratories and training centres can no longer cope with the tasks awaiting them. New institutes are being established, but the number of patients is mounting at a higher rate.

Some Technical Terms

Before going into the details of ethical problems, the technical premises and the main technical terms must be clearly understood.

The terms *restoration* and *conservation* are almost synonymous. In the U.S.A. the word 'conservator' is preferred to 'restorer' because it is rightly averred that one cannot restore to its original state a painting, hundreds of years old, that is noticeably changed or damaged. On the other hand the restorer does a little more than just conserve when he restores, as far as possible, the original aspect of a painting by removing dark and cloudy varnishes and overpainting.[1] The word

---

[1] *Manual of Conservation and Restoration of Paintings* (International Council of Museums), Bibliography, *Section 4* (28), said in the resolution passed at its first General Biennial Conference in Paris 1948: 'Noting that museum directors are unanimous in agreeing that paintings should be restored to an appearance corresponding as closely as possible to their original state. . . .'

conservator sounds more impressive but there is a difficulty that has so far held up the introduction in Europe of the term 'conservator' instead of 'restorer'. In some countries such as France, 'conservator' or 'conservateur'[1] is a title or rank equivalent to or directly below the director, equivalent to 'Keeper' in Great Britain and 'Kustos' in Germany. For the time being we may perhaps go on using the word 'restorer'. It will not confuse anybody, though it is true that it claims a little too much if taken literally. On the other hand, if the term 'conservator' were exclusively adopted, the attempt at restoring, at least as far as feasible, the original aspect of a painting might gradually be abandoned, a tendency already alarmingly evident, particularly in some museums abroad.

Any measure of restoration is preceded by *Examination*.

The word *Restoration* might conveniently be said to comprise five different measures :

1. *Preservation* of sound paintings
2. *Treatment* of ailing paintings
3. *Cleaning*
4. *Retouching*
5. *Re-varnishing*.

These various activities of the restorer can again be distinguished under two headings : consolidation, the *technical* or constructional on the one side, and the *aesthetic* or 'artistic' on the other. The two often overlap, for varnish removal may be necessary to prevent flaking, or work on the support itself may be necessary for the sake of appearance only.

Which of the two aspects is to be given priority cannot be doubted. A painting must in the first place be saved from decay and made sound and only in the second place need it be cleaned. In recent years the controversies on the cleaning of paintings have created the impression that varnish removal matters more than preservation work. The results of cleaning (or not cleaning) are visible to all and make sensational topics in newspapers and conversation, whereas consolidation passes unnoticed. Though it is often more urgent and vital, and can result in worse damage if neglected or ill done, nobody talks about it because it is carried out in remote workshops and mostly on the backs of the pictures by devoted and unassuming craftsmen (though many leading restorers in this country and in the United States do their own consolidation work).

Varying Emphasis in Different Countries

The emphasis on the one or the other category of procedure will vary according

[1] See ibid., p. 15, where the word 'conservator' is used for the director in charge of the paintings as distinct from the restorer who works under him.

to prevailing conditions. In one country the aesthetic part of the problem assumes greater importance, in another, the technical. For instance, in France and England the accumulation of darkened (and often tinted) varnishes, applied to the masterpieces through the ages, reached during the nineteenth and twentieth centuries appalling proportions. The material deterioration was comparatively slow and unspectacular, and — alas — often the results of neglect or inadequate treatment went unnoticed under the darkening varnishes.

By contrast, in the U.S.A. nearly all the paintings that were acquired in Europe for private collections and later for the more recently created museums arrived already looking their best and technically well cared for. The European dealers through whose hands those thousands of masterpieces had passed had seen to that. Thus the aesthetic part of the problem was mainly settled beforehand. The public in the States had not known large collections of pictures covered with 'patina', genuine or false. There was little prejudice to overcome and the American conservators soon had to concentrate on the technical conditioning of the treasures. These quickly began to deteriorate through the totally different climatic conditions, extremes of cold and heat and the inordinate overheating in most houses and museums. It was many years before adequate air conditioning plants began to be installed in the museums. In the meantime the most common ailment of pictures, the flaking of the paint, became very prevalent, and our American colleagues, with their natural technical bent, rapidly improved the methods of transfer, the only radical cure. In the States to this day the restorers have little time for anything but consolidation and only a few are interested in *integration* (careful retouching of gaps) and *compensation* (reconstruction of missing design).

Similarly in Italy technical preoccupations prevail, but for other reasons. Despite devoted efforts the lack of sufficient funds has made it impossible to keep all of the country's enormous wealth of treasures in good repair. Moreover, during the last war some of Italy's finest wall paintings were bombarded to fragments and the putting together of these vast jigsaw puzzles is the first thing that comes to an Italian's mind on hearing the word 'restoration'. In comparison with the urgency and scope of the fabulous salvage work of frescoes[1] for which there are not nearly enough restorers, the question of cleaning pictures, which looms so large in the rest of Europe, appears much less important.

In addition to these troubles, many of Italy's most famous frescoes, which had not suffered from the war and had kept comparatively sound for over four centuries, have in recent years suddenly started to disintegrate at an alarming rate because of the increase in air pollution. If they are not to be lost com-

[1] Ugo Procacci, *Del distacco degli affreschi e della loro conservazione* (Florence, 1957).

pletely they must be detached from the walls immediately and transferred to new supports. This has been done most admirably with a great number of them.

Another recently discovered phenomenon causes much concern: on many early Italian pictures the paint is beginning to fall off in minute flakes; I have seen alarming examples in Florence and Siena. An organism, not yet identified with certainty, is by some specialists believed to be the cause; others blame the noxious fumes in the cities. Woodworm is yet another scourge that spreads in Italian panel paintings to an extent unknown in Northern Europe. The Istituto Centrale del Restauro in Rome and the Technical Department of the Soprintendenza at the Uffizi in Florence are tackling all these problems energetically but, owing to the low salaries and the consequent shortage of restorers and scientists, it will take a long time for them to be solved.

Collaboration of Restorers and Art Historians

The restorer's work, particularly at a museum, entails a great deal of collaboration with art historians. Present practice at the National Gallery is described by the Trustees in their Foreword to the Report of 1960–2: 'The decision to clean a picture is a decision of the Trustees alone. It is taken only after the Director and Chief Restorer have presented a full report on its case history and condition prepared by the Restorer who will carry out the work and the Head of the Department of Painting concerned, who is called upon to explain to us the reasons for the cleaning.' This is amplified by the Director in the body of the report (pp. 77–8). 'The administrative procedure followed before varnish is removed . . . involves no dictation to the restorer concerning technical procedure. This varies with every individual picture, and the work comes to an end when the restorer is satisfied. Throughout the treatment he is in consultation with the art historian concerned, whose duty it is to follow it, and he can also call on the Scientific Department for relevant data. But it is the restorer himself who decides how far the removal of varnish and other accretions is practicable.'

I myself had introduced in 1935, together with elaborate and systematic documentation, the practice of calling in a witness, art historian or scientist of the staff, at critical stages of an important restoration.

The Various Types of Restorer

When I am asked: How can one become a picture restorer? I must first find out what sort of a restorer the person in question would want to be, in order to know what apprenticeship or training to suggest. Why don't we do the obvious thing and give everybody the same ideal training and let him find his own bearings later? Simply because facilities are extremely scarce and we must choose

C. National Gallery No. 3948, Titian, 'Madonna and Child', 75·5 × 63 cm., during cleaning. In two horizontal bands the varnish has been removed. Note how the cloudy and irregular varnish makes the painting look much worse preserved than it is and blurs the contours of the Virgin's shoulders and veil and of the Child's head; and how the dark yellow of the varnish kills the delicate blue of the gown, making it impossible to guess correctly the true colours and intentions of the artist. The powerful three-dimensional effect is visible only in the cleaned strips.

the most suitable candidates to fill the few vacancies available. Provided the candidate has the necessary gifts and qualifications, into which of the two main categories is he likely to fit? Would he, like an artist, be happy doing his best, whether paid much or little, and work with small prospect of promotion in a museum, on the finest pictures? Or would he be interested in more profitable work mostly of lesser quality for the trade? This is of course a theoretical distinction, which is rarely found undiluted in reality, and I have known a few exceptionally gifted and high-minded colleagues who have done well out of first-rate work as 'commercial restorers' most of their lives. Yet it is obviously easier for the official museum restorer with a safe salary and guaranteed pension to live up to the highest principles. Half of the week I am a commercial restorer myself and I know how difficult it is to keep to the high standards of the museum when working for dealers or private owners, who often prefer quicker superficial cleaning and retouching to slower and more conscientious work.

In the quiet atmosphere of a public picture gallery nothing matters but quality; speed is of little importance and the young assistant has ample opportunity to develop his gifts. At best he will become an all-round man, versed in the use of both empirical and scientific data. Or he may in the course of years become a specialist on the methods of the old masters; a consultant on matters of condition and authenticity[1] for prospective purchases for his own and other galleries; and an expert witness in court and insurance cases. Or he may undertake lecturing, teaching and writing, and giving technical advice to contemporary artists. Professor Kurt Wehlte of Stuttgart, who ran the most comprehensive courses on modern painting materials and methods, is also a competent picture restorer. I know of about a dozen centres in Europe and the U.S.A. which have restorers of this ideal type, each excelling in one or two of these specialities, and there must be many others.

Whether a public picture gallery should have its own appointed restorers or employ them on a free-lance basis depends on the situation in the different countries and cities. Both solutions have their advantages and disadvantages. An increasing number of museums in the British Isles are appointing their own restorers. This is preferable where apprentices can be taught in the tradition of the Gallery and where there is only a small number of free-lance restorers to choose from. The United Kingdom has all the London restorers, more numerous than anywhere else in the world, to draw upon. As far as I know, the principal German galleries never commissioned outside restorers.

Up to 1946, when the Conservation Department was founded, the National Gallery employed only private restorers or firms together with their assistants,

[1] See Appendix B for an example of a professional report, p. 290.

and many British museums still do. This has the obvious advantage that one can change over should a preferable specialist appear.

The Restorer-Craftsman

The craftsman who saves a valuable painting from decay by transferring it to a new support renders a greater service than the restorer who cleans and retouches it. But for reasons already given, the man who does the *preservation* work gets much less credit for it than the cleaner and retoucher, though often his difficulties and responsibilities are no less formidable. His kind of work will be described in some detail in Chapter 6, Preservation and Consolidation.

As a rule all the work on a given picture is now done under the guidance of or in consultation with the general restorer, at least in large museums, but it is good practice to leave the difficult and ticklish work of blister-laying, lining, transfer and wood work to the *specialist craftsman*. He will probably make a better job of it than the 'artist-restorer' who only does this kind of work occasionally; just like a pianist, the reliner needs to 'keep his hand in' by daily practice. Moreover, the most successful cleaners and retouchers, mostly artists by birth and training, are usually too busy with their particular skill, and once the best technical methods have been developed by them the more mechanical side of picture restoration can be learned by an intelligent craftsman.

There are a number of restorers, particularly North American, who rightly pride themselves on doing everything to a painting themselves, but it must be an exceptional man who can fulfil all the different tasks with equal perfection and concentration. On the other hand we must not forget that we owe some of the most valuable technical innovations precisely to these American colleagues.

The Task and Rank of the Restorer

As a rule the conscientious restorer will, at least at the beginning of his career, carry out himself all the various treatments a painting needs, though he may later prefer to delegate the preservation work to the specialists.

What the exact position of the restorer should be in a museum will depend partly on the qualifications and the personality of the man available. On the organization of the Restoring Department at the Metropolitan Museum in New York, Mr. Murray Pease has published an exemplary paper.[1]

At the Kaiser Friedrich Museum in Berlin, as chief restorer I had the same rank and title as the keeper, that is to say, immediately under the director himself. After five years of service the title 'professor' was due. Though my salary

[1] Murray Pease, 'The future of museum conservation', *Museum*, III, No. 3 (Paris, 1950), pp. 233–42, and reprinted in *The Care of Paintings* (UNESCO, Paris, 1951), Bibliography, *Section 4* (44).

and pension were at the higher civil servant level, they were still well below what I had been earning in my free-lance restoring practice; therefore I was officially allowed to continue to work for private clients during my spare time in my home studio. (Similar arrangements exist in most countries where the salaries are inadequate). Complete cleaning was always a matter of course and the director left it to me to decide how far to carry the retouching in every case.

While sometimes the responsibilities of a 'chief', 'head', or 'senior' restorer may be more confined, in most galleries his regular duties would be :

(a) to clean and restore[1] the most important of the gallery's pictures, though he may want to confine himself to cleaning and retouching only, leaving the consolidation work to the craftsmen.

(b) to train and supervise assistant restorers and apprentices, and to delegate work to them.

(c) to advise the director, the art historians, and the scientific staff, and to collaborate with them in all technical questions. If he is an artist and connoisseur he may also advise on other matters.

(d) to train the master craftsmen and to assign work to them and supervise it.

(e) to interpret X-ray photographs and other laboratory results, in collaboration with the scientists.

(f) to strive continually, together with the scientists, to improve restoring methods, partly by suggesting subjects of research.

(g) to keep up to date by reading the foremost international technical periodicals, by exchanging experiences with leading fellow restorers abroad, by travel and by study of the pictures and the studios and laboratories abroad (special funds ought to be available for these important activities) and by attending congresses.

(h) to receive visitors, especially from abroad, and explain the restoring practices of the museum.

Cleaning, retouching and varnishing should be done by the same person. All these three measures require artistic judgment and skill. Occasionally however one may find, for instance in a firm of commercial picture restorers, the head of the firm doing nothing but the cleaning and the assistants doing the retouching — each what he is able to do best.

How much freedom the restorers are to be given in their work will also depend on the director and on the prevailing circumstances. In general, the character of a restorer and his approach to art are as important as are his qualifications and

---

[1] The term 'to restore' is not interchangeable with 'retouch'. 'Restoring' is the wider concept, embracing everything, consolidation, cleaning, retouching and varnishing.

experience. Indeed, when I began my career as a restorer, forty-seven years ago, the trustworthiness of a restorer was about the only safeguard, even in the most important museums.

Today it is supplemented by many modern and wise precautions, some mentioned earlier: by arranging to have witnesses present at decisive moments, by detailed photographic and written records and more frequent visits by the gallery director or his deputy. But despite all this and because of the very nature of the work, the director or the trustees, or whoever bears the responsibility for the restoration work, must inevitably leave things to a large extent in the hands of the senior restorer (see pp. 236–7).

Choosing a Restorer

For this reason it is vitally important to take the greatest care in choosing the right person in the first place and entrusting him with important work only after complete confidence has been established. Of two otherwise equal candidates for assistantship, I would choose the dawdler rather than the man who gets things done quickly, but who may easily get the wrong things done. What matters is that even the seemingly unimportant things must as nearly as possible be done to perfection. The good restorer is a perfectionist by nature in so far as his own work is concerned (but he must never try to perfect a picture). Not everybody seems to think so. While most collectors collect original paintings I have met one, from the continent, who collected restorations. He had 'discovered' a highly dubious and fragmentary Titian. When he asked me to restore it, he showed me photographs of three previous restorations of this picture; he obviously hoped I would 'titianize' it more successfully than my predecessors.

The restorer's is also the compromising profession par excellence (in striking contrast to the creative artist who must be uncompromising), for everything the restorer does is but the lesser of two evils.

A restorer should never overplay the bad condition of a picture brought to him. He should always be completely frank but as optimistic as the circumstances allow.

A charming little skit on this point was once performed for me by two of my young students. One of them dressed up as myself, wearing my spectacles. The other appeared as a client who carried an empty antique frame hanging over his forearm, saying: 'I admit, Mr. Ruhemann, there is not much left of the picture, but I am sure you will make a good job of it.' The one acting me replied: 'Don't worry, the picture presents no problems.'

Let me quote from *The Care of Pictures*[1] by George L. Stout, '... Is he

---

[1] George L. Stout, *The Care of Pictures* (New York, 1948), Bibliography, *Section 4* (34).

(the restorer) a person of good education, of sound judgement and of reasonable inclinations? Does he explain his work in a way that is frank and rational, or does he hide behind affectations of peculiar taste and sensibility? Does he maintain full records? Does he insist on complete exploration of the condition and is he clear about the facilities for examination — physical, optical, chemical and photographic?'

From all this it is clear that the restorer should be a connoisseur and an artist of sensibility; further, he must possess integrity, tact, humility and self-discipline. I repeat: his character matters at least as much as his abilities.

The Keeping of Records

In museums one of the junior restorers usually looks after the dossiers or records of the physical state of the paintings. He sees to it that all restorers and craftsmen write reports on even the smallest treatments and that the necessary photographs are entered in the folders.

An early example of conservation dossiers, on which those in the National Gallery are partly based, is described by G. L. Stout.[1] The National Gallery dossiers, the form of which has been gradually evolving since 1935, measure $17\frac{1}{2} \times 13\frac{1}{2}$ inches. The dossier for Leonardo's 'Virgin of the Rocks', to give an extreme instance, consists of seven volumes and contains as many as 144 photographs of 12×10 inches.

Special forms for collecting statistical facts concerning cleaning methods and the techniques of the masters are mentioned in the appropriate chapters, and a few examples are shown in Appendix B, pp. 309 ff.

The Restorer's Studio

For the benefit of anybody who has to choose or design a restorer's studio I reproduce an architect's plan (with grateful acknowledgement to my brother) of the one built for me at the National Gallery under Sir Kenneth Clark's régime. For sharp and detailed observation powerful light is even more important than strong magnification. High side windows are imperative for a restorer's studio, if possible joining on to a low top light and running along the whole length of the wall. But the top light must not extend over the whole of the studio roof: one third or half of it away from the side window should be opaquely covered. Light coming from every side is useless for restoring and creates distressing reflections. The walls must be painted dark and matt. Very dark coffee brown has proved more agreeable than black. (On this colour pictures look surprisingly well.)

---

[1] G. L. Stout, 'A Museum Record of the Condition of Paintings', *Technical Studies in the Field of the Fine Arts*, III, 4 (April, 1935), pp. 200–16, Bibliography, *Section 9 (3)*.

PLAN OF RESTORER'S STUDIO

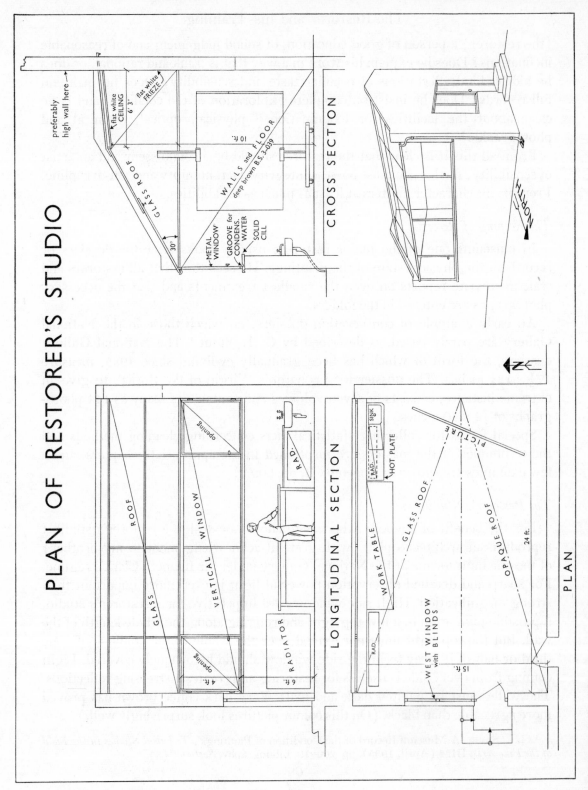

preferably high wall here →

flat white CEILING
flat white FRIEZE
6' 3"

GLASS ROOF

30°

10 ft.

WALLS and FLOOR
deep brown B.S. 3-039

METAL WINDOW
GROOVE for CONDENS. WATER
SOLID CILL

CROSS SECTION

NORTH

ROOF

GLASS

VERTICAL WINDOW

opening

opening

4 ft.

6 ft.

RADIATOR

RAD.

LONGITUDINAL SECTION

SINK
RAD.
HOT PLATE

WORK TABLE

GLASS ROOF

PICTURE

OPAQUE ROOF

24 ft.

WEST WINDOW with BLINDS

RAD.

15 ft.

N

PLAN

The Restorer and his Training

In artificial lighting the restorer must also have the most powerful available, provided that excessive ultra-violet radiation is avoided. The window panes should all have an ultra-violet filter. Where this is not yet installed, the pictures should be covered when not being worked on.

Fluorescent lighting has one disadvantage: it is too diffuse for certain jobs and, like the conventional studio top light, not concentrated enough. For anything to do with the surface texture of a picture, such as puttying, treatment of flaking and for varnishing, a small concentrated source of light is needed of which one can clearly see the reflection on the surface of the picture. Also for observation or retouching of fine detail a stronger, better-focused lamp is necessary.[1]

Direct sunlight is still unequalled and the ideal studio should therefore have one small window where the sun shines in for part of the day.

If one has seen certain subtleties in the strongest illumination and with powerful magnification, one can then often discern them in weaker light and with a weaker lens, as one's power of observation improves. On the other hand, a restorer who gets used to working in inadequate light sees fewer and fewer minutiae, his power of observation and his fastidiousness decline. I do not say this lightly, for I have actually seen several sad cases of this developing in British and foreign galleries.

We are still dreaming of the ideal studio lamp, yet I have once heard a museum official argue against purchasing a stronger lamp for the restorers, saying that 'if the restorer sees too much he does too much'. He meant of course too much cleaning and retouching. This remark exemplifies a characteristic attitude: the acceptance of voluntary self-deception as a desirable state of affairs, coupled with groping in the dark. Surely, if a restorer should succeed in a comparatively dim light in cleaning and retouching just enough to please the curator in question, it would be a coincidence. Is that desirable? Or is it preferable that the proper limit to his operation should be set by self-discipline in the fullest knowledge of the relevant facts, obtained in the strongest light available?

Simple logic as well as experience shows that the better the lighting conditions, the better the restorer's work will be. However, exceptional cases may occur; for instance when, in order not to do any unnecessary spots of retouching, one would finish the job in the gallery where the picture is to hang eventually and where the light may be dimmer than in the studio.

[1] Since this was written the *Xenon Gas Lamp* has been invented; it gives a ray almost as powerful as sunlight and of similar hue. Unfortunately it is still expensive and complicated and has been known to explode.

Background

THE TRAINING OF RESTORERS[1]

I have always advocated the creation of international training colleges for restorers at university level, in London, Paris and other capital cities. This measure would do much to raise the general standard in our profession, and would guarantee a succession of highly qualified restorers for all the major picture galleries.

In the absence of such colleges, there are at present three main ways of entering the profession : as an apprentice to a private restorer or firm, as an apprentice to a museum or as a pupil at one of the few schools of restoration in existence.

New York was given its *training centre* at university level[2] for restorers in 1962. Paris and London are still without one. The Courtauld Institute's Technology Department now specializes only in science for restorers and courses for art historians (see Appendix A, pp. 287–8).

The Restorers' College under Professor Eigenberger at the Kunst-Akademie in Vienna is of older standing; but there the emphasis has always been on traditional practice rather than tuition in scientific examination and modern methods, which prevail in the Training Institutes in Rome — where exemplary work is being done both in restoring and in training — in Stuttgart, Zurich and Brussels (see Appendix A, pp. 287–9).

I do not think that before 1946 any of the British picture galleries had their own appointed restorer, so until then the only training available in Great Britain and the Commonwealth was in one of the established firms of free-lance picture restorers; however, they were apt to stipulate rather stiff terms, a high premium and seven years' commitment.

When in 1946 I was asked to take over the Technology Department of the Courtauld Institute, I felt I was filling a gap in starting at the Laboratory a course in restoration of paintings, mainly destined for future museum restorers. To watch the restoring work at our 'Lab.' was also considered an excellent education for the young scholars of art history in the Institute, some of whom were to become museum curators. The maximum number of restoring pupils (many of them foreigners) at one time was seven; by 1961 eight of the students had already become museum restorers, several in Great Britain and the Commonwealth; most of the other students had turned to free-lance restoring.

---

[1] See also Cesare Brandi, 'Il fondamento teorico del restauro', *Bollettino dell' Istituto Centrale del Restauro*, I (Rome, 1950) pp. 5–12, see also Bibliography, *Section* 7 (34) in which this article and other of the author's writings on the same topic are included; and G. L. Stout, 'Cleaning and restoration of pictures, the viewpoint of the conservator', *Alumni*, XIX (Bruxelles, 1950), No. 3–4, p. 283, Bibliography, *Section* 4 (42).

[2] The Conservation Center, Institute of Fine Arts, New York University, commenced courses September 1962. See Bibliography, *Section* 8 (11), and Appendix A, p. 288.

Special summer courses were given for gallery curators, museum staff, curators of the National Trust and the Ministry of Works, who look after many great houses and their treasures.

Selecting Candidates

From thirty-five years' teaching I have learnt that the greatest problem is how to select the most suitable recruits. A training institute, particularly if it is attached to a University, should of course demand University entrance standard, but the many candidates who have not reached it should also be catered for, at least for the present, while the dearth of qualified restorers lasts.[1] Professor Rotondi, the director of the Istituto Centrale del Restauro, in his excellent lecture at the 1961 Rome conference, rightly stressed the necessity of admitting non-restorers in charge of works of art to shorter courses.

I do not agree with those of my colleagues in the U.S.A. who hold that anybody with an intelligence a little above average can be taught to be a good restorer. He can only be taught the teachable things, and talent, sensitivity, flair and a sharp eye are not among them. They can be developed, but only where they are inborn. Any candidate for the post of apprentice restorer at the London National Gallery has to prove first that he can see and paint. (If the present lack of connoisseurs among art historians is to be cured, undergraduates ought to be set similar tests before being admitted to the faculty of art history.)[2]

Should the restorer be an artist?

This brings us to the important question : should a picture restorer be an artist by nature and training? I have no doubt that he should, though one of the most efficient restorers at the National Gallery was no professional painter but he had exceptional patience, artistic gift and sensitiveness; several outwardly very successful restorers seem to have managed well without any apparent artistic gift or training; but these are exceptions. However, opinions on this point differ. Monsieur F. M. Kahn[3] believes that a painter let loose on an old master's

[1] The Society of German Picture Restorers sent me an excellent summary on their attitude towards training. For candidates who have Higher School Certificate, they suggest altogether 5–6 years of training: 2 years at art school, followed by 2 years with a museum's restorer and 2 years at a special Training Centre. For boys from Secondary schools or with the Lower Certificate, 7–8 years altogether : 2–3 years with craftsmen in the field of art, gilders, church decorators etc.; 2 years with an officially recognized restorer and 2 years at the Training Centre. The Society does not favour the introduction of a Final Examination and an official diploma, but instead certificates, written by the principals of the different training institutes or workshops through which the candidate has passed.

[2] Michael Levey, Keeper at the National Gallery, wrote in *The British Journal of Aesthetics* (April 1963, p. 188) 'Today's art history students are all-knowing and non-seeing.'

[3] Guy Iznard, *Les Pirates de la Peinture* (Flammarion, Paris, 1955), p. 49.

picture would paint too much on it. This could be true only of one without respect and understanding of great art and without self-discipline. I hope this type of restorer has about died out. Monsieur Germain Bazin, Chief Curator of Paintings and Drawings at the Louvre Museum, holds that 'restorers must be painters'[1] and so do most curators I know.

It is not so much that the restorer must know how to paint retouchings, as that he must be able to identify himself profoundly with the masters whose works he treats, and he must be thoroughly familiar with all the painter's materials, which is almost impossible without years of practical experience as a painter; above all, in seeing a dirty, damaged and repainted picture he must be able to visualize how it was intended to look; how it will eventually look depends even more on artistic feeling and aesthetic tact than on his mastery of the materials and the ways in which they have to be used. Here I should like to make it quite clear that the restorer ought to discipline his personal taste when he cleans and allow it to restrain him from retouching too much or too coarsely and from applying too thick and shiny a varnish.

It is quite true that those rare qualities that make the greatest artist, genius, originality, and dynamic energy, would not make a good restorer; they will not be found among the candidates who, like myself, lack precisely some of these gifts and have given up the hope of becoming first-rate painters.

In a training course, those students whose bent and talents make them apt rather for the more mechanical consolidation (this really most important part of restoration work), would soon sort themselves out and their further training could be specialized accordingly. If a student is too impetuous in his cleaning, this may be a sign that he is not suited for the profession; if his retouching does not improve sufficiently (be it 'deceptive' or 'visible') it must be due to a lack of talent and in both cases he should be encouraged to specialize in consolidation work or to choose another profession.

At one of the leading Institutes the test for artistic qualification consists of nothing but an outline drawing from one or two pictures. In my opinion the candidate should at least be able to make a good drawing of a hand from nature, and not only his eyesight but also his colour vision should be as carefully tested as his integrity of character, before he is accepted as a student. The Louvre Museum has an excellent and elaborate scheme for the entrance examination to its Restoration Studios, including a copy from an old master's painting and an art historical essay; their candidates for apprenticeship have already gone through a thorough training at an Art College.

---

[1] Guy Iznard, op. cit., p. 49.

The Restorer and his Training

Science for Restorers

Another important and controversial problem is how much scientific training a restorer needs. Some people contend that a two or three years' course in science is necessary; others, among them Norman Brommelle who is both a scientist and restorer of some standing and now Keeper of the Department of Conservation in the Victoria and Albert Museum, believe that all the science a picture restorer requires could be taught in a course of a few weeks, perhaps with the help of a handbook on 'Science for Restorers', which remains to be written. I for one certainly agree. With this another question is connected: should picture restorers be trained together with restorers of *objets d'art* of metal, stone or wood and other archaeological treasures? My answer is they should perhaps attend part of the science courses together, especially elementary ones, but there are so many things which only the one kind of specialist needs to know, that it would be a great waste of time and effort to make the groups combine for that part of the training which is unnecessary for them. One lifetime is not long enough for learning to restore well.

I myself know only the science that I learned at school and what I picked up as I went along. The more intricate part of it is now wonderfully taken care of for us by the museum scientists. However, I have often deplored my lack of scientific training, particularly in systematic preparing, handling and testing of materials.

A restorer who masters all the relevant science and uses all the scientific aids can still be the worst of his profession; one with no scientific training can still be one of the best if his talent is great. He will of course have to be intelligent enough to make use of every help he can get from scientific methods. One of the first things a restorer should be taught by scientists is the discipline of systematically painting out samples of every substance, adhesive, medium, pigment or varnish etc. that comes into his hands; this must not be done on glass only, but also on canvas and proper grounds, etc. Had I done this from the beginning of my career I would today possess an invaluable archive and far greater assurance on certain points.

Other Desirable Subjects

I find training in connoisseurship and in the ethics of conservation indispensable. A close contact, in regular seminars, with outstanding art historians will benefit both sides. Guided visits to galleries and picture sales should be on the syllabus as well as lectures on the methods of the old masters and on the detection of forgeries.

Another point on which opinions diverge is whether an official training centre should accept commissions to restore pictures. I am in favour of it, because no medical school can work without patients. The risk would be negligible if the difficult and valuable cases were left to the teachers to work on for demonstration purposes.

Every student should make at least one copy of part of a masterpiece under the teachers' guidance.

I have found it most useful to know sufficient French, Italian and German to enable me to read all the relevant literature and to make travel more useful.

After finishing the, say, three years' course at the training institute and passing a stiff final examination[1] the student should work another three years at the restoration department of a museum or with a free-lance restorer of renown, before he starts on his own and is entrusted with valuable pictures.

I have always been in favour of museums taking on volunteers, including foreigners, perhaps on an exchange basis, and this system has worked most satisfactorily at the Berlin Museum where I introduced it, at Munich, Brussels and in Yugoslavia.

The Importance of the Teacher

Finally I would like to stress that in our field, even more than in an ordinary school, not only the success of tuition but also the design of the syllabus will to some extent depend on the teachers available; apart from the elementary ones, certain subjects (for which prominent specialists are at hand) will occupy a comparatively larger place in the programme, at least until eminent and more versatile teachers emerge from among the younger restorers. In the meantime the problem is urgent because the awareness of the problems of conservation has grown everywhere much more quickly than the number of highly qualified restorers.

It is only the great museums and related institutions who can deal with the problem. It should be possible for them to ensure that the knowledge of the older and more experienced restorers in their institutions is shared by a larger number of the rising generation. This would guarantee the continuance of sound tradition, in principles and methods, more than the most systematic or scientific university courses.[2]

Whatever the syllabus and staff of any new training institute for restorers, and wherever started, it should be founded on a generous scale and should preferably be run by a picture restorer who has excelled in his profession: if he has some

---

[1] See Appendix B for a suggested test paper, p. 315.

[2] Paul Philippot, 'Zur Situation der Gemälde-und Plastikrestauratoren & zum Problem ihrer Ausbildung', *Museums-Kunde* (Verlag de Gruyter & Co., Berlin, 1963), No. 3, Bibliography, *Section 8 (9)*.

command of science, all the better. Where no restorer with the suitable personality and experience is available, an art historian who has spent much time with restorers and scientists should, in my opinion, be the director.

It goes almost without saying that the syllabus of a training institute will vary greatly in different countries.

Technical Training of Art Historians

Every modern college of art and every training centre for restorers has lectures on art history in its syllabus as a matter of course. On the other hand, few university departments for the History of Art include technical courses.

The following important pronouncement by one of the leading Museum directors on the Continent expresses lucidly what I have in mind when I recommend technical training for art historians. After the 1946–7 controversy, Dr. Georg Schmidt, the director of the Basle Kunst-Museum, who had distributed a detached but critical assessment of the National Gallery's Cleaned Pictures Exhibition, wrote: 'Indeed we art historians realize, however excellent our historical training may have been, that we never had any tuition of the technique of the old masters or the technique of restoration and cleaning. It may be too late for our generation to acquire the long experience necessary to become proper judges in these matters, but we should at least try to help create adequate training and facilities for study for the younger generation. All we can do is to try to learn as much as we can — in refresher courses etc. — so as to be able to appreciate and assess the advice given us by the technical specialists.'

The Technology Department of the Courtauld Institute of Art (London University) founded in 1934 was a new departure in the suggested direction. It was primarily intended to provide relevant technical knowledge to the art history scholars studying at the Institute, and in this respect was to my knowledge the first of its kind.[1]

The Institut Royal du Patrimoine Artistique at Brussels, under the energetic and versatile directorship of the late Paul Coremans, developed into a training centre of international renown, for scientists concerned with the preservation of art treasures, for restorers and to some extent for art historians.

Studies in Conservation published obituaries[2] by three close professional friends of Paul Coremans. I cannot add much to these detailed and moving appreciations of Paul's person and achievements. I did not work as closely with him as did Plenderleith, Rivière and Rawlins, but only followed and admired from

[1] Similar courses connected with their Universities now exist in Milan, Rome, Munich, Utrecht, New York and Bristol, and probably elsewhere, unknown to me.
[2] Vol. X, No. 3, August 1965.

afar his great contributions to our field. He will go into history on many counts, but perhaps above all for his research (together with Gettens and Thissen) into the media of the van Eycks and their contemporaries. It has put an end to centuries of legend and guesswork and inaugurated an era of positive knowledge in this matter.

CHAPTER 3

The Exhibition of Cleaned Pictures at the National Gallery

The 1947 Exhibition of Cleaned Pictures at the National Gallery was probably the most important event of its kind in the field of picture cleaning since the cleaning of the Frans Hals paintings at Haarlem in 1919. Yet it was not an innovation: the Louvre in Paris anticipated the National Gallery by exactly 150 years with a little exhibition of this kind, possibly the first one to be held. I quote from an article by M. J. Friedländer:[1]

'When Napoleon gave his great example to later "leaders" and took a great number of works of art from Italy to Paris, the gentlemen at the Louvre were violently attacked. They had dared to have renovated precious Italian paintings. To defend themselves against this reproach, they wanted to exhibit a Perugino and a Carracci, half cleaned, so that the public would see how necessary the cleaning was and with how much caution and art it had been carried out.'

The exhibition in London[2] was also arranged to inform the public. Only, instead of two half-cleaned pictures, five were exhibited; three pairs of companion pictures were also displayed, one cleaned, the other not cleaned. A large number of ordinary and special ray photographs and the equipment used were also shown, to illustrate the methods and safeguards applied. The plan for the exhibition was set up by the Director of the National Gallery, Philip Hendy, together with the restorers and the staff. After careful preparations the exhibition was opened on October 9th, 1947, in two large rooms of the National Gallery.

Altogether seventy pictures which had been cleaned during the preceding ten years were exhibited. It is probably no exaggeration to say that this was one of the most instructive art exhibitions ever held. From the beginning to the end it was crowded with visitors from all over the world.

[1] M. J. Friedländer and W. Martin, 'The Awakened Night Watch', quoting a Berlin newspaper article of March 19th, 1796: in *Maandblad voor Beeldende Kunsten*, 22 (1946), p. 197, see also Bibliography, *Section 5* (8), (10).

[1] See also pages 228–9.

Background

It is characteristic of Philip Hendy's independence of thought that at the beginning of his career he wrote the catalogue of the Gardner Museum, Boston, in which he introduced a daring innovation, the mention of the pictures' state of preservation.[1] In this later venture of his, *The Catalogue of the Cleaned Pictures Exhibition, London, 1947*, the condition and technical history of the pictures form the main part of the booklet. The staff of the Gallery, Martin Davies, Neil MacLaren and Cecil Gould, helped to compile the material and the restorers contributed the technical information.

In this unique little book many of the arguments for and against the thorough cleaning of paintings may be found.[2] (For illustrations, see plates 10–22.)

International Repercussions

The exhibition naturally aroused a good deal of comment, overwhelmingly but not exclusively favourable. But we at the Gallery were especially interested in the reaction of visitors from the Continent. Many artists and museum officials came to study the London attitude to the problems of restoration, and especially to the question of whether complete or partial cleaning was more desirable.

Two Schools of Cleaning

M. René Huyghe, at that time Curator of Paintings and Drawings at the Louvre, and Professor Cesare Brandi,[3] then Head of the Istituto Centrale del Restauro, Rome, who were in those days worried that the London example might set off a craze for cleaning, and that it might not always be done by competent hands, proffered in several meetings and lectures a few impressive and at first sight rather convincing arguments:

(1) 'What has been removed cannot be replaced; what has been left can be removed later.' But this implies that the restorer may be unable, in general, to distinguish between what is original and what is not. He may indeed find himself in that position, in which event he will not proceed. However, in the case of an experienced cleaner this may be fairly said to be the exception rather than the rule.

(2) 'Most old paintings are like ageing beauties who can no longer stand the full light of day and we therefore keep the curtain drawn.' It is surprising how

---

[1] This had been suggested a generation earlier by Justi and Glück (in *Giorgione*, Vol. II, p. 36), but as far as I know never carried out.

[2] On the desirability of scrupulous cleaning for technical reasons see also Morton Bradley, *The Treatment of Pictures* (Art Technology, Cambridge, Mass., 1950), paragraphs 2.02, 2.03; 2.021 to 2.022. Bibliography, *Section 4* (41).

[3] Cf. *Museum*, III, 3 (Paris, 1950), Bibliography, *Section 4* (44).

10. National Gallery No. 279, Rubens, 'The Horrors of War', 49 × 76 cm. In the light rectangles the dark varnish has been removed.

11. The same after completed cleaning (1948). See above. 'I am afraid, when a freshly painted picture has been so long fastened up in a box, that the colours may very well have gone dull, and particularly that the flesh tones and whites may have become a little yellow. However, Your Lordship will easily remedy this by putting it out in the sun, and leaving it there at intervals.' Rubens writing from Antwerp to Sustermans, court painter in Florence, about this painting on 12 March 1638.

12. A case of cleaning criticized. National Gallery No. 54, Rembrandt, 'A Woman bathing in a Stream', 61·8 × 47 cm., before the cleaning in 1946. Note the rather dark, highly finished and not very well modelled hand.

13. The same picture after removing the dark varnish and the overpainting. An original hand as sketchy as the shift has come to light.

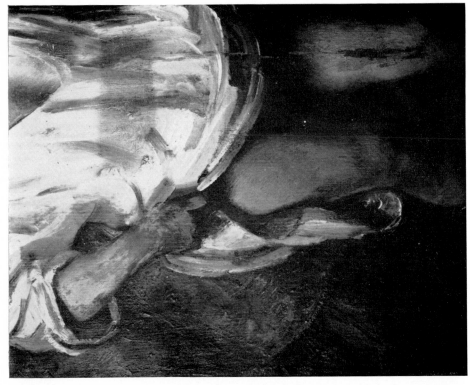

15. Detail from an ultra-violet photograph taken during cleaning. The dark varnish has been removed except in a horizontal rectangle on the abdomen; remnants of the over-painting on the hand appear now, like the obvious retouching on the leg, as dark patches.

14. Detail of an X-ray photograph taken in 1927 (compare with plate 13) already showing the sketchy or unfinished state of the original hand and the dark gap across the wrist, for which the cleaner had been held responsible.

much better preserved most of those beauties prove to be than they looked before the curtain was drawn back and the veil and make-up removed. Nothing makes them look more worn and aged than a superficial toilette which leaves the wrinkles in the flesh paint emphasized by ingrained dirt. Moreover, as the New York Metropolitan Museum puts it so well: 'The common visual defects produced by deterioration and attrition are not "counterbalanced" by obscuring varnish. Any material that will render damages less apparent must also obscure the healthy remainder of the painting, thus mitigating one type of disfigurement by adding another.'[1]

(3) As for the fallacy that many old masters applied or desired a 'patina to improve their pictures', I refer again to the great masters' own words[2] in the catalogue of the Exhibition of Cleaned Pictures. Such practices may have prevailed in the earlier nineteenth century, but there is no evidence that they were frequent before the eighteenth century (see also p. 236). However, dealers and fakers may well have put toned varnishes on in the seventeenth century.

A great old master, after proudly putting the last touch to his work, would hardly expect Time to finish or improve it. Nor would he be likely to have said to his patron in delivering the commission: 'This is not quite right yet, but in ten or twenty or perhaps fifty years it will look much better and more as I want it.'

The famous French restorer and author Horsin Déon in 1851 had this to say about the policy of the Louvre:[3]

'It is understandable that the romantic amateur loves the rust and haze of the varnish, for it has become a veil behind which he can see whatever he desires: ... under this smoky and grimy crust I shall perhaps find a masterpiece. How can one resist such a lure? How can one not prefer the deceptive hope of a treasure to a cold and mediocre reality?

'But in a museum like ours, the finest in the world, the pictures must be shown sincerely, clean and in full light; show them openly, that is how you will confound those scholars, clever with words, but less erudite than skilful in usurping other peoples' knowledge.

'Yes, we repeat, our pictures can bear the full light of day, and we must add, that the duty of their curators is to show them to us with all their qualities, without heeding the clamours of ignorance.

---

[1] *Museum*, III, 3 (1950), Bibliography, *Section 4* (44).

[2] See also Dürer's letter to Jacob Heller, p. 234. To these must now be added the thorough and scholarly refutations by Denis Mahon and Joyce Plesters of some erroneous interpretations of literary sources (*The Burlington Magazine*, CIV (1962), pp. 452–70 incl.), Bibliography, *Section 7* (26), (28).

[3] From Horsin Déon, *De la conservation et de la restauration des tableaux* (Paris, 1851), p. 55, Bibliography, *Section 3* (43).

Background

'We must even say that it is a necessity to put the pictures right, for this museum, created for study, is today disastrous to young artists who go there seeking inspiration.'

By now some of the opinions expressed under the shadow of the controversy of 1946–7 may have been modified in the light of new experience. But no major declarations on the subject have since appeared, and some of the statements made nearly twenty years ago still need clarification. In particular, René Huyghe's article 'The Louvre Museum and the Problem of the Cleaning of Old Pictures' and Professor Brandi's contribution on 'The Restoration of a Sebastiano del Piombo'[1] (see also pp. 217 ff.) have had and still are causing wide repercussions, some of their surmises having found their way into technical books.[2] Of course they are both valuable warnings to rash and inexperienced cleaners.

In his article on the theory of restoration Professor Cesare Brandi has laid the theoretical foundation of the desirability of 'patina' on paintings.[3] Because of my admiration for his invaluable organization of some of the stupendous salvaging work of Italy's treasures and of the Istituto Centrale del Restauro in Rome, I have for years hesitated to draw attention to some errors in other papers of his in *The Burlington Magazine* of July 1949 and in *Museum*, III, No. 3, 1950, p. 212 (see Bibliography, *section* 4 (44) and *section* 7 (10)). Both these papers have come to be regarded as the main pillars to support the desirability of semi-cleaning and the respect for patina on paintings. MacLaren's and Werner's challenge[4] of Brandi's arguments and misinterpretations of technical details has never been invalidated. Their statement that 'there was no evidence of easily soluble and tinted varnishes until much later times' still holds good and has just been confirmed again by Denis Mahon's and Joyce Plesters' elaborate research.[5]

Here follows Brandi's main evidence for the desirability of patina on paintings:

Baldinucci (rather late, in 1681) says under 'Patena': 'e quella universale scurità che il tempo fa apparire sopra le pitture, che anche talvolta la favorisce.'

I suggest the word *anche* in this context be translated by 'even': 'Patina even suits certain pictures well'. Thus Baldinucci neither takes the 'suiting well' for

[1] *Museum*, III, 3 (1950). Bibliography, *Section* 4 (44).

[2] E.g. by Guy Iznard, op. cit., p. 48. M. Iznard also mentions as 'excellent results' of cleaning in the Louvre two classic examples of timid undercleaning: the 'Vierge aux Rochers' by Leonardo and the 'Concert' by Giorgione.

[3] C. Brandi, 'Il Restauro secondo l'Istanza Estetica', *Bollettino dell' Istituto Centrale del Restauro*, XIII (Rome, 1953) pp. 1–8. Reprinted in book form together with other writings by the same author, and on allied topics, see Bibliography, *Section* 7 (34).

[4] Neil MacLaren and Anthony Werner, 'Some Factual Observations about Varnishes and Glazes', *The Burlington Magazine* (July 1950) pp. 189–92, Bibliography, *Section* 7 (11).

[5] Published in their articles in *The Burlington Magazine* CIV (1962), pp. 452–70, and pp. 460–70, Bibliography, *Section* 7 (26), (28).

granted nor does he apply it to the majority of paintings. The patina does indeed suit certain pictures only too well (*favorisce*).

In his article in *Museum*, Professor Brandi says that a Sebastiano del Piombo at Viterbo could not be cleaned with anything stronger than turpentine (that is to say: without harming the paint). This is obviously based on one of those misunderstandings which so often occur when persons little versed in technical matters witness the cleaning of a picture. Every restorer knows that you cannot remove from a painting varnish more than twenty years old, let alone damage or endanger the paint, with pure turpentine or slightly stronger solvents. The only old work which has been through my hands where the original paint reacted to turpentine was a Stubbs (dated 1780) and even that I managed to clean safely with undiluted acetone.[1]

This erroneous statement of Brandi's had for fifteen years served as a basis for theories that have caused a great deal of confusion and harm. In the meantime he has immeasurably widened his experience, to the point at which in the last few years of his directorship he allowed the restorers of his Istituto to go further and further with the varnish removal from great masterpieces. Now anybody can go and admire the exemplary cleaning achieved under Professor Brandi's regime for the galleries of Siena (Duccio's 'Maestà') and of San Marco in Florence, or one can walk into the Istituto Centrale del Restauro in Rome which he created out of nothing and where so much fine work was done while he was director. One had been able to examine there perfectly cleaned masterpieces by Duccio, Simone Martini, Ambrogio Lorenzetti, Piero della Francesca, Giovanni Bellini, Antonello da Messina, etc., which no longer show any trace of 'patina'.

The theory of picture cleaning had preceded the practice of it. Now the practice seems to have overtaken the theory, which at present is lagging behind and will probably continue to do so for some little time to come: I shall not be surprised to read denials of the great progress I have just mentioned. However, on the whole matters are improving almost everywhere.

In case this chapter should have convinced some readers so well of the desirability of cleaning pictures that they feel tempted to try their hands on their own treasures I must repeat here a strong warning. Far more damage has probably been done by enthusiastic amateur cleaners than by professional restorers. J. Guillerme writes in *L'Atelier du Temps*[2] p. 105 (Hermann, Paris 1964): 'The cleaning of paintings can with certain amateurs become just as compelling a passion as the love of patina.'

[1] A portrait of Sir Joshua Wedgwood, belonging to Sir John Wedgwood, Leith Hill; it is probably painted with a medium based on resin and wax.

[2] Bibliography, *Section 2* (23).

Background

Which of these two passions is likely to have caused more physical damage in the course of time can hardly be doubted; but if one were able to compare in percentage terms the loss of the master's intentions, on the one hand by ruinous cleaning and on the other hand by the retention of the 'patina' the latter might easily win the contest. Indeed might it not be worthwhile to go seriously into this question? It is true, while the damage done by reckless cleaning is irreversible the patina which has for centuries falsified the majority of paintings can be removed; but how many erroneous judgements in the literature of art may not be due to patina? How many styles may even have been based on it? I have only mentioned one striking example, Delacroix (p. 51), but there must be many more in earlier times; after all, in periods when pictures were not scrupulously cleaned, one or two generations after their creation they were only known as already considerably changed by dirt and darkened varnishes.

Some student of the history of art, less interested in iconography and history than in the aesthetic, as it were, the timeless aspect of the great masters' paintings, will perhaps find here a rewarding subject for his thesis. Much spade work in the field he would find already done by Joyce Plesters and Denis Mahon (*The Burlington Magazine*, Nov. 1962). They have dug up and turned over scores of doubtful interpretations and translations of texts and terms related to patina; in fact they have gone through practically all the relevant sources and have not found anything to substantiate assertions that any great master covered his pictures with an overall toned varnish or wished them to become mellowed by time.

Now that the 'Rokeby Venus' by Velázquez at the National Gallery in London has been cleaned, one is able to compare it with Manet's 'Eva Gonzálès' (National Gallery No. 3295) which hangs in the next room but one. This picture has also been cleaned recently and one cannot fail to observe how much less luminous and poorer in nuances is Manet's flesh paint than Velázquez'. Does perhaps the same explanation apply here as in Delacroix's case? As Delacroix was inspired by Rubens so was Manet by Velázquez and like Delacroix he probably never had a chance of seeing his idol's works without the distortion of patina.

16. National Gallery No. 54, Rembrandt, 'A woman bathing in a stream'. Detail of the woman's right hand after the removal of the overpaint, two times magnified. See p. 80 and Plates 12–15.

17. National Gallery No. 852, Rubens: 'Le Chapeau de Paille', 79 × 55 cm.,
during cleaning in 1946. The dark rectangles are left uncleaned for photographing. The dark patches in the clouds along the vertical join on the right
hand side of the painting are probably original retouchings where Rubens
tried to bridge the join of his own extension of the initial panel. A similar
horizontal join runs through the sitter's right hand.

18. The same picture after cleaning, in ultra-violet light, showing Rubens'
own retouchings as dark patches in the clouds on the right.
See chapter on the Exhibition of Cleaned Pictures.

19. Detail of 17 before cleaning, taken in 1934, showing the dark streaks of the preparation appearing through the flesh paint on the forehead.

20. The same detail after cleaning. It had been alleged that the dark streaks had been caused to appear by the cleaning and that other original touches had disappeared.

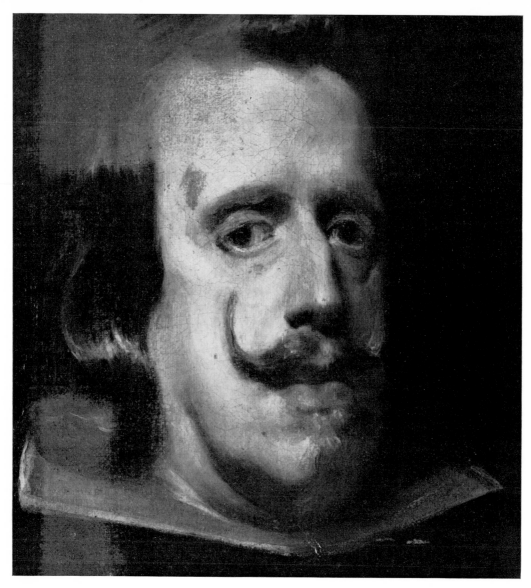

21. National Gallery No. 745, Velázquez: 'Philip IV of Spain' bust portrait, 64·1 × 53·7 cm. Detail, approximately half of full size, taken in ultra-violet light during cleaning. The dark spots on the temple and below the sitter's right eye are old retouchings, which in ordinary light showed only slightly through the dark varnish. The milky rectangles left on the forehead and on the collar are old varnish, which has been removed from the rest of the picture except for small remnants showing light fluorescence here and there.

22. The face after cleaning. This photograph, taken in ordinary light, shows the excellent state of preservation of the painting. Note how much smaller the actual holes are than the retouchings that covered them.

23. National Gallery No. 566, Duccio, 'The Virgin and Child with Saints', 42·5 × 34·5 cm. Detail, two times magnification, after removal of a yellow varnish, before removal of a 'grey layer' sometimes called 'original patina' which covered the whole painting. Many of the colours were indistinguishable.

24. The same detail after complete cleaning, before retouching. The darkness of the 'grey layer' was almost entirely caused by dirt collected in the fine cracks of the varnish. This is proof that it could not have been intended by the artist. See p. 234.

Part II

TECHNIQUE AND ETHICS
OF RESTORATION

CHAPTER 4

Anatomy of a Painting

Before learning anything about the treatment of paintings, their anatomy and the relevant technical terms must be understood. What a painting consists of and how it is constructed has been so lucidly and exhaustively explained by George L. Stout that I cannot hope to do it better. He has most generously allowed me to quote extensively from his small classic, *The Care of Pictures*,[1] in which much useful — and no unnecessary — detail is to be found. He writes:

'If you take a piece of paper and make a mark on it with a piece of charcoal you have, in about the simplest terms, the structural parts of a picture. In this the paper serves as a *support*, the thing on which the picture is carried, and the charcoal will do to represent the other structural part, the *design*. A great many pictures have been made since the earliest recorded times and are still being made with only these two main parts. The charcoal alone is a *pigment*, one form of carbon black. Substitute for it a mixture of pigments and add enough *sticking material* (or *adhesive*) to hold these mixed powders in place after they are dry, and you have *paint*.

The most common supports . . . are *wood, fabric* and *paper*. All of these are organic materials and all are somewhat alike, or they share the basic substance, cellulose. In paper and fabric the fibres have been removed from their original position of growth and have been twisted, woven or felted into new relations.

The use of *grounds* brings in a somewhat more complex type of picture construction, for the ground is by definition and general understanding never a direct part of the design. It is a smooth, flat coating put over the support. For the most part the ground is a device of European painters. It may have come into wide use during the Middle Ages when much of the surface of a painted panel carried gold leaf and when a very smooth preparation was needed to imbed this leaf and to permit burnishing and tooling it.

The color or tone of grounds is usually white or light. This allows for easy development of the drawing. The material which gives this tone is a white powder, and many such materials have been used for the purpose: gypsum, chalk, China clay and white pigments. To make the powder hold in a firm layer on the support, some kind of binder or *adhesive* is needed, and the usual one is a skin *glue* or any animal glue. The reason for the choice of a water-soluble adhesive is largely that it works better — dries quicker and

---

[1] George L. Stout, *The Care of Pictures* (New York, 1948). It has been out of print for years and I wish this plagiarism to be regarded as an homage to the insuperability of George's writing. Bibliography, *Section 4* (34).

Technique and Ethics of Restoration

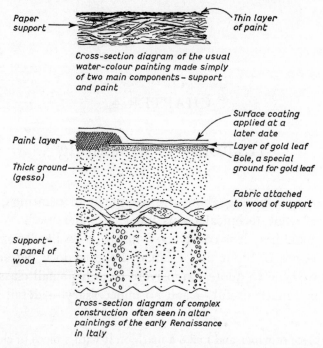

Paper support → Thin layer of paint

Cross-section diagram of the usual water-colour painting made simply of two main components – support and paint

Surface coating applied at a later date

Paint layer →

Layer of gold leaf

Bole, a special ground for gold leaf

Thick ground (gesso) →

Fabric attached to wood of support

Support – a panel of wood →

Cross-section diagram of complex construction often seen in altar paintings of the early Renaissance in Italy

smooths more easily — and also that it keeps the white tone of such inert materials as gypsum or chalk. These look drab and brown when mixed with oils. Oils can be made, however, with *white pigments* such as white lead or zinc or titanium white, often mixed with chalk or another inert filler, and are now fairly common on prepared artistic canvas. Probably the greatest cause of deterioration in the older, aqueous grounds is the presence of glue which reacts quickly to changes in relative humidity and is a good food for mould and micro-organisms. There is less glue in *canvas* supports that have *oil grounds*, but often glue is used on these as a sizing before the ground is laid.

In a structural sense there is no difference between a ground and a paint. The different terms merely indicate different functions or uses in the construction of a picture. Ground is a smooth, even coat the purpose of which is largely mechanical. The *paint*, whether applied by a stick, a brush, a pen, or a printing press, contains the drawing and development of the pictorial idea. Whether the material is ground or paint, it is usually composed of two very different substances — the *pigment* and the *binding material*. The difference between these two components needs to be kept clear because there is a tendency to use the word 'pigment' in place of the word 'paint'. *Paint*, to repeat, is a mixture of *pigment and medium*. Pigments have to be thought of as *powders*. Seen under a microscope they are lumps or grains. To get a clear idea of a paint film or paint layer, imagine chunks of coal piled together in a shallow box with some kind of sticky material like tar to hold them together. This is essentially the appearance of a paint film when studied under a microscope. If the coal is relatively large in quantity and there is only enough tar to cement it at adjacent edges, the mixture is *lean*. If there is an over-supply of tar, so much that it flows over the tops of the lumps and the lumps themselves float in it, the relation would resemble that of a *rich paint*. Lean paint is *mat* and *granular*. It is found in most wall painting and in pastels. *Rich* paint is *glossy* and *smooth*. It is found in the translucent glazes of some painting done with oil as a medium.

100

Anatomy of a Painting

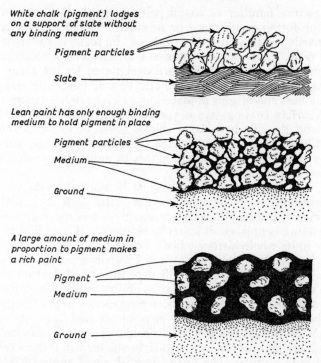

White chalk (pigment) lodges
on a support of slate without
any binding medium

Pigment particles

Slate

Lean paint has only enough binding
medium to hold pigment in place

Pigment particles

Medium

Ground

A large amount of medium in
proportion to pigment makes
a rich paint

Pigment

Medium

Ground

Pigment materials are many and varied, and little would be gained by a catalogue or a long description of them. Some are taken directly from the *earth*. Certain of these are coloured by iron, yellow, brown, or red; they are *ochres* and *umbers*. Some are synthetic preparations like white lead or cobalt blue, and among these pigments are those that go back in time to ancient Egypt. Some are *dyes* precipitated on a *base*, like the old madder or the modern alizarin crimson. All come to the paint maker or to the painter as *powders*, and these have to be combined with some kind of medium, a material that will bind them in a layer and will hold them where they belong in the design.

The number of materials used for *mediums* in Europe has been greater probably than in the Far East. *Egg* yolk and egg white, *gum arabic*, exuded by the acacia tree, and finally the *drying oils* have been added to the more ancient *glues* and *waxes*. Oil as a binding medium may have come into use in the early Middle Ages. By the fifteenth century it was well known. It probably had a number of sources — walnuts, poppy seeds and flax seeds or linseeds. To be satisfactory as a medium an oil must be able to dry to change from a fluid layer to a hard film. This is brought about not by evaporation and return to a hard state, as in glue or gum, but by a chemical change in the presence of air — an *oxidation* and polymerization. Oils so constructed that they can make this change are drying oils. It is a common failing of all such materials, since all of them are organic in nature, to deteriorate and become weak and brittle. Those which are mixed with water at the time of application are subject to the action of water at later times and are also subject to damage by mould. Oil is only moderately susceptible to mould growth and very slightly to water, but it follows a constant course of oxidation which renders it more brittle, more translucent, and more yellow as time goes on. Of all the known binding materials East and West, *lacquer* and *wax* seem to have the nearest approach to permanence.

Technique and Ethics of Restoration

The kind of picture familiar as an oil painting in the Western world is regularly coated with a film-forming substance or mixture referred to as a *varnish*. The word 'varnish' is ordinarily related, however, to those film materials that are made of resin or of mixed oil and resin. There is less confusion if all substances which may be used for the outer, transparent coating of a picture are designated by the term 'surface coating'. Under this term other materials — synthetic resins, pure oils and waxes — can be included. The numbers and origins of materials which have been used traditionally in the compounding of surface coatings are beyond the reach and far beyond the necessity of description. Among the oils have been chiefly those of linseed, walnut, poppy seed, soya bean and China wood; among waxes have been beeswax, paraffin, ceresin and carnauba; among resins have been the hard fossils, amber and copal, and the soft resins — mastic, dammar and sandarac.

The difficulty with a drying oil, as this must be noticed in the care of pictures, has already been mentioned — its tendency to get brittle and dark with age. The same tendency to deteriorate is found in the resins and in them is much greater.

As soon as a picture is finished, it starts to *deteriorate*. Those first few days or months are the only time in its whole history when its condition is perfect. The change in it will be produced by inevitable circumstances and by chance acting on the materials from which it is made. The rate of change will depend a good deal on the relation of the picture's surface to conditions in the air, on its ability to withstand dust, wear, injurious gases, light and dampness. In Asia it has been the practice to put things away, somewhat removed from these conditions. Movable pictures are laid in covers or rolled and kept in boxes. In the West certain kinds of pictures, like prints and drawings, are kept boxed or, like water colours and pastels, are regularly shielded in frames behind *glass*. Other kinds are coated with varnish. The use of varnish or of some surface coating has increased as cities have become more smoky and as the need for it has become more evident. There are good signs that painted altar-pieces, even before the time when oil got to be the prevailing medium, did not always carry a surface coating.

The traditional coating for the surface of a picture is varnish, made by dissolving or fusing a natural resin in a fluid that will let it be brushed.

Although the trees that furnish them are of many species and far apart geographically, the *resins* have a number of common characteristics. They have a glassy structure. They can be melted by heat, are not dissolved in water and are fairly resistant to chemical reagents and to the micro-organisms or moulds that cause decay.

The kinds of resins that may have been used in the past are fairly large in number. For convenience they are put into two broad classes: hard and soft. Copal and amber are *hard resins*. They need to be fused, melted in oil at a high temperature, to get them into a fluid and ready for application. The *soft resins* can be dissolved in organic solvents and because of that the solution is often called 'spirit varnish'. Some go into *turpentine* and other *hydrocarbons*; some work better in alcohols. Most of them are from the Mediterranean region or from the Far East. One of the two most common is *mastic*, found in Portugal, Morocco, and the Canary Islands in small quantities, but mainly from one island, Chios, in the Greek Archipelago. The other common soft resin is *dammar*, taken from a tree grown in the Malay States and in the East Indies.

Whether it is hard or soft, oil-fused or spirit-dissolved, the resin produces a film that is only more or less clear. At best, it has some color and some slight cloudiness. In a thin layer this does not show, and, when first put on, a varnish can be considered as a transparent film like glass. Before many years, however, clarity diminishes. The glass seems to be coloured yellowish brown. It may get faint bluish streaks, and it begins to look rough, shot through with cracks, and ends by being a kind of veil or screen rather than a clear film. The *deterioration* of varnishes made out of natural resins is quick or slow, covers a few years or many years partly in consequence of the kind of resin used and partly as a result of housing — general cleanliness, light, and relative dryness. The phenomena of deterioration have been studied with much care, and the basic causes are considered to be *oxidation*, or autoxidation, molecular rearrangements and association, and the loss of volatile essential oils.

Blemishes and discolouration in surface coatings can be noticed by one or more of three different attributes or earmarks. The first, and the easiest to explain, is the ordinary accumulation of *dust* and grime from the air. Whatever settles on the wall around a picture naturally tends to settle on the picture also. If the varnish is slick, dust will be apt to drop off or fail to lodge there in the first place. But some will stick, and it may hold tightly enough once it has got fixed in place. A speck of dust may become a small focus for condensation of atmospheric *moisture*, and certainly dampness improves the chances for a surface to hold any grime that may come its way.

The second earmark of deterioration is *darkening*. Practically nothing can be done to prevent this as long as the material is in contact with the air. Many of the soft resins are mixed with small amounts of oil to reduce their brittleness, the hard or fossil resins have been fused with oil in their preparation, and the complex process of darkening in oil adds itself to that of the resins in most picture coatings. Darkening as such can usually be gauged by looking at the relative value of a white area in a picture, a lace or linen cuff or frill, a highlight, or a cloud. Hold a white handkerchief beside one of these spots and notice how near it comes to reflecting the same amount of light. Along with the natural darkening of the materials of surface coatings goes the *stain* that was often put into them when they were made up and applied. In the technological history of European painting there is not much to show that varnishing of pictures, as an application to the whole surface, was a fixed practice until late, perhaps the seventeenth century. There are few pictures to be seen today which still carry varnish as old as that. In most, the surface coatings have been taken off and replaced. Often blemishes were found in the paint underneath or there were uneven streaks of grime which were not removed. It seems to have been a common practice to smooth out breaks and irregularities by tinting the varnish with a thin, weak stain. Occasionally this is found in an independent layer, a pale brown scumble put over a whole surface. More often it is an actual coloring put into the first layer of the surface coating. Some of the artists and artisans who have worked on pictures frankly resorted to this treatment as a means of saving time and pleasing the owner. The colouring of the varnish was known in the workshops by various names such as Old Master Glow or Toner.'

From this masterly analysis in general terms let us see what a detailed examination of an individual picture reveals.

TECHNICAL ANALYSIS OF AN EARLY PAINTING BY BOTTICELLI

(No. 592 National Gallery, 'The Adoration of the Kings')

I have already given some reasons in the Introduction why a thorough study of the masters' methods must form the basis of any steps taken towards restoration.

Technique and Ethics of Restoration

The following excerpts from an account I originally published in *Studies in Conservation*[1] will give the reader an idea of some of the problems involved and of how one may set about trying to solve them. I have quoted only what is directly relevant to cleaning and restoration.

This particular kind of research attempts rather more than an anatomic dissection of a painting. It ventures into the realm between technique and style and tries, as it were, to catch the master during his work, at the moment when his brush strokes begin to assume meaning and to express form.

The purpose of the original article was, apart from suggesting a pattern of observation, to investigate and describe in detail the technical construction of a painting by a great Renaissance master and to attempt the reconstruction of all the main stages of its creation.

On the whole, our interest will be focused upon the way in which the master uses paint to obtain his particular visual effects; that is to say, chiefly on the comparative tone value and the sequence of the layers of paint, and upon the way he handles it. For the purpose of our enquiry it is less important to know what medium or pigment the painter used than whether he painted a passage opaque or translucent, dark over light or vice versa, wet in wet, or wet on dry. However, this is not to say that we shall withhold any information as to materials that comes to notice.

The painting (Plate 25) lends itself particularly well to an analysis of this kind because it is not only unfinished but, in places, so abraded that the lower paint-layers can be clearly seen even with the naked eye; moreover, it shows many striking irregularities. But these very conditions make it all the more hazardous to draw generalized conclusions from this one case. All we can say is that Botticelli seems to have painted this particular picture in this particular way. A great many similar analyses will have to be collated before wider deductions can be drawn. It is disappointing that no such cases have come to our knowledge since the publication of the article already mentioned. It may be hoped that *Studies in Conservation* will give a new stimulus to contributions in this field.

Questions Arising from Preliminary Observation

It would be interesting to find out eventually whether Botticelli used any special means of expressing his particular vision and to see whether he differs from contemporary Florentine masters as much in technique as he does in style. One would not be surprised to find in his method more of an earlier tradition than in the works, say, of Ghirlandaio. How does he realize his very characteristic vision in this picture? The decidedly linear design with sharply bounded colour

[1] *Studies in Conservation*, II, 1 (1954), pp. 17–40, Bibliography, *Section 9* (2).

fields; the relief-like modelling which does not attain full sculptural effect; the comparatively soft and light shadows, and the colours which are luminous and broken at the same time? The refined differentiation of many similar colours is quite striking; there are more than ten different reds in the picture, and as many different blues. It is interesting to ask how Botticelli obtained them, since we know that he had neither ten different red nor blue pigments at his disposal.

Examination

The painting is first examined for its condition. For instance, it is obvious that one must be certain that original paint is being observed and not a retouching.

The scrutiny and description of the construction begins from the support — in this case the panel — and proceeds upwards (see cross-section, Fig. 4). The

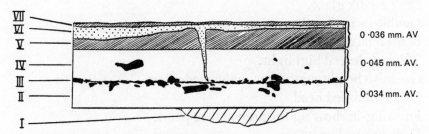

Fig. 4. Cross section of red paint, sleeve of the man, centre, who is raising his crown.

monochrome underlayers, or preparatory constructions, extending over the whole surface are dealt with together, whereas the actual colour-layers are dealt with passage by passage, according to their colour.

Most of the technical terms used here are now widely accepted or self-explanatory. As a rule, a new 'layer' connotes paint applied over a ground or paint already on the panel in a more or less dry state. The term 'layer' must, however, not be understood too rigidly. Our description is bound to be a simplification, and what we call a 'layer' may again consist of several coatings, or it may in places be interwoven or blended with the previous stratum.

A 'flat wash' means a broad coating with no direct gradation of colour or tone in itself, but it may vary in thickness and translucency and thus in value (tone). A clear distinction is drawn between a layer containing its own *heightening* (rendering of light) wet in wet, obtained by admixture of lighter paint, and, alternatively, one in which a lighter under-layer showing through fulfils the function of the heightening, like the white paper in water-colour technique.

Technique and Ethics of Restoration

Details of Plate 26 (Panchromatic detail of heads and horses)

1. White horse, finished in grey.
2. Yellowish horse, left in brown monochrome undermodelling stage, with white heightening.
3. Light heightening. }
4. Grey scumble over yellow imprimatura. } grey horse.
5. Pentimento-drawing-in of different head dress.
6. Heightening of green underpaint left bare for light areas (no pink highlights).
7. Incised architectural lines.
8. Worm hole, filled with putty.
9. Black contour, drawing-in stage.
10. Brown-pink glaze.
11. Double incised outline.
12. Black final accents over pink paint.
13. Thick pink final highlight.
14. Greenish heightening from undermodelling.
15. Highly finished head.
16. Drawing-in showing through mauve paint.
17. Dark brown line on top.
18. Dark top layer flaked off on edge.
19. Black abraded.
20. Streaky tempera handling.

25. National Gallery No. 592, Botticelli, 'The Adoration of the Kings', 50 × 136 cm., after cleaning. See p. 104.

26. Detail of the same picture. See key, opposite page.

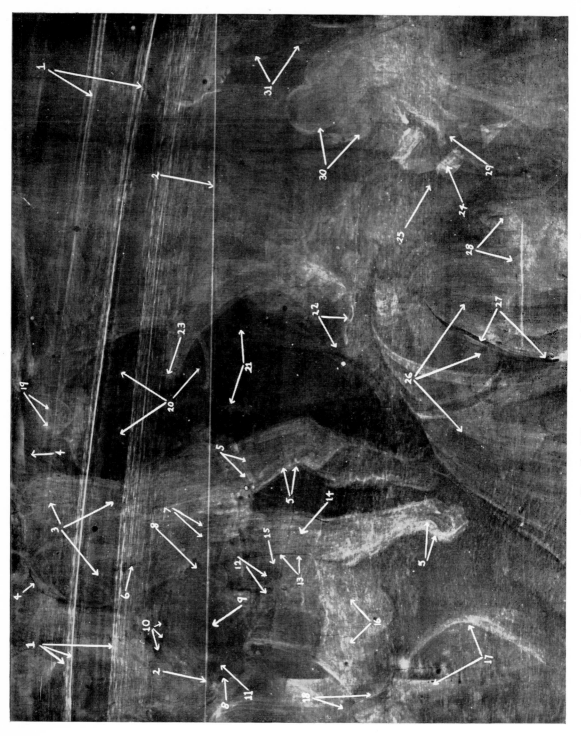

27. Detail of X-ray photograph. See key opposite.

Anatomy of a Painting

1. Oblique white lines : wood grain, probably filled with priming.
2. Join, probably with glue and some dense filler.
3. Thin white underpaint under this whole figure.
4. Outlines scratched into dry paint (see ragged edges).
5. Repeated groping or tentative outlines.
6. Triangle between waist and arm scratched out down to the imprimatura and never covered with paint again.
7. Very thin white heightening in the hand.
8. Particles of Botticelli's colour layer have flaked off; in the original the brown form stage lies bare; as there is no heightening here the patches show dark.
9. The face of the kneeling King shows dark because there is no light under-modelling except for the nose tip and the eyeball.
10. The dark patches show where the paint has been scraped away exposing the yellow ground, to represent the crown.
11. Dried paint flaked off, gap repainted by Botticelli.
12. Later paint losses retouched recently.
13. Incised outline of arm holding the crown, to correct the contour.
14. Light grey underpaint and dense vermilion.
15. Light grey underpaint and transparent carmine.
16. Thick grey of stone wall.
17. Pentimenti, probably folds, now covered over.
18. Incised sceptre, never carried out in paint.
19. Marked white heightening; one of the sculptural heads.
20. No light underpaint under red.
21. Heightening under crimson.
22. Heightening under crimson.
23. Pentimento : grey rock plus heightening for red sleeve, now overpainted with dark red by Botticelli.
24. Pentimento : architectural detail now overpainted by Botticelli.
25. Ground used for light in face (no heightening).
26. Losses in light underpaint.
27. Contour scratched through underpaint.
28. Losses in light underpaint.
29. Losses in light underpaint.
30. Heightening in Child's flesh.
31. Losses in light blue.

Details of Plate 28. What one can see in a hole $4\frac{1}{2} \times 3$ mm.

1. Lilac paint.
2. Blue pigment particles of glaze.
3. Edge of the gap in the lilac paint layer.
4. Lilac 'promontory'.
5. Pink underpaint.
6. Light grey heightening of undermodelling.
7. Transparent brown undermodelling.
8. Lighter part of undermodelling.
9. Stroke of brown undermodelling showing bluish through lilac paint.
10. The same stroke of undermodelling lying bare in the gap.
11. Sharp crack in the paint.
12. Crack with rounded edges in the softer ground.
13. Fine cracks in top paint.
14. Large crack through paint layers and ground.

Method of Investigation

The analysis of the painting begins with general observations, advancing by degrees towards minute and, eventually, miscroscopic detail.

Even a cursory examination raises a number of intriguing questions; in some passages the upper layers seem to be missing; have they been worn away or were they never painted? Why are some of the heads more forcibly modelled and others so much flatter and softer? Is this again due to damage or were they always so different? Some of the corrections of contours are obviously done by scraping. Were they made by the master himself or by a later hand? Many lines of the initial drawing-in do not coincide with the final painted contours. Is this kind of groping exceptional in this period? There are a number of little depressions with sharp angular edges, as if paint had flaked off, but the top paint seems to traverse them uninterrupted. Are they losses, overpainted by the master or by a restorer? Are the differences of hue in the various blues partly due to wearing, or were perhaps some left unfinished?

Condition

On both the perpendicular ends of the painting, strips of about $\frac{3}{4}$-in. width have obviously been added at a later date (plate 25). These were left, but all other accretions were removed from the painting before this investigation was started. All the observations were carefully checked by two witnesses before they were entered in the tables. Most observations were made in small gaps found in

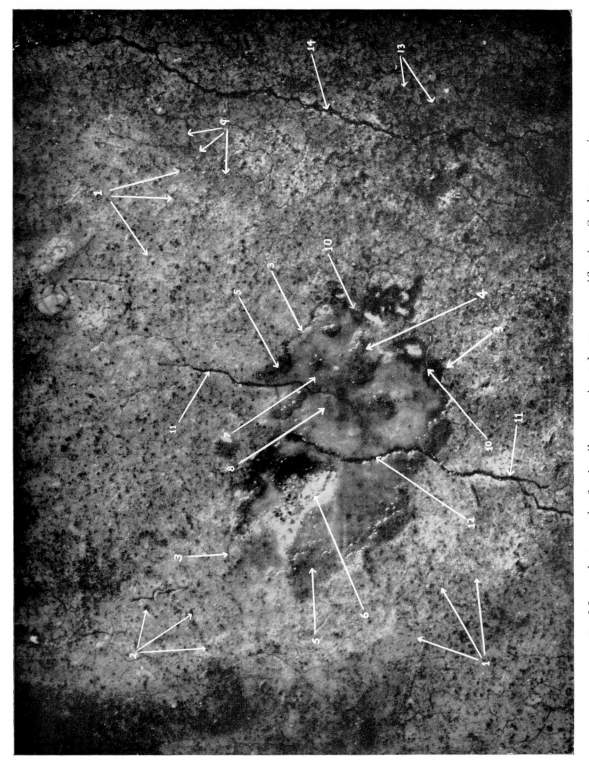

28. Macrophotograph of a detail, approximately 30 × magnification. See key opposite.

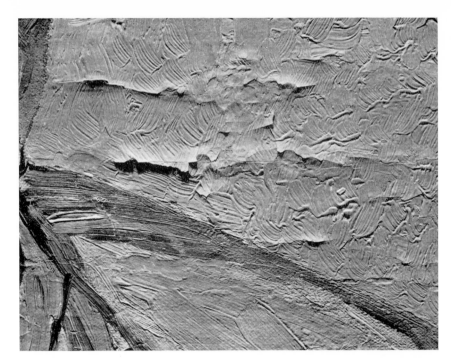

29. Typical flaking paint on a van Gogh, photographed in raking light.

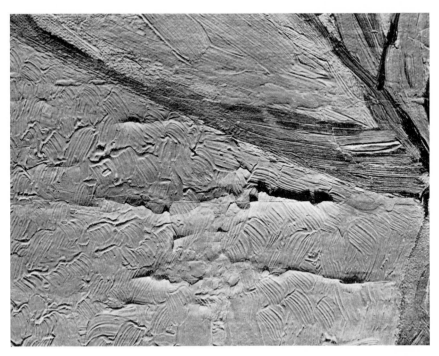

30. The same photograph printed upside down. If the book is held so that the light from a lamp falls on it in approximately the same direction as it does on plate 29, on plate 30 the flakes will appear concave instead of convex. See p. 153.

the upper or lower paint layers. Eventually a sufficiently clear idea could be formed to permit a description to be made of how this painting was in the main executed.

Medium

The medium of the layers so far described and also of the subsequent colour layers shows in most places the characteristics of egg-tempera. The fine 'early' craquelure is also typical of tempera. Another interesting piece of evidence has been found: namely, perfectly round microscopic craters in the body paint, probably burst air bubbles which cannot occur in oil paint.

Part of the fine crackle (plate 28, no. 13) in the undermodelling and in the colour layers may well have developed while the painter was still at work. Some tempera paints crack in a very similar way a few minutes after application. As a matter of fact, there is in a number of places a striking proof that the paint of the underpainting had not only cracked, but also flaked off, before the master had finished: the presence of small depressions (found with 10 × magnification), with sharp ragged edges. The upper paint layer bridges the hollows without interruption. These places show as dark spots in the radiograph (plate 27, no. 11), because in them the lead white of the underpainting is missing. This discovery forces us to revise our habit of regarding an overpainted loss in the paint as proof of later tampering. Though it is known that the original crackle often imparts its own character to overpainting, the homogeneous appearance of the paint in these hollows under high magnification, and the test made, preclude the possibility that it is later retouching by another hand. The microsection (Fig. 4) shows a similar phenomenon, namely, original paint run into a crack in lower layers.

The green underpainting in the flesh portions is quite visible in St. Joseph's head which seems never to have been finished in flesh colour.

Monochrome Form Stage

This, i.e. the design and modelling, is carried out in brown or green with whitish heightening.

Colour Layers

On top of this, in a completely independent process, the actual colour was applied and developed in several layers.

Certain passages appear less substantial or complete than others. They might all have been unfinished or abraded. The whole of St. Joseph, the Virgin's blue garment, the fragment of a wall in the foreground, the first head on the left edge of the picture, and three or four hands are unfinished, so is probably the rock in the left-hand upper corner.

The technique in this picture is traditional, almost to the point of anachronism, and at the same time highly unorthodox and original. On the other hand the artist follows his predecessors in relying for the evolution of the form on an elaborate undermodelling. Wherever the actual colour he is using is translucent enough, he makes almost every stroke of the understructure tell in the finished phase. Micromeasurements on the section (Fig. 4) will give an idea of the extraordinary thinness of the upper layers.

Changes the Painting has Undergone Since it Left the Master's Workshop

The $\frac{3}{4}$-in. wide strips of paint added at the left and right end of the picture show a paint so dark and so different in style, colour and texture from the original, that they must be regarded as later additions.

Pentimenti

There are a number of minor and major *pentimenti* in the picture, which cannot have been so obvious when the artist had finished his work. Some of them are in the preliminary outline stage, others in the colour stage. One group of figures 7 in. long was first started as much as $1\frac{1}{2}$ in. higher than it is now. i.e. 8 per cent of the total height of the picture. This appears in a radiograph, not reproduced, but is just visible in plate 25 on the stone wall. Here the first version had been already carried to the grisaille stage. In another place the earlier design shows remnants of finished painting, namely, carmine glazes on vermilion. The painter seems to have filed off some of the paint before overpainting the passage. Where figures or parts of garments overlap, corrections are frequent. In one place there are on top of one another: the brown undermodelling, the grey underpaint, a yellow layer, another grisaille, a carmine coating, a third grisaille, and finally a blue. The uppermost of these grisailles shows a fresh start from the beginning; drawing-in outlines in brown are found superimposed upon it.

Apparently these *pentimenti* were overpainted by the master in a paint that has lost some of its covering power with time, possibly oil paint. Oil paint, as is well known, becomes progressively more transparent with time, because the refractive index of the oil increases; it is, however, quite possible that a similar change may occur in tempera paint. Though a fresh egg only contains about 11 per cent of egg oil, in Botticelli's time most painters probably used the yolk only, which, fresh, contains 22 per cent of oil, but after evaporation of the water nearly 50 per cent would be present. At any rate, the *pentimenti* must have shown through eventually, and this again may have led — as often happens — to the alteration being suspected to be by a later hand, and to its being made still thinner in an attempt at scrubbing it away. Yet what overpainting is left on the *pentimenti* here is doubtless original paint.

One change the picture has undergone with time may be of interest, particularly to curators. An orange-coloured stain was found in all the cracks; it extends a little way into the priming under the paint and, near the larger and deeper cracks, it affects also the lower ground strata. It was also located in the 'foam craters' mentioned above. The position, colour, and transparency of the substance suggests that it is a kind of varnish or oil (coloured or discoloured) which permeated through the fissures when it was liquid. This seems to show that a darkened or tinted varnish can penetrate and spread over a small area beneath the surface of the paint. This might in some cases amount to a considerable and irremediable disfiguration of a painting; it usually affects the whole extent of a painting and is an irreversible effect of darkening varnish.

Reconstruction of the Method

This section, here omitted, describes in detail the following strata and phases: panel, gesso, priming, monochrome form drawing-in (tentative outlines); undermodelling in greenish brown; heightening in white or grey; green underpainting in flesh areas; colour layers.

The detailed article will be published in the second book on the Masters' Methods which is in preparation.

Conclusion

It is gratifying that our expectations have not been wholly disappointed and that our conception of the gradual construction of this painting has been clarified to a certain extent. But it may be that the entirely unexpected features will prove the more fruitful: the air craters, to distinguish tempera from oil paint; the penetrated staining as a warning; the unruly scratching as a possible sign of originality and the tentative outline as a symptom of sustained creative inspiration. Another new point found is that the green underpaint of the flesh parts is here shaded wet-in-wet, an interesting development of the usual earlier procedure in which a plain green wash was heightened and shaded in subsequent separate layers.

It has not been feasible to settle all the problems which this picture presents; for instance, many more analyses will be needed to know whether Botticelli used plain egg as a medium or an emulsion of egg and oil, and if the glazes contain egg as well as oil. Yet the present scrutiny may have yielded sufficient evidence to show that the work was constructed in the order and manner described in this paper.

It cannot yet be said that Botticelli always painted in this, or even in a very similar way; the material available for comparison is still too scanty. However, it is perhaps not premature to state that this is far from being an isolated case. Indeed it is, in its fundamental characteristics, typical of the Renaissance, in that it shows the indirect and gradual forming of the final effect in separate, mostly translucent, phases or layers — in striking contrast to types of direct technique, of which the Impressionist is the most characteristic example.

This basic difference cannot be a matter of chance, but is surely conditioned by a profound difference of conception. The Renaissance master constructs his forms and figures (after careful study of nature) from memory or imagination — he builds them up, as it were, from within, in several layers; he first establishes the form in monochrome, and then adds the colour in a separate phase, whereas the Impressionist renders the surface or the outward appearance of things, by means of one direct application of solid paint, which gives form and colour at the same time.

CHAPTER 5

Science and Restoration

Today people are apt to talk and write as if the treatment of pictures were often carried out in the laboratories of the scientists. In reality they are cleaned in the restorer's studio, their fundamental ailments in the wood or canvas are remedied in the master craftsman's workshop and they are eventually retouched and re-varnished in the restorer's studio, where the skill of the restorer is still the most important safeguard for the safety of the pictures.

Nevertheless the whole process of picture restoration has greatly improved since, in the late nineteenth century, several eminent scientists responded to an appeal made by those in charge of paintings.

As I have already mentioned, nowadays every measure of restoration in museums and in the workshop of the serious private restorer is preceded and accompanied by a thorough examination, carried out in both studio and laboratory.

Though in the nineteenth century several great scientists, including Faraday, Pasteur, Chevreul, Pettenkofer and Eibner, had done research on paintings, a hundred years ago the restorer and examiner of paintings had little more to help him than a lens and a monocular microscope. Since then many scientific aids have been added to his equipment or to that of the scientists who are now assisting him, and assuring a longer survival of the works of art through their research on air conditioning, safer lighting, ever more lasting varnishes, and so on. Moreover, the analysis of the masters' techniques and of stylistic details has been much developed. Outstanding examples of this kind of research are the detailed restoration reports by Paul Coremans, 'L'Agneau Mystique au Laboratoire', Centre National des Recherches *Les Primitifs Flamands* (Antwerp, 1953) pp. 130 f. Bibliography, *section* 27 (50); and by the leading specialists of the Istituto Centrale, Rome, in their *Bollettino*, XXXVII–XL (1959) on Duccio's 'Maestà' in Siena, Bibliography *section* 5 (42).

Technique and Ethics of Restoration

Purposes of Examination

The technical examination of a painting has three main objects: first to ascertain, and at the same time to record in writing and by photography, its state of *preservation*; second, to verify which parts of it, if any, are later *additions*; third, to find out details of the technique and *method* used by the master. Obviously all three kinds of observation will help greatly in guiding the cleaner and restorer in his work; and the written and photographic documents, recording each step, will safeguard the practitioner and the other persons responsible against criticism. Moreover the discipline of making systematic notes has a most salutary psychological influence on the execution of the work. For less important routine work summary records may suffice,[1] but for museum work more elaborate forms ought to be used.[2] On printed forms, however, over-elaborate queries tend to be left blank. If ample room is left for special information or comments, complication of the form can be avoided.

RECORDS

The National Gallery's dossiers have the following headings: Gallery number; attribution; subject; summary of recorded previous treatment; present condition; support; paint and ground; varnish; treatment proposed; examination made by ... and date; proposed treatment approved and date. Many pages are filled with photographs, 37×30 cm., 29×22 cm., or colour slides 25×20 cm. Lately 35 mm. transparencies are often added.

The dossiers consist of twenty-two pages and as many as seven volumes have been filled for one picture. Often one or more pages are added of notes on the method of the master observed before or during the treatment.

It was found imperative to have detailed captions under every photograph, making it quite clear what particulars they show. It is surprising how soon one can without such explanations forget why a photograph was taken.

All dossiers should contain at least a sufficient number of photographs, taken before the treatment, to give a good idea of the picture's condition, and one (or more in important cases) taken after the cleaning, showing all the losses unmended. The ideal would be to include also an ultra-violet photograph[3] taken

---

[1] Such as those described by George Stout in 'A Museum Record of Condition of Paintings' — *Technical Studies*, VII (1939), pp. 200–216, Bibliography, *Section 9 (3)*.

[2] A fine example of a report made before the treatment of an important painting, far more elaborate than our routine dossiers, was published in the *Bulletin de l'Institut du Patrimoine Artistique*, V and VI (Brussels, 1962, 1963): '*La Descente de Croix de Rubens, Etude Préalable au Traitement.*' It contains an ingenious method of recording the curvature and shrinkage of the panel and temporary support, Bibliography, *Section 5 (56)*.

[3] See plate 21, p. 94.

after retouching. If this is not always done, it is mostly in order to avoid the risk of injury through very long exposure to ultra-violet light necessary for photography. A brief inspection of the actual picture in ultra-violet light will usually suffice to show the new retouchings, which will appear as dark patches.

The National Gallery now has a dossier for each of its 2,000-odd paintings, though as yet some contain little more than short notes on acquisition. These files will provide invaluable historical documentation and together constitute something like a unique practical treatise on restoration methods. Since, in important cases, every pigment, medium and varnish used on the pictures is recorded, they will also help to check in years to come the durability of the materials employed.

To give some idea of the scope of these dossiers, here are details of material collected for two important paintings :

The dossier for 'The Virgin of the Rocks' by Leonardo, cleaned and restored in 1948, contains one preliminary examination report (February 1948), another after cleaning tests had been made (May 1948), a third made by the Scientific Adviser, a supplementary report (also May 1948), and finally one made after the cleaning (January 1949). Two months went in the examinations, the taking of photographs, tests etc. The cleaning and retouching took eight to nine months. There are one hundred and twenty-eight photographs, of which nine are 29 × 24 cm.; seven details 3 × magnified; six details 50 × magnified. There are also six colour slides of details and three colorimetry test sheets to record the colour of the varnish before cleaning.

The dossier for 'Margaretha Trip' by Rembrandt (National Gallery No. 1675) has altogether fifty-three photographs; three high magnification photomicrographs; two colour slides; two diagrams from micro-sections; four detailed reports of chemical analyses, partly carried out on cleaning swabs (from which the removed varnish was extracted); a systematic chart of special comparative cleaning tests with two pages of explanation; and a description of the method by which Rembrandt built up the various layers.

SCIENTIFIC AIDS TO PICTURE EXAMINATION

The following systematic list shows the most important of the current scientific aids available for examining paintings and the particular purposes served by each device. The items are arranged more or less in the order in which they would be applied. The enumeration begins with ordinary surface observation and with the simple aids and goes on to the more complicated processes and to the deeper layers of a painting.

This enumeration probably contains most of what a layman may want to know about the matter. Those who are more deeply interested in it can consult the copious technical literature. The most practical and most important publications that have come to my knowledge are mentioned in the footnotes and in the Bibliography. Some applications of the methods enumerated are illustrated here. Other relevant illustrations in the book with further explanations in the captions are mentioned in the last paragraph of each item.

In my opinion, this equipment, operative in a successful examination of a painting, would, in order of importance, be good lighting; a good pocket lens (6 times magnification), Number 6 on the list; a binocular low power microscope, No. 8; and an ultra-violet lamp (No. 9). The last two every restorer ought to have by his easel; the ultra-violet lamp if only to check the progress of cleaning and to remind him in retouching that every touch of his brush will show as a dark spot in the ultra-violet light.

Nobody at all interested in the finer technical aspects of old paintings should ever be without the 6 times magnification *pocket lens*. It is however almost useless unless it is held in the proper way: nearly touching one's eyebrow, absolutely parallel with the picture plane and taking care not to cast a shadow on the area being examined. I have known several famous experts who in their ripe old age regretted not having known these seemingly trivial details at the beginning of their careers. However, it cannot be stressed too much (and will therefore be repeated) how wrong it is to rush at a picture with magnifying glasses and X-rays before enjoying and examining it in ordinary light at normal viewing distance. The most impressive detail will be useless if it is not understood within the context of the whole, and some important point may strike the examiner on seeing the picture for the first time which might never be discovered later, even with the most powerful lens.

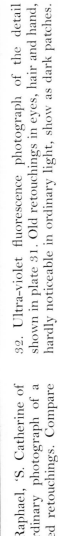

31. National Gallery No. 168, Raphael, 'S. Catherine of Alexandria', 71·5 × 55·5 cm. Ordinary photograph of a detail, showing slightly darkened retouchings. Compare following four plates, all taken before the recent cleaning. See pp. 125–130.

32. Ultra-violet fluorescence photograph of the detail shown in plate 31. Old retouchings in eyes, hair and hand, hardly noticeable in ordinary light, show as dark patches.

121

34. National Gallery No. 168. Infra-red photograph of the same detail. The rays penetrate the retouchings and the original paint layer and faintly show the hatched black thin lines of the monochrome form stage underneath.

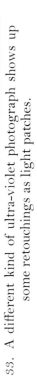

33. A different kind of ultra-violet photograph shows up some retouchings as light patches.

METHOD	PURPOSE
Observation with the unaided eye: 1. In natural or artificial daylight. 2. In sunlight (or with the Xenon lamp), for dark areas.	1. Revealing irregularities and flaws in design, tone and colour; general deterioration, damages and additions.

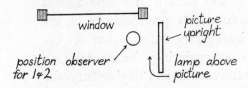

METHOD	PURPOSE
3. In reflecting light. 4. In raking or tangential light.	3 & 4. Revealing irregularities in surface texture, such as wrinkling, cupping, too smooth areas of puttying and retouching, bulges, dents, etc., and sometimes over-painted thick paint. See pp. 152, 158.

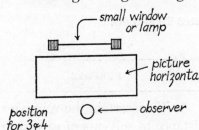

Records

1. Detailed description; photographs in black and white and in colour. Photomacrographs (up to 10 × magnification) and photomicrographs (from *c.* 10 × upwards) can be taken directly with the camera in all these types of illumination. Enlargements of ordinary smaller photographs are not so sharp.

Notes

1. Daylight, or the best quality colour-matching, fluorescent lamp, or the Xenon lamp may be used (6000 K colour temperature).

2. In addition to a north light or general lighting, a restorer's studio should have a small south-facing window for sunlight. In both methods 1 and 2 the picture should be tipped forward to avoid reflections.

3 and 4. For this kind of observation the diffuse light from a sky light is unsuitable; a dark room is preferable.

Reflected light: the simplest and quickest way of finding an interruption of the normal surface texture of a painting is to hold it horizontally between the source of light and oneself (a small lamp is more effective for this than a window). The light is reflected from the more or less shiny surface and reveals fillings and retouchings which seldom match the original texture accurately. *Raking or tangential light* (hitting the picture in a line almost parallel with its surface) also accentuates prominences in the paint surface and often affords interesting information on the technique of the master and on overpainting. Incidentally, it shows up every bit of fluff caught in the varnish and 'dry' or 'sunk-in' patches.

See Bibliography for literature on artificial lighting and light sources.

Illustrations on other pages: pp. 112, plates 29 and 30.

METHOD	PURPOSE
Using simple equipment: 5. Cleaning test: removal of surface dirt and discoloured varnish from minute areas of the picture.	5. To ascertain the relative resistance to solvents of varnish, retouchings and original paint. Only to be carried out by an experienced restorer.
6. *Observation with the pocket lens.* A pocket lens of good quality is held close to the eye and parallel with the picture plane before focusing on the picture surface. 3–10 × magnification can be obtained. 6 × is best for general use. 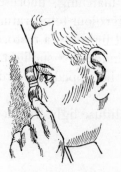	6. Reveals small irregularities, cracks (clear, blurred or overpainted), retouchings, etc.

METHOD	PURPOSE

7. *A binocular magnifier* such as is worn by surgeons and has a magnification of as little as 2 ×, will serve for the examination of larger areas, though it is more often used in retouching. It gives a stereoscopic image.

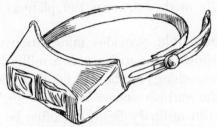

8. *Binocular microscope* (mounted on a stand). This gives a stereoscopic image, the usual magnification being c. 15–30 ×.

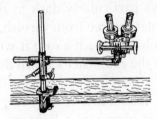

8. Shows in depth details of condition : reveals microscopic cracks and the different layers of the painting; such features as altered signatures can be examined. The instrument is also useful for removing samples from the picture for microscopical and chemical examination and for stereoscopic photomicrographs. Especially strong light is indispensable.

Using Laboratory equipment

9. Ultra-violet fluorescence (mercury lamp with Woods glass filter over it)

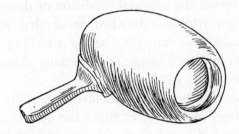

9. U.V. light excites different types and degrees of fluorescence in different substances; e.g. varnish generally has a milky fluorescence, clean original paint is generally dark; repaints fluoresce differently from original paint, usually showing as dark spots although appearing identical in ordinary light (see pp. 84, 121–2, and plates 15, 21, 32, 33, 87, pp. 84, 94, 121, 122, 226).

METHOD	PURPOSE
9a. True ultra-violet. Photographs and photomacrographs may be employed.	9a. Only visible by photography. Visible light from fluorescence is removed by a filter on the camera, so giving a true picture of ultra-violet absorption and reflection. Less useful than method 9. See p. 122, plate 33

9. *Ultra-Violet radiation.* The ultra-violet light provides information only upon the very surface of the pictures. It shows old varnishes as a milky haze which obscures other features; sometimes retouchings can be seen faintly through this, but usually only retouchings over the varnish appear as dark blotches. Interference with the original, not obvious in ordinary light, can often be discovered in this way, before removing the varnish. Conclusions have to be drawn with the utmost care. Old retouchings frequently do not show distinctive fluorescence at all and, on the other hand, some dark spot may not be a retouching but original paint that normally shows particularly dark in the ultra-violet light; or it may be an isolated patch completely free from varnish, or even a patch of varnish regenerated by a touch of alcohol. In such a case it will be not so much the darkness as the inconsistent mark of the retoucher's brush that might decide the issues. See plates 15, 18, 32, 87.[1]

10. *Infra-red rays* penetrate a little deeper than ultra-violet rays, but not nearly as deep as X-rays. Whereas the effect of ultra-violet light can be seen directly on the picture and that of X-rays on the screen, the infra-red viewing screens are not very satisfactory and the result can only be studied properly on a photograph for which special filters and plates are needed. Retouchings are not usually shown up directly as dark patches but they are often penetrated by the infra-red rays (see plate 54) which thus reveal the original condition or design underneath. This is particularly useful on widely retouched areas that are abraded. In exceptionally favourable cases one can get, before touching a picture, however overpainted and dirty, an infra-red image of it, looking almost as the picture will appear after cleaning (see plates 37–8, p. 146).

Unpleasant surprises during cleaning can thus be largely avoided, especially if X-ray examination is used at the same time. However, at times the accretions can be so thick and complicated that the infra-red rays fail; the X-ray examination

[1] Certain pigments, e.g. some lakes, zinc white and Indian yellow, show a fluorescence of a characteristic colour.

also may be impeded by an impenetrable lead white ground and then nothing short of varnish removal and removal of the retouching will reveal the true condition of the painting. To this must now be added *Infra-red Luminescence* in the photography of pictures and other art objects, using blue-green filters, on which an article by F. Bridgman and H. L. Gibson appeared in *Studies in Conservation* (Vol. VIII, No. 3, August 1963). It gives results very similar to ultra-violet luminescence, but seems to penetrate varnish layers more readily. This development shows how rapidly our arsenal of weapons against uncertainty increases.

X-RAY PHOTOGRAPHY

11. *X-rays* are the best known and the most spectacular of the technical aids in picture examination. Indeed, some people still believe that one need only expose a picture to them in order to know all about it, including date and artist. It is true that several impressive discoveries are due to X-ray photography, but it can be said that most cases are disappointing, because nothing of any interest is revealed. At any rate this method deserves a longer explanation. Röntgen himself or friends of his examined paintings with X-rays soon after their discovery in 1896. (See pp. 36, 84, 108, 168, 177.)

Extensive tests have been made and there seems to be fairly general agreement that the amount of radiation used on pictures (of any of the main three types of rays) is innocuous when kept to a certain minimum exposure.

To obtain an X-radiograph, a photographic film is laid on the picture and X-rays are sent through it from the back. The rays are absorbed by the white (lead) and other dense pigments usually prevailing in the lighter parts of the picture, in proportion to the atomic number of the chemical elements present and to the thickness of the layers. So the film remains on the whole whitest where the paint is thickest, that is in the highest lights; it turns grey where there is less light or less thick paint, i.e. in the half-tones; and it turns dark in the shadows, which contain no dense paint to speak of. Dark paint is normally not recorded. Only holes right through support, ground and paint show quite black.[1] The X-rays do not reveal any separate under-layer, but only the sum of dense paint of all the superimposed layers. However, when a piece of design appears in the X-radiograph that is invisible on the picture, this design naturally belongs to a covered, lower stratum. This applies not only to entire passages of a composition, but also to individual brush strokes which can in this way at times be identified as belonging

---

[1] Unless there happens to be such a hole, it is impossible to judge how near to perfect black the most transparent and darkest patch of paint ought to register on every particular exposure. So a spot of maximum black ought always to be produced by cutting off a small corner of the film before printing. The ideal or maximum white is usually supplied anyway by the lead letters, such as 'TR' for 'top right' which most X-ray films show.

to lower layers. For such delicate distinctions a great deal of experience in painting technique and interpretation of radiographs is necessary and the X-ray photograph must be perfectly sharp; only when the film is in close contact with the picture surface can this be achieved. The risk of the wrapped film injuring the picture is negligible. Stereoscopic X-ray photographs can at times help considerably in discriminating between different layers of a painting[1] (see No. 14 on the List of Aids).

If and when an X-ray photograph resembles surprisingly an ordinary photograph of the picture, it is because, as already said, it so happens that often the painter builds up his 'lights' with thick and dense paint (usually containing white lead), which stops the X-ray and therefore comes out light on the film; that he applies the half tones thinner and that most dark paint used for shadows does offer hardly any resistance to the X-rays and therefore shows dark also on the X-ray film.

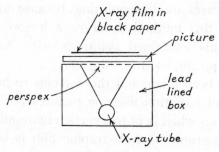

Yet it is not always so simple; sometimes light and dark appear almost reversed in the X-ray photograph. This is so because the ground, particularly on paintings earlier than the eighteenth century, is not made with white lead but with chalk-like whites that allow the X-rays to pass and to turn the film dark. Now, some masters use the white of this chalk or 'gesso' preparation in the manner water colour painters use the white of the paper by only slightly tinting it with a more or less transparent paint. When painting like that transparently on a perfectly white ground, they need hardly any thick white paint for their light areas. But if the background, say a sky, is painted with blue that for greater luminosity is usually underlaid with lead white, a face on the picture which in ordinary light shows light on dark, may in the radiograph appear dark against a light background (plate 35). Further interesting complications shown up by

[1] Rudolf Kozlowzki, 'La Microstéréoradiographie', *Studies in Conservation*, V (1960), pp. 89–101, Bibliography, *Section 31* (39).

Augusto Vermehren, 'Sulle possibilita stereo-strato-radiografiche di un nuovo tipo di apparechio a raggio X in dotazione presso l'Istituto Centrale', *Bollettino dell' Istituto Centrale del Restauro*, XI–XII (Rome, 1952) pp. 121–3, Bibliography *Section 31* (27).

X-rays such as 'pentimenti' and 'tentative outline' will be described in a further book on the methods of the masters and forgery.

X-ray photographs often seem to show what one might take for a sketchier and bolder phase underneath the surface; but this impression is in many cases produced only by the fact that contrasts of light and shade are usually exaggerated by the effect of X-rays, so that what seems a separate subjacent phase is often the main paint layer appearing freer, with stronger contrasts than it shows in the painting in ordinary light.

Overpainting may at times have been done by the original master himself (see plate 18). In the chapter on Cleaning various methods are described for deciding whether an alteration is by the master or a much later addition. Equally important for the restorer is that the X-rays will help to find out and at the same time to record photographically, all the complete losses of substance, holes or *'lacunae'* in the paint and ground, injuries, worm holes and channels in the wood, which show white if filled with lead putty and dark if not; also tears in the canvas, etc. Without special experience the layman may from an X-ray photograph get the impression that a picture is a' ruin, when in fact it is perfectly preserved, because any irregularity on the reverse may show as clearly as if it were on the front in the paint layer. In the same way the pattern of the wood grain or the image of battens on the back of a panel may seriously impede the 'reading' of an X-ray photograph. This difficulty is being partly overcome by methods for blurring out all but the chosen plane (which will usually be the paint layers) from the X-ray image.[1]

A third and most valuable aspect of the X-rays is that they help the explorer of paintings to find out otherwise hidden facts about the way a certain master has built up his work, perhaps in several layers, and they may reveal or accentuate certain peculiarities which can be of great help to the style critic and art historian. The interpretation of X-ray photographs requires a detective mind and long experience. Even now, after thirty-six years of practice in every kind of photograph with special rays, we are sometimes faced with features that we cannot readily explain.

To give just one instance: incised lines naturally appear dark in the radiograph, because there is less body of paint in the way of the rays. Yet we have seen incised lines mysteriously show white on the radiograph. The painter will probably be the first to explain: some dense pigment must have run or been rubbed into the groove.

An art historian can easily learn from the scientist the few facts necessary to handle the apparatus and to understand how X-rays produce an image. Much more difficult would it be for the art historian to learn from the painter all the

[1] See footnotes, p. 128.

intricacies of technique that must be understood for a proper interpretation of an X-ray photograph. Rarer still would be the scientist who can master all the complicated criteria that both the art historian (or the style critic) and the painter-restorer apply to the analysis of an X-ray photograph. On every X-ray film or print the data of exposure, voltage and current should be mentioned for purposes of comparison. It should be made clear that the X-ray photographs that we normally see and which we reproduce are not directly printed from the original X-ray film but from an intermediary negative made from it.

This is perhaps all that need be mentioned here with regard to the use and interpretation of X-radiographs, except possibly that two or three pigments, such as vermilion and Naples yellow, may appear about as light as white lead in the radiograph because they are of similar density or atomic weight.

(See pp. 84, 108, 145, 177, 199, 210).

METHOD	PURPOSE
12. Mercury lamp (used without a filter).	12. Reveals details in very dark areas. (Not often used.)
13. Sodium lamp.	13. Sodium light penetrates the varnish layers, and may be used as a substitute for sunlight.
14. *Stereo- and microstereo-radiography:* a Polish invention made in 1952, of great promise and useful particularly for objects other than pictures. 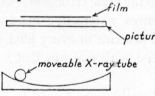	14. This gives a three-dimensional image of the various layers of the painting, as distinct from the image given by ordinary radiography which is the sum of that of all the superimposed layers. Microstereo-radiography can give a stereoscopic enlargement (up to *c.* 14 ×). Two films or prints have to be viewed through a special binocular viewer.

METHOD	PURPOSE

15. *Monocular microscope: c.* 40–200 × magnification is the most useful range.

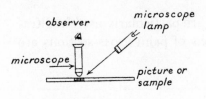

15. Sometimes useful for viewing pigment particles, etc., on the picture surface, but more often used for the examination of detached samples and in chemical microscopy. The refractive index of pigments, fibres, etc., can be measured.

Strong illumination of the right type is necessary.

Photomicrographs can be taken by attaching a camera to the microscope.

16. *Chemical microscopy and microchemistry:* this includes examination of particle characteristics and measurement of refractive index (e.g. of pigment particles), chemical tests carried out under the microscope and 'spot tests' on solutions of the material examined.

16. Determining the chemical composition of minute paint samples, particularly identification of pigments. Also tests can be carried out to discover the type of media present. Fibres of canvases and woods of panels can be identified.

17. *Microscopical examination of paint cross-sections:* the minute fragment of paint (usually less than 1 mm. in diameter) is first embedded in plastic, then one edge exposed by grinding or cutting so as to provide a plane surface for focusing under the microscope. Transparent sections, prepared by grinding down both sides of the embedded sample, can also be made for study by transmitted light.

17. Reveals the layer structure of the painting. Overpaints over layers of dirty varnish or over old cracks filled with dirty varnish can sometimes be seen. Some chemical tests can be carried out on the surface of the section. Paint sections also provide valuable information on the artist's technique and may be permanently mounted and kept for reference.

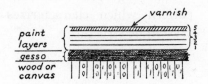

Notes. 16 and 17. An indispensable check and complementary to the restorer's findings. This method can sometimes provide one of the few possible 'hundred-per-cent proofs' in, for example, cases of forgery or overpainting. The size of sample required is even less in the case of pigment grains.

15–17. Colour photomicrographs are particularly useful. Ultraviolet and infra-red photomicrographs of paint cross-sections are also sometimes taken.

METHOD	PURPOSE
18. *Polarizing microscope:* photomicrographs can be taken recording the characteristics of pigment particles, etc., viewed by polarized light.	18. Useful for examination of crystalline pigment particles (the most often quoted example of its use is in the detection of doubly refractive calcite crystals in natural ultramarine — absent in the synthetic product). Also useful in the examination of textile fibres from canvas.
19. *Spectrography:* a photographic film or plate shows a spectrum in which different lines correspond to different chemical elements.	19. To determine the metallic elements in pigments.
20. *X-ray diffraction analysis:* this may be carried out either on the picture itself, using the back-reflection method, or else on a detached sample by means of the X-ray diffraction powder method. 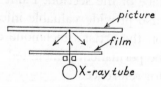 *Back reflection method*	20. Distinguishes between different crystalline forms, even of the same chemical composition; e.g. distinguishing rutile from anatase titanium oxide. Also useful for identifying the inert components of gesso grounds, e.g. distinguishing gypsum from the anhydride form of calcium sulphate. A photographic record shows a pattern which characterizes the crystalline structure.

METHOD	PURPOSE
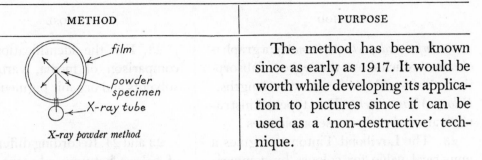 *X-ray powder method*	The method has been known since as early as 1917. It would be worth while developing its application to pictures since it can be used as a 'non-destructive' technique.

Note: To use the term 'non-destructive' for methods which do not require taking samples from the picture may be slightly misleading; it could be understood to imply that methods for which a sample has to be removed from the paint are destructive. Removing a particle, less than a millimetre in diameter, from a painting can hardly be said to destroy the painting or even part of it, particularly when the sample is taken (as it usually is) from the very edge of the picture or from an injured spot which would have to be overpainted anyhow. (See p. 111).

METHOD	PURPOSE
21. *Chromatography:* this is a method of distinguishing between chemical compounds by their rate of flow through an absorbent medium. The resulting chromatograms can be photographed in either black and white or colour. The method of chromatography was described in 1903, but not developed until 1931. Paper chromatography, as distinct from column chromatography, was first described in 1944. 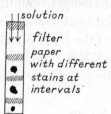	21. The identification and separation of media, varnishes and solvents. The method is also applicable to organic pigments and dyestuffs. It sometimes affords information where all other methods of analysis have failed.

METHOD	PURPOSE
22. *Infra-red spectrophotometry:* a graph is obtained which shows the degree of absorption of infra-red at different wavelengths. *Colour Measurement:* Two types of instrument are currently in use on pictures :	22. For the identification and comparison of media, varnishes, solvents and organic pigments.
23. The Lovibond Tintometer gives a numerical value for colours by comparison with standard colour filters; in the case of the improved Lovibond–Schofield Tintometer this value is in international (C.I.F.) units.	23 and 24. Recording differences of colour between adjacent areas before and after cleaning; also fading or darkening occurring on exposure. Useful too for making comparisons between the original picture and colour reproductions.
24. Visual spectrophotometers give a spectrophotometric curve showing the distribution of wavelengths in the colour of the specimen. A simple type, the EEL Reflectance Spectrophotometer, giving a limited number of points on the curve, has been used in the National Gallery.	

In addition to these methods which are in fairly general use, there are a number of newer scientific methods of examination rarely used or still in an experimental stage as far as applications to pictures is concerned. These include ultra-violet spectrophotometry (which has been applied for investigating the characteristics of picture varnishes), X-ray topography, X-ray fluorescence analysis and the use of the electron microbeam probe.

This impressive list will give the reader an idea of the vast contribution science has made to the methods of examining works of art. Methods of preservation and restoration have benefited no less from the scientist's work. He has revolutionized, or rather created, artificial lighting, air conditioning, more lasting synthetic retouching media and varnishes. The laboratories are continuously finding and testing new substances and adapting them for the restorer's use.[1]

The establishment of the Honorary Scientific Advisory Committee in 1934[2] provided a solid authoritative backing for the National Gallery's policies in matters of conservation. Its original members were (the late) Sir Henry Lyons, F.R.S. (Chairman), (the late) Sir William Bragg, F.R.S., and Dr. H. Plenderleith. It has continued meeting ever since, including the war years and now consists of twelve distinguished members.

[1] See National Gallery Report 1938–54, pp. 56 ff. and 108.   [2] Ibid.

Science and Restoration

New Materials

How careful we have nevertheless to be in adopting newly invented materials is shown by the case of a methacrylate varnish[1] which proved disappointing, and by that of the pigment Titanium White, which was greeted as stable when it first came on the market (about 1920). It was eagerly adopted everywhere because of its great advantages over the other whites: greater stability, opacity and tinting power (whiteness). I noticed that some of my light retouchings turned slightly grey-pink after a while and then, in about 1930, this completely unexpected drawback, which is due to an effect of this particular crystalline form of anatase of titanium dioxide on the paint media, was officially published. Fortunately the other crystalline form — rutile — of titanium dioxide was introduced fairly soon after and seems now to be one of the most lasting pigments on our palette. Even so, only the empirical test of time will really tell how it lasts.

The most important benefit, however, is to be expected from the scientists' long-term research into the reaction of varnish and paint films to cleaning solvents and the search for improved varnishing methods.[2]

EXPERIENCE OR EXPERIMENTS

After having made it quite clear how much the restorer owes to modern science and how indispensable the collaboration of studio and laboratory is, a certain clarification is necessary regarding the parts played by each. As I mentioned earlier some people have been left with the impression that pictures are restored by scientists in the laboratory and that science can solve most of the restorer's problems. Others have resented the interference of the scientist with the 'artistic' activity of the restorer. The fact is that scientific discoveries and still more so the new scientific approach made a tremendous impact on the work of the restorer and it is only natural that at first the actual and the potential contribution of science were somewhat exaggerated. Then came disappointments and, as happens so often in life, the disappointed himself was to blame; he had expected too much. The belief is still widespread that a scientist cannot err. Admittedly he is, thanks to his training in systematic thinking and working, less prone to error than the non-scientist; but he is not entirely immune to the danger of wrongly interpreting facts.

[1] See Arthur Lucas and Norman Brommelle, 'Failure of synthetic materials in picture conservation', *Museums Journal*, LIII (1953), pp. 149–55; Bibliography, *Section 18* (9); and Garry Thomson, 'Some Picture Varnishes', *Studies in Conservation*, III (1961), pp. 64–79, Bibliography, *Section 16* (16).

[2] See Robert L. Feller, Elizabeth H. Jones and Nathan Stolow, *On Picture Varnishes and their Solvents* (Intermuseum Conservation Association, Oberlin, Ohio, 1959). Bibliography, *Section 16* (20); and Garry Thomson, 'Some Picture Varnishes', *Studies in Conservation*, III (1957), pp. 64–79, Bibliography, *Section 16* (16).

Technique and Ethics of Restoration

In an attempt at improving on empirical methods a well-known painter whom I know tried out an ingenious method of painting, based entirely on scientific grounds, optical and technical; the results did not look very different from a good colour reproduction because the imponderable potentialities of paint, which cannot be measured in the laboratory, had been disregarded: all the infinite and subtle effects of *impasto* and *scumble,* of playing off thick against thin paint, heavy pigments against light ones, etc., which have not been found by science but in centuries of laborious practice and experience and cannot be pinned down in scientific terms.

Yet in a sense science has always played a considerable part in painting; in the Italian 'primitives'' ingenious invention of the green underpaint under the flesh colour; in Uccello's and Piero della Francesca's and Alberti's perspective; in Dürer's and Leonardo's study of proportion and so forth.[1]

It is idle to play off empiricism against science: they form no antithesis. Each must be given its proper place in restoration and it must be kept in mind that certain century-old experiences and certain obvious facts do not need scientific checking, whereas, I repeat, all laboratory findings do need practical verification. Every serious scientist admits that the testing conditions in the laboratory are often too far removed from those prevailing on paintings, where much too many variables prevail. For instance, the most ingenious forced tests on paints and varnishes, though they afford invaluable indications, cannot completely replace twenty-five years or more of natural weathering.

Another fallacy is that some people are apt to regard any opinion based on the use of a scientific instrument as being a 'scientific verdict'. In fact the instrument is only an aid to the expert in arriving at the right conclusion. What is for instance scientific in the use of radiographs for restoring purposes or for the detection of forgeries is the discovery of the rays and the construction of the apparatus. To tell what certain white or black passages in the X-ray photographs mean is largely a matter for the paint technician and the style critic.

Ideally the *laboratory* of the scientists and the *studio* or workshop of the restorers would be next to one another, as they have been in my case for many years now; there would be frequent visits to and fro. The restorer may want to put an urgent question or to have a special cleaning mixture or varnish made up.

---

[1] The much admired scientific device used by the Neo-Impressionists or Pointillists has proved disappointing. It consisted of putting small dots of pure colour side by side instead of mixing the colours. The expected greater purity and luminosity of the colour effect did not always materialize. Gauguin had already pointed out that large spots of colour 'tell' better than small ones. In the 'Festschrift' for Professor J. Wilde's sixtieth birthday (Courtauld Institute 1951, but never published), S. Rees Jones has explained the scientific reasons: spots below a certain size change colour in the viewer's eye at a distance.

The scientist may want to watch, say, how a certain solvent or retouching medium that he is working on behaves in the hands of the restorer, and so on.

When these two departments of a museum work so closely and harmoniously together as they now do at the National Gallery, the progress is palpable and comparatively rapid and great improvements are emerging all the time.

An excellent example of this is the history of Paraloid-B72.[1] In February 1962 our laboratory provided us with this synthetic resin. A friend and fellow-restorer, Alexander Dunluce, had brought over a sample for us to try out as a retouching medium. Judging by our trials, the long industrial tests and the scientists' calculations, it looks as if B72 may be the fulfilment of the restorer's dream: a paint that will stay put, with which one can match a tone, and which will not change either in drying or varnishing or with time. Much experimenting is however necessary to overcome the handling difficulties (see also p. 254).

I would like to make, here and now, a point that will come up repeatedly in this book and one that may surprise many art lovers. In trying to decide whether a given passage is by a certain master himself, or by a later hand, purely stylistic criteria, which are usually considered to be too vague, can often be more conclusive than technical or scientific ones; in fact, they are sometimes no less scientific though they do not belong to the field of chemistry or physics but to that of aesthetics or logic.

A characteristic instance occurred when the 'Allegory' by Bronzino was cleaned at the National Gallery. One of the most disturbing things, apart from the dark and yellowish varnish, was a poorly drawn veil on Venus's body (see plate 6). Nobody doubted that it was a much later addition and ought to be removed. The question of a scientific test hardly arose. Cupid was caressing Venus's nipple and she put out her tongue for his kiss. Both these details had been painted out later and the overpainting had come away easily. The loincloth was obviously added much earlier, probably in the seventeenth century. But several weeks of scientific examination and deliberation did not solve the question whether the twig which covered part of Cupid's buttocks was original or not.

When I was asked I argued: why should Bronzino, who was obviously not prudish about the particulars mentioned, have narrow-mindedly covered up Cupid's behind and spoiled his composition? The sprig now formed the strongest contrast of light and dark in the picture and drew with its restless design attention to the very edge of the picture. Brommelle pointed out the inferior quality of the twig.

Everybody concerned agreed with these arguments, and the twig was re-

[1] Paraloid B-72 is manufactured by Rohm & Haas (U.S.A.).

moved (see plate 7). In the process the propriety of the decision was splendidly confirmed : '. . . samples of paint from the myrtle leaves. This area was examined and the results given below confirm the restorer's [Brommelle's] judgment in wishing to remove the myrtle. Cross sections of the paint showed that these two layers passed over a deep crack in the indisputably original paint layers beneath and that the crack was filled with old and dirty varnish.'[1] Later a copy of the painting was found, of unknown date. The absence of Venus's veil and of the sprig across Cupid's buttocks was further proof that these were later additions.

Incidentally, this example also shows how the prejudices of one particular epoch could be perpetuated, and how historical truth could be distorted considerably if pictures were not cleaned thoroughly and some of the varnish, and with it later additions, were left on them. In this case, for instance, the notion might well have survived that Bronzino's period was far more prudish than the picture now clearly attests. Without the tinted varnish obscuring them the falsifications would probably have been discovered and the truth found out much sooner.

The way it was found out provides an excellent example of how common sense, style criticism, art history, knowledge of paint technology and science can, and always should, work fruitfully together in solving special problems.

DIGRESSION ON COLOUR PHOTOGRAPHY

Colour photography is one of the scientific inventions we are employing more and more, both in studio and laboratory.

For many years now I have been using *colour slides* of paintings in lectures. Though they do not render the shades perfectly, they certainly convey a far truer idea of a picture than a black and white photograph, and they are particularly useful for showing details of brushwork, etc., which even a careful observer would not be able to see so clearly on the original; the enormous and yet remarkably sharp magnification on the screen allows for more leisurely study than the more strenuous examination of the original with a magnifying glass. Moreover, the slide can be made with the most suitable angle of lighting ('raking light') for showing up texture effects, brushwork, etc.

In the last few years colour films have become so reliable that slides, say, of a partly cleaned picture can even be used in the dossiers to record a fair impression of the tone of the varnish before its all-over removal and lately at the National Gallery 35 mm. colour films have often been employed. For absolutely accurate

[1] From *The National Gallery, July 1956–June 1958* (Published by the Trustees of the National Gallery, London, 1959), p. 70.

D. National Gallery No. 270, Titian, 'Noli me Tangere', 109 × 91 cm. Detail of the Magdalen with two cleaned strips revealing that her figure had at a later date been narrowed by more than a third by over-painting it with background. When this had been removed the original paint, which it had protected, came out far better preserved than most other parts of the painting, which had been irregularly abraded during earlier cleaning attempts. (See *The National Gallery 1956–1958*, pp. 77–79.)

recording Tintometry or Colorimetry has of course to be used in addition (see p. 134).

Colour photographs on paper are still far from faithful enough for our purposes, but half-tone colour reproductions printed in four colours (or more, in special cases), have been so much improved lately that they can serve as most useful illustrations to the text and as approximate records, if carried out by highly skilled engravers and if the proofs are vetted by a specialized expert who combines knowledge of the printing process with a high degree of artistic appreciation and colour sensitivity.

In order to realize the importance of this point, it is necessary for the reader to know something of the colour printing process. For the benefit of those who may not have studied this subject, I will outline briefly the various steps involved in half-tone colour reproductions (which is the method commonly used for the purpose under discussion and used in this book).

The Process[1]

1. Half-tone colour consists of printing, one on top of the other, impressions made by four separate metal plates, each one being inked with a separate colour; yellow, red, blue and black. By grading the relative intensity of these four colours (from 0 to 100%) on a white ground, it is theoretically possible to reproduce any colour (and indeed any tone of any colour) though in practice this is not always true, as I hope to show.

2. The four *copper plates* are sensitized (somewhat as is a camera film) so that, by a process of photography and consequent etching it is possible to produce on the copper a covering of minute, raised dots, larger dots in the darker areas, down to the infinitesimal dots in the lighter areas of the picture. These dots pick up the printer's ink and deposit it on the paper, more or less of it, corresponding to their varying sizes.

3. By means of colour filters on the camera lens *colour separation negatives* are taken of the three primary colours and one in black, and these negatives are printed down on to the sensitized copper plates, one for each colour. On the red block, for instance, larger dots will develop only where red exists on the picture being reproduced; and relatively smaller dots in those areas which contain *some* red (such as brown) and almost non-existent dots on those areas where there is no red. The four separate plates are printed one on top of the other to make the complete colour image.

4. However, in most cases the relatively crude mechanical method is not

[1] See H. Ruhemann, 'The Masters' Methods and Colour Reproduction', *The British and Colonial Printer*, 25th May, 1951), p. 542; Bibliography, *Section 23* (7) and Appendix D, pp. 348–54.

sufficiently sensitive. The first, unretouched proofs are normally far too brown and dark. That is where the art of the 'engraver', etcher or retoucher comes in; with infinite skill he reduces the dots by etching them with an acid, where there is too much of any colour. An operation still more difficult is that of increasing the size of the dots by rubbing them down — where he finds for instance his red too weak — and so on with each plate. Every dot is a minute raised cone shape, so the more he crushes it the larger its surface becomes. Thus, in order to get more red into a purple area, he will intensify the red by rubbing that area of the red plate.

An approximate match will often suffice for commercial purposes, but when the subject is a work of art, where every shade of colour plays its important part, the artist must step in. Let me explain.

Very few of the foremen engravers who vet the proofs are painters born with an exceptionally sensitive eye for colour shades and fewer still have acquired the indispensable knowledge of the technique and intention of the masters, old and modern, whose work is being reproduced. Many a painter with the appropriate gift could find here a fascinating and gratifying way of making a comfortable living. He could easily acquire the necessary experience in colour printing.

The majority of even the most successful colour prints could still be improved considerably by such an artist.

It is well enough known that no artist can hope to render in his painting 'the total visual effect' of nature if only because the contrast of light, say, between a white cloud and a dark tree seen against the sky is in reality hundreds of times greater than can be attained with pigments. In order to show one aspect of the visual world he has to sacrifice others, and the greater the painter the more deliberately he often emphasizes one or two facets of nature that inspire him, at the expense of others.

But the colour printer is immeasurably more limited. With his ink and paper and with the tremendous reduction in size he has to work in, he cannot even emulate the painter, let alone nature; he is often forced to neglect more than one characteristic of the master's style or technique in emphasizing his salient points. Without being a specially trained painter it is difficult to know what is important and what is not. The engraver who does the delicate final retouching of the block has to know that for instance he must under no condition lose the cool half tones in the flesh of a picture by Rubens or the white glitter in a Renoir. Such knowledge is difficult to acquire by anyone who is not a painter. Often reproductions do not look like the work of a master but like that of a copyist who has missed the original's peculiarities and special merits. Of course, until fairly recently, before the old masters' pictures were cleaned, even the keenest eye could not properly see the bold touch of Titian or the subtle tones in Rembrandt's, Rubens' and Velázquez' flesh paint and it was comparatively easy to produce a fair reproduction of any old master's picture while brown prevailed all over in most of them.

During the last two decades enormous progress has been made in the art of colour printing; superb results have been achieved; but with today's immense increase of coloured magazines and cheap art books where speed of production is unavoidable, the improvement in the reproduction of paintings does not seem to keep pace with the advance in technique. One still sees all too often a reproduction, say of a van Gogh picture, with black outlines where they should be of varying colours, or a garish travesty of Rouault's lovely king of which Braun & Cie have made such a splendid facsimile long ago.

Just as in sound reproduction we are not always availing ourselves of the high quality attained and are allowing our ears to be blunted by careless and over-loud tuning in, so in a similar way, our eyes are in danger of becoming insensitive to all but the crudest and loudest colours.

Another thing that at present prevents most colour reproductions from reaching the attainable degree of perfection is that the regulations of the printers' Unions prohibit one man from doing the whole job from the beginning to the end. It seems difficult to believe, but it is a fact that, in the majority of cases, the etcher or engraver who does this crucial work has never seen the picture he is reproducing; he works from more or less well-matched small colour slides, taken in artificial light of the wrong hue and usually not projected in proper magnification, nor in the proper colour of lighting. It is truly amazing that under these circumstances such excellent results are often achieved.

It would be well worthwhile to try seriously to remove these obstacles to progress, since colour reproduction has come to play a part in our lives second only to reproduction of sound, whatever those may say who still regret this fact and who understandably would rather buy mediocre originals than reproductions of fine originals.

UNESCO, for one, have fully recognized the importance of good colour reproductions of works of art.[1] In 1949 they invited me to suggest ideas concerning colour reproduction and I submitted to Sir Julian Huxley, the then Director-General, a scheme for an *International* UNESCO *Art Prize*. The prize-winning pictures bought during five or ten years were to be reproduced large

[1] And so has *Which?*, the journal of the Consumers Association. In their December 1962 issue they published an admirably organized piece of research into the comparative merit of colour reproductions.

size and in the best available way and to form a travelling exhibition. This plan has, for many reasons, remained utopian,[1] but what has been carried out is admirable enough : the excellent catalogue of all the best colour reproductions and the magnificent volumes of colour reproductions of the folk art output of the various nations.

Another, greater, task seems to loom for UNESCO, perhaps no less utopian and far-fetched than my first plan. The possibility that some of the finest master-pieces may one day be exterminated by the H-bomb has to be seriously faced. Does not this thought suggest the urgency of producing as quickly as possible large colour facsimiles of all the greatest pictures and distributing them so widely that they cannot all be destroyed ? However, two conditions would have to be fulfilled : the reproduction would have to be of insuperable quality (many more plates than four would of course be used and better processes than half-tone) and the originals would all have to be cleaned first, lest a misleading memory of them should be perpetuated; and it is of course this last point that I am particu-arly concerned about and that made me put in this digression.

At all events, even if, as we all hope, the H-bomb should not be exploded in earnest, there remains a similar duty for UNESCO or any of the other big foundations. The greatest frescoes in Italy that can for some reason not be saved from disintegration must at all costs be perpetuated by life-size colour repro-ductions. Where this is not possible first-rate copies should be commissioned. A beginning has already been made in Italy on objects of less urgency with the Ravenna Mosaics and in France and Yugoslavia with frescoes. These copies would offer a worthy opportunity for Art College prize winners in Italy and abroad to show and improve their skill.

To frescoes, incidentally, an often-heard objection levelled at reproductions does not apply, that 'the texture of a painting cannot be rendered properly'. Of drawings and watercolurs facsimiles are now often made, which even the expert can distinguish from the original only with difficulty. To avoid error and fraud the reproduction is therefore usually marked with a special stamp.

The same degree of perfection should be possible with frescoes, which have no marked impasto brushwork. What texture they have is mostly the grain of the wall and that could be very closely matched by a cardboard or paper of a similar texture.

Perhaps it is the colour reproduction that will save the great masterpieces from oblivion. Of the coloured ink may come true what Shakespeare says of the verse in black ink to his beloved :

[1] UNESCO, for some years now, has chosen a picture by a young artist at each Venice Biennale and paid him a fee-prize.

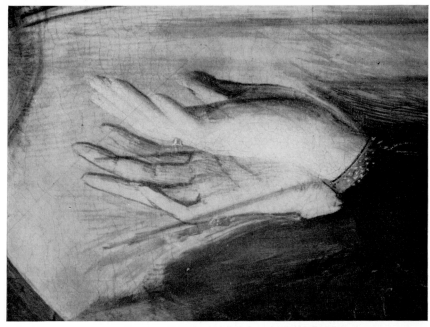

36. National Gallery No. 186, van Eyck, 'The Marriage of Giovanni Arnolfini and Giovanna Cenami', 81·8 × 59·7 cm. Detail in infra-red light, revealing an earlier position of the hand which van Eyck abandoned at the drawing-in stage and over-painted partly with the hand now visible in the picture and partly with background colour.

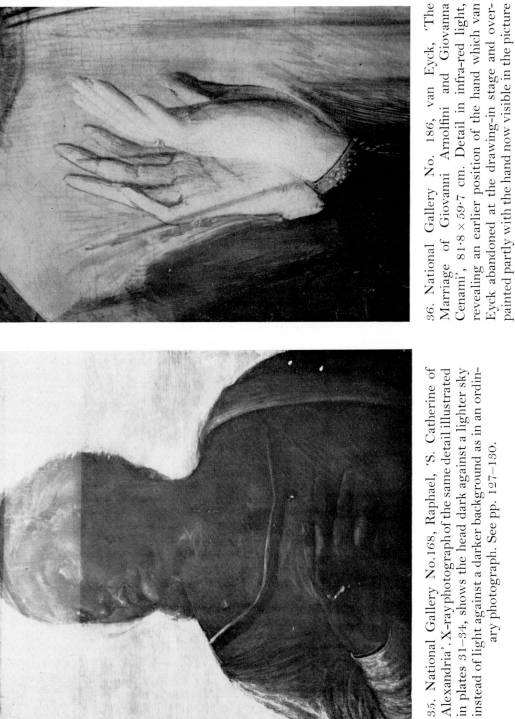

35. National Gallery No.168, Raphael, 'S. Catherine of Alexandria'. X-ray photograph of the same detail illustrated in plates 31–34, shows the head dark against a lighter sky instead of light against a darker background as in an ordin-ary photograph. See pp. 127–130.

38. The same detail in the same condition as shown on plate 37, taken in infra-red light. The rays take no account of the layers of dirt and varnish and show the picture almost as it would appear after their removal. See p. 126.

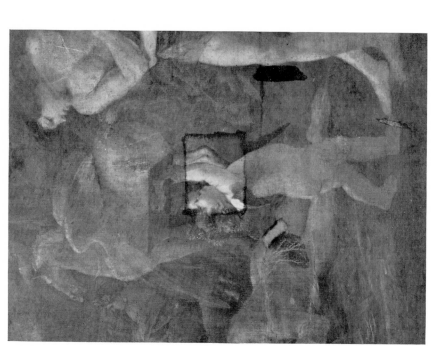

37. National Gallery No. 65, detail from Poussin, 'Cephalus and Aurora', 96·5 × 130·5 cm. Ordinary photograph taken after the old cloudy varnish had been removed only in a small square.

146

Science and Restoration

'... When rocks impregnable are not so stout,
Nor gates of steel so strong, but Time decays?
O fearful meditation! where, alack,
Shall Time's best jewel from Time's chest lie hid?
Or what strong hand can hold his swift foot back?
Or who his spoil of beauty can forbid?
O, none, unless this miracle have might,
That in black ink my love may still shine bright.'

CHAPTER 6

Preservation and Consolidation

Preservation

From the general historical and technical background of restoration, with the examination and recording that precede it, we come now to the actual treatment of a picture.

As to the principles that should guide the restorer there is little disagreement: the main ones were agreed upon at the Conference in 1930[1] and could be condensed in this form: *'To preserve and show to its best advantage every particle that is left of a painting.'*

Some Fundamental Rules

1. Preservation is more important than cleaning.

2. The restorer must try by all available means to get as clear an idea as possible of the condition of a picture (and record it) before he begins treatment.

3. He must not interfere with the intention of the master so far as it can be ascertained, nor finish unfinished passages nor try to 'improve' intrinsic shortcomings.

4. He must try to recover as far as possible the original appearance of a painting where it is obscured. *The intention of the master is the guiding standard.*

5. He must never introduce, in mending, retouching or varnishing, any substance that does not remain removable without risk to the painting, that is to say, no glues, no paints or varnishes which get too insoluble with time.

6. He must do the minimum that will suffice to preserve the picture in good condition, while making its full enjoyment possible. An old master's work should not be made to appear flawlessly preserved if it is not so. It is comparatively easy to make a picture look intact, but not easy to avoid that 'freshly restored' look, which can be so disturbing. I shall go into further detail on the ethical questions involved in the chapter on Retouching (pp. 255–268).

[1] See *Manuel de la Conservation et Restauration des Tableaux* (Paris, 1938), pp. 15 ff. Bibliography, Section 4 (28).

7. He must if possible avoid introducing anything alien to the aesthetic quality of the original paint (e.g. difference of transparency, or any colour not figuring in it).

8. Speed must not be considered. The beginner does well to work slowly; speed develops with practice without deliberately striving for it.

Consolidation

Consolidation consists largely of fixing scaling paint and of preventing further scaling, by reinforcing deteriorated or damaged panels and canvases; the most frequent measure necessary is the fixing of loose paint particles. At the National Gallery, until sufficient rooms were air-conditioned, three specialized craftsmen spent most of their time doing this.[1]

Since this was written the air conditioning of the National Gallery has been steadily progressing and now (March 1967) more than half the pictures are hung in air-conditioned rooms, and all the early paintings, which needed a healthy and steady climate most urgently, have been installed in them. The percentage of ailing panel pictures has since gone down by about fifty per cent, but the craftsmen are still much occupied with fixing detached paint.

Loose paint particles (plate 39) are fixed by introducing an adhesive (usually one that melts with heat) under the surface. Nowadays this is done in most of the museum workshops and private restorers' studios by means of electrically heated spatulas (up to about 60° C or 140° F) with automatic temperature control (see plates 40 and 41) melting size or more often, the same wax-resin mixture that is used for lining, into the cracks. The pricking of blisters with a needle, which was done lavishly in the past, is seldom necessary. When unavoidable a hot needle should be used.

Lining and Transfer of Canvas Painting

As painting on canvas did not become general practice until the middle of the sixteenth century, the transfer of pictures from wood to canvas is not likely to have been invented earlier.[2] The same applies to 'lining', the sticking of a deteriorating canvas painting to a second canvas for reinforcement, not, as some text books say, 'transfer' to a new canvas.

The transfer of canvas paintings to a new canvas, which is very rarely necessary, was probably thought of a little later. 1729 is the earliest date mentioned for the

[1] The first of the National Gallery Reports: *The National Gallery 1938–1954* contains interesting information on the ailing pictures and on the measures adopted to treat them, air conditioning, etc., pp. 21–5 and on pp. 56 ff. on the foundation of the Conservation and Scientific Departments.

[2] N. Brommelle, 'Material for a History of Conservation', *Studies in Conservation*, II (1956), pp. 176–88. See pp. 182–3; Bibliography, *Section 2* (16).

operation.[1] It consists of removing the original canvas from the back of the paint layer, which has first been secured by a firm temporary *facing* of paper and fabric stuck on to the surface, and then glueing the back of the paint on to a new canvas. The method is much like that used in fresco transfer.

The most difficult and tiresome part of the lining or transfer process is the removal of old lining canvases and hard adhesives, which is often done in weeks of painstaking scraping, centimetre by centimetre.

Invention of Wax-Lining

In 'relining' (or rather 'lining' when carried out for the first time) the new canvas is coated with adhesive and at first gently attached to the back of the old canvas. Then the picture is ironed from the back in order to melt the adhesive and to force it through the old canvas and into the ground of the painting. The older method, and one still much in use for special purposes, employs an aqueous glue compound.[2] A *wax-resin* mixture was used in Holland on Rembrandt's 'Night Watch' in 1851 (see p. 79, note 1). Déon mentions a slightly earlier case.

The main advantage of this innovation was that the adhesive used permeates at the same time the original canvas and the paint layers from the back and fixes any loose particles.

Another advantage of the wax-resin method is that when carried out on a hot table the securing of loose paint by impregnation can be done first in a separate process at the melting temperature of the adhesive. The joining of the two canvases can then be achieved at a much lower temperature. The laundry irons used in the past had to be kept unnecessarily hot to melt the wax mixture repeatedly.

Wax-lining has been in wide use on the Continent since the 1870's.

To secure loose paint on canvas pictures the adhesive can usually be introduced from the back, through the canvas. In cases of extensive and recurrent flaking the entire painting has to be impregnated with the wax-resin adhesive. Indeed, the main use of *lining* is this permeation of the original canvas, of the ground and of all the fissures and pores of the paint itself. If the original canvas is not too brittle, the second canvas can sometimes be omitted and a mere impregnation may suffice. The linings carried out with the older method, using glue and flour-paste mixtures, are less successful in securing all the loose paint during treatment, because, unlike the wax adhesive, the water-soluble glue mixtures do not always

[1] Horsin Déon, op. cit., p. 155.
[2] This adhesive usually contains flour paste, glue and, as a plasticizer, Gum Elemi or Venetian turpentine. Mr. Howard at the National Gallery prefers instead of the plasticizer a subsequent impregnation of back and front of the picture with wax.

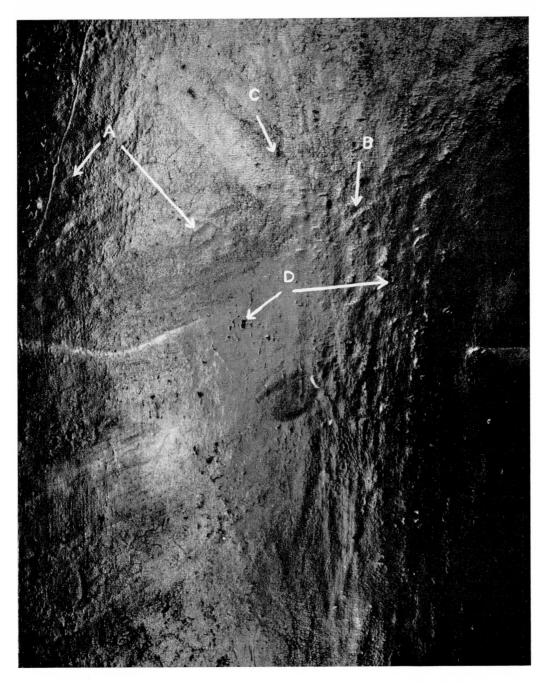

39. National Gallery No. 1093, Leonardo da Vinci, 'The Virgin of the Rocks', 189·5 × 120 cm. Detail photographed in reflecting light showing : A. Areas of cupping. B. Areas of blistering. C. Small-scale craquelure with incipient flaking. D. Loss of paint through flaking. This scaling of the paint recurred, despite many treatments, until the old 'curling' varnish was removed. See p. 149.

40. Flaking paint particles being reattached by using electrically heated spatulas of different sizes to melt an adhesive and make it penetrate beneath the loose fragments. See p. 149.

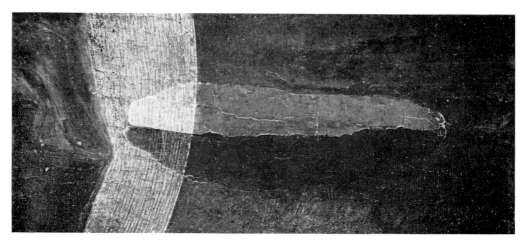

41. National Gallery No. 3913, detail from Giovanni Bellini, 'The Virgin and Child', 78·5 × 58·5 cm. Large blister (shown almost original size) taken in side lighting. In diffused light the blister would not be easily noticeable (compare plates 42 and 43).

sufficiently penetrate through the ground to the back of the paint, but mostly harden on the way during the ironing and, though the painting may look perfectly flat after the ironing (if inexpertly done often too flat!) the flaking is not really cured and will recur. Another disadvantage of glue lining is that anything that goes wrong is far more difficult to put right than with wax, which can easily be melted again. Another drawback of glue or paste is that they are hygroscopic and cause under unfavourable conditions continued expansion and contraction of the canvases as well as mould growth.

In order to save the pictures unnecessary handling, or to save time, or to save their clients expense, some restorers do not recommend lining unless it is urgent; others line every valuable painting that comes into their hands as a precaution and now that modern methods have excluded practically all risks, there is little to be said against this.

In my opinion nearly all van Gogh's pictures belong to a type that should, even if an immediate necessity is not apparent, be relined, for two reasons: first, often the all-too absorbent canvas (frequently without sufficient ground on it) on which van Gogh painted has drained too much of the oil out of the paint and left it in places almost as dry and powdery as pastel colours; here the wax impregnation will bind and hold the loose particles. Secondly, on the majority of van Goghs the paint is badly cracked and flaking, probably also due to the cause just mentioned and to the excessive *impasto* (thick paint). This flaking can be permanently remedied by the permeation with wax-resin adhesive, which takes place during the lining. I have seen several important van Goghs that had travelled overseas for an exhibition or for sale with extensive loose paint areas and a few small losses, and have wondered whether these have not occurred during the journey.

Hot Table and Vacuum-lining Method

Whichever adhesive was used, until recently relining was carried out on an ordinary firm surface, padded if necessary to protect impasto. This lining on a cold table had several disadvantages: it was extremely difficult to apply the adhesive evenly on the canvases; uneven heat distribution caused sudden change of tension in adjacent fields; there was uneven pressure during cooling; the relatively heavy ironing necessary caused danger to impasto, and often a complicated bedding was necessary to protect the paint surface. It was always opaquely covered and it was impossible to watch the progress; there was a danger of air pockets forming, by melting out too much wax in places, which only showed later; the movement of the iron could cause folds to appear in the paint surface.

153

Technique and Ethics of Restoration

The hot table and vacuum-lining method[1] described in detail in Appendix D (pp. 335–9) overcomes most of these disadvantages, and in particular meets the most serious objection to lining in general: the risk of crushing the relief of the brushwork. This suffered all too often in the past, particularly when ironing on the front was necessary; fortunately more care is being taken now. However, even the traditional method of using felt, a bed of sawdust or sacks of fine sifted sand between iron and picture usually avoided such damage. In the case of pictures by van Gogh the exact maximum temperature must be ascertained that can safely be applied. Some of his paint seems to contain wax or some other ingredient, which melts at comparatively low temperatures.

As the majority of paintings on canvas are executed in oil colour the impregnation with wax-resin mixtures will not alter the refractive index of the paint, that is to say, make it appear darker, as a drop of oil darkens blotting paper. On the other hand, a matt and porous tempera painting, as well as some size-paintings on cardboard, e.g. by Vuillard or Bonnard, turn noticeably darker through saturation with wax. However, a great number of old tempera paintings, during injudicious treatments in the past, have already been so drenched with varnishes and oils, that an additional permeation with wax could make little or no difference. For very light modern paintings one would make up a specially colourless mixture of bleached beeswax and colourless resins.

Another disadvantage of wax-lining is that it does not always keep badly cupped[2] and tough paint surfaces sufficiently flat. A skilful restorer can often obviate this by first ironing the picture with slight moisture (though certain types of paintings would suffer from such treatment). The steam developed makes all the layers of the picture limp and if it is then relined with wax before the moisture has completely evaporated, it will usually remain flat; if it does not, a second lining with wax or with a glue composition will succeed. The latter will stick well if a sheet of packing paper is first ironed on to the wax-backing to form an insulation.

Yet another drawback of wax when used on panel pictures is sometimes mentioned: it is very difficult to make glue stick on a waxy surface and in some cases glue may have to be used at a later date.[3] Fortunately the wax can be removed more easily than is often alleged. Usually it is only a matter of patience

[1] H. Ruhemann, 'The Impregnation and Lining of Paintings on a Hot Table' and 'Restoration of "La Haie: Landscape near Arles" by van Gogh', *Studies in Conservation*, I, 2 (June, 1953, Bibliography, *Section 11* (13), *Section 5* (24) respectively), pp. 73–81. Also 'Vacuum Relining using a Heated Rubber Mat', *Studies in Conservation*, V, 1 (1960), pp. 17–18; Bibliography, *Section 11* (22). See also Appendix D, pp. 335–44.

[2] See illustration on plate 39.

[3] This objection is becoming less valid as wax-resin cements are being more widely adopted for woodwork on pictures.

and of using enough solvent, the right temperature and enough blotting paper or absorbent paste for melting it out. In a similar way the allegation can be met that wax-relining reduces the transparency of the paint by spreading over the surface to which it has penetrated through the craquelure. Surplus wax can easily be removed from the surface, as it is always soluble in the mildest of solvents, rectified paraffin ('White Spirit').

The fear that wax-lining will not last in hot climates is also exaggerated.[1] The curator of a picture gallery in India once came to see me for advice: all the glue-composition linings on their pictures had completely disintegrated in the damp heat. I told him of an experiment I had carried out before the war for the Government of Singapore, where heat and moisture are extreme. I made about six token linings of small squares of canvas, using several glue-paste-balsam compositions and different wax-resin combinations of varying proportions. I held the samples in the steam of a boiling kettle for several minutes. The only squares which did not come apart with pulling were a pair stuck together with a specially hard wax-resin mixture containing a large proportion of carnauba wax. Eventually the pictures at the Indian gallery were lined by a young British restorer whom I had trained in wax-lining. Since the invention of the vacuum method with its enormous advantages, the balance has tipped heavily on the side of wax-lining.

Badly cupped canvas paintings are sometimes stuck on to hardboard to keep them flat. This method is called 'marouflage'.[2] It is satisfactory for museums, but not popular in the trade.

Transfer of paintings

From about the twelfth to the sixteenth century nearly all pictures not executed directly on the wall were painted on wood. Many of the panels have disintegrated from rot and woodworm and it stands to reason that it must have occurred to craftsmen early on to save the paint layer by detaching the support from it, and transferring the paint to a new panel. The first recorded operation of this kind is ascribed by Horsin Déon[3] to the 'Citoyen Hacquin' (a 'découverte toute nationale') who worked for Napoleon I and transferred among other famous pictures Raphael's 'Madonna di Foligno'. The procedure described is still much the same today, except for the adhesives used. I have closely examined a version of the 'Belle Ferronnière' frequently ascribed to Leonardo which

[1] *I.I.C. News* (June, 1961), p. 11, report from the Battioli Institute, Rio de Janeiro, Brazil.
[2] R. E. Straub and S. Rees Jones, 'Marouflage, relining and the treatment of cupping with atmospheric pressure', *Studies in Conservation* (1955), pp. 55–63; Bibliography, *Section 11* (14).
[3] Op. cit., p. 9.

Hacquin also transferred to canvas and seems to have signed and dated on the back (1777). It is still in perfect condition.

Removal of the old canvas and of deteriorated gesso grounds is comparatively easy, but some tough oil grounds have to be laboriously abraded until the reverse of the actual paint lies bare. Among the two thousand odd paintings of the National Gallery only five have been transferred of recent years; but seven more, all on panel, are awaiting transfer.

When the edges of a canvas are so torn or weak that it would not bear renewed stretching, *strip-lining* is often sufficient: a strip of canvas, one to two inches wide, is stuck on to the edges at the reverse side of the picture overlapping only about $\frac{1}{4}$ inch into the exposed surface of the picture.

Small tears on unimportant pictures are often mended by means of patches on the reverse, applied with wax adhesive. They do not have the disadvantage of producing bulges as glue or gum patches do. Some extremely thin material, such as muslin, must be used and the edges should be frayed.

Transfer of panel paintings

Transfer of panel paintings is normally done with valuable works where the paint and the ground have been repeatedly flaking in large areas and where local treatment will not avail (see plates 42–46). Though the process often involves a small risk of losing minute particles of paint, it is by no means so alarmingly dangerous as it must seem to the layman who may wonder how the paint layers can be removed intact from the panel. In fact this cannot be done, one can only remove the panel from the paint layers.[1] It need hardly be said that the operation must be carried out by specially experienced craftsmen-restorers.

As in lining, the paint film is first secured by a *facing*. Fine strong tissue paper is stuck on to the face of the picture with one of various adhesives, either soluble in water or in turpentine or the like, according to the case.[2] Synthetic resins such as some methacrylates could be most useful for this purpose. They must be tough enough to withstand the handling during the transfer and must be easily removable when it is finished. Several layers of paper and often silk or plastic materials are applied in the same way so that eventually a firm board is formed. Sometimes an actual board is stuck on top of this facing. The picture is then turned

---

[1] In *Gemäldekunde* (Leipzig 1920) Frimmel, Bibliography, *Section 4* (5), mentions that Picault in Napoleon's time used a method, dissolving the gesso between panel and paint gradually with hot water from the edge, also that Dr. Büttner Pfanner zu Thal removed a painting from its copper support by a galvanizing treatment.

[2] Alexander Dunluce tells me that several modern paintings could not be faced safely with either of these adhesives; in the vacuum method Melinex (a non-sticking plastic sheet) used as a loose insulation proved sufficient.

42. National Gallery No. 599, Giovanni Bellini, 'The Madonna of the Meadow', 67 × 86 cm. Before the cleaning in 1949. The ordinary lighting shows up little of the irregularities recorded in the next plate. See pp. 156 to 161.

43. Photograph in reflected light (taken at about the same period) showing the buckled and split surface. Complete transfer, removal of the original panel and the ground was necessary; the deteriorated condition of both had already caused damage to the paint layer. See pp. 156–161.

44. The back of 'The Madonna of the Meadow' photographed during the transfer, after removal of panel and gesso. Some of the paint layers can be seen in reverse. Several details of clouds, trees, animals and figures had not been drawn in the first stage. See p. 161.

45. After cleaning and before retouching, showing all the losses, mostly caused by the deterioration of panel and ground.

on its face and the reverse can be worked upon safely. If pronounced impasto is present a papier mâché mould is indicated. It can easily be made from layers of tissue paper and thin gesso.

The original wood is gradually chiselled off. The last paper-thin layer is moistened a little to soften the ground adhesive and is pulled off in small strips. When the ground has too far deteriorated to be saved by impregnating it with the adhesive with which it was originally made up (usually glue), it can be slowly removed by careful moistening and scraping until the lowest of the actual paint layers is reached. Eventually a new ground as nearly as possible identical with the original one is applied on the back of the picture and then a new support is stuck on to it.

Sometimes it is possible to see at this stage in reverse the entire *build-up* of the painting (plate 44) and to read off all the successive applications, the *drawing-in*, the *monochrome form stage* and the *underpainting*, all seen from the back, a fascinating and, as the reader will imagine, highly instructive sight. Apart from minor cases I was fortunate to have occasion to watch the transfer of 'The Madonna of the Meadow' by Bellini, and the semi-transfer of 'The Nativity' by Piero della Francesca, both processes carried out at the National Gallery workshop in 1949 by Richard Buck,[1] who was called in from the U.S.A. to show us his own ingenious wax-balsa wood method.

I am inclined to agree with Mr. James Roth, Conservator of the William Rockhill Nelson Gallery of Art, Kansas City that 'partial removal of the wood will achieve partial results, but complete removal and transfer to a new inert support appears a more logical and permanent solution'.[2] If some of the old wood is left (more than 1 mm.) often new fissures and flaking occur.

The 1948 exhibition in Florence, of paintings which had suffered through the war and were being restored at the workshops of the Soprintendenza at the Uffizi, presented another wonderful opportunity of seeing Italian colleagues' highly developed methods of restoration and at the same time studying the underpainting methods of the old masters, including those on works by such artists as Fra Angelico, which were exhibited after the removal of wood and ground, with the backs of the paint layers exposed. I must mention here with gratitude the kind welcome my Italian fellow restorers gave me and the generosity with which they shared their experiences with me, particularly professors Vermehren, Lo Vullo and Tintori.

[1] Now Director of the Intermuseum Laboratory, Oberlin, Ohio, U.S.A.
[2] *Exposition of Painting Conservation*, Brooklyn Museum, 1962 ; Bibliography, *Section 6*, under 'Brooklyn, New York'. The *semi-transfer* of the Piero della Francesca did not leave the picture quite flat nor absolutely stable.

Other treatments for panel paintings

If for some serious reason total transfer is not indicated, the method of leaving a minimum of the original wood (less than a millimetre) has often proved effective. After the panel had been thus reduced in thickness, it was glued on to plywood.[1] As early as the 1920's, the Berlin wood specialist F. Böhm treated numerous paintings in this way for export to the inclemencies of the American climate.

P. Hermesdorf recently published[2] his account of an improved 'semi-transfer', a combination of the Böhm method with Rosen's or Buck's wax cement idea, which seems bound to work and last well.

Cradling

Many remedies have been tried to arrest the shrinking and consequent warping of paintings on panel.[3] The failure of the *cradling*, much used for this purpose in the past, has lately been discussed by several authors.[4] It consists of rows of battens glued in the direction of the wood grain to the reverse of the panel, through which thinner battens are running loosely at right angles. The main rule in panel work is that any wood stuck on must follow the original grain with its own. This system did prevent panels from warping but often caused splits along the edge of the fixed battens and a 'washing-board' wave in the original panel. Bellini's 'Madonna of the Meadow' (plate 43) and Piero della Francesca's 'Nativity' at the National Gallery, were extreme examples. Cradling is rapidly being replaced by more innocuous and effective remedies, such as the reduction in thickness of the panels described above. An alternative for reducing the expansion and contraction of the panel in varying humidity is to apply a 'moisture barrier' of some suitable substance such as wax or polythene, since complete saturation of panel and paint does not so far seem feasible. Immersion in hot molten wax (keeping the surface of the picture outside it) has been recommended by David Rosen, but prolonged exposure to heat is dangerous and the depth of penetration is disappointing; even under vacuum pressure, the wax penetrates only a few millimetres at best. The latest experiments published[5] appear to show that complete

[1] See David Rosen, 'Notes on the preservation of panel pictures', *Journal of the Walters Art Gallery*, IV (1941), pp. 123–7; Bibliography, *Section 10 (6)*.

[2] 'A new Process of Semi-Transfer for Paintings on Panel', *Uber die Erhaltung von Gemälden & Skulpturen*, ed. Rolf E. Straub (Schweizerisches Institut für Kunstwissenschaft, Zurich, 1963); Bibliography, *Section 10 (34)*.

[3] Morton C. Bradley, *The Treatment of Pictures* (Art Technology, Cambridge, Mass., 1950), paragraph 1.0724. Bibliography, *Section 4 (41)*.

[4] 'The Care of Wood Panels', *Museum*, VIII (Paris, 1955) pp. 139–94 (A report on the problems of wood panel picture supports, with contributions from members of the ICOM Commission for the Care of Paintings). Bibliography, *Section 10 (17)*.

[5] Christian Wolters and Hermann Kühn, 'Behaviour of Painted Wood Panels under Strong Illumination', *Studies in Conservation*, VII (1962), pp. 1–9. Bibliography, *Section 10 (31)*.

impregnation is neither desirable nor necessary, and that beeswax, perhaps in combination with aluminium powder, is still a favourite as a moisture barrier.

The Istituto Centrale del Restauro, Rome, published several ingenious inventions for new cradles made by Signor Carità.[1] At the National Gallery most of the complicated and difficult consolidation work described in this chapter is now being carried out by the craftsmen, led by the mastercraftsman Mr. L. Howard (see plate 49).

For further information on panel treatment I recommend George Stout's admirable résumé on the subject published for I.C.O.M. in *Museum*.[2]

When paintings are taken down from the wall temporarily, for photographing, cleaning etc. a Sundeala board, cut to the proper size, should be somehow fixed to the reverse to reduce the risk of injury. Against shrinking and warping some moisture barrier should be applied to panel pictures.

Difficult Problems

Unusual and unorthodox methods sometimes have to be invented to solve particular problems. For example on one occasion a work of a great eighteenth century master was brought to me, badly disfigured by a coarse wrinkling due to excess of oil used by the master as vehicle. I was asked to get the paint even. I could easily have ironed it completely flat, but not without making the raised wrinkles look like crushed sausages. I thought of a compromise which after a few trials proved workable : from several of the more normal areas I took four or five wax mouldings (casts) measuring about 2 inches × 3 inches. These were turned into copper moulds by plating them in an electrolytic bath. I then insulated the picture surface with talcum and pressed the heated copper moulds firmly onto the worst-wrinkled passages with a carpenter's screw. The heat softened the paint (which from softening tests on the edge I had reason to believe contained some resin) and the treated areas showed after the treatment the texture of the less distorted parts. They were still wrinkled but no longer to a disturbing degree, and complete flattening had been avoided.

On another occasion I had to deal with a still more unusual condition : a valuable painting on wood showed in an important area a deep depression of about $\frac{1}{2}$ inch diameter. It was the only flaw in the picture; it could not be remedied from the front, so, after the area had been secured with a thin tissue paper facing, the picture was screwed on to an absolutely even board; a hole the size of the depression was cut out of the panel from the back, exactly behind the depression;

---

[1] Roberto Carità, 'Proposte per la parchettatura delle tavole', *Bollettino dell' Istituto Centrale del Restauro*, XVI (Rome, 1953), pp. 173–88. Bibliography, *Section 10* (13) and (18).

[2] 'The Care of Wood Panels', see above p. 162 and note 4. Bibliography, *Section 10* (17).

great care was taken not to bore far enough to reach the paint layer. The last bit of wood next to the ground was removed by scraping with a specially shaped instrument; then some sticky and non-shrinking wax putty was introduced and the cut out 'stopper' gently hammered back into place. The hard smooth table prevented it from bulging out at the surface. The operation was wholly successful.

A much more difficult and responsible job, carried out by Arthur Lucas, Chief Restorer at the National Gallery, was the mending of Rubens' large landscape 'Château de Steen', which split in two during a frost spell (plate 48). This needed great ingenuity.

The original picture consisted of a great number of rectangular panels glued together in the most unorthodox way (with the wood grains at right angles). Where the panels had split apart, they had at once warped considerably. For the mending operation the picture ($54 \times 92\frac{1}{2}$ inches) was held upright between four improvised columns. Firm wooden screwing devices were placed against front and reverse at several points and the screws were very gradually turned, over a period of about six weeks, so as gently to force the protruding parts back into the picture plane. The air was kept appropriately moist. When everything was flat and straight, the joins were glued together and small 'buttons' glued diagonally across the back of the joins in such a way that they would give and come off before tension in the re-drying original panel could cause another fissure.[1]

Relative Durability of Old and Modern Painting Materials

The reader will have marvelled at the amount of handling old paint seems to stand, including even the application of heat and all sorts of solvents. The paint layer is indeed usually the toughest and most lasting of all the strata of which a picture consists.

In centuries of trial and error and of steady improvement on their forerunners' methods the old masters made their paint amazingly resistant, and to improve on them would indeed be difficult even for modern science.

On the whole the pigments in general use until the seventeenth century were fairly permanent and they underwent comparatively few changes. White lead goes black under certain circumstances but this happens rarely in oil and tempera paintings and is avoidable (e.g. by a wax finish) in some cases curable by treatment with hydrogen peroxide. Copper green and several dark browns often darken with time, madder pigments fade under certain conditions, ultramarine bleaches in contact with acid. These latter four deteriorations are irreversible, as well as modifications in the paint layer, such as bleaching and abrasion caused by injudicious cleaning or ironing. The more or less fine cracks which most old

[1] This repair was carried out in 1949 and is still in good condition in 1967.

46. 'The Madonna of the Meadow' after cleaning and retouching.

47. An extreme case of bitumen craquelure in a nineteenth-century painting, approximately 50 × 60 cm. In drying, the brown paint had shrunk apart forming gaps in places up to an inch wide. Photograph taken in *raking light* to show the irregularities in the texture.

48. National Gallery No. 66, Rubens 'Château de Steen', 137 × 234 cm.
Detail showing the state of the crack. See p. 164.

49. To replace worm-eaten panels the method shown in this model is now sometimes used. A core of a honeycomb system of paper stiffened with resin is glued between two sheets of hardboard. This makes a light support for very large paintings needing transfer. See p. 168.

166

paintings show are also irreversible. Where the *craquelure* is too disturbing it can be mitigated by careful retouching.

Considering the many ancient pictures, which look almost as if they had just been painted, there seems to be little need for improvement in painting technique. On the whole it is wiser for the painter to keep, as far as they are known, to the media the Renaissance masters used with such success rather than to experiment with new ones before they have been tested for at least twenty-five years.

On the other hand, the old masters were by no means infallible in their technique. Even some of the greatest have made mistakes. A number of Leonardo's and Titian's paintings show serious wide shrinkage or *'early cracks'* as they are termed which appeared during the drying of the paint, sometimes before the masters had finished the pictures, and probably because they had painted over a layer which was not yet quite dry or contained a bituminous brown (Plate 47). Excessive oil in the paint has caused considerable wrinkling also in certain Titians and Leonardos and in many Watteaus, again during the drying of the paint (see plates 50 and 51).

Other technical mistakes become apparent only after many years; certain areas, particularly of half shadows, were painted too thinly and have become so translucent with time that the green underpaint (in some early Italian pictures[1]) or a brown-red ground, for example in certain Piazzettas and Poussins, now shows through too much. For the same reason many Caravaggios and Riberas have darkened considerably all over. This as well as the appearance of *'pentimenti'* (an early design grinning through, which the master had overpainted) may be due to the rise in the *refractive index* of the oil medium which becomes more transparent with time. For the same reason the dark outlines of the *drawing-in* often eventually show through.[2] (See plate 26, detail 5.)

Of the two or three novel paint media which have been produced in modern times, only the silicate medium (for outdoor paintings, patented by A. W. Keim, 1878) seems to have certain advantages over the media known in the Renaissance.[3] The method of adding a considerable proportion of soft resins, such as mastic, to the paint medium which has spread alarmingly since the nineteenth century has proved disastrous (see Bibliography and p.191; also Appendix D, pp. 355–9).

As for *supports*, the synthetic *'hard'* or *'fibre'* *'boards'* of the *'Sundeala'* type are certainly an important contribution to the painter's materials; they do not warp or shrink like wood and are more insect-resistant. In addition they are a great

[1] H. Ruhemann and Ellen Kemp, *The Artist at Work*, p. 31.

[2] See Technical Analysis of an early painting by Botticelli, p. 103 (Bibliography, *Section 9* (2)), and H. Ruhemann, *Artist and Craftsman*, p. 25.

[3] The synthetic resin B72 may prove to be another one.

asset to the restoration of paintings, in providing a new support, preferable to plywood, to which pictures can be transferred, or on to which certain canvas paintings can be mounted if they cannot be kept flat in any other way (p. 155). Thin fibre boards should also be kept fixed to the stretchers at the back of canvas pictures, almost touching the canvas, to protect it from slashes and blows.

The honeycomb support, now often used for the transfer of large panel pictures, must be mentioned here. It consists of a honeycomb system made of resinated paper (plate 49); it is available in different sizes of cells. This system glued (with Araldite) between two Sundeala boards forms a very firm and comparatively light support on to which the paint layer of the original can be transferred, with wax-cement or any other suitable adhesive.

The construction can be reinforced at the reverse with wax-impregnated canvas and aluminium battens.

This method, used at the National Gallery for over ten years, has proved most successful so far.

Paper is also a modern painting support or ground which was seldom used by the old masters, except for water or size colours, e.g. in the Orient. The few oil paintings on paper by Rubens, van Dyck and others I have seen were all exceptionally well preserved, they showed hardly a crack, and the few tears might not have occurred if the paper had been mounted on hardboard instead of on a wood panel which, in shrinking, produces bad waves and sometimes tears the paper.

The *Grounds* (often called 'primings' or 'preparations') have changed little since the Middle Ages. Gesso, a mixture of powdered gypsum and glue, prevailed in the Mediterranean, chalk (whiting) and glue in the Northern countries. Gesso was found to be too brittle to be used on canvas and after about 1500, when canvas had been widely adopted, white lead oil paint soon replaced the gesso ground. Later, in the sixteenth century, red brown earth pigments were introduced for tinted oil grounds; the same materials are still in use today.

Among publications on modern painting materials and methods Professor Kurt Wehlte's works and Ralph Mayer's *The Artist's Handbook*[1] are the most detailed and reliable that I know (see Bibliography, p. 447). Unfortunately Wehlte's have not yet appeared in English. Extremely useful advice is to be found in the question and answer section of his periodical *Maltechnik* (Callwey, Munich). Professor Max Doerner's famous book contains advice that needs partial modification (see Appendix D, p. 355).

Gesso grounds usually last well but are of course, like paint and varnish layers, subject to cracks caused by stresses in the support and sometimes to deterioration through damp, mould and microbes. The only real cure for bad cases is removal

---

[1] An excellently revised edition appeared in 1964. Bibliography, *Section 18* (3).

of the panel and the ground and transfer of the paint layer to a new support, as described earlier, with a new ground, as similar as possible in composition and colour to the original one.

CHAPTER 7

Technique and Ethics of Cleaning

M any people believe that the cleaning of paintings is a modern idea, but considering how quickly pictures get dirty and unsightly, some simple cleaning must obviously have been done ever since pictures were first painted. Most early pictures were probably cleaned soon after their creation and then countless times again and again, together with every other object in the church or wherever they were. It seems safe to assume that it was a long time before they were regarded as too delicate and too precious to be touched by the unskilled and were therefore exempted from the general cleaning as they fortunately are at present. The foregoing applies only to the surface dirt that comes off with dusting or soap and water (but see the warning against this on p. 189). That darkened and dirty varnish layers did not yield so easily was, no doubt, soon realized and people either gave up and left them or, undeterred, used stronger and stronger scrubbing methods. Many cases of early damage by 'overcleaning'[1] are known, and textbooks even up to the late nineteenth century are full of recipes for removing tough varnish layers which must also remove some of the paint.[2]

New Cleaning Agents

The introduction of safer cleaning agents, such as acetone and ammonia-wax paste, brought great advantages. In the nineteenth and twentieth centuries industrial research found a great number of very varied new solvents which have rendered cleaning much less hazardous than it used to be.

Distinguishing original from later paint

The cleaning is one of the most responsible and difficult tasks for the restorer. To allay the often legitimate misgivings of the art lover, and to show how all possible means are used to make our work safe, I shall list some of the very

[1] See Philip Hendy's note on p. 191.
[2] See Bibliography, *Section 3*, pp. 376–395.

170

50. Early Leonardo da Vinci, 'Virgin and Child'. Alte Pinakothek, Munich, No. 7779 (1493). Detail showing wrinkling caused by excess of oil in the master's paint. See p. 167.

51. National Gallery No. 1093, Leonardo da Vinci, 'The Virgin of the Rocks', 189·5 × 120 cm. Detail, showing shrinkage cracks due to faulty original technique, in the fingers and on the right hand edge of the photograph. The light patch above the head shows a fingerprint (probably Leonardo's) in the underpainting, which here lies bare. See p. 167.

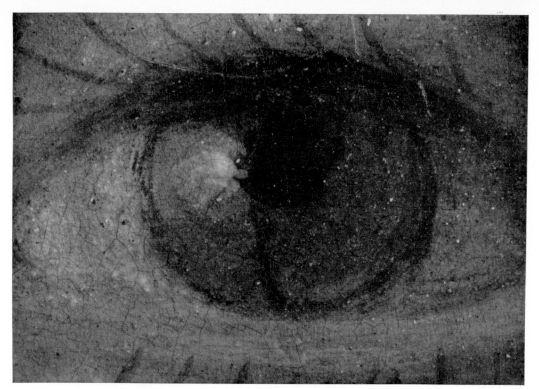

52. National Gallery No. 189, Giovanni Bellini, 'The Doge Leonardo Loredan', 61·5 × 45 cm. Detail of the sitter's right eye, ten times magnified, showing eyelashes added later and starting from the eyeball instead of from the outer edge of the lid. See p. 182.

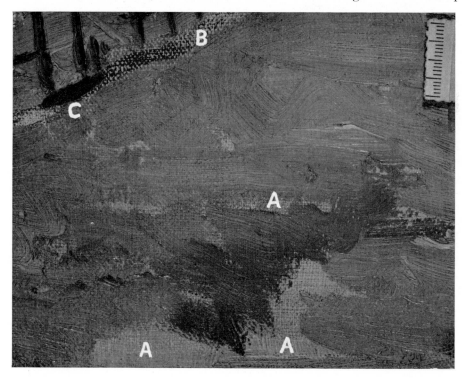

53. Detail from a painting by Manet (Barber Institute, Birmingham; for size see the 4 cm. scale in the top right hand corner). A. Areas of canvas left uncovered by the artist. B. Area of canvas where paint has been scraped off by him. C. Partly overpainted by Manet after scraping. The expert easily distinguishes such areas from 'overcleaned' passages.

54. National Gallery No. 1675, Rembrandt, 'Portrait of Margaretha de Geer, Wife of Jacob Trip', 130·5 × 97·5 cm. Infra-red photograph taken before the cleaning in 1956. The infra-red rays penetrate the dark varnish applied by an earlier restorer and reveal a curved chair leg which he had painted over some slight damage. He left the other, original, leg straight. Both straight legs are now visible on the original at the National Gallery. See pp. 126 and 182.

55 (*above*). National Gallery No. 854, J. van Ruisdael, 'A Pool surrounded by Trees', 107·5 × 143 cm. A large area of the well preserved lake was solidly overpainted with a light grey (on the left in this detail).

56 (*left*). Enlarged detail of the over-painted area. The craquelure of the original has broken through the over-paint. See p. 183.

58. Another detail from the same picture. The head, down to the top of the neck, has been completely re-painted. The craquelure is missing, and the style is harder than in the original, resulting in lack of soft transitions and of roundness of form. Brush-strokes are less certain. The old varnish, in which false cracks were painted, has been removed above a line through the mouth.

57. National Gallery No. 565, Follower of Duccio, 'The Virgin and Child with Six Angels', 189 × 166·5 cm. Detail. There are areas of repainting, distinguished by lack of craquelure, extending down from the left side of the head, and including the base of the neck, to the bottom of the detail. See p. 183.

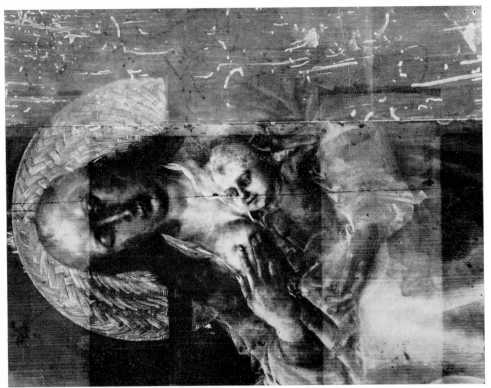

60. X-ray detail. The added panel can be distinguished by the greater opacity of the paint and by the worm channels, partly filled with white lead, partly hollow (dark). See p. 183.

59. National Gallery No. 2609, Campin, 'The Virgin and Child before a Fire-Screen', 63·5 × 49 cm. A missing panel, 9 cm. wide, down the right hand side of the picture has been replaced. It shows an inferior woolly style, particularly in the Virgin's hair and sleeve. On the painting itself differences in craquelure between the original and later panels can easily be seen.

62. Detail from a seventeenth-century painting. The difference in texture, having less prominent canvas grain as well as a perpendicular groove along it, gives away the retouching on a triangle from the shoulder down to the elbow. See p. 184.

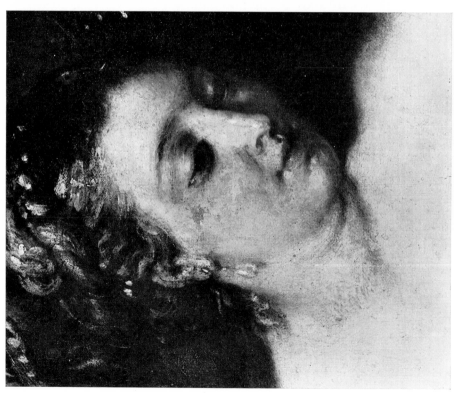

61. National Gallery No. 46, detail from Rubens, 'Peace and War', 198 × 295 cm. A number of retouchings can easily be discerned because they have darkened. See p. 183.

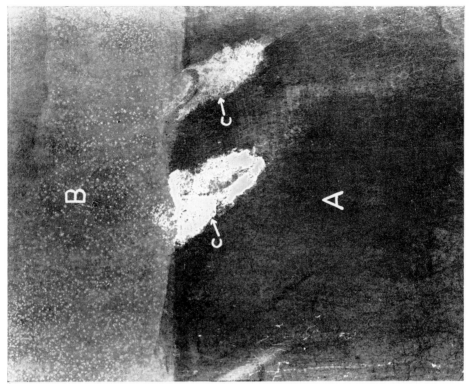

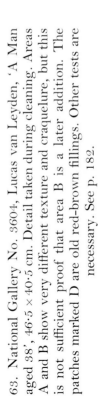

63. National Gallery No. 3604, Lucas van Leyden, 'A Man aged 38', 46·5 × 40·5 cm. Detail taken during cleaning. Areas A and B show very different texture and craquelure, but this is not sufficient proof that area B is a later addition. The patches marked D are old red-brown fillings. Other tests are necessary. See p. 182.

64. On area B varnish and repaint have been removed. Area A is uncleaned. One indication that it is overpainted is the 'blanching' in the two patches marked C. It was produced by wetting with acetone and then immediately with saliva. This treatment was extended for an equal length over area B, where no blanching occurred. See p. 186.

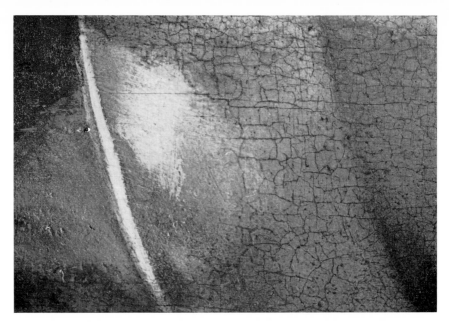

65. Detail from a copy of a painting by Dürer (private collection). The network of dark cracks is confined to the varnish and disappears with its removal. See p. 184.

66. Detail from a picture ascribed to Adriaen van de Velde (private collection). The white patches appeared during the cleaning; they are probably some ingredient of the varnish precipitated during its removal. They were easy to remove with the usual solvents. See p. 186.

numerous ways in which the cleaner of paintings distinguishes between original and later paint.[1] Many of the tests described are used for other purposes in addition to the detection of later paint: some have already been described in Chapter 5; others will be given in detail in the appropriate later chapter. Although it has led to a certain amount of unavoidable repetition, I have gathered many of them here for the reader's convenience. This account gives an idea of the process of cleaning and at the same time serves as a useful complement to the notes on scientific aids (pp. 120–134).

CRITERIA FOR DISTINGUISHING ADDITIONS FROM ORIGINAL PAINT[1]

Although our modern methods of distinguishing what belongs to a painting from what does not have much improved in recent years, it must be admitted that there is no absolutely safe test for this purpose. I must say again that ultimately the success of a restoration may depend, within limits, much more on the ability and experience of the restorer than on the methods used. However, it would be wrong for a restorer to rely either entirely on his flair and experience or exclusively on science. Every available approach and aid must be used.

It has often been suggested that the swabs used in cleaning should be tested to see if any trace of the original paint has been removed. Though frequently useful, this method rarely turns out to be conclusive, for several reasons; one often finds traces of pigment, usually of the same brown or black pigments used by old masters and modern restorers alike; any pigment found in the swab might be from a later retouching or tinted varnish and not from the original paint; finally, where no tinted varnish or later retouching was present, a microscopic trace of original pigment may have come off through friction. On the rare occasions when doubt exists as to the nature of a particular passage, the swab method is sometimes used with success, but more often microscopic cross section tests are made before deciding on its removal. It is important that scientist and restorer should assess together the practical relevance of the microscopic finding to the actual case in hand. Recently in the swabs used to clean a Titian no pigment particles were found, but a trace of iron, which suggested to the analyst Joyce Plesters the presence of bitumen, a transparent colour often used by restorers to give their varnish a 'golden glow'.

It goes almost without saying that wherever any doubt remains, the layer or passage in question should be left untouched. Fortunately the cases are rare where

---

[1] Based upon an article of mine of this title in *Studies in Conservation*, III, 4 (1958). Bibliography, *Section 27 (73)*.

uncertainty persists for long as to whether a given layer of varnish or paint ought to be removed or not. Alterations or additions made by the painter himself or within his period can usually be recognized as such, and are in any case often painted in the same technique as the original work, equally tough and altogether homogeneous. An example is shown in plate 53.

Few of the criteria will offer conclusive proof if used in isolation, but a number of them together will nearly always mount up to convincing evidence; in the majority of cases many will be operative at the same time. Varnish will not be treated separately, for we are chiefly concerned with additions of later paint, though many of the criteria apply to both paint and varnish.

The items are arranged roughly in the order in which one might use them during the examination of a painting.

HISTORICAL AND ICONOGRAPHICAL CRITERIA

It is important to know as much as possible of the technical history of a painting before restoring it. Sometimes records may be available that mention old alterations still present in the picture; or conversely a passage of colour may be described which is no longer apparent.

Many instances are known where early copies or engravings of a picture under scrutiny show certain divergences from its present composition. A recent example from the National Gallery dossiers is Bronzino's 'Allegory' (National Gallery, No. 651), (see plates 6 and 7, and pp. 137–8).

It is often possible to date a picture to within a few years, from furniture, architecture, and costume; and restorers' additions to the composition can thereby be detected. For example no special knowledge was needed to spot that the costume in plates 80–83 and the chair leg in plate 54 were not of the period. A similar example is seen in plate 52.

DIFFERENCES VISIBLE IN ORDINARY LIGHT TO THE NAKED EYE, OR UNDER LOW MAGNIFICATION

Before using magnifying lenses one should first look at a picture in daylight at ordinary viewing distance. The inconsistencies that may first be discovered can be discussed under two headings — luminosity and style.

Luminosity

It is exceptional to find a painting where a striking overall darkening is in the paint itself and not in a discoloured varnish. Such a painting will usually turn out to be a later copy or fake. This is easily explained; firstly, copies are often made from originals covered with darkened varnish and dirt. Second, the copyist's technique is usually inferior, so that his work suffers more obviously from the effects of time, of which darkening is one. Third, whereas the original painter, intent on creating form, manipulates light as his principal means, his copyist tends to imitate lines and silhouettes rather than to create volume, with the result that copies are often in a lower key (and consequently flatter).

The darkening of retouchings, either by chemical change or by the accumulation of dirt on the retouchings themselves is well known (plate 61). More rarely, on the other hand, retouchings fade or bleach.

Style

Stylistic and aesthetic criteria are frequently the most valid and convincing of all. This is not surprising, for after all the style of an old masterpiece is more difficult to emulate than its technical features. It is perfectly possible to work with the identical materials and to imitate fairly deceivingly the effects of ageing, cracks, and wearing. But it is unthinkable that anybody at the present time could match the style, let alone reach the standard of, say, the greatest painters of the Early Renaissance. It is well known that, however skilful he may be, a restorer in making a major reconstruction unwittingly puts something of his own period's style into his work. This becomes more apparent with time.

An attempt at making a reconstruction in the style of an earlier period is shown in plates 57 and 58. In this case the divergence in style may have been augmented by the gradual darkening of the shadows in the new parts.

It is often, however, difficult to prove by visual means alone that an entire passage has been overpainted, particularly when the original cracks have broken through the repaint.

This had occurred in an area of extensive overpainting, differing little in style from the original, on Ruisdael's 'Pool surrounded by Trees' (plates 55 and 56). That it did not belong to Ruisdael's paint became evident only during the cleaning, when the solvent which had been proved not to attack any original paint, began to dissolve the passage in question. Further examination then revealed the extent of the repaint.

In contrast to the modelling on the Duccio 'Transfiguration' (plates 89, 90) which was too hard in style, that on Campin's 'Virgin and Child' (plates 59, 60) is distinguished by a lack of precision resulting in excessive softness and woolliness. The brushstrokes show at the same time a loss of spontaneity characteristic of the laborious work of the imitator.

In the majority of cases technical proof of spuriousness is ample, but numerous instances could be quoted where doubt persisted until stylistic evidence tipped the balance.

Paint structure and texture, craquelure

Up to this point criteria have been described which come into play while the restorer examines the picture as it lies before him. He may now turn to his low-power binocular microscope, or to cautious tests on the picture.

Retouching will usually differ from original technique by the build-up of the layers of the painting (fig. 4). Comparatively few restorers take the trouble to investigate the various strata of an old master's paintings, except in a very superficial way. This is, of course, one of the reasons why retouchings are so rarely well-matched in the first place.

Irregularities in the texture are most clearly revealed by using a small concentrated source of light rather than the diffuse light of a studio. Most retouchings are smoother than the surrounding original, because the canvas texture or wood grain is interrupted by them (plate 62). For similar reasons, deterioration in the original paint such as wrinkling will be absent from most retouchings, or alternatively the retouching may have wrinkled and not the original.

The network of cracks that most old paintings show is usually missing or very different in retouching and overpainting. The differences in the two-dimensional pattern are easily seen, both when the fissures in the new paint have occurred naturally and when they have been produced artificially. Though drawn, painted, or scratched 'cracks' are often deceiving enough to the naked and untrained eye, they can always be distinguished under low magnification. As already mentioned, however, the original cracks may break through an overpainting (plates 55, 56). Yet even when the original cracks have broken through the later addition, differences in the structure of the fissures can sometimes be discerned at 5 to 15 × magnification. For instance, the 'lips' of cracks in old paint are almost invariably raised, whereas they are usually drawn-in downwards on later paint which contains much resin, as of course also in resin varnishes.

Varnishes often have a craquelure of their own, differing considerably from that of the paint (plate 65). But there is not always absolute certainty, even in this case. In my technical analysis of an early painting by Botticelli (p. 105) a spot is shown where a fragment of paint had obviously fallen out while the picture was still being painted. Undoubtedly Botticelli had painted across the gap, slightly lower in level. In another place on the same picture the original glaze had run into an already existing crack in the paint. The bulk of the paint in this picture is egg tempera, which is known to dry with fine fissures within a few minutes.

Strips added to pictures will usually be covered with later paint, and by analogy with the paint on these strips, false paint on the original may often be detected.

DIFFERENCES REVEALED BY SPECIAL EQUIPMENT

Raking light

Variations in the surface of a picture, such as those associated with over-painting, can often be revealed by raking light[1] (plate 62) and in such cases a magnification of from four to eight times is useful. In Chapter 5 (pp. 117–47) I have given details of the various ways in which scientific equipment helps us to distinguish later additions. Ultra-violet light, infra-red and X-ray photography are especially valuable.

DIFFERENCES REVEALED BY CLEANING

Solubility

The relative resistance of original paint and paint of doubtful origin can be tested with the usual restorers' solvents, and a restorer's accumulated experience with the solvents he normally uses can be put to diagnostic use in this way. Such a test is, of course, only confirmatory, and in any case must be used on certain vulnerable reds and greens with all the restorer's normal caution, and possible variations in solubility of the different layers of original paint must be taken into account.

The solubility test is comparatively reliable on old paintings executed in plain oil paint or egg tempera; it grows more and more precarious the more resin the old paint contains, until it becomes impracticable on such works as Reynolds', where the paint contains soft resin varnish and the varnish may contain oil.

Moreover the cleaner may be faced with highly misleading exceptional cases where the whole picture has been covered (probably by some restorer) with a shellac, milk, egg-white glue or modern plastic varnish which resists the usual cleaning solvents.

'Feel' (Softness, tackiness)

Except on paintings containing a high proportion of soft resin in the medium (i.e. mainly from the eighteenth century onwards) the paint will never be turned sticky by the solvent in the way that varnishes always are. The swab of the cleaner first glides over the still hard varnish, then is held up in the softened varnish and eventually again glides over the hard original surface, freed from varnish.

Sound

The experienced restorer can, in wiping gently over the surface of a picture

[1] M. Hours-Miédan, *À la Découverte de la Peinture par les méthodes physiques* (Arts et Métiers Graphiques, Paris, 1957), Chapter 1. Bibliography, *Section 27* (68).

with a swab, distinguish, mostly without being consciously aware of it, the different sounds of the various stages of varnish removal just described, and this can, in a minor way, be a guide to the physical differences between original paint and later layers.

Powderiness

Virtually all natural varnishes, unlike plain oil films, can be tested for their readiness to turn into white powder by scraping with a sharp scalpel.

Pure old oil, or for that matter, egg tempera paint, cannot be powdered in this way, except with undue pressure.

The proper degree of pressure can be easily ascertained on the edge of the picture.

Adhesion

As a rule a much later application of paint does not adhere so firmly to the old paint as the different layers of the original adhere together. This difference will often act as an indication; it is often due to an intermediate layer of grime.

Blanching

Certain solvents, notably those of high evaporation rate, leave, after evaporation, a whitish effect called blanching on the area cleaned, or being cleaned (plate 66). It consists of a precipitate in powder form of parts of the varnish removed.[1] This effect has some diagnostic value. The same or a similar effect can be produced by quickly wiping with water or saliva an area that has been wetted with acetone (plates 63 and 64). This kind of 'blanching' (remnants of varnish) can be removed by wetting with ethanol and immediately wiping dry with clean cotton wool.

Superficially similar in appearance is a kind of blanching which occurs frequently in varnish films during blister treatment with size. Unfortunately sometimes the paint also absorbs some of the warm moisture and turns whitish, and is then very difficult to regenerate.

Repairs Over Damage

One of the most conclusive proofs of a later addition is an obvious repair or damage occurring below the layer in question (plates 67, 68).

Melting Test

In rare cases an exceedingly tough retouching can be found to soften slightly

[1] But see also p. 197.

E. A nineteenth-century painting 'Italian Lake' by Herring, approximately 75 × 45 cm. Private collection, England. An example of how surface grime can disfigure a picture more than darkened varnish. On the left side of the painting the dark yellow surface dirt and the old varnish underneath it have been left untouched. The right-hand side of the picture has had the surface dirt only removed, leaving the slightly yellowed varnish, except in a square in the top right hand corner, another in the sky, left of the tower, and a small one on the awning of the boat where the old varnish has also been removed.

when wetted with a suitable solvent and touched with a heated spatula (at a temperature not greater than about 60° C.). The temperature and the length of operation must be tested on the edge of the picture. The original paint, which is usually harder, must first be tested to make sure that it does not melt under the same conditions.

THE PRACTICE OF CLEANING

The cleaning can be begun only when every particle of paint threatening to fall off has been fixed. In some cases, however, most of the varnish has first to be gently removed to make a proper penetration by a fixing adhesive possible,[1] and the impregnation may have to be repeated by warming and pressing the picture a second time after removing the varnish completely. In many cases, before lining operations are begun, old retouchings and putty fillings have to be eliminated.

Three Phases of Cleaning

The cleaning of pictures consists of three different phases :
1. Removal of surface dirt
2. Removal of varnish
3. Removal of retouchings.

Removal of Surface Dirt

It is not generally known that *surface cleansing*, which is the removal of the grime from the top of the varnish film, can do as much to brighten up a painting as the removal of the varnish itself, and sometimes more (see plates 69–73). It so happens that an accumulation of soot and dust, particularly on the light parts of a painting, looks much like yellowed varnish, especially when the picture has been hanging for a long time over a fireplace or in a smoking room. The use of soap and water is to be strongly discouraged because it may cause irremediable harm to certain types of pictures in seeping through fissures in the paint and loosening it by dissolving the ground between paint and canvas. Alkaline wax emulsions are often used for removing this surface dirt.[2] The widely used

---

[1] Mr. Howard, the Master Craftsman of the National Gallery, tells me that even a much fissured varnish film always impedes penetration of the adhesive because the cracks close up as the film melts through the heat used in the treatment of flaking. Only the loosest scales, with wide open cracks, can be fixed before the cleaning.

[2] 'C.R.P.' (Cleaning, Reviving and Preserving) paste (C. Roberson, 71 Parkway, London, N.W.1) solves the problem of how to remove with a minimum of alkali and moisture all the surface dirt from the top of the varnish, leaving the varnish film intact and refreshed.

mixtures of much diluted wax and varnish have the great disadvantage of removing only part of the dirt and fixing the rest. Moreover they dry so slowly that they collect a great deal of dust before they are hard. It is always imperative to remove all the surface dirt before attempting the actual varnish removal, because soot, together with humidity from the air, forms a slightly greasy film which frequently offers a certain resistance to the usual varnish solvents. The restorer who is not aware of this may use unnecessarily strong agents to break through this insulating layer (plates 71–73). Otherwise dust and soot offer no serious problem in a well-kept Gallery, particularly where air conditioning exists.

Removal of Varnish

The current method of varnish removal is based on the fact that the majority of paintings, because the medium contains much oil or egg, are tougher than most varnishes, which consist largely of soft resins. George Stout says,[1] 'Dried oils do not respond to even the strongest of organic solvents, and the hard resins with them are about equally impervious.' (See p. 203.)

Certain 'strong' solvents for resins, such as alcohol and acetone (which do not usually dissolve old tempera and oil paint) can, by dilution with turpentine or petroleum solvent (rectified paraffin, usually called white spirit), be made milder in steady gradation to suit individual cases. However, Ian Graham has proved in a paper 'The Effects of Solvents on Linoxyn Film' published in the *Journal of the Oil and Colour Chemists' Association*, XXXVI (1953) p. 500, that 'some mixtures show a curve of swelling [of films immersed in the mixture] rising to a maximum very much higher than even the sum of swellings due to each solvent alone' [e.g. 2 parts ethyl alcohol : 3 parts turpentine]. But Graham continued : 'however . . . the speed of penetration of the restrainer will be very much slower than that of the acetone or alcohol alone.' By careful and repeated tests on minute areas a proportion can often be found which will, with reasonably careful handling, remove all the varnish, particularly on Renaissance works, without endangering the paint.

There is no 'safe' solvent mixture or method one can recommend for a group of paintings, let alone for all paintings. *Every case is different, and often different areas in the same painting react differently.* Strictly speaking, it is also wrong to call any particular solvent 'strong' or 'weak'. For instance, waxes and the modern A.W.2 or M.S.2 varnishes dissolve in the 'mildest' of solvents (white spirit), but the much 'stronger' solvents, alcohol and acetone, have little effect on them.

The enumeration of tests and criteria shows how the risk in cleaning paintings can be reduced to a minimum; but one cannot give too strong a warning against

[1] In *Care of Pictures*, p. 21. Bibliography, *Section 4* (34). See also pp. 202–3 of present book.

inexpert attempts to clean a picture of any value. Innumerable masterpieces have been spoiled by *'over-cleaning'*[1] in the past, before respect for the old masters' works had properly developed; and only about two generations ago many an amateur restorer or painter thought he could easily replace by overpainting what he had removed by *'over-cleaning'*.

Only a highly skilled restorer can safely remove the varnish from a painting. Nowadays the qualified restorer is aware of his limitations and knows that only self-discipline and an ever-alert conscience will save him from making mistakes.

Certain categories of paintings, especially of the later eighteenth and early nineteenth century, as well as many modern ones, are painted with an admixture of soft resin (of which more modern varnishes generally consist) and are therefore as easily dissolved as the varnish over them. If the varnish contains a hard resin, such as copal, as it often does, it can be even harder than the paint. In the past copal could be dissolved only in hot oil, so that an old 'copal varnish' is really copal-oil varnish. One of the main pitfalls in picture cleaning is the fact that, as I mentioned just now, the paint surface does not always react uniformly all over. Some parts may be more vulnerable than others.

For example certain scarlet reds, particularly vermilion and red lead, tend to rub off with even the mildest solvents. This is probably because the pigment when in powder form does not 'take' the oil well during the grinding, so that the particles are not sufficiently bound by the medium.[2] Yet with the trick of rolling the swab, described later, such red passages can usually be safely cleaned. Crimson (madder) colours are, by contrast, remarkably tough even in thin glazes. Thus on vermilion red garments one often finds crimson glazes which resist stronger solvents than the body colour underneath them.

Another colour that is sometimes difficult to clean is green. Many landscapes in European Renaissance paintings are executed in copper-resinate green and how to clean this is one of the main problems in varnish removal.

The difficulty is not only that it contains a considerable proportion of a resin which can occasionally remain soluble but it also often goes brown with time in its uppermost transparent layers. This makes it doubly difficult to distinguish these glazes from darkened or from later tinted varnish. Removing inadvertently some of the original green (and now often brown) glaze can only be avoided by continuously checking the progress of the varnish removal in ultra-violet light and by frequent chemical *spot tests*. Both these aids will warn the cleaner in time

[1] Footnote by Philip Hendy :
Personally I don't recognize the possibility of 'over-cleaning'. You clean either not enough, or completely. After that you damage. You cannot make pictures too clean or 'over-clean'.
[2] Theodor v. Frimmel in *Gemäldekunde* (Leipzig, 1920), see Bibliography, *Section 4* (5), mentions this phenomenon. It also occurs in tempera paint.

when he breaks through the varnish layer he wants to remove. However there are at the National Gallery many paintings on which such glazes have survived earlier harsh cleaning methods (National Gallery Report 1960–61, pp. 60–63).

The old copper-resinate glazes are in many cases so dark brown and opaque that some art dealers and collectors, and in extreme instances a few gallery directors deliberately have part of them removed in order to recover at least some of the original brighter colour beneath. This is possible where these greens are underpainted with a lighter and more solid green. Unfortunately it is almost impossible to reduce the browned glaze evenly and avoid leaving the green area cooler (bluer) in hue than the artist may have intended.

The *Safety Margin Test*[1] can be used only by experienced restorers. It was evolved in imitation of the engineer who allows for a safety factor in calculating the strength of a girder. He will test it, not for the actual weight it will have to carry, but for a six times greater one. In a similar way I have suggested that one should, wherever feasible, test the resistance of a painting to a solvent stronger than is needed for achieving one's aim. The most frequently used cleaning agents consist of a 'strong' or active solvent such as acetone or alcohol, acting vigorously on resin films, but not on oil or tempera; this active solvent is diluted with a liquid such as rectified paraffin (white spirit) which neither dissolves old varnish nor old paint, but one need not necessarily keep to the weakest possible concentration as this might imply unnecessary friction. On the whole the shortest possible contact of the cleaning solvent with the paint is desirable. As long as one does not let oneself be lulled into an undue feeling of assurance and continues to apply all the other possible tests and safeguards, the Safety Margin Test tells the cleaner the precise degree of vulnerability of the painting or of its parts as well as the comparative resistance of varnish and paint. The aim is to see that none of the original paint can be removed by the solvent used, even by a stronger concentration. This can often be achieved. I am glad to see that even the scientist[2] who had made one of the main contributions to ending 'empiricism' in cleaning attaches importance to such trial and error methods; he says: '. . . Failing this [greater knowledge of the chemical composition of old paint films] it would be necessary to compile a compendium of empirical data on the action of solvents on pictures of known authorship, age, period and so forth. Such knowledge, together with the research already carried out, would be extremely useful.'

I believe that it would be a good idea to establish under the aegis of the I.I.C. a small committee of, say, two restorers and two scientists who would formulate

[1] H. Ruhemann, in *Manuel de la Conservation et de la Restauration des Tableaux* (Bibliography, Section 4 (28)), p. 128.

[2] Nathan Stolow in Feller, Jones and Stolow, *On Picture Varnishes and their Solvents*. Bibliography, *Section 16* (20).

a standard method of testing and of charting. These charts could then be used by cleaners all over the world and the results be collated. (See Appendix B, pp. 308–313.)

While these preliminary tests give the cleaner an increased assurance, they must never be entirely relied upon. As we have seen, the cleaning test is only one of the many criteria the experienced cleaner applies to distinguish the original paint from later material.

If one finds an old oil painting which is not dirty and yellowish in tone, it is very probable that it had been cleaned not long ago, unless it had been sealed under glass since it was painted. To find a picture which has never been restored in the past is extremely rare. Even in such countries as Italy and Spain, where one would expect to find in the churches absolutely untouched pictures (I am told by my fellow restorers there) they usually turn out to have been, if not crudely mended, covered with a film of milk or oil with which some priest has tried to 'refresh' the picture. Both these kinds of application invariably cover layers of dirt, etc. and turn so hard with time that they are sometimes impossible to remove without at the same time endangering original paint.

In a large museum where the earlier masters' works prevail, the cleaning of the majority of pictures should offer no particular difficulty to a restorer who has learned to distinguish subsequent retouching from original paint. The ideal of every restorer may often become fact and, after all the dark varnish has been removed he may find that his last swabs, soaked in solvent and wiped over the picture, remain white. But in collections of eighteenth and nineteenth century and contemporary paintings, many more difficulties arise. Here it will rarely be a case of the cleaning mixture ceasing to act when reaching the paint, but rather a case of the operator knowing how to stop in time.

Yet, even when the varnish is almost as hard as the paint it is often possible for the experienced cleaner to remove it by skilful choice and dosage of solvents, by not having the cotton wool swab too wet or too dry, and by adroit handling, without doing the slightest harm to the paint. One of the main rules is to avoid friction; another that the active solvent in the cleaning mixture should be the one which evaporates more quickly than the diluent. By far the most generally used diluent is a petroleum distillate usually sold under the names 'turpentine substitute' or 'white spirit'. By this is meant a distillate of petroleum having a boling point range of about 160–170° C. The British Standards Institute has laid down a standard for commercial white spirit (British Standard Specification 245 : 1956. *White Spirit*) which specifies the required boiling point range, limits of impurities and non-volatile constituents, absence of colour, etc., and if purchased from a reliable dealer white spirit should fulfil this standard, but it is safest to specify the boiling point range or see that it is given on the container. I should prefer to see a term like 'petroleum distillate' used for this solvent instead of 'turpentine substitute' or 'white spirit'. The name 'turpentine substitute' dates from the time when petroleum solvents were regarded as inferior cheap substitutes for turpentine, whereas nowadays not only are they useful solvents in their own right, but have to a large extent displaced turpentine in industry. The term 'white spirit' (although approved by the British Standards Institute and also recently acquiring some currency abroad) tends sometimes to be confused by foreigners with ethyl alcohol. Unfortunately this is by no means the full extent of the confusion in the international terminology of petroleum solvents. In America petroleum solvent corresponding to the white spirit described above is generally called 'naphtha'. Professor A. P. Laurie once caused considerable confusion by translating the French 'essence de pétrole' as 'petrol' which in this country means the fast-evaporating, low-boiling range petroleum fraction used as motor fuel and which has no application in picture cleaning. Although the term 'essence' in French when used alone indicates petrol, the terms 'essence de pétrole' or 'essence minerale' generally indicates what we know as white spirit. Another misunderstanding has sometimes arisen with terminology of solvents, though to a lesser extent. In America the volatile petroleum used as fuel for cars which we know as petrol used often to be termed *benzine*, and in Germany is still called *Benzin*. This has sometimes been confused with *benzene* (alternatively, but correctly, named *benzol*), a different solvent. Whereas petroleum products such as white spirit belong to the class of chemical compounds known as aliphatic or long-chain compounds, benzene is a single chemical compound (formula C_6H_6) of the aromatic or benzene-ring series. Benzene, although a good solvent for a number of materials, is not used in picture cleaning, partly because of its high toxicity, but mainly because when mixed with alcohol in certain proportions, instead of behaving like a diluent and reducing the solvent action of the alcohol, it actually increases it. As well as the white spirit of boiling point range 160–170° C. mentioned above, a higher boiling point petroleum fraction (about 220° C.) sometimes finds use in restoration for certain retouching techniques, for wax finishes and to reduce the evaporation rate of ordinary white spirit. It is often sold under the name of 'kerosene' (the quality 'odourless kerosene' is purer) and is also useful as a slow-evaporating diluent for oil paints.

Every restorer chooses solvents and evolves methods that suit him best. Often a 'dangerous' substance will produce better results when used by safe hands than a 'safe' agent in careless hands. A clumsy manipulator can cause damage with the mildest of solvents.

Technique and Ethics of Cleaning

Up to recently our methods of choosing cleaning solvents and of using them were almost entirely empirical. It was only by trial and error that we vaguely worked out what properties the ideal solvent should have. That it should dissolve varnish but not paint was of course the first postulate. That it was a utopian one for oil-resin paint we soon realized on logical grounds, but certain 'strong' solvents, such as alcohol and acetone, seemed to work extremely well on practically all pictures earlier than the eighteenth century. Of course scientists, mostly working for the paint manufacturing industry, had made it easy for us to choose suitable resin solvents; they had made long lists of them, arranged according to their various properties apart from solvent power: boiling point, rate of evaporation, penetration and so forth.

By experience with hundreds of paintings I eventually came to the conclusion that the most desirable features for achieving something like 'discrimination' between varnish and paint were: prompt effect on resin and resin-oil varnishes, fast evaporation, little penetration and spreading power. Of all the many liquids I tried, acetone had these properties in the highest degree by far. George Stout was probably the first to prove by an ingenious testing method,[1] which re-enacted closely the conditions prevailing in actual varnish removal from a picture, including friction, that acetone had about three times more solvent effect on a hard copal varnish than on a one year old linseed oil film whereas alcohol, though slower, had the same effect on both. This agrees entirely with my forty years' experience on every type of easel painting. Recently, with a scientist as controlling witness, I made the following comparison on a tiny spot on the very hard old varnish over a red garment in a seventeenth-century picture. To remove the varnish entirely with a swab wetted in pure ethyl alcohol, I had to wipe it 150 times; but only 15 times when the swab was wetted with pure acetone. Neither solvent removed any pigment, both left the paint with the same slight gloss. This was only a repetition of an experiment I had made many times before.

List of Cleaning Solvents[2]

The following are given in approximately the order of their solvent power for varnish films beginning with those with the mildest effect:

[1] In *Technical Studies in the Field of the Fine Arts*, IV (1935–6), pp. 146–61, 'A Preliminary Test of Varnish Solubility'. Bibliography, *Section 14* (4).

[2] A warning of the danger of toxicity of some of the solvents mentioned must be given. Whereas in ordinary use ethyl alcohol, acetone, petroleum solvents such as white spirit, and turpentine are harmless, methyl alcohol and benzene as also the less common solvent dioxane, are quite dangerous poisons either when inhaled or absorbed by the skin. Recent findings indicate that toluene and xylene are much safer and that reported cases of poisoning were almost certainly due to presence of benzene. Chlorinated hydrocarbon solvents are also of varying degrees of toxicity, but, as mentioned above, these are not recommended in any case for use in picture restoration. A word must also be said about fire hazards. Since almost all the organic solvents

Paraffin hydrocarbons (aliphatics): hexane, octane, petroleum distillates; white spirit (synonyms: turpentine substitute, naphtha, rectified paraffin, petroleum solvent) all these, including turpentine, used in the ordinary way, have no appreciable effect on old varnish or paint.

Essential oils: turpentine, oil of spike, oleo-resins, sl.[1]

Aromatic hydrocarbons: xylene, toluene, benzene. f.(Benzene used alone has little effect on most old varnish films.)

Alcohols: n-butyl alcohol, n- and iso-propyl alcohol,* ethyl alcohol,* methyl alcohol, f.

Diacetone alcohol (a keto-alcohol) sl.[2]

Esters: methyl, ethyl, butyl and amyl acetate.

Ketones: Acetone* (dimethyl ketone), f.

Ethers: (Di-ethyl ether etc., being hydrophobic are better solvents for waxes and fats than for resins.)

Cellosolve (ethylene glycol monoethylether), cellosolve acetate (ethylene glycol monoethyl ether acetate)[2] and dioxane (a cyclic diether) are all strong solvents for organic coating material, particularly those in which wax or oil is present.

Chlorinated hydrocarbons: carbon tetrachloride (tetrachlormethane), ethylene dichloride (1, 2-dichlorethane), chloroform methylene chloride (dichlormethane), are all solvents for organic coatings. In addition to dissolving resin varnishes they are capable of swelling or even dissolving oil media.

The above are all *neutral* organic solvents (i.e. having neither acid nor alkaline reaction). In addition the following *alkaline reagents* have a dissolving action on varnish and paint films. This is not a simple solvent effect (as is the case of the above solvents where the dissolved solid can be recovered virtually unchanged by means of the evaporation of the solvent) but a disruptive effect in which the chemical bonds of the molecule of oil or resin are broken. Alkaline solvents are generally only used for the removal of stubborn repaints or retouchings.

Alkaline reagents: morpholine, dimethylformamide, ammonia solution (in water, alcohol or wax paste), sodium hydroxide solution.

---

used are inflammable materials, care must be taken not to smoke while using them or to have open fires or electrical appliances with exposed elements in studio or workroom. The use of ether (diethyl ether) should be avoided, since this solvent is not only highly inflammable, but its vapour can easily give rise to serious explosions.

* The three solvents marked with an asterisk have in my experience proved the most widely useful, mostly diluted with white spirit in various proportions.

[1] 'f'= fast evaporating. 'sl'= slow evaporating.

[2] Slow evaporating solvents, such as diacetone alcohol and cellosolve do the same and moreover can turn practically insoluble old paint films into soluble ones by their slow but insidious penetration and slow evaporation.

Blanching and Leaching

Among many other solvents alcohol and acetone are often used in varying dilutions to test the difference between old and modern paint. Before S. Rees Jones (to him together with George Stout must go the credit of starting the ball rolling) began scientific research into the behaviour of solvents on paint films, a certain disturbing phenomenon was much discussed. It was first vaguely called 'blanching' (see p. 180). After removing varnish, when the solvent had evaporated, the surface of the picture frequently appeared mat in places, and often white. It was at first believed that this effect was more often and to a much higher degree caused by acetone and not at all, or less, by alcohol. In fact a great number of weaker solvents produce the same effect, and alcohol certainly does. What may have misled some restorers in the past is the practice of adding to the usual mixture of methylated spirit and turpentine a little varnish, in order to keep the two incompatible ingredients in a kind of clear suspension. The fraction of this varnish remaining on the picture after evaporation of the solvents usually concealed the 'blanching', which consists mostly of a deposit of remnants of the old varnish, and is probably caused by the fast evaporation of the solvent. (This deposit is often readily removed with turpentine or with the same solvent as used before.) Other factors are also involved. In a cleaning test with various solvents on Michelangelo's 'Madonna and Child with S. John and Angels' (No. 809, National Gallery) a persistent blanching occurred. It was by microanalysis ascertained to be calcium sulphate, the substance of the gesso apparently brought to the surface through the wide cracks in the paint by the evaporation of the solvent.

Stolow has expanded Rees Jones' research and published the results in a paper of great potential importance.[1] But he himself stressed at the 1960 Rome Congress that it was too soon to draw any practical conclusions from it. This particular research is in its infancy and the laboratory tests used are very far removed from what happens during actual cleaning of paintings. The samples tested were comparatively young paint films and they were immersed in the pure solvents for a considerable length of time. In the actual cleaning of a picture the surface is in contact with a solvent for a matter of seconds only during the wiping or rolling with a swab. The solvent evaporates immediately, acetone three and a half times faster than alcohol or any other suitable cleaning solvent.[2] This is the greatest advantage it has over alcohol; it usually evaporates before it can do any harm. With acetone one can even clean completely and with perfect success paintings done with oil-resin mixtures, such as Morlands, Constables, Stubbs

[1] In Feller, Jones and Stolow, op. cit. Bibliography, *Section 16* (20).

[2] A. K. Doolittle, *The Technology of Solvents and Plasticizers*, 1954 edn. See tables of physical properties of solvents, pp. 380–416.

and certain exceptionally vulnerable Renoirs; but very special skill is needed. This is impossible with alcohol, which does not dissolve hard varnishes quickly enough, remains much longer on the surface and often has time to penetrate into the paint film and soften it. I asked one of the foremost restorers of the Louvre, when he visited me in January 1962, what he used when he wanted to clean gradually and leave a little varnish on a picture. He replied: 'Acetone with a diluent.' On my question: 'Why not alcohol?' he mentioned the same well-known disadvantages.

Stolow has proved that certain solvents, and acetone in particular, can 'leach out' (a much more accurate term than 'blanching') small amounts of 'leachable matter' from the paint medium of dried oil films, under the comparatively unrealistic conditions of his experiments. And we can take from this the useful warning that the same thing may happen during the actual cleaning of pictures if only to a much lesser degree. The only conclusion we can draw from this at present is that we must do our cleaning thoroughly instead of, by semi-cleaning, inciting renewed and unnecessary repetition. Neither Stolow nor anybody else has ever asserted that pigment is being removed by this leaching. At any rate the visible effect of it, a lack of gloss that may occur on the treated spot, is completely nullified by simple varnishing, though we must keep in mind that unnecessary weakening of the paint structure by repeated extraction of leachable matter must be avoided as far as possible. Stolow himself has in his paper said that leaching seems at present often unavoidable, and that one should now try to go back, in a more scientific way, to the old idea of *nourishing* the paint film. He suggested several new substances more promising than oil which was excessively used for this purpose in the past.[1]

One point should be made clear: alcohol also leaches the paint film, and so little less than acetone as to make no difference for any practical purpose.

In a recent publication in German, edited by R. E. Straub, *Über die Erhaltung von Gemälden und Skulpturen* (Zürich 1963), Mr. Rees Jones says on p. 53: 'It can however be assumed with certainty that these effects (leaching etc.) observed on artificially aged oil films are far less pronounced than on the old films with which the restorer is usually faced.'

I cannot think on what evidence he bases this surmise. All the details of experiments published by Stolow and all practical experience seem to warrant the opposite assumption: that on actual oil paintings cleaned in a normal conscientious way the leaching must be expected to be far less than in the forced laboratory tests. Indeed it is doubtful whether it will not be so little that it will not be

---

[1] M. C. Bradley suggests linseed oil for counteracting blanching but advises avoidance of its use if possible (op. cit., paragraphs 7.05 and 7.13). Bibliography, *Section 4* (41).

68. This X-ray photograph of a detail shows that the entire mantle was overpainted across the holes where the original solid blue had flaked off. The holes show here as dark spots. Through the removal of this and other widespread repainting, the whole picture re-appeared of equally high quality. The dark spot on the Child's cheek is a hole through all ground and paint layers. See p. 186.

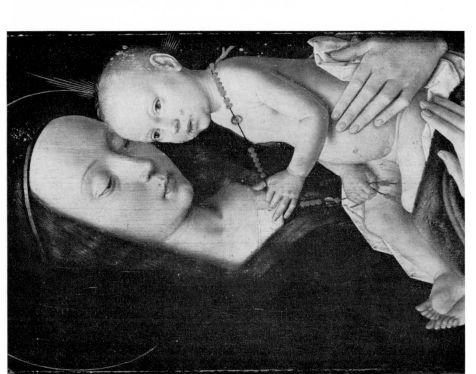

67. National Gallery No. 3066, Studio of Gérard David, 'The Virgin and Child', 32·5 × 21 cm. Before cleaning the picture seemed to lack quality except in the hair and jewellery. Four little indentations showed on the Virgin's shoulder.

69. National Gallery No. 852, Rubens, 'Le Chapeau de Paille', 79 × 55 cm. Detail photographed in 1963 showing the amount of grime that had settled on the surface in the course of fifteen years, since the cleaning illustrated on plates 17 to 20, despite the regular careful dusting. In the light rectangular areas the surface dirt has been removed. See pp. 189–190 and 279.

70. Detail from a life-size early nineteenth-century portrait. In two horizontal bands the surface dirt has been removed from on top of the varnish with a slightly alkaline wax paste. Note how much lighter the cracks in the white shirt have become. See pp. 189–190.

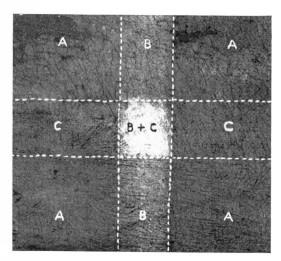

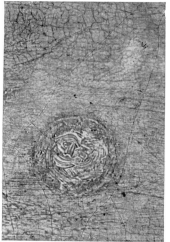

71. Detail from a nineteenth-century sunset landscape before cleaning. A. uncleaned; B. surface dirt removed; C. band cleaned with acetone which removed the dark varnish only in the square B + C where no grime layer was in the way of the varnish solvent.

72 (left). Detail from another part of the sky. 'A black sun'. Accumulation of grey grime in the grooves of the brushwork, which was thickest and roughest on the sun, made it appear even darker than the surrounding sky.

73 (right). The same detail of the sun after cleaning. See pp. 189–190.

measurable or demonstrable. A scientist must beware of not being taken in by his own deliberately exaggerated token experiments. We are here touching on the core of the whole problem of cleaning, and at the risk of being repetitive and tedious I must make this quite clear: in order to prove the potential danger of leaching in picture cleaning the scientist does everything to produce a maximum of the leaching effect he wants to show. The cleaner, in removing a varnish film from a painting, does the opposite, he tries to avoid leaching altogether, or where it is unavoidable, to keep it to the minimum.

He makes the contact of the solvent with the varnish film and paint as brief as possible by choosing the solvent which dissolves the varnish most rapidly (acetone) and is absorbed by the softened varnish; this in turn is immediately absorbed by the cotton swab rolled quickly across the surface. The acetone evaporates so fast that, if properly used, it has no time to penetrate into the paint film and so to harm it.

The laboratory test excludes this fast evaporation, the one variable that makes the cleaning operation on even the most difficult cases (see p. 203) possible and innocuous. Moreover, the oil and paint films tested in the laboratories were immeasurably younger than the pictures with which the cleaner has usually to deal.

Until a great number of systematic cleaning tests on actual old pictures and in the careful cleaner's technique described have been collated, Stolow's experiments will have to be regarded as largely academic.

In the same article Mr. Rees Jones reproduces a photo-micrograph (20 × magnification) of a spot from a picture, showing widened cracks. The caption says: 'Through the disrupting action of the solvent the lower layers of this painting have been partly exposed.' No data of the picture or the method of cleaning it are given.

I publish here two photo-micrographs, also of magnification 20 ×, taken from a spot on Rembrandt's 'Old Man in an Armchair' (plates 78, 79). One was taken before the removal of the varnish, the other after the varnish had been removed by means of pure acetone (using the rolling method to avoid friction).

The object of these photographs was to discover if any widening of the cracks or any other loss of paint could be detected by strong magnification. This cleaning technique had of course been proved safe in many tests on similar paint. The spot was particularly chosen because it contains some often vulnerable vermilion, apart from white and yellow. Neither Mr. Rees Jones nor Mr. Lloyd Jones, in their articles on the same topic in *The Burlington Magazine*,[1] makes it clear

[1] S. Rees Jones, 'Science and the art of picture cleaning', *The Burlington Magazine*, CIV (February, 1962), pp. 60–62. Bibliography, *Section* 7 (29). P. L. Jones, 'Scientism and the art of picture cleaning, *The Burlington Magazine*, CV (1963), pp. 98–103. Bibliography, *Section* 7 (37).

enough that the high percentage of leaching they calculate from their experiments would not apply generally to old paintings in actual cleaning. Any layman reader might easily get this misleading impression.

'Dry Cleaning'

An often recommended but seldom used method of varnish removal still remains to be mentioned. It is sometimes, aptly, called 'Dry Cleaning'. Before starting it the surface dirt must be removed from the picture. If wax paste has been used for this purpose, the residue must be thoroughly removed with turpentine or toluene. Dry varnish removal is done in the following way: one crushes a grain of mastic or colophonium resin over the surface of the picture to be cleaned, and on a small area, rubs it with the tip of the finger until it turns the varnish film into white powder. This powder will, in turn, pulverize the varnish on the adjacent area and so on until no more powder is produced. This method may sound ideal but it has several drawbacks: while it is perfectly successful on certain pictures painted with plain oil or egg, having a completely smooth surface, it will not break up a varnish film containing too much oil or wax; nor will it work safely if the paint film contains so much resin varnish that it will itself be abraded almost as soon as the varnish film. Also it is obvious that on a painting with a rough irregular texture the protruding spots would be worn clean first and the depressions not at all; the result would be a very freckled and woolly appearance.

Difficult Cases of Cleaning

The skilled restorer finds as a rule no particular difficulties in removing with solvents by means of a bristle painting brush all the ingrained dirt and old varnish from the depressions of the canvas grain or the grooves of a high impasto. It is merely a matter of patience. Particularly tough accretions can, after softening with the usual solvents, applied if necessary in paste form, be taken off with a pointed quill, which would bend before scratching the paint.

The attrition method just described is often advocated as the safest for removing varnish films, but it is safe only where the removal by solvents would in any case be safe. Special difficulties arise only on pictures painted with a high proportion of soft resin ingredient; then both the dry and the wet method of varnish removal are precarious, because the paint film as well as the varnish film contain resin, though probably in different proportion. Reynolds's paintings are the best-known instances of this, and many of them cannot be cleaned properly.

I mentioned at least one existing solvent which 'discriminates' between resin films (varnish) and oil films (paint), for instance acetone; this quickly dissolves the former but not the latter; but one can hardly expect to discover a solvent which will discriminate between one soft resin film and another.

However, it is often possible to find a way out of the quandary. For instance, I once had to clean a French eighteenth-century picture, of which the paint yielded almost as soon as the varnish; it was obviously painted with much resin added to the oil paint. I tried dry cleaning, but found that with prolonged friction the paint began to come off. I realized however that it did so only as a result of considerable pressure. Gentle friction removed only the varnish layer and not the slightly oilier paint surface. By making distinctive use of the two main active 'variables' of the friction process, pressure and friction, I solved the problem. A disadvantage of this method is that the white powdered varnish prevents one from seeing accurately what one is doing. To check the progress one can remove it from time to time with dry cotton wool and very slightly wet the surface with water.

In a similar way the worst problems in cleaning with solvents can sometimes be resolved, for instance, the removal of a comparatively hard resin varnish from an oil-resin paint film. The two main operative variables here are : swelling and wiping or friction. The time factor is a third. A strong solvent applied to the hard varnish film will swell it but will not remove it without the customary wiping action of the wet swab. The paint film may also be swelled, but not as quickly as the varnish film (see also p. 190). Thus, by exploiting the slight time lag and by avoiding friction altogether this problem can be solved in the following way : the cotton-wool swab is rolled round the thin handle end of a long brush, it is soaked with a powerful and fast evaporating solvent and it is not wiped or rubbed, but it is rolled over a small section of the surface very fast, not more than three or four times. In rolling the swab over the surface the solvent is applied; and in rolling it back, with a slight pressure, the softened varnish is absorbed by the swab. Great experience and skill are of course needed for this potentially dangerous operation, but I have successfully cleaned in this way some very vulnerable modern paintings as well as some seventeenth-century pictures (they are fortunately rare) in which under perfectly resistant paint a more vulnerable original priming was affected by the solvent penetrating through the cracks. This could also easily happen on a painting transferred with an adhesive based on resin or oil resin mixtures.

This method came in very useful on an unusual case, a Corot. A few lines representing branches seemed to have been applied on the finished painting with a Conté crayon. I tested one and found that it would come off with the slightest friction. So I decided to clean with pure acetone by rolling. This was wholly successful.

Two Modern Cleaning Methods

Two more recently invented cleaning methods are worth mentioning. One is, unfortunately, like varnish removal by friction, safe only where solvents would be safe too. It was devised for pictures where ordinary solvents are risky, by the ingenious restorer Robert van Eyck.[1] The method, which works admirably on tough old oil paint, is striking and perhaps capable of development. A semi-liquid mixture of a 'plastic', the synthetic resin Melvic, and a resin solvent is applied thickly on the surface of the picture and left for a short while to act and dry to a rubber-like thick film. This can then be peeled off from the picture together with the entire varnish film. An obvious disadvantage is that one works, as it were, 'blindly'. The paint is covered while the resin solvent acts and thus some of the safety criteria mentioned earlier do not apply; but I daresay by long experience one might learn to judge the strength and concentration of the mixture and the duration of its action so accurately that no trace of original paint will come off with the varnish. Where risk is involved, a gradual effect could be obtained by making several brief applications.

The other recently invented cleaning method has been called the '*Re-forming Method*', probably to distinguish it from the 'Regenerating' Method invented and patented by Professor von Pettenkofer of Munich in 1864, which restores the transparency and coherence of disintegrated varnish, and at times of paint films, by exposing the surface of a picture to alcohol vapours in a box. I quote from Miss Elizabeth H. Jones, 'The Removal of Varnish' :[2]

'His (Pettenkofer's) process had limitations which are now well known : the long exposure necessary, with its risk of swelling the paint film beneath, and the rapid return of the undesirable surface characteristics. In his procedure no effort was made to remove the grime. The discolouration of the aged coating was probably increased by the application of copaiva balsam, used in an attempt to prolong the effectiveness of the treatment . . . [copaiva balsam darkens considerably. H. R.].

'Morton C. Bradley Jr. first noticed in 1949 that a coating regenerated by spraying with solvent was more readily removed than it has been before treatment.'[3]

From his suggestion, in ten years' work, Miss Jones developed the re-forming method to its present perfection. Not only has she, together with her assistants,

---

[1] For a full description of the method, see R. E. Straub and S. Rees Jones, *Über die Erhaltung von Gemälden und Skulpturen*, Zürich/Stuttgart, 1963, p. 51. Bibliography, *Section 10* (34).

[2] Feller, Jones and Stolow, op. cit. part IV, p. 177. Bibliography, *Section 16* (20).

[3] As far back as 1910 L. Kainzbauer recommends in a little book : *Öl-Tempera-und Fresko-Gemälde* (Vienna), Bibliography, *Section 4* (3), (see also Bradley, op. cit., par. 2.081, Bibliography, *Section 4* (41)) first regenerating tough overpainting (by Pettenkofer's method) which will then yield to turpentine.

successfully cleaned in this way over a thousand pictures of different types, including oil-resin paintings (I have, for instance, myself seen a Delacroix, notoriously difficult to clean, impeccably done by her using the re-forming method), but she has also by painstaking scientific tests investigated the mechanism of the process and proved its innocuousness. The initial misgiving that the paint layer beneath the varnish treated might be unfavourably affected, has been allayed. It is apparent that the solvent sprayed on to the surface is (like the acetone in the rolling technique) absorbed by the varnish film, which it swells before it can swell the paint surface. This seems to explain why even paint of a vulnerable type is not affected by the re-forming method. However, it is with some hesitation that I publish details of this process in a book which is destined for laymen as well as professional restorers. Though it is probably one of the safest of all known cleaning methods it can still cause havoc in unskilled hands.

Again I quote from Miss Jones' paper (pages 177–8 and 197):

'The varnish layer must first be cleaned of dust, grime or wax. A mixture of strong and comparatively slow-evaporating resin solvents is sprayed on to it for about two to four seconds, until the varnish film becomes slightly tacky to the touch. After a period of from one hour to one week, removal of the softened varnish is done by the usual process (rolling); only a far weaker solvent, usually toluene, will now suffice to remove it than would have worked before the spraying, less mechanical action will be needed and the danger of abrasion is thus reduced.'

It is obvious that after the 're-forming' of a varnish film one must wait till all, or nearly all, the strong solvent sprayed on has evaporated, before starting the mechanical removal of the film with a mild solvent, otherwise it would be made stronger by the remnants of the strong spray solvent left in the swelled film. With experience one may gauge by smell or touch whether the film is dry enough to be removed.

How, then, one may ask, is it possible that the varnish film when dry and hard again, is still swelled enough to be removed with a milder solvent than would have been possible before the spraying? The scientists who have helped Miss Jones in her tests (with their intricate modern methods, e.g. radio-active tracers to follow the progress of the solvent molecules through the varnish film) have given the answer (op. cit. p. 197).

'Even after evaporation of all the solvent applied, the swelling has broken a number of secondary linkages of the molecules and it may take as long as six months for the original number of bonds in the aged film to be re-established. In the case of an oil-resin paint coated with an oil-resin varnish, the paint usually contains a higher proportion of oil to resin than does the surface coating (varnish).

The concentration of solvent molecules applied by the re-forming spray can never be as high at the level of the paint as it is at the surface of the varnish coating. Although re-forming causes a very limited improvement in the rate of solubility of an oil-resin surface film, even a slight improvement may be of assistance to a conservator faced with one of the most demanding tests of his skill and judgement. This method is not a "magic cure-all" which solves all the complex problems involved in the cleaning of paintings. We hope, however, that the re-forming technique and our greater understanding of it can become another useful tool in the hands of a trained conservator.'

I can attest that it certainly has become that.

Removal of Retouchings

The ideal method of removing retouchings would theoretically seem to be a scientific one which would eliminate the human factor of possible error and automatically remove everything that did not belong to the work of the master. From what we have learned about the construction of paintings, it is clearly most unlikely that a method will ever be found which will discriminate unerringly between the original paint and later additions. But from time to time ingenious restorers with a scientific bent invent methods which lie on the road towards the unattainable goal. I have just mentioned two of these.

The greatest problems in cleaning begin when the varnish has been removed and the restorer is faced with the task of getting rid of tough old retouchings which are often much harder than the hardest oil varnish, and at times as hard as the oldest oil paint. Incidentally, these tenacious retouchings are a striking proof of the insolubility of old oil paint, mentioned by the scientists. It is then that the cleaner has sometimes to resort to solvents or softeners which might eventually endanger the original paint. They are usually alkaline. Most branded cleaning agents sold at artist colourmen's, etc., are of this kind. They frequently not only soften the paint, but alter it chemically, leaving it soft and sticky, and sometimes water soluble. I earnestly advise those who really love their pictures never to use these concoctions.

I have published in a professional periodical a formula for a *wax paste*[1] which has proved useful for removing hard old varnish and grime films, as well as some tough retouchings, whether executed in oil or tempera, without attacking the original paint. Its special advantages are: it 'opens up' certain films that do not respond to the usual solvents; it 'stays put', does not run or spread, so that the cleaning operation can be confined if desirable to minute spots; its action can

---

[1] H. Ruhemann, 'A Record of Restoration', *Technical Studies in the Field of the Fine Arts*, III (1934–5), pp. 2–15. Bibliography, *Section 9 (2)*. See also Appendix C, p. 318.

be accurately modified by the concentration of the mixture, the thickness of application and the length of time it is left to act; the strong ingredient evaporates fast but is held *in situ* by the wax as long as desired; when the layer of hard varnish or overpaint is sufficiently softened it can be removed with a mild solvent, sometimes with water.

When even this method is not successful, one has to resort to 'mechanical removal', scraping or chipping off the disturbing accretion with an instrument. This may sound alarming but it is often safer than any other technique. In the studios of the Soprintendenza at the Uffizi in Florence the major part of the cleaning, even the varnish removal, is done with a fine scalpel or a similar instrument. This process is naturally very slow and can only be done safely under a strong (6 to 12 times) stereoscopic magnification (binocular microscope), in direct sunlight or with a special microscope spotlight of daylight colour.

Scraping is far more arbitrary and hazardous than splitting. That mechanical removal can be done at all is due to the fact that it is possible to split one layer, of varnish or dirt for instance, from a dissimilar one, but not dirt from dirt or varnish from varnish except in very rare cases when the lower varnish layer contains much more oil which makes it tougher and more insoluble; and in such cases usually solvents can be used safely.

I have fortunately only three times had to resort to the use of the scalpel in cleaning an entire picture. One of them was by Degas.[1] A vague remnant of the composition was all that was visible of the original, which was daubed over with up to eight layers of stone-hard, dark oil paint $\frac{5}{16}$ inch thick in places (plate 74). An X-ray photograph (plate 75) revealed a most delicate design and exquisite details characteristic of Degas; that the X-rays were able to penetrate such thick layers of overpaint can probably be explained by the fact that, luckily, zinc white had been used instead of lead white in the overpainting. By using the radiograph as a guide I was able, after months of careful splitting under a stereoscopic magnification of seven times, to uncover a delightful early Degas (plates 76–77). It was exacting but thrilling work. Art historians corroborated my explanation that Degas himself, when he was getting old and almost blind, must have repeatedly overpainted his own early work, which he had left unfinished and which had suffered some damage in the background. Here we have a freak case of overpainting which it was legitimate to remove, though it had been done by the master himself. The courageous art dealer who had bought the overpainted picture at a sale brought it to me and said: 'I bought this on speculation. It is worth nothing as it is. I am prepared to throw it away. See if you can do anything with it.'

[1] Benedict Nicolson, 'The Recovery of a Degas Race Course Scene', *The Burlington Magazine*, CII (1960), pp. 536–7. Bibliography, *Section 5* (48).

From this brief survey of the complicated process of the cleaning of pictures the reader will now understand how not only diverging views but also mis-understanding and confusion could easily arise, but he will, I hope, be better able now that he is acquainted with some of the underlying physical conditions, to form his own idea on what can and what should be done in the matter of cleaning pictures.

ETHICS OF CLEANING

I suppose there are few museums left which do not clean their paintings at all, and in some galleries they may be left dirty or half-cleaned, not so much because of a deep-rooted conviction but through lack of means and of competent staff or through force of habit or inertia. It has already been seen why these problems exist to a much lesser extent in the United States.

Progress in Cleaning

Some of the leading galleries are now beginning to clean important works, not only half-way but thoroughly. I have seen the first well-cleaned pictures by Correggio, Delacroix, Poussin and Rembrandt in the Louvre; and the Uffizi in Florence have for the first time cleaned a Rubens thoroughly.

Less than ten years ago clean pictures still stood out as disturbing exceptions in the large exhibitions at the Royal Academy, the Orangerie in Paris etc. Some of the museums which lent paintings to exhibitions had them cleaned for the occasion. Now it is often the dirty paintings that strike one as the disturbing exceptions.

Indeed, a large number of famous masterpieces have of recent years been scrupulously cleaned abroad.

In Belgium, Ghent: van Eyck's 'Adoration of the Lamb'; Antwerp: Rubens' Triptych with 'The Descent from the Cross' among twenty other important pictures; all these thanks to the late Paul Coremans's enthusiastic endeavours. Holland, in the Mauritshuis, The Hague: Vermeer's 'View of Delft', and many other great pictures have been transformed by thorough cleaning. In the Rijksmuseum in Amsterdam the 'Night Watch' by Rembrandt and many other masterpieces have been strikingly improved. This also applies to many in the Louvre, where a number of pictures of most schools, except Venetian sixteenth century, have been completely cleaned during the last few years: also a number in French provincial museums.[1] In Italy much thorough cleaning has been done,

---

[1] In the exhibition held in 1965–66 at the Petit Palais in Paris of sixteenth-century European paintings from public collections in France the majority of pictures had been cleaned, a number of them recently.

74. Degas, 'Aux Courses, Les Jockeys', 45 × 36 cm. Private collection, England. Before cleaning, showing clumsy overpainting, squat figures of jockeys and a tall man in the foreground. Compare with the three following plates. See p. 207.

75. Detail of an X-ray photograph of the same picture revealing competently drawn horses' heads, jockeys in different positions and two delicate figures in the foreground.

76. Ordinary photograph during cleaning. Layers of hard overpainting have been chipped off; the figures in the foreground and a horse's head (on the right) are emerging.

211

77. After complete cleaning. The two figures in the foreground have reappeared in good condition. See p. 207.

except in Venice.[1] In Bologna and Perugia many pictures have been cleaned. In Florence, among many others, Masaccio's 'Madonna with St. Anne'. Siena: Duccio's great and enormous 'Maestà' (already mentioned); the Piero Polyptych from Perugia. Naples: almost the whole of the Capo di Monte museum, including Masaccio and Bellini. The Titians there are being tackled now. Rome: all Raphael's Stanze frescoes and his oil altarpiece 'Madonna di Foligno' (an extremely bold piece of work), the huge Titian altarpiece in the Vatican (bolder still) and, above all, the many supreme frescoes in Florence, Assisi, Pisa, etc., have been tackled 'with a far greater courage than we have ever needed' (quoted from a letter by Philip Hendy). Further, Spain: many pictures in The Prado and Escorial completely cleaned, e.g. Rogier van der Weyden, Tintoretto, El Greco, etc. Germany: some pictures in Berlin and provincial Museums thoroughly cleaned, though few in Munich and Dresden. Some have been cleaned in Vienna.

All this is not surprising in view of the answers to a questionnaire distributed in 1950 by the International Council of Museums.

One of the first tasks of I.C.O.M.'s Commission on the Care of Paintings was the drawing up and distribution of a questionnaire intended to reach as many institutions connected with conservation as possible. The questionnaire was framed with the intention of discovering the views and practices of the foremost picture galleries in the world concerning picture restoration. Copies of the questionnaire were sent to the Commission's representatives for distribution among the institutions of their countries. Replies were received from 14 institutions of 10 nations. There were no replies from Norway, Russia, Spain or Switzerland. From France only the Louvre replied; in Italy, where several museums have restoration departments of long standing, the only reply — and that the briefest — came from the Istituto Centrale del Restauro.

I am sure that the balance of replies to the question 'Do you, wherever possible, remove all old coatings and retouches?' must have been very different from what had been expected by those curators of institutions who answered in the negative or not at all. Nine museums returned an unqualified 'yes'; three an unqualified 'no'. A further nine to eleven qualify an answer which is affirmative in the main. The proportion of affirmative replies would probably have been greater still had the questionnaires reached all the public picture galleries and museums in the main countries. Alas, in two or three countries only one gallery seems to have received them.

[1] Since this was written a number of highly important masterpieces in the Galleria dell' Accademia in Venice have been completely cleaned thanks to the enlightened new Soprintendente Professor Valcanover. See Bibliography, *Section 6* (27).

Technique and Ethics of Restoration

It is understandable that gallery directors were deeply worried by cleaning tests on certain eighteenth- and nineteenth-century French or English paintings where original paint yielded almost as quickly as the varnish. They and their cleaners thought perhaps that the same thing was happening when attempts were made on earlier works, where in fact the original paint had not nearly been reached, and they were still removing only brown varnish which is often not easy to distinguish from translucent brown paint.

Eventually curators realized that on a large number of paintings the dark accumulations had become too disturbing to be left altogether and they suggested removing only the upper layers of accretions but leaving a thin layer of old varnish.

Let me repeat the main *Arguments against Part-way Cleaning*:

1. It is rarely feasible to leave an even layer, because varnish does not yield evenly while being dissolved, worn or scraped off, but in patches, particularly on paintings which are not quite smooth.

2. This makes it necessary to repaint the 'patina' where more has come off than in other places.[1]

3. Semi-cleaning is entirely arbitrary, depending on the taste of the cleaner or curator.

4. Semi-cleaning is not necessarily safer than thorough cleaning. As I have said before, by the nature of his method the habitual semi-cleaner cannot know his job thoroughly, in the sense that his experience helps him in distinguishing between a pigmented varnish, added by a later hand, and an original glaze; he cannot know how genuine old paint really reacts; he is condemned to groping in the dark. On the other hand a restorer who has cleaned hundreds of pictures right down to the original paint, will have a surer understanding as to where the danger begins and how to avoid it. The responsible restorer does complete cleaning at least as cautiously and subtly as the more superficial and imprecise semi-cleaner; the latter can easily inadvertently over-clean the raised points of the

---

[1] In his evidence to the 1853 Commission on the National Gallery Henry Farrar said that he himself practised partial cleaning with solvents and corrected the consequent unevenness with tinted varnish. [In 1964 leading restorers in Italy told me that this was still their practice] (*Report from the Select Committee on the National Gallery, together with the Minutes of Evidence* (London, August, 1853), p. 74). He worked with a clear conscience. If he had ever looked at the pictures in ultra-violet light he would probably have realized with a shock what a large amount of new paint there now was. Corradini (see Bibliography, *Section 14* (6)) writes: 'we endeavour to leave on the picture the customary thin layer of the old surface coating ['as slight as breath'— *hauchdünn*]. Yet it may not be giving away too much if we call this endeavour rather theoretical than practical.'

214

texture while the rest of the surface is still dirty. Examples of this are not lacking.

5. Admirers of 'patina' demand that well-preserved original varnish if it were ever found should be left untouched, and indeed we restorers had taken this for granted until 1947, when a case reported by the restorers of the Uffizi in Florence seemed to overthrow this rule : on removing (with an instrument) an inferior overpainting of the sixteenth century from a more valuable work of the fourteenth century a varnish was found on the latter which had to be regarded as original or at least of a date earlier than the overpainting. This varnish was so dark and opaque that it had to be removed in order to see the original painting. Many cases of 'original' varnish or 'original' patina (a 'toning' imagined to have been applied by the master himself) have been found to lie over drops of wax, underneath which the perfectly clean original paint appeared. This is clear evidence that there was no 'patina' on the picture when it was hung in the church and the candle wax dripped onto it. In one case it had been alleged that the 'acidity of the wax had eaten away' the patina or that the dark film had been torn off in removing the wax drop, but there was no dark film at the bottom of the drop, nor does wax contain enough free acid to eat away paint or varnish.

Moreover, one rarely finds an original varnish film on old pictures; it has nearly all been cleaned away in the past. I have in forty years had perhaps three seventeenth-century Dutch pictures where an old varnish film could possibly have been original, but it had always distorted the colours considerably.

6. If one leaves any dark or yellow varnish it means leaving old retouchings, which one almost invariably finds underneath it and which show the varnish film to have been a restorer's addition. The alternative would be to remove the darkened retouchings which are, with few exceptions, ill matched in the first place and also discoloured, and then to match the new ones to the varnish tone. This unsatisfactory practice was in fact fairly general in the past as well as another : that of leaving the old retouching while slightly improving it. As this was usually done with oil or resin paint it soon darkened again and as a result we have innumerable pictures covered with retouching, widened with every new restoration, vaguely matched, not to the original but to darkened older retouchings; already the first retouching usually impinged on well-preserved original paint. Thus the disfiguration wrought by old retouchings is often far worse than that due to the varnish film. The expanse of original paint that is uncovered by removing them is often substantial.

In other words leaving any perceptible varnish amounts to a renunciation of possible discovery. Signatures are often found only in removing the last traces of dirty varnish on the edges of pictures, and sometimes even under overpainting.

7. 'Under-cleaning'. This is the term commonly given to a particular con-

dition which for the layman is difficult to distinguish from wearing of the actual paint, the consequence of genuine 'over-cleaning' so-called because in both cases the raised spots of the texture are lighter than the depressions or grooves (see plates 80–81). In the first dirt and dark varnish have been left or rubbed into them, in an attempt to leave part of the 'patina'; in the second dark paint has been worn away from the protuberances and left in the depressions. Rembrandt's late self-portrait in the London National Gallery[1] (plates 84 and cf. plate 85) and the 'Fête Champêtre' by Giorgione in the Louvre are characteristic examples of 'under-cleaning'.

Curiously, Professor Laurie,[2] who was the first to make and use for purposes of comparison and attribution large detail photographs of Rembrandt's brushwork and that of his imitators, was delighted with the dirt in the grooves: he thought it emphasized the brushwork. In reality by its fortuitous irregularity it makes it impossible to follow any touch of the master's brush from beginning to end. 'Under-cleaning' is worse than leaving a picture untouched, when the false tone is at least more or less even and self-explanatory.

This condition had led restorers and curators to regard as badly preserved pictures which often, on being properly cleaned, turn out to be in exemplary condition. Most picture galleries abound with such spotty, woolly and lifeless-looking pictures. If, to boot, the relief of the brushwork has also been flattened by ironing and drowned in excessive thicknesses of varnish, as is frequently the case, then what is still visible of the master's intention is little more than the effect of a colour reproduction which had been made with too coarse a screen and which has turned out too brown.

It can easily be imagined to what unnecessary disfigurement this 'under-cleaning' can lead, in the way of distorted effects, squints, dirty finger nails and wrinkles. It often produces hard dark outlines where they were never painted, for instance in Rembrandt's 'Adoration' — where one of the figures also displays a disturbing squint (plate 86). (Over-hard dark contours are often characteristic of bad workmanship, particularly in periods when soft modelling prevailed.) This is an ironical illustration not only of how 'Time also paints' (a saying often quoted to defend semi-cleaning) but even of how 'Time also draws'.

I have seen notable examples of so-called 'artistic cleaning', when — out of excessive caution — only the lighter parts had been freed of the darkened varnish, where it was easily distinguished. This resulted in contrasts stronger than the artist could have intended, and in the light passages looking 'chalky'.

[1] Since this was written, the picture has been completely cleaned.
[2] A. P. Laurie, *The Brushwork of Rembrandt and His School* (London, 1932). See also Bibliography *Section 28* (1).

8. Only the restorer who has seen many perfectly clean pictures can train his sensitivity to subtleties in the master's works. One is not likely to produce retouching of the high quality required unless one is much of the time in close touch with clean and pure painting.

I have already spoken of the time wasted in vain efforts to leave an 'even skin' of 'original patina' and of the dangerous lure of the varnish veil left or put on again. It would need almost superhuman integrity to do highly conscientious retouching work when it is going to be obscured anyway by a tinted varnish and surrounded by bad old retouchings 'left for reasons of safety'.

9. Much to be pitied are the poor copyists one sees in front of the most famous pictures, uncleaned or semi-cleaned, in vain straining their eyes to see how the master painted and trying to match hues produced by dark varnish which are impossible to reproduce and not worth copying.

Another interesting, and to me convincing, argument is this: has it never occurred to those who advocate leaving 'patina' on pictures that it does not apply to the greater acreage of paintings, the frescoes? They have never been varnished and therefore do not acquire with time a warm 'harmonious tone'; the dirt is being removed from them as a matter of course. So, if the idea of a deliberate or desirable 'patina' cannot be true of frescoes, why should it apply to easel painting? Nobody claims it for miniatures, manuscript illuminations, water colour paintings and pastels, which all have preserved their luminous colours.

These are the main technical reasons why incomplete varnish removal is usually unsatisfactory. More important still are the aesthetic arguments as to why it is not desirable: for instance the loss of colour, light, third-dimensional effect, atmosphere and many crucial imponderables which a remnant of dark varnish or 'patina' would obliterate. I am putting the word 'patina' in inverted commas because I believe it should not be used in earnest in connection with paintings. Some of the reasons why I believe this may already have emerged in the foregoing chapter.

'Patina' on Paintings

Even if the word *patina* may have been used in connection with paintings (as for many other things) for over three hundred years, the fact that an error is repeated, no matter for how long, whilst it may make it more acceptable, does not necessarily make it less wrong. *I still contend that the equivalent of a painting, covered with a yellow varnish, is not a bronze covered with a green patina, but one covered with a layer of mud, thick enough to hide its true form.* The bronze patina is not an accretion, but the decomposed surface of the bronze itself, turned green through oxidation. What is often, and confusingly, called 'patina' on paintings is merely an accumulation of extraneous darkened varnishes and dirt. What might legitimately be called the patina of a painting is the alteration caused by time in the paint layer itself: fading and darkening of colours; increased transparency; the veil of craquelure; etc.

This true patina certainly cannot be taken away from a painting without destroying it; but this is not true of what is — in our opinion — wrongly called 'patina'.

Patina on a sculpture or a building adds something to them without substantially interfering with the main thing, their form, while it alters one of the essentials of a painting, its colour (and often more). It can add a false poetry or 'harmony' to indifferent paintings, and at times a flattering veil of varnish may prompt a too optimistic attribution, but it can only detract from the quality of great masterpieces.

Paul Philippot, in his article[1] on the training of restorers, has advanced a subtle defence of 'patina': he gives warning of the dangers of 'presenting an ancient work as materially new. This artificial annulment of history introduces between the reality of the work and its appearance a contradiction which falsifies its authenticity.'

This, I think, is based on a fashionable fallacy: that a painting is no more than a piece of furniture or of any other applied art.[2] But unlike the antique *objet d'art* an old painting depicts something of a bygone period and of its atmosphere and colour. It conveys something of the personality of the painter, subtleties as well as more obvious features. To bring out all these individual qualities to the full is far more important than to preserve accretions of dirt or varnish, or 'patina' if you like, which they have in common with every old trinket or chair.

Moreover, however hard you try, you cannot make an old painting look like a new one unless you entirely overpaint it. The main thing you must avoid is to varnish it too shinily, or to feign perfect preservation. As for cleanliness, do you exhibit valuable porcelain or Limoges enamels obscured by a darkened layer?

The true 'patina', the *craquelure* for instance and other intrinsic changes which these have in common with paintings, cannot be removed anyway; only a spurious craquelure will sometimes disappear with the varnish (see plate 65).

Why then should any detail or shade be lost of the truest and most precious testimony of bygone ages that we possess? And why allow any of the artist's subtly calculated effects to be nullified by 'patina' left on his picture, and often indeed applied in the nineteenth century, or even in our own day?

[1] In *Studies in Conservation*, V, 2 (May, 1960), pp. 61–70. Bibliography, *Section 8 (5)*.
[2] See H. Ruhemann, *Artist and Craftsman*, pp. 16 ff.

Technique and Ethics of Cleaning

Some Consequences of Semi-Cleaning

I believe that the worst dangers attached to thorough picture cleaning can be avoided and that, save in a few exceptional cases, they are no greater than in semi-cleaning. In galleries which have no cleaners at their disposal with sufficient skill or experience to avoid those risks, the cleaning must necessarily be postponed or confined to the safest, that is, the toughest, types of paintings, but where facilities are adequate, there is ethically little justification for leaving on a masterpiece a fortuitous or artificial 'patina' that could be removed without risk.

Curiously enough the curator or restorer who goes in for incomplete cleaning can hardly escape being condoner and perpetrator at the same time. I have already said that those who practise semi-cleaning have almost invariably to paint some of the 'patina' back again, where 'too much' had come off. I have actually quite recently witnessed a restorer in a famous institution doing exactly this: he cleaned and painted alternately every few minutes.

We cannot very well be expected to revere as genuine patina and to preserve religiously not only the dirt, the darkened varnishes and retouchings of earlier restorers, but also the pigmented varnish recently painted on by restorers after the last part-cleaning they have attempted. Another important point must be seriously considered. No other single factor plays so much into the hands of forgers, slapdash restorers and dishonest dealers as a dark veil of varnish. It obviously makes it much less difficult to distinguish the real from the false and the good from the bad when the obscuring film has been removed.

For this reason a responsible gallery director will always do his best to have a picture which has been offered for purchase 'stripped' of old varnish and repaints before concluding the deal. However helpful X-rays, etc. are in forming an idea of a painting's condition, they are not an absolute safeguard against surprises. How many mistaken purchases for public and private collections might have been avoided if pictures had not in the past been considered acceptable when coated with a brown varnish.

Emotional Factors

One of the comments most often heard is: 'I liked the picture better before the cleaning.' It has become clear that many critics blame the last cleaner for things they do not like in a cleaned picture. Naturally the shock of being confronted suddenly with the truth plays a great part. One is dazed by the unfamiliar brightness, like one who has lived in a dark room with closed shutters which are suddenly opened. People who have never seen subtle shades of colour or tone do not know that they exist, and when they face them in a newly cleaned painting they do not observe them because they have not learnt to see them and do not expect them. When they become accustomed to a cleaned picture they are apt to say: 'It is toning down.' It is true, all varnishes used until recently did darken with time, but even then in a well-kept gallery this effect would become just noticeable only after about fifteen years, as I have had occasion to witness.

Probably all these psychological factors have combined to form the policy still prevailing in certain important galleries and in many small ones, of gradually accustoming the public to cleaner and cleaner, but never entirely clean pictures. In a particular museum, at least one picture has been cleaned three times in fifteen years; a most reprehensible practice not only from the point of view of preservation, but in this way a policy of straightforward cleaning is postponed and perhaps thwarted for ever and harmful errors are being perpetuated. It is pathetic to see some of the best restorers wasting years trying to preserve so-called 'patina' and cleaning second- and third-rate works, whose cleaning worries the curators less, while in some of the famous galleries in Europe the greatest masterpieces are still left partly hidden under dirty varnish. One cannot blame people who turn against cleaning after seeing on some third-rate picture a disappointing quality appear, hitherto mitigated by a charitable veil of dirt.

As for the often heard and read assertion that many old masters, particularly Titian and Rembrandt, finished their pictures with vulnerable glazes, meaning easily soluble applications based on soft resins, this is not borne out by experience. They were too intelligent to use such a vulnerable medium on the surface where the glazes would be the first to be attained by injury. Nevertheless the cleaner is always on guard for exceptional cases of technique or passages made more vulnerable by earlier restorers' treatment. Those who have studied the completely cleaned Rembrandts and Titians in the National Gallery were able to see the wealth of subtle glazing touches which have all survived the cleaning, unimpaired — and which were not visible before.

This is also the case in the Louvre, where several Rembrandts have recently been admirably cleaned without hurting those allegedly vulnerable 'glazes' of madder or brown. The fact is that the risks involved in cleaning these masters' works have been grossly exaggerated. This was not a bad thing as long as too many unqualified people tried their hand at restoring.

As for the other notion that any great old master put an all-over toning or artificial patina over his finished picture, it is difficult to imagine anything smacking more of amateurish subterfuge than an all-over toning down;[1] and is it not an admission of partial failure to hope for time, 'patina' and hazard to

[1] Friedländer, in *On Art and Connoisseurship* (English Edn., 1942, p. 269) called it 'the cheapest kind of harmony'. Bibliography, *Section 7* (5).

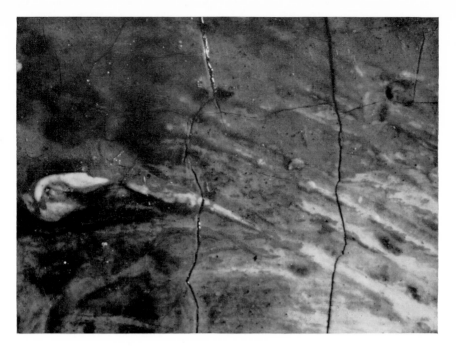

78. Detail from the sleeve of 'An Old Man in an Armchair' by Rembrandt (National Gallery No. 6274) approximately twenty times magnified; before varnish removal. See pp. 198, 201.

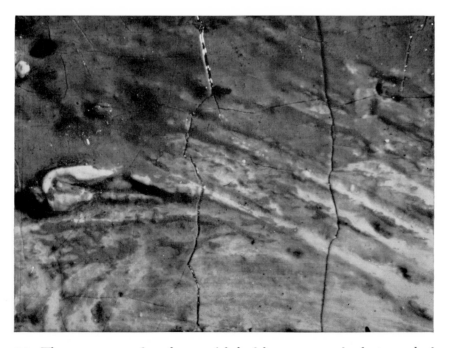

79. The same area after the varnish had been removed, photographed under identical conditions to check whether the cleaning has widened the cracks. See pp. 198, 201.

81. Detail from the same picture. In a horizontal band across the face the dirty varnish has been completely removed; at the same time the scarf over the woman's head and shoulders came away. It had aroused suspicion for stylistic reasons. An authentic pearl ear pendant is coming to light. See p. 182.

80. Unknown master, Italian or Spanish, seventeenth-century portrait, approximately life size. City Art Gallery, York. A typical case of 'under-cleaning'. The accumulation of dirty varnish left in the depressions of the texture creates the impression that the paint is worn. Compare with the three following plates. See p. 216.

82. The picture after the whole of the modern over-painting had been removed, including S. Appolonia's attributes. It was seen that a secular portrait had been turned into a saint. See p. 182.

83. The original painting, after cleaning and retouching.

223

84. National Gallery No. 221, Rembrandt, 'Portrait of the Painter in Old Age', 86 × 70·5 cm. Detail. Dirt and dark varnish left during a superficial cleaning in the depressions of the paint texture interrupt the brush strokes with a fortuitous pattern of irregular spots and cause a woolly effect. The picture has now been completely cleaned. Compare following plate. See p. 216.

85. Rembrandt, 'Self Portrait', 114 × 94 cm. The Iveagh Bequest, Kenwood, No. 57. An example of scrupulously thorough cleaning (carried out by the late Horace Buttery). Almost every brush stroke can be followed from beginning to end.

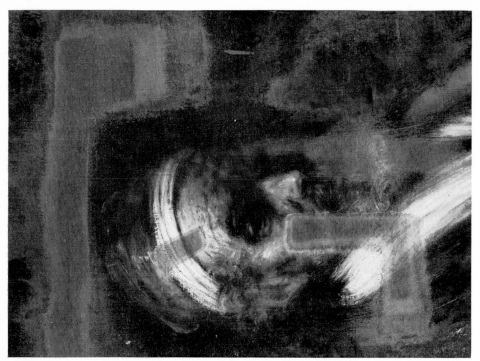

87. National Gallery No. 1674, Rembrandt, 'Portrait of Jacob Trip', 130·5 × 97 cm. Detail taken in ultra-violet light. The rectangular hazy areas show four different layers of dirt and varnish. The left side of the sitter's face and beard shows a perpendicular cloudy remnant of varnish, which was invisible in ordinary light, so that I had thought the cleaning in that area was finished. See pp. 126 and 230.

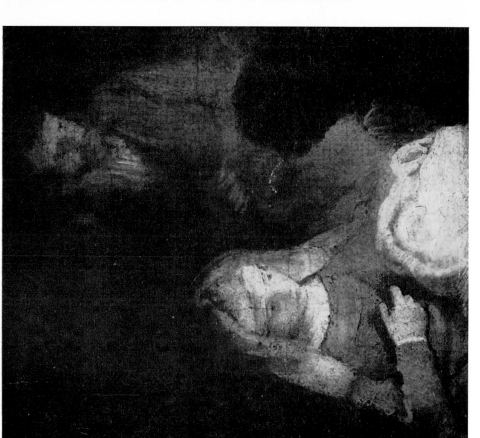

86. National Gallery No. 47, Rembrandt, 'The Adoration of the Shepherds', 65·5 × 55 cm. Detail, showing that 'Time also draws'. Dark varnish, accumulated in furrows of the brushwork, produces lines which Rembrandt never painted : e.g. under Joseph's right eye, making him squint downwards. Along the Virgin's headband, around her left index finger and along the Child's forehead and cheeks disfiguring dark lines have been 'drawn' by time. See p. 216.

improve one's work? In my experience time is precisely the friend of bad paintings and the enemy of fine ones, and not the reverse as one quotation alleges. I have often instinctively left brown varnishes on some old ikons because I regarded them as antiques rather than major works of art, even before I learned that the brown lacquers that cover them were put on by their makers who copied them from older darkened ikons.

Perhaps it will help to reconcile lingering differences of opinion to take into account which paintings may be treated no differently from antiques and which deserve to be shown in all their distinction.

It is obviously less important if second-rank pictures are left half hidden under 'patina' and embellishments, when no subtleties or overpainted original of great merit can be uncovered by entirely cleaning them. Though we well realize that historians, often not seeing much more of them than the subject matter, would be unable to find out how subtly or how coarsely these masters really painted. Scholars could not even always be sure of the subject matter of a half cleaned picture. On the 'St. George and the Dragon' by Tintoretto (National Gallery No. 16) the river had been turned into a meadow, not by local overpainting, but precisely by what our critics would call 'patina' — a tone covering the whole picture surface. Superficial cleaning had not revealed this fact.

At all times painters, paint technicians and art historians, among them Vasari (1511–74) reported or rather speculated on the great masters' methods and were often wide of the mark. This was demonstrated only in our lifetime by revealing the pictures. Some of these false guesses can be found in the most widely read text-books, e.g. in Max Doerner, *The Materials of the Artist* (Ed. London, 1935) p. 320; and C. L. Eastlake, *Materials for a History of Oil Painting*, I, p. 252. (Bibliography, *Section 4* (8) and *Section 3* (40).)

What made matters worse was that, in order to legitimize the popular 'golden glow' that used to cover the majority of pictures, such old texts were invoked and often misinterpreted; but fortunately not everybody shares the reverence of some for everything written or said a hundred years ago or earlier. A great deal of nonsense has been uttered at all times and an artist's offhand remark need not be regarded as a considered opinion. It is more than likely that some future expert will publish as 'evidence' this recent statement by one art scholar: 'taking away the patina means wilfully destroying the work of art;' and he may equally accept as true the nonsense published in some of the 'Letters to the Editor' of the London newspapers of 1947. If such misguided utterances are made by a President of the Royal Academy, a fashionable artist or a well-known author, they become 'evidence'.

A Lesson from Correggio

In an article in *Museum*[1] Professor Brandi makes a very true statement; but with a false and slightly demagogic insinuation : 'If we were to remove from one of Correggio's paintings that nuance which is so light that it seems to be no more than the intervening air, simply in order to see the first paint layer applied by the painter in preparation for the glaze and for the varnish, the very essence of Correggio's style would be destroyed.' What experienced restorer would ever try to uncover Correggio's or, for that matter, any other master's 'first' application and remove an 'imperceptible' and 'ethereal' tint in so far as it is original ? The Louvre offers a most useful lesson : next to a very dirty Correggio, painted in oil and heavily varnished, hang two distemper (probably size) paintings, Allegories, by the same master, which were apparently never varnished or cleaned and seem to be in an excellent state of preservation. They show gay, bright colours which are to my taste a little sugary. The obvious question that arises is : 'Did Correggio paint his size pictures light and colourful and his oil paintings dark and brown ?'[2] A small cleaning test would quickly answer the question. It is naturally to be expected that a somewhat darker and browner tone will appear on the oil paintings, as oil paint has in itself a deeper, more saturated tone and darkens a little with time. Since this was written, the Louvre has got ahead of the National Gallery in cleaning their first Correggio ('Le Mariage Mystique de Sainte Catherine d'Alexandrie'). It has come out almost as colourful as the tempera paintings (but deeper in tone) though some of the cool bright quality of the colour is still partly reduced by remnants of varnish.

The reason why the opposition to cleaning was so strong in this country and why the decisive battle was fought here may perhaps be explained by two facts. The practice of adding soft resins (particularly for the finishing touches) which, however old, remain easily soluble, may have started in England. So probably did the habit of imitating the old masters' 'golden glow' with an all-over brown wash or varnish which is actually resin. There is also evidence for the practice in the nineteenth century of applying an aqueous solution of liquorice, tobacco extract, etc., to the surface of the picture which was probably afterwards varnished on top of the brown wash (not only in England either, see Secco-Suardo (1894 edn., vol. II, pp. 318–19) and Horsin Déon, pp. 150 and 151.[3]).

[1] Cesare Brandi, 'The Restoration of the "Pietà" of Sebastiano del Piombo', *Museum*, III, 3 (1950), p. 210. Bibliography, *Section 4* (44).

[2] This was answered in the affirmative during the cleaning recently of two Correggios at the National Gallery.

[3] Bibliography, *Section 39* (43) and (49) respectively.

Technique and Ethics of Cleaning

The late eighteenth- and nineteenth-century painters did not know that what they admired and tried to emulate was varnish darkened by time, or often actually transparent brown paint daubed on by restorers. To have been deceived by these accretions on the pictures is not in the least shameful. Everybody has been taken in by them, including even at times those experts who were aware of their existence (see pp. 216 and 237). It is impossible, even for someone with great specialized experience,[1] to guess accurately what they hide, and to form a proper idea of the masters' style and intention.

The main point I wish to make is that it was simply the unclean and unclear state of the paintings which has created the false concepts of some masters' styles, for instance that blurred outlines and an all-enveloping vague 'tone' were the regular thing and part of many old masters' intentions. This idea could not survive a study of paintings which have been restored, as nearly as possible, to their original state by scrupulous cleaning. Such 'subtle tonal unity'[2] was introduced only in the nineteenth century by Carrière and Whistler, who were probably inspired by dirty pictures (pp. 50–1), as well as by fog.

Another reason why the protests against varnish removal were perhaps more violent and numerous in England than in the rest of Europe, where similar battles raged at almost the same time, was that nowhere else was the change and consequent shock so great. Never had so many recently cleaned pictures been exhibited together during the nineteenth century. In admiration of the 'golden glow' more and more of it had been painted on to the masterpieces. Reports exist that 'gallery varnish' and 'liquorice' were washed over the pictures in the National Gallery to reduce the 'shocking crudeness' revealed by varnish removal.[3] (A significant story is told in Chapter 1 of similar practices in the Berlin picture gallery, and were rife in Italy by the seventeenth century.) The use of soft resin in both varnish and paint (see pp. 236–7) explains why so many paintings of the British School have been damaged by cleaning in the past. However justified the outcries and warnings regarding these cases were, one must not generalize and believe that the cleaning of all types of paintings is always dangerous; this is only so when done by unqualified and inexperienced persons.

Many erroneous ideas concerning the risk of cleaning paintings are due to writers on the subject even quite recently reiterating their predecessors' guesses and errors without checking them. During the fixing of flaking paint this is often ironed with spatulas at temperatures up to 60° C. or 70° C. That the paint on

---

[1] E.g. Eastlake and Doerner. Bibliography, *Section 3* (40) and *Section 4* (8) respectively.

[2] A greater 'tonal unity' is not necessarily 'more subtle' but, on the contrary, subtleties are obscured by a dark and cloudy varnish.

[3] Norman Brommelle, 'Controversy in 1846', *The Museums Journal*, LVI (1957), pp. 257–62. Bibliography, *Section 2* (17).

works by, for instance, Rubens and Rembrandt, does not show any tendency to melt is proof that two of the many imaginative guesses in textbooks are wrong, namely, that these artists added wax or a considerable amount of soft resin to their oil paint (see p. 237). During the cleaning of Rembrandt's, 'Portrait of Jacob Trip' (National Gallery No. 1674) we applied a number of additional tests (see Criteria, pp. 181 ff.) and safeguards, of which the checking of the progress of the varnish removal under ultra-violet light is perhaps the easiest to illustrate. Plate 87 shows an area by the sitter's left cheek where a haze of varnish remains (invisible in ordinary light), and where I thought I had finished the cleaning. As the ultra-violet photograph shows, I had not in fact reached the actual paint.

The concern of curators who prefer to keep their pictures dirty and intact rather than risk having them harmed by unqualified cleaners is only too legitimate, and indeed the most serious objection to the cleaning of pictures is based on the fear that it may not be possible without removing some of the original paint.

As far as it can be done with words I hope to have dispelled, or at least substantially allayed misgivings concerning the risks of cleaning.

While we must never relax our striving towards perfection, the present degree of safety in cleaning methods, at least as practised by the leading restorers and in the progressive museums, is greater than is often supposed. It goes without saying that whenever scientific or other tests show that the complete cleaning of a particular masterpiece presents problems which cannot be solved by methods known today, we must wait till some future scientific discovery may enable it to be treated safely. Fortunately such cases are becoming rare.

The present practice at the National Gallery is to preserve very full documentation in the dossiers and on some of the cleaned pictures one or two 'witnesses', remnants of the untouched dirt and varnish film, about half an inch square, are left on the edge, almost covered by the frame. For instance, on Leonardo's 'Virgin of the Rocks' at the National Gallery, one can still verify in this way that, before the cleaning, the white flowers were brown and that it was impossible to guess that they had yellow centres. The entire picture was distorted in the same way. Such tangible indications of the advantages gained should not be overlooked.

As for the belief concerning artificial 'patina', no documentation has as yet been produced to establish that a final all-over 'toning-down' or veiling was, before the eighteenth century, a practice of creative artists of any stature (as opposed to fakers and restorers).

All endeavours to suggest that such a practice could have existed make it clear that, in order to attempt to understand the aesthetic aspect of a work of art, knowledge of its condition and technique can only be an advantage. It is relevant to know, for instance, whether one is faced by a genuine varnish darkened by age or by a transparent tinted varnish deliberately applied by a restorer. It is equally relevant to be able to distinguish a titivated picture from a pure one. Otherwise one is liable to take dark and cloudy accretions for Leonardo's 'blurring of images', or to equate the present condition of the 'Bacchus and Ariadne' with Titian's intentions — grotesquely distorted as it now is by the clumsy retouchings and pigmented varnishes of past restorations.[1]

The point is well illustrated by Benedict Nicolson in *The Burlington Magazine* of August 1949, p. 224, in an article on some Titians; he concludes: 'The photographs . . . taken before and the other since the recent cleaning should be enough to convince diehards that cleaning in such circumstances is essential, if we want to discover the truth.' It is futile to attempt to discuss the 'purely aesthetic' aspects of painting without taking into account the technical side. There is no aesthetic quality in a painting which is not at the same time physical matter. On the other hand everyone at the National Gallery abhors the attitude of treating masterpieces as documents or laboratory objects. It goes without saying that the National Gallery, like every other gallery, judges and treats every case individually. In reality, the policy at the Gallery is undogmatic to the point of inconsistency. Often gold backgrounds are left dirty where they have lasted better than other colours in the picture. We have, for instance, left a much later hand on the 'Virgin of the Rocks' by Leonardo, for the sake of instructive interest (see plate 88); recently the portrait of Captain Orme by Reynolds had to be left only partly cleaned and the faded face helped by slight glazing (National Gallery No. 681).

In two cases disturbingly darkened glazes were left untouched because they were undoubtedly original: 'The Circumcision' by Bellini (National Gallery, No. 1455) where the garment of the female saint on the right is painted with copper-resinate of which the top layer has gone dark brown and opaque; and on Aelbert Cuyp's landscape (National Gallery, No. 53) a glaze over the skirt of the woman which has turned very yellow, probably through injudicious use of oil or dryers by the master. Naturally the conservation of our heritage is the overriding consideration, but, we must also consider that a great masterpiece, however well kept, fails in its purpose to the extent to which part of its quality is concealed and for as long as it remains so.

In an allusion that every restoration brings a picture nearer to its death an American road sign has been quoted: 'Death is so permanent!' Precisely because 'Death is so permanent' and, indeed, perhaps imminent, nobody has the right to

[1] The recent highly successful cleaning of this picture (1967) by Arthur Lucas has confirmed this assumption.

withhold unnecessarily any of the quality of our finest heritage while both the picture and the viewer are still alive.

Of course the criticisms have not been in vain. They have served pitilessly to expose the confusion in the art world caused by the dark accumulations on the pictures for generations.[1] But the best thing that has come out of it all is that art historians, scientists and restorers have for the first time been forced into making a concerted effort to clear up matters systematically. I expect the November 1962 number of *The Burlington Magazine*[2] to go into history as a classic pioneer work of this kind.

I have already implied that more harm has been done to art in general by not removing the dark varnishes than by removing them conscientiously. The varnishes with which we replace them will darken very little, perhaps to the regret of some art lovers, who are still in the grip of a romantic love of patina. Perhaps a future generation will again, in emulation of the periods that abhorred bright colour, cover up our discoveries and overpaint the pictures with yellow varnish. But I do not really believe that the outlook is quite so gloomy. The recent courageous cleaning on the continent inspires hope for continued enlightenment.

A Balance

All things considered, of two pictures of the same high quality the clean one is the better picture if only because it fulfils its purpose better, to convey unblurred the master's intention and the result of his efforts. This is why the act of cleaning teaches one so much about quality.

I do not subscribe to the often heard evasion that it is *only* a matter of taste whether one picture is better than another.[3] If this were so, the endeavours of all the museums who have tried to the best of their ability to collect only the finest available of its kind would have been futile. Though the bias of fashion may at times prevent the connoisseur from seeing this clearly, I believe that in the upper regions of excellence the difference in quality exists as absolutely as that

[1] A characteristic example is the theory that Leonardo was 'The inventor of the deliberately blurred image, the *sfumato* or veiled form that cuts down the information on the canvas and thereby stimulates the mechanism of projection.' (See *British Journal of Aesthetics* I, 4, September 1961, pp. 231–8. Bibliography, *Section 7* (23).

[2] It includes the following articles: Joyce Plesters, 'Dark Varnishes — Some Further Comments'; Denis Mahon, 'Miscellanea for the Cleaning Controversy'; J. A. van de Graaf, 'The Interpretation of Old Painting Recipes'; Michelangelo Muraro, 'Notes on traditional methods of cleaning pictures in Venice and Florence'; and G. Thomson, 'Notes on "Science and the Art of Picture Cleaning".' See Bibliography, *Section 7*, (28), (26), (31), (27) and (30) respectively.

[3] H. Ruhemann and Ellen M. Kemp, *The Artist at Work* (Penguin Books, 1951), p. 64, tries to illustrate this point with tangible examples; also *Artist and Craftsman*.

between a clean picture and one covered with brown varnish, which inevitably appears of a lower merit because some of its qualities are hidden or obscured. And, of course, if the same brownish tone covers two works of different quality it makes good and bad more alike. This can hardly be stressed too often.

However, while it is not advisable to cover or to leave covered all pictures with the same 'gallery tone', it would be foolish to advise the same general cleaning policy to all galleries and for all pictures.

The decision on whether to clean all pictures in a gallery or only some of them completely or partly and how and when to do it will in every case depend on :

1. The history of the collection.
2. Its size and importance.
3. The quality or relative excellence of the pictures.
4. The urgency of treatment for reasons of conservation. It is not well enough known that an old varnish sometimes in contracting pulls off loosening particles of paint and must therefore be removed (p. 21).
5. The degree of distortion through accretions.
6. The taste of the director and trustees.
7. Public opinion.
8. The degree of vulnerability (or risk) in every case.
9. Whether a restorer is available who can clean a picture without harming and who can retouch it without disfiguring it. (Non-darkening retouching, etc.);
10. Who will in cleaning and retouching subordinate his own taste to that of the master;
11. Who will put preservation and consolidation before cleaning;
12. Who will retouch tactfully and sparingly.
13. It also depends on whether the pictures are to be exhibited in a strong or a dim light.

Where the available restorer does not live up to these postulations, it is far better to confine oneself to keeping the pictures in good repair, but leaving them uncleaned.

One of the erroneous ideas caused by the tone found on old pictures is that all the 'Primitives' produced discreet, subdued colour schemes; the truth is that the colours of many early pictures (for instance those of Lorenzo Monaco) are emphatic and according to certain tastes unharmonious. Therefore some people, when looking at one that has been cleaned, naively assume it must have been 'over-cleaned'. This is one of the many instances where a prejudice has created a false assumption and engendered new prejudices.

There may be those who would prefer to see the strong colours of a Lorenzo

Monaco (or, for instance, of a Bronzino or a Baroccio) subdued by a haze of yellow varnish and dirt. But one can hardly approve of a museum yielding to such a subjective attitude, for is not one of the duties of a picture gallery to serve the purposes of the true history of art? (See p. 232.)

The National Gallery based its case for the thorough cleaning of masterpieces mainly on primary evidence: that is, the evidence of the paintings themselves, obtained by thorough and scientific examination. To quote only one example: the so-called patina found on many early Italian paintings is a kind of varnish gone dark grey largely through a net of fine cracks, filled with dirt in the course of time (plates 23, 24). This cannot possibly have been the artist's intention.[1]

The second kind of evidence of the artist's intention, no less first-hand and indubitable, on which a cleaning policy can be based is his own word. I am quoting here only one example, Dürer's classic letter to his patron and friend Jacob Heller[2]: p. 50. Speaking of a picture of a Virgin and Child he has delivered '... painted with seven layers of ultramarine — will last 500 years clean and fresh if you keep it clean. . . . And when in about one, two or three years time I come to see you, the panel will have to be taken down. If it is then well dried, I would again varnish it with a special varnish which one cannot make anywhere else! thus it will last another hundred years longer than before. But do not let anybody else varnish it again, for all other varnishes are yellow, and one would spoil your panel. . . .'

The Formation of Policies

Although the art historians in charge of pictures are officially responsible for the policies regarding cleaning[3] they naturally form their ideas in the first place from what they are told by their restorers and what they see them do. We must remember that when the present restorers of the older generation began their careers, no proper schooling existed in the profession; scientific aids had only just begun to be taken up by it and the potential museum director had little opportunity of any experience or training in technical matters.

The inexperienced and over-timid cleaner, not knowing the difference between a restorer's tinted varnish and an original glaze, becomes worried when beginning to remove the varnish and stops lest he remove some of the original paint. In perfectly good faith he declares that the brown, showing on the last cotton

[1] E. H. Gombrich, 'Dark Varnishes, Variations on a Theme from Pliny', *The Burlington Magazine*, CIV (February, 1962), p. 53. Bibliography, *Section 7* (24).

[2] Albrecht Dürer (letters in German) *Quellenschriften für Kunstgeschichte*, I, p. 36, letter to Dürer's patron and friend Jacob Heller.

[3] For further points of logic regarding semi-cleaning, see M. C. Bradley, *The Treatment of Pictures*, paragraphs 2.00 to 2.021. Bibliography, *Section 4* (41).

wool swab he used for his tests, is actually a trace of a 'delicate original glaze'. There is little doubt that this is the starting point of the whole theory and practice of part-cleaning. The next step is for the cleaner to tell the director, who in turn lays down a rule that 'no picture in his museum should be completely cleaned; at least a thin layer of old varnish must be left, so that the top layer of the original paint is not reached by the cleaning.' Finally, the decision is made public, and the policy of non-cleaning or semi-cleaning is fixed for generations. Thus the cleaner is prevented from making any progress in his experience. In fact, of some galleries it could be said that up to recently their restorers had never been face to face with real original old masters' paint — only with varnish of varying thicknesses and antiquity.

There is one important point which may affect a gallery's policy. The more pictures a gallery comprises, the more difficult it is to follow a systematic policy of cleaning, because the demands of maintenance and repair will be keeping the curators and restorers too busy to envisage within the foreseeable future a programme of thorough cleaning of all the masterpieces in the collection.

In the London National Gallery with its 2000 pictures, it is just possible to work out a plan for the cleaning of most of the major works without neglecting the necessary work of preservation.

The situation is very different in a gallery like the Alte Pinakothek in Munich, which comprises 15000 paintings (the smaller part of which are on exhibition). Here a programme of proper storing and maintenance had to come first[1] and a policy of doing as little as possible in the way of cleaning has developed naturally during the last decades. Only for special reasons or occasions are pictures cleaned.

Even when, in 1960, the large 'Höllensturz' by Rubens was damaged by a maniac, the picture was not cleaned but only the worst damage was retouched. This decision is quite understandable: the picture is extremely large and shows many darkened retouchings. It would have been an enormous undertaking to clean the whole painting and to re-do the retouchings, of which moreover the majority would be much above the eye level of the viewer.

One factor which may, perhaps subconsciously, influence the cleaning policies is the comparative brightness in which the pictures are hung.

In relatively dimly lit galleries, as for instance in Rotterdam, Munich and Vienna, the disfiguration of the pictures by yellowed varnishes and darkened retouchings will be less disturbing than in lighter ones; though it may of course be argued that in the darker galleries it would be all the more necessary to show the pictures in their full original brightness.

[1] Dr. Christian Wolters has recently created a modern reference section which surpasses even many American ones in efficiency of arrangement.

Technique and Ethics of Restoration

On the other hand, the restorer who knows that the results of his efforts are not fully appreciated in a comparatively dark exhibition room cannot be blamed if he does not attempt to clean or retouch to perfection; but the quality of his work will, as I have said before, depend ultimately more on his conscientiousness and on how good the lighting is, not in the gallery, but in his studio.

One group — the professional copyists in certain galleries — whom one would expect to be the first to demand it, are passionately opposing the removal of the brown surface coatings. One can sympathize with them, because their stock of copies would become valueless if the originals were revealed in their true brightness. It is fortunate that the firms producing colour reproductions had not accumulated a sufficiently large stock to form a weighty impediment when the possibilities of proper cleaning became known. They are now on the contrary frequently urging directors of galleries to have popular masterpieces cleaned before making their colour blocks. On many occasions their earlier reproductions became obsolete through the cleaning of an original, and indeed when comparing the old reproduction with the new one it is hard to believe that for so long almost everybody seemed satisfied with the disfigured image.

THE VICIOUS CIRCLE OF VARNISHES

This brings us to the crux of the whole matter, to what I call 'The Vicious Circle of Varnishes'.

Let me try to recapitulate how in my opinion all the mistaken hypotheses and practices originated.

1. Varnishes on old paintings darkened with time[1] (of their ingredients, both resin and oil do so).

2. The dark varnishes were admired and restorers resorted to deliberately pigmenting their varnishes.

3. When accumulations became excessively dark and distorting, the attempt was made to remove them; they came off easily, but, not knowing the difference between original paint and addition, the restorers concerned were scared. Finding brown pigment in all their cleaning swabs they were confirmed in their belief that they had removed traces of the original paint or glaze.

4. They declared that it was now proved that the old masters finished their pictures with all-over brown washes or glazes, that these were very delicate or vulnerable because they contained soft resin and therefore came off easily.

---

[1] Garry Thomson reminds me of the important fact that the light has to pass twice through a varnish, on the way to the picture surface and on its way back to the viewer, so that the light absorbing effect of a dark varnish is doubled.

5. It was then officially proclaimed, first by the cleaners, then by their directors, that it is impossible to clean old masters' paintings (except superficially) without at the same time removing some of the original paint.

6. The textbooks on technique of painting and on restoration adopt this error and new mistaken theories are based on it and win wide acceptance. (Bibliography *Sections 3, 4, 7* and *8* include many examples.)

7. Technical terms and art historical hypotheses become confused: Patina, Sfumato, Tone, Harmony, Chiaroscuro, etc.

8. Textbooks conclude: old masters painted with admixture of soft resin therefore contemporary painters should do the same.

9. Modern paintings, containing excessive quantities of this unstable, darkening and never completely hardening ingredient (mastic or damar resin), deteriorate faster than old straightforward oil paintings.

The vicious circle is closed: what used to be a false conjecture has become a reality: the picture galleries are now full of relatively modern canvases which are painted with a considerable proportion of soft resin and virtually impossible to clean because they are no harder than the varnish covering them.

The nineteenth-century French and English paintings and also some eighteenth-century English ones, which have afforded the most frightening cleaning experiences, are early examples of the group which forms the last link of the fatal circle.

The connection between the links of this formidable chain of errors would never have been discovered and denounced if the misguided prophets of 'part way', 'semi', 'artistic', or 'nuancé', cleaning had been heeded everywhere. They were themselves victims of the vicious circle; their judgement was impaired by the veil they tried to perpetuate on the works of art in their care.[1]

---

[1] In 1962 I had a striking confirmation that the 'Vicious Circle of Varnishes' is more than a theory: Dr. Christian Wolters, director of the Doerner Institute in Munich, very kindly allowed me to make cleaning tests on copies made after old masters in the 1930's and 40's by pupils of Doerner (see Bibliography, *Section 4* (8)) in his famous 'Misch-Technik'. Mr. Ostenrieder, in charge of the special Department of the Doerner Institute, had seen some of these paintings being made and was most helpful with first-hand information. The copies had notes attached to them giving dates and the materials used.

The tests showed that:

(1) approximately 20 years old mastic varnish could not be entirely removed with toluene, one of the mildest solvents for varnish films.

(2) that from none of the 4 pictures tested could the varnish (which had darkened considerably) be removed without removing at the same time paint (applied with admixture of a high proportion of resin).

Further details of these tests are given in the Appendix B (pp. 306–8).

Technique and Ethics of Restoration

One powerful argument in favour of varnish removal which I have not mentioned yet may not belong under the heading 'Ethics of Cleaning' but it certainly comes under 'Gains through Cleaning'. In 1930 the art historian Dr. Römer coined the phrase 'Bloodless Acquisition' and Osbert Lancaster commented on the Cleaned Pictures Exhibition of 1947 'Fifty new pictures, cost nil, a bunch of new masterpieces'.

This point of view is particularly valid when the cleaning makes it evident that a picture is by a greater or rarer master than had been believed before, as for instance in the case of the 'Adoration of the Magi', National Gallery No. 1160, catalogued as Bonifazio in 1929, and as Giorgione in the catalogue of the Venetian School of 1959 by Cecil Gould.

But even when the reverse happens, the disappointment will, at least in a museum, be offset by the satisfaction of having discovered the truth.

When in 1962 the true brilliance of certain blues in two or three pictures by Titian was revealed by cleaning, it was also a kind of disappointment to a number of art lovers. We agree with the critics that these blues without their veil of dirty varnish do now appear a little out of balance, perhaps partly because some of the greens have turned brown with time; however, we have to consider that those blue distances may always have been too strident for some people's taste. The blueness of distances was a great discovery in the Renaissance and the painters may well have exaggerated it as the Impressionists exaggerated the blue shadows they discovered, much to the annoyance of their contemporaries. In every large picture gallery one can find many paintings by Renaissance, Romantic and Impressionist masters, with distances seeming no less 'out of balance' than those in the criticized Titians, and where there is no question of this 'discord' being due to any alteration by time. Many of the greens in the cleaned Titians are still very strong.[1] These blues of distances or skies must always have been much stronger than any that one can observe in nature.

Though it is true that certain greens in old pictures have originally been greener and less brown than they are now, there are numerous Renaissance pictures in which the greens seem to have changed only slightly. I believe that one factor which turns greens into browns is often forgotten: autumn. In a number of Renaissance paintings certain foregrounds (e.g. in Tintoretto's 'St. George') and in trees, the demonstrable admixture of brown ochres entitles one to suppose that they were intended to be brownish-green from the outset.

Moreover, as has been pointed out elsewhere, *lapis lazuli* (genuine ultramarine) was as expensive as gold, and one can understand the reluctance of such

[1] This is also the case in the 'Bacchus and Ariadne'.

a painter as Dürer to tone it down (see his letter, page 234).[1] It should be borne in mind that Dürer (1471–1528) was still alive when Titian painted those of his pictures which continue the colourful tradition of the fifteenth century.

THE IMPORTANCE OF RETOUCHING

In many picture galleries on the Continent, probably another generation of curators will take the credit for finding the proper balance between prudence and courage in their cleaning policies. As enlightenment, experience and confidence spread among them and as more restorers are systematically trained, it will probably not be long before we see the important masterpieces shake off the last remnants of obscuring grime.[2] Nothing can now hold up this development except perhaps setbacks such as unsuccessful restorations, including unsuccessful retouching. But too little or no retouching will also delay progress because it leaves the masterpiece in a condition acceptable only to a small minority of scholars and to most people less acceptable than before the cleaning. In the same way as unintentionally visible, clumsy retouching, much deliberately visible inpainting, unless it is superbly done, will retard the universal acceptance of complete cleaning.

One progressive curator on the Continent told me that after long hesitation he had had a highly important early masterpiece cleaned very competently; it came out considerably finer, brighter and comparatively well preserved. However, the restorer was not a good retoucher and when he had finished, the 'lacunae' (losses) which cleaning almost invariably reveals on old pictures, were covered with disturbing ill-matched inpainting, which degraded the quality of the original, as unsubtle retouching always does. This disappointing experience has put the Gallery director off cleaning (but I hope only till he finds a restorer who retouches as competently as he cleans). It is curious how even a small retouching of inferior quality or ill-matched style can antagonize a sensitive scholar. How Friedländer tended to reject fine originals with small flaws of this kind as not by the master's hand is a good instance of this.

On the whole, the success or failure of methods in the future will depend more on the tradition and experience handed down in the picture galleries than on the teaching in training centres outside the museums.

[1] However, the blues in the Titian and Giorgione distances are very far from the brilliance of pure ultramarine or azurite. During the retouching of Giorgione's 'Adulteress' in the Glasgow Art Gallery (the attribution to Giorgione is contested by some art scholars) I realized that these blue pigments, where they are not broken by admixture of other pigments, are considerably reduced by yellow grounds, or under-paintings in a dimmer blue which show through the ultramarine glaze. This was the traditional method.

[2] Since this was written I have revisited the Louvre and found to my delight that a great many pictures had been beautifully cleaned, particularly in the 'Exposition des Réserves' and among nineteenth-century works.

CHAPTER 8

Technique and Ethics of Retouching

We can now understand why it may be difficult for a public gallery to adopt a policy of scrupulous cleaning without coupling it with careful retouching. Before, however, discussing the technique of retouching, I cannot stress too much the necessity of preliminary photography to the fullest possible extent. As I have already suggested, old paintings are very rarely found in which the cleaning does not reveal some losses previously unsuspected, at least by the layman. These, however, can mostly, if not all, be revealed before cleaning by photography of different kinds (see pp. 125–30). In this way also the restorer may protect himself against himself, that is against the too easy assumption that all losses revealed by his cleaning must necessarily have been there before, under the obscuring varnish. The first step in cleaning should always be the fullest possible photographic record; and normal photographs should be taken again after the cleaning and before the retouching. This second record gives a permanent and accurate key to the condition of the picture, which will be invaluable if further treatment becomes necessary.

Stopping (filling) of holes

Though the filling of holes with a 'putty' might seem a matter of minor importance, the physical and aesthetic success of a retouching depends on it.

The putty must stick and last perfectly, both on panel and canvas paintings. A plain gesso mixture tends to crack and flake when used on canvases. The following formula found by trial and error has proved most satisfactory:
in volumes: 2 parts gilder's whiting, 1 part stand-oil mixed on a warm slab; if the result is soft, add more whiting (or pigment for tinted ground), till you obtain a hard consistency difficult to knead; too much oil would retard drying; add *ca.* 1 part glue of normal viscosity (thickness). Brand glues sold in tubes, such as seccotine, are perfectly satisfactory in this mixture, but most plastic adhesives are not. Add a little zinc white as a preservative for the glue and approximately 5 per cent of beeswax or relining wax mixture. If too soft, add whiting or pig-

ment. The slab must be just warm enough to melt the wax. The finished putty should be kneadable like bread crumbs. It must immediately be put into a container with a screw top; a small piece of rag moistened with water containing a drop of acetic acid as antiseptic will keep it usable for weeks.

For flesh parts, skies and other luminous areas the putty should as a rule be white (some lead or titanium white can be added).

On large canvases with many 'flake gaps' a great deal of time can be saved by matching the putty to the (often brown) colour of the original priming, ground or undermodelling (but in a slightly lighter shade).

The putty is pressed into the holes by means of a small metal modelling-spatula or a scalpel, squeezed well against all the edges and kept accurately to the hole. All surplus round the edges must be carefully washed away with silk damped in water or turpentine. The surface can immediately be smoothed with the cleaned instrument dipped in talcum powder. The texture of the original canvas or even the brushwork can be imitated (using talc for insulation) by pressing into the putty a piece of canvas of a suitable grain pattern, or better still a plastic mould which has been made from it or from a characteristic bit of the original surface. The wax ingredient in the putty (and in the tempera medium) allows one to do this even at a later stage with a warm spatula. If it is desired to leave the filling easily traceable, it can be left at a slightly lower level. This has the added advantage that any retouching that may have spread beyond the actual lacunae can before it is quite hard be scraped off without removing it from the depression.

In imitative or 'deceptive' retouching (or *compensation* as the Americans call it) the matching of the texture is of importance; for, however well you match the surrounding colour, your patch will look quite wrong and fall short of the quality of the original if you leave it too smooth or in some way dissimilar.

TECHNIQUE OF RETOUCHING

Fundamental Rules

Retouching, or 'inpainting' as the Americans aptly call it, should be kept to the minimum necessary to restore the coherence in composition and the character of a damaged painting. No new paint must be allowed to cover the smallest part of well-preserved original. The picture should never be given a spurious look of perfect preservation, nor should it be varnished too thickly and with too much gloss.

Where there is no fundamental loss of paint but only an ill-defined wearing of the original surface 'stippling-in' is required. For this, only easily-removable paint media should be used, the water-colour medium gum arabic, a wax resin mixture or Paraloid B72. Egg tempera, the most unchanging of all retouching media,[1] does get rather hard with time but may be used in sharply defined gaps. If it is applied over an insulating preliminary varnish and if a little wax is added it can easily be softened at any later time and safely scraped off. The finished retouching should be left a fraction on the light side wherever this does not too much interrupt the original modelling, in order to avoid as much as possible interfering with the master's intention. The retoucher should use a mahlstick, to avoid smudging the surface. Many a gifted apprentice has failed through lack of neatness; matching his own smudges; using the magnifying glass at an angle; working in semi-darkness, etc.

Other rules, of ethical implication, will be discussed presently.

Inpainting, particularly of larger missing parts, should be executed as nearly as possible by imitating the original build-up. With stereoscopic magnification (binocular microscope) of five to twenty times it is usually possible to see within small gaps of the paint, or where the upper coatings are worn, the usually lighter, solid underpainting, and sometimes below this a monochrome under-modelling (in most cases brown). Though it may at first seem unnecessarily complicated, the student will soon realize by experience that any attempt to match the exact hue and quality of the original paint directly or in a different way must fail and he can save a great deal of time and frustration by imitating from the outset all the main stages of the master's process. Details of the old masters' infinitely various methods, which we have discovered in the course of this kind of careful matching, I hope to describe in a second book.[2] It is obvious that such knowledge must form the basis of the restorer's work, both in cleaning and retouching. Before he starts cleaning, he must, as far as it is possible, know what layers to expect, and he should always begin by writing down a systematic account of them. Unless he does this he might for example be tempted to try to remove an original top layer that resembles in tone a dirty varnish; though in most cases he will be warned by a greater hardness of the original film and by the presence of modelling or gradation in the original glaze or scumble. Often the old varnish will make it impossible to ascertain certain details of technique. These should then be clarified by cleaning tests on minute areas.

At about twenty times magnification one can often discern even the pigment

---

[1] B72 may prove another stable retouching medium.

[2] One example of such an analysis has been published in *The Burlington Magazine* (December 1964) H. Ruhemann and J. Plesters, 'The Technique of Painting in a Madonna attributed to Michelangelo.'

particles and discover whether for instance a master used black or blue, vermilion, red ochre or madder in his flesh paint. In doubtful cases one can take from the very edge of the picture, or from the edge of a loss, minute samples of original paint (one has to be careful not to be deceived by an earlier retouching); a sample of a fraction of a millimetre is sufficient for the specialized chemist to confirm or disprove by means of a microsection or by microanalysis the restorer's observations on the various strata of the paint and often to contribute valuable new information.[1]

No ideal retouching medium is yet known

We are now coming to a subject on which I cannot give any definite recommendation, the paint media to be used for retouching.

For painting our own pictures oil, watercolour or egg tempera paint, if properly used, are sufficiently reliable.

For the painter the slight changes which come with ageing are negligible at any rate in his lifetime. The new picture may darken a little all over and certain colour fields change more than others; but no abrupt dark patches will appear, if reasonable care is taken in the choice of pigments and media and in the method of application. The restorer is faced with an entirely different problem; he has to match definite spots or passages in a picture already aged, and his retouching will now also change with time and sooner or later stand out as a disturbing dark patch, at least if he paints in the normal way with oil colour.

The question is often discussed whether a tempera painting should be retouched in tempera and an oil painting with oil colours. I have mentioned elsewhere that oil paint is unsuitable for retouching because it darkens and one cannot with fresh oil paint imitate the glass-like effect of aged paintings. Tempera glazed with a non-darkening resin medium or with water-colour enables one to match this effect much better. It was not always possible even to decide from the appearance of a picture in which medium it was executed. Whole libraries of guesswork have been written discussing the medium of the Van Eycks. Coremans', Gettens' and Thissen's truly fundamental research[2] should settle this riddle for good.

Unfortunately the microscope or the chemist cannot yet give us much definite information on the exact composition of the media used in an old picture, where many colours seem to have lasted perfectly.

For paint media testing methods are in their infancy; though the National

[1] Joyce Plesters, 'Cross-sections and chemical analysis of paint samples', *Studies in Conservation*, II 3, (1956), pp. 110–57. Bibliography, *Section 27 (65)*.

[2] Coremans, Gettens, Thissen, 'La Technique des Primitifs Flamands', *Studies in Conservation* I, (October 1952), 1–29. Bibliography, *Section 27 (45)*.

Gallery laboratory is making comparatively rapid progress in improving them and in identifying some of the media.[1]

Yet even if we knew definitely, as we sometimes think we do, that a certain bit of old paint that looks perfectly preserved is executed with pure oil or with pure egg tempera it would not help us much in our retouching. Scientists have already found ways of reaching the moon; but they have not yet invented the perfect paint medium for a paint with which one can match a hue relying on it not to change in drying, with varnishing or with time.[2] Water-colour and egg-tempera paint do not generally darken, once one has finished the retouching and varnished it, but the touch one puts on will turn a little lighter in drying, and again darker than it was initially when burnished and varnished. One can rarely gauge the change at the first attempt, and often has to try five to ten times, by drying with a hair dryer, and by means of a small brush wetting the patch with white spirit to see how it will look when varnished. At times a touch of dark tempera or water-colour will not acquire full saturation when wetted with white spirit but will turn disappointingly dark with varnishing. No suitable volatile liquid with a higher refractive index seems to exist; the only way out I can think of is to try with very diluted varnish, which you can largely rub off with a silk rag, before continuing to paint.

Almost every restorer tries to obviate these complications by composing all sorts of emulsions of oil and egg and resin or by reverting to oil paint; and almost every time, if he is conscientious enough to check his retouchings after some years, he sooner or later regrets it, and eventually decides that the cumbersome tempera technique is not only the best but in the long run the quickest for obtaining a non-darkening retouching, at least in body paint. The frequent testing necessary makes it difficult to avoid some irregularity and sullying in the preliminary varnish; but this can be removed by dry attrition, as described earlier.

It is very tempting to cling to the belief that oil or oil-resin paint can be relied upon not to darken 'if used in a special way'. But, even if an oil retouching does not darken noticeably, it nearly always remains shinier than the rest and therefore appears to be darker. The not uncommon method of using resin and pigment only is not much better. It darkens in a few months nearly as much as oil, sometimes more, and acquires a slimy appearance with time.

I have recently seen many years old oil-resin retouchings which had not

[1] M. Hey, 'The analysis of paint media by paper chromatography', *Studies in Conservation*, III (1958), pp. 183–93. Bibliography, *Section* 27 (72).

J. S. Mills, 'The Gas Chromatography Examination of Paint Media. Part I Fatty Acid Composition and Identification of Dried Oil Films', *Studies in Conservation*, XI, 2 (1966), pp. 92–107. Bibliography, *Section* 27 (107).

[2] But see note on Paraloid B72, p. 137.

noticeably darkened because they were carried out in elaborate glazes over a light ground which, in becoming more visible with time as the covering paint turns more translucent, offsets the gradual darkening of the retouching. However, this admirable technique does not allow any imitation of the character and texture of the original paint, which in important reconstructions is in my opinion as necessary to match as the colour. This I have found possible only with tempera (and in small patches sometimes with water-colour).

Thus the oil, or oil and resin technique, which is still widely used though its disadvantages were exposed as early as 1708 by Luigi Crespi[1] does not achieve well enough the aim that some of the foremost galleries set themselves: to re-establish as nearly as possible the original aspect of a masterpiece.

There is however one retouching paint for the final glaze which can be matched directly and which darkens far less than oil paint: wax-MS2A resin colour.[2] It does go a little darker in drying (which takes about half an hour; it is possible to see this change taking place by using a hair dryer): it darkens only slightly with time. One can soon learn to allow for the initial darkening, which is of course physical, not chemical, and may be due to change of refractive index during solvent evaporation or to the pigment particles sinking or rising. This point has passed unnoticed for a long time because when one varnishes the picture, in a darkened retouching — which has perhaps gone a little mat and therefore appears lighter than it really is — the medium is re-swelled by the final varnish and again turns lighter. The retouching then seems to be as well matched as it was in the first place, but it will darken once more as the diluent evaporates from the varnish. Perhaps this drawback could be remedied by adding to the paint some volatile liquid of a high refractive index while executing the retouching.

Wax has for centuries been known as the most permanent of paint media. It was Mr. Arthur Klausner[3] of Paris who first thought in modern times of grinding pigments in dissolved wax only. This paint, as opposed to oil paint, remains indefinitely soft in tubes and has the additional advantage that if it has hardened on the palette it can be dissolved again with rectified paraffin (usually called white spirit), which serves as diluent during painting, just as water colours are dissolved with water. As the wax colour alone would dry too mat, the brush has to

---

[1] Letters to Francesco Algarotti, published in Gio Bottari's *Raccolta di Lettere*, III (1759), p. 297.

[2] See also Rolf E. Straub, 'Retouching with synthetic resin paint', *Museums Journal*, LXII, (1962), pp. 113–19. Further comments: 'A note on A.W.2 and M.S.2A', *Museums Journal*, LXIII (1963), pp. 123–4. In my opinion both these articles slightly over-rate this resin-retouching method. Bibliography, *Section 15* (10).

[3] Klausner Wax paint. See H. Ruhemann, 'Une méthode de restauration à la cire neutre', *Mouseion*, XVII–XVIII (1932) pp. 167–8. Bibliography, *Section 15* (2).

be dipped in thinned dammar, or better still MS2A varnish.[1] The exact proportion of resin necessary to obtain just the wanted degree of gloss is a matter of experience. If a touch should dry too mat, one can put it right by varnishing it individually by means of a soft small brush (after about one hour's drying), with very little varnish on it, and touching each spot only once. Wholesale varnishing is only safe with a spray gun.[2] This is the one great disadvantage of wax-resin retouching. To retouch with wax-resin medium have ready on the palette (of ground glass for preference) some very thin AW2, MS2A, or MS2B varnish with about 3 per cent wax, and with the finger grind the powder pigment into this mixture until no more grain can be felt.

That the restorer should on the whole grind his own paint from levigated powder pigments is understood. He must know the exact composition of all the materials he uses.

Wax-resin paint is a little too transparent to be used successfully in painting light over dark or for pastose or 'body' paint, but it is excellent for the finishing glazes over tempera underpainting.[3] Light colours can be made more opaque by adding rutile-titanium white.

One can make any of the more opaque colours more transparent without getting them slimy by grinding a little kaolin with the pigment. This excellent technique was suggested by Norman Brommelle.

Glazing over a lighter tone seems the only way of imitating that glasslike quality which oil paint acquires only with age and which certain misguided painters of the late nineteenth and early twentieth century tried to imitate by adding quantities of resin to their paint.

None of the branded tempera colours I know is suited for our purposes. They all seem to contain glue or other admixtures which soon make the tints change a little.

Personally for tempera I separate the yolk from the white of the egg and mix, with a spatula, about the volume of a small pea of thin wax paste (white beeswax in white spirit c. 1 : 3) to the yolk which is then placed with the white in a wide-necked bottle and well shaken. Distilled (or boiled) cold water up to the volume of the egg, with a drop of acetic acid for preservative is added.[4] This egg mixture can be further thinned with water for painting. One cannot give too

---

[1] Manufactured by Laporte Industries Ltd, Ilford, Essex, England. It was discontinued and replaced by a similar material, MS2B, but has recently been re-introduced.

[2] See H. Ruhemann, paper read at Rome Conference 1930, op. cit., Bibliography, *Section 4* (17). A very satisfactory spraying unit called 'Chiron' is marketed by Line (Wallpapers) Tottenham Court Road, London.

[3] After several years, retouchings carried out by this method have also been found to turn slightly yellowish.

[4] Wehlte in reply to a reader's enquiry recommends 'Raschit, watersoluble', a few drops of a 10% solution (*Maltechnik*, No. 3 (1963) p. 84).

strong a warning against the many quite unnecessarily complicated emulsions recommended in text books. The more ingredients, the more chance of trouble.

If you paint too wet or with too much medium the paint will crack in drying. A drop of oxgall may be added to the water to make this paint stick better on oily surfaces; if it does not 'take' well rub the surface first with oxgall. It is important to add sufficient egg medium to the pigment; otherwise the paint dries too mat (and will easily rub off) or absorb too much varnish, which would make it darken with time.

The ideal is to match everything in tempera, but this needs a good deal of experience and patience. Final glazing with water-colour is preferable to resin. The usual way is to leave the finished, burnished (with silk) for proper gloss, and varnished underpaint a little too light and too 'cool' (blueish), and then to glaze it very thinly with water colour or resin down to the precise match, but leaving it even then always on the light side. The tempera underpainting must of course have all the necessary pastosity and texture. With a special brush or an instrument all the typical oil impasto can be imitated closely, far better than with oil paint, by modelling in the semi-dry application. The wax ingredient facilitates this. Each layer must be insulated with thin varnish before painting over it and this varnish must be well dry to the touch before painting on it again. Polyvinyl acetate diluted in methyl alcohol is a useful medium for this purpose.

Pigments

One is often asked: 'How can you ever hope to match those luminous colours of the old masters with modern pigments?' As a matter of fact modern science has given us twenty odd pigments equivalent in hue to those of the old masters, but far more lasting. What — alas — we have lost is the tradition of conscientious craftsmanship, the way to use the materials.

All the same, we still lack a completely permanent transparent deep brown, a substitute for Van Dyck brown (which is fugitive). A mixture of black and alizarin orange imitates this successfully but this too is not completely permanent.

On the whole it is better to use the pigments which were used in the original (read what Brommelle has to say about 'metameric' match[1]); but the superior or equivalent modern pigments may be used safely; the original hues can be matched very closely with them.

However, the transparency and vibration of certain colours, especially in skies, cannot be matched except with the coarse grain pigments peculiar to the old masters.

The rate of drying is of little consequence for restorers, given the fast drying

[1] N. S. Brommelle, 'Colour and Conservation', *Studies in Conservation*, II (1955), p. 78. Bibliography, *Section 23* (9).

media with which the pigments are ground and the thinness of their applications in retouching. Here follows a list of lasting pigments which are all chemically compatible with each other. They will suffice for retouching purposes. The ones not mentioned seem to me too unreliable or unnecessary.

SHORT LIST OF LASTING AND COMPATIBLE PIGMENTS FOR RETOUCHING

m signifies a pigment of comparatively modern invention, the earliest being Prussian blue, discovered in 1704.

I. *Opaque Pigments*

m Titanium white (rutile form)	Titanium oxide was introduced as a pigment early in the present century, but the light-stable rutile crystalline form was not readily available until later. Replaces lead white.
Yellow ochre	
Brown ochre	
Venetian red	
Indian red	
Vermilion	
Raw umber	
Burnt umber	
m Prussian blue	Invented 1704. It is not an opaque pigment in the true sense, but its high tinting strength gives it good hiding power. It replaces the more fugitive indigo, and, to some extent in mixtures, blue copper pigments such as azurite and blue bice.
m Opaque oxide of chromium	Invented 1809, but not introduced as an artists' pigment until c. 1862. Replaces less stable opaque greens based on mixtures of copper pigments, such as verdigris, with lead white or yellow lead oxide.
Ivory black	

II. *Intermediary, semi-opaque pigments*

m Zinc white	First introduced as a non-poisonous substitute for lead white c. 1779. It has

248

	a limited use alone in oil painting, but in retouching is useful for the imitation of translucent scumbles for which titanium white would be too opaque.
m Cadmium yellows and oranges	Introduced as pigments in 1829, but not commercially produced until 1946. Can be used to imitate yellow lead oxide, lead-tin oxide, red lead, orpiment, realgar, chrome yellows and oranges, Naples yellow, all pigments which are either impermanent or obsolete. Raw Siena.
m Cadmium red	Introduced in 1907, in supply by 1912. A substitute for vermilion. In addition to the scarlet form there are useful crimson and maroon shades.
m Mars yellows, reds and browns Light red (a variety of red ochre)	Artificial iron oxides giving a wider and more reproducible range of colour and different degrees of opacity than the natural ochres nowadays generally available.
m Ultramarine (artificial)	The synthetic pigment was produced in 1828 and rapidly replaced the expensive natural lapis lazuli ultra-marine. It is of equal permanence, but has the advantage that different shades of blue, including purplish and greenish tones, are obtainable.
m Cerulean blue	Invented c. 1800 though not available as a pigment until c. 1860; can be used to imitate the now-obsolete azurite blue.
Green earth (terre verte)	Has very little colouring power and is rarely useful in retouching
m Davy's grey	A finely powdered slate with colour and properties which make it useful in retouching where black plus white would be too heavy.

249

III *Transparent pigments*

m Indian yellow (coal tar)

m Hansa yellow

Lakes of modern synthetic dyestuffs which replace the fugitive and now obsolete yellow vegetable-dye lakes such as 'Dutch pink', Persian berries lake and quercitron lake as well as the more fugitive gamboge and saffron and the now unobtainable natural Indian yellow.

m Viridian (transparent chromium oxide)

First made in 1838, commercially available as an artist's pigment c. 1860; used to imitate the now obsolete verdigris, malachite, green copper resinate and emerald (Paris) green.

m Cobalt blue

Invented 1802, available as a pigment c. 1820–30. Used to imitate azurite and smalt. Not strictly a transparent pigment (in the sense of having a low refractive index) but has rather slight hiding power.

m Cobalt green

Invented in 1780, but not available as a pigment until c. 1835; substitutes for malachite and other copper greens. See above under cobalt blue for remarks about degree of transparency, applicable also to this pigment.

m Alizarin crimson (synthetic madder lake)

A synthetic form of alizarin, the principal and less fugitive colouring matter in natural madder, for which it substitutes. Introduced in 1826.

m Alizarin orange

A lake pigment of a modern synthetic dyestuff; when mixed with black it produces a useful translucent brown for the imitation of bituminous brown glazes and brown oil paint which has become more translucent with age.

Within the last year or so, certain modern pigments, already used in industry but not yet introduced into the usual range of artists' colours, have been tested in the National Gallery and Victoria and Albert Museums with a view to their use in retouching. One of the most successful is the range of Cinquasia (alternatively called quinacridone) pigments[1] made by Dupont. These are transparent or semi-transparent crimson and violet pigments, synthetic organic dyestuffs of comparatively recent invention. Industrial tests have shown them to be greatly superior in light-fastness to either natural or synthetic madder lakes, for which in many instances they may prove to be useful substitutes, but they are less transparent and less dark. Tests are also being carried out on lake pigments of a number of other modern dyestuffs of high degrees of light fastness in the transparent yellow-orange-crimson range of colours, which up to now has been the weakest part of the painter's palette with respect to fading. Another useful modern pigment is Titan yellow (nickel titanate), an opaque lemon yellow used in colouring ceramics. It may substitute for pale cadmium yellow, the latter having been known to turn white in certain exceptional conditions and generally to be less chemically stable than was once supposed.

Retouching Method

I must stress here again that for good retouching the best possible lighting obtainable is imperative; at least a very high window with unobstructed sky shining in. Atlas Northlight 6300° k colour temperature fluorescent tube affords an excellent substitute for daylight, if at least four long, high wattage tubes are fitted in one reflector. Most of the fluorescent tubes are said to go yellower after thirty hours' use, but this change is negligible. Where no sunlight is available Sunora Xenon Gas lamps can be used for working on dark passages, but are said to explode sometimes and are costly. However, I have had very satisfactory reports from two museums which have been using Xenon lamps for several years.

Binocular 2 times magnification surgeons' lenses with shade are most useful (see illustration, p. 124).

For retouching I recommend the following procedure:

Where a picture has been relined or treated with wax its surface, after thorough cleaning, should be carefully wiped with turpentine or xylene to remove the wax.

Apply a thin preliminary varnish; MS2B has the advantage of quickly drying on a wax relined picture (and even on a wax finish) whereas mastic or dammar often take weeks to harden properly on the slightest remnants of wax.

---

[1] Since this was written some of the crimson and violet pigments in the Cinquasia range have been put on the market as artists' colours.

Monochrome Undermodelling

I. Reconstruction of missing design in transparent *monochrome brown under-modelling*,[1] in resin paint; varnish thinned with white spirit, with admixture of very little stand oil (only for this phase), to facilitate even application and quick hardening. Instead of stand oil, ordinary oil colour may be used, from which excess oil has been drained out by spreading it on blotting paper. A mixture of burnt siena and raw siena broken with a little black produces a good semi-transparent tone. I strongly recommend this phase, even where such an under-modelling may not have been ascertained in the original. The advantages are:

1. A great number of Renaissance paintings (and many others) seem to have a transparent monochrome brown undermodelling (over a black or dark brown drawing-in).[2]

2. A brown undermodelling in the *lacunae* (gaps) facilitates considerably the matching of the colour layers which must follow; if the varying tone values of the original are well matched in this undermodelling the transitions from dark to light in the following colour layer will often come about by the dark undermodelling showing through; this will save much mixing for half tones.

3. In reconstructing all the missing design (however small the gaps may be) of the original the restorer will form a clear idea of it already in this preliminary stage and he can do in it all the necessary correcting of his drawing, and then apply the actual colour with all the more assurance and freshness (more in the way the old masters did it) without much fumbling; light details can be washed out from the brown to uncover the white ground or putty.

4. Certain subtle hues in skies and some greys can be achieved only by such undermodelling showing through the paint; it is impossible to reproduce them in any other way. The same holds good of the cool middle tones often found in flesh paint, which are due to the Turbid Medium effect.[3]

5. When the missing design has been reconstructed in this way the gaps are no longer so disturbing, the picture looks more complete, is easier to judge as a whole, and this also makes the restorer, particularly in a long and difficult job, more confident.

6. This method actually speeds up the process of retouching considerably, though it may at first seem a detour (see advantage no. 9).

7. It is difficult to apply an even smooth wash of a darker tone over a light

---

[1] Two fine examples of paintings left unfinished in this stage are in Florence: Leonardo's 'Adoration' in the Uffizi and a large Fra Bartolommeo in the Museo San Marco.

[2] H. Ruhemann and E. M. Kemp, *Artist at Work*, pp. 18, 19.

[3] *Artist at Work*, p. 17.

ground (white putty), it is easy to apply a smooth lighter wash over a darker tone.

8. This method produces soft contours (a major concern of most painters) automatically, partly because the final painted outline rarely tallies entirely with the drawing-in or undermodelling contours.[1]

9. After reconstructing missing parts of the composition and stippling-in light spots in worn or chipped areas in this way, with transparent brown, the restorer may find that the picture already looks whole enough and he may decide to go no further and dispense with the matching of the actual colour, at least in some parts.

10. This method will help to avoid one of the most frequent mistakes found in larger reconstructed passages: over-modelled details within half-tone and shadow interrupting the consistent roundness of the larger form (e.g. in a sleeve).

11. One can with the undermodelling colour stain disturbing light cracks, which will then need no further retouching.

When the undermodelling is finished the picture should look almost intact on a black and white photograph taken at this stage.

If in the original a grisaille exists, it can be painted over the brown undermodelling in the reconstruction.

It is nearly always possible to find in the picture an original passage that can serve as a guide for the reconstruction, sometimes by using a pocket mirror to reverse left and right. Only after having carefully scanned the whole picture and then other paintings by the same master for a piece to copy should one make a drawing from nature. To reconstruct freely from memory is rarely satisfactory.

II. According to the layers found in the original, one or more applications follow of rather thick and opaque or semi-opaque body colour in tempera. Impasto must be built up gradually and not too wet. This main colour layer should not be even and mechanical but as freely painted and as completely modelled as possible. Cool middle tones must be placed where they belong and will mostly produce themselves automatically over the dark of the undermodelling, if it has been carried far enough into the half-light areas. Warm where cool should be will completely disrupt the modelling. The modelling must not be left to the next phase.

At this stage the picture should look finished except for the former gaps being a little too cool and light. Burnishing of all tempera retouchings with artificial silk, tight around the index finger, or with an agate stone, is necessary to prevent

[1] H. Ruhemann, *Artist and Craftsman*, pp. 12 and 24–6, where the term 'groping or tentative outline' is suggested in distinction to '*pentimento*'.

'sinking in' of the varnish. It is for the same reason that the pigment powder must be ground on the palette with the finger until no more grains are felt.

II*a*. Thin varnishing of retouched areas only.

III. Final glazing with wax in MS2B (see also p. 137) resin or with water colour. Very thin and slight, always on the light side. Use Davy's grey in preference to black; light red (instead of brown or yellow) with cobalt or cerulean blues. Add kaolin to reduce the strength of the glazing hue.

Having the picture flat against the light, varnish carefully the individual mat spots (after 1 hour), with a soft brush and varnish of normal thickness.

III*a*. Final varnish. This can be applied with a brush over tempera or water-colour but not over wax-resin retouchings. Only a spray gun can be used on these.

This is one of the reasons why some restorers go on using oil retouchings which can, after a few days, be varnished with a brush.

The synthetic resin B72, or Paraloid (see also p. 137), which is well worth trying out both as a retouching medium and as a varnish, dries hard enough in a few minutes to allow varnishing with a brush, if varnishes dissolved in white spirit, for instance AW2 or MS2B, are used. Paraloid varnish, shiny or rendered mat by admixture of wax can be sprayed on immediately, but sometimes wets and spreads unevenly.

Paraloid B72 when dissolved in xylene instead of toluene, and diluted and re-dissolved with xylene during retouching, dries slowly enough to make it easily usable. To retard the drying still further, Shellsol E (Shell) can be added. B72 paint has remarkable covering power; it darkens very slightly on drying only when applied with too much diluent, or when the B72, dried to a rubbery consistency on the palette, is not given enough time in re-dissolving. It does not alter in tone at all on being varnished (unless it has been applied with too little medium and dried mat). According to experience (about twenty years in the States) and to laboratory evidence, it is not likely to darken or crack at all with age. It does not bloom.

B72 is the only medium I know with which one can match a tone directly and which will 'stay put'. It has, however, disadvantages which seem difficult to overcome:

1. A rubbery consistency which makes it awkward to handle : the second touch (unless applied at least 3 minutes later) will remove the first.

2. If sufficient medium is used to make the retouching dry shiny it will nearly always be too bulky (raised), though this can be sometimes remedied by subsequent scraping. It is preferable to paint with B72 very much diluted and rely for the gloss on MS2B varnish on the individual retouchings, or on polyvinyl-acetate diluted with methyl alcohol (suggested by Margaret Hey).

3. These bulky touches are further swelled if a final varnish is used which contains Shellsol or stronger solvents.[1] Thus only polycyclohexanone varnishes which keep completely dissolved in paraffin (white spirit), like AW2 or MS2B can be used.

4. Used as varnish B72 often does not wet well and forms a marked 'orange peel' texture. Attempts to overcome this grave drawback are in progress.

About B72 as varnish see p. 254.

ETHICS OF RETOUCHING

Excessive Retouching in the Past

In the past it was taken for granted that holes in pictures had to be repaired and the gaps repainted, whether small or large. Restorers often did not hesitate to conceal all traces of damage as best they could. It was customary for the retouchings to be much broader than the loss they were meant to hide and they usually encroached widely on well-preserved original paint; often they spread unnecessarily over the entire surface, so that eventually little or nothing of the original remained visible.

Modern Compunctions

In the 1920's the opinion began to be expressed in professional journals that any kind of retouching was an illegitimate and presumptuous interference with the original master's work (and should be forbidden), for instance by V. Bauer-Bolton,[2] Conservator in Riga, and a pioneer in modern attitudes to restoration. So far the earliest instance seems to have been found by Professor Gombrich[3] quoting from Filippo Baldinucci, *Vocabolario Toscano del Arte del Disegno* (Florence, 1681):

'There have been many, however, who were by no means inexperienced in matters of art and who held that the best paintings should never be retouched, either much or little, by whoever it may be. For it was difficult for the restoration, be it small or large, not to show up sooner or later, however small it may have been, and it is also true that a painting that is not untouched is also very much discredited.'

Compromise

However, it was soon realized that it was possible to satisfy, by various

---

[1] Diethylbenzene is still more satisfactory as a retarder than Shellsol.
[2] V. Bauer-Bolton, Hamburg 1914. Bibliography, *Section 15* (1).
[3] In *The Burlington Magazine* of February 1962. Bibliography, *Section 7* (24).

compromises, both the extreme purists and, at the same time, the public who want to enjoy their pictures whole.

Some scholars thought that art lovers who did not mind a missing limb in an antique sculpture would soon get used to holes in a picture. But it is not as simple as that : in a statue there is nothing in the place of a missing hand or foot; in a picture, the 'lacuna' forms an irregular patch which disrupts the continuity of the whole composition and assumes an active part in it.

Justi in 1908, Glück in 1910 and Bauer-Bolton in 1914 condemned secrecy and advocated the mention of the condition of the pictures in public gallery catalogues,[1] which would make 'invisible' reconstructions more legitimate.

Visible Retouching

At the first International Restorers' Conference in 1930, I read a paper advocating 'Compromise — or Visible Retouching' for certain cases.[2]

Whereas in the case of cleaning, half-way measures are in my opinion only admissible on paintings of little artistic value, in retouching it is quite the contrary : the more important a picture the more a compromise is indicated, and the less a 'deceptive reconstruction' of a large missing portion is justifiable. Naturally one of the main points to consider is : how much invention would be necessary in each case to reconstruct the missing part.

As one can easily see, a decision depends on a number of factors, and it is no use being dogmatic. For instance on a given picture I might make one compromise retouching for one owner, a different one for another, and a complete reconstruction for a third. Personally I have sometimes used different solutions in various parts of the same picture. What matters most is to restore the possibility of enjoyment and the coherence of the picture for the particular kind of people who are likely to see it most; this will vary from a sophisticated capital to a small provincial town. It also matters whether a picture is valued for its aesthetic excellence, its historic, topographic or sentimental content, as in a family portrait, etc., or as a commercial asset. One of the main points to consider is how good an artist the available restorer is. The complete reconstruction of a major part of a museum picture should never be attempted (e.g. an entire hand or head). However accomplished a draughtsman and painter the restorer may be, he can never match the original style, even if he were given a chance of practising his

---

[1] These early suggestions were put into practice by Philip Hendy in his catalogue of the Isabella Stewart Gardner Museum, Boston, Mass., in 1930.

[2] H. Ruhemann, 'Visible Retouchings', International Congress, International Museums Office (Rome, Oct. 1930) : and '16 Compromise Solutions', *Mouseion*, XV, pp. 19–21. Bibliography, *Section 4* (17).

version a hundred times like the pianist who tries to render a masterpiece to perfection; the musician at least finds detailed guidance in the score.

This raises the question whether a picture gains or loses in value by retouching. It can do both. The trade value of a picture, together with its potential enjoyment value, will naturally rise if the retouching successfully eliminates the disturbing effect of the damage and blends in technique and style perfectly with the original, or rather well enough for the most fastidious eye. The price of the picture will fall if offensive gaps are left unmitigated or if the retouching is badly matched or covers original paint.

On the other hand an indifferent work, badly and widely retouched and covered with a tinted varnish, will often fetch a higher sum than if sold again after it has been nicely cleaned, retouched and revarnished. The first time it was perhaps bought on speculation in the hope that a good cleaning and restoration would raise its value; instead its intrinsic mediocrity may have been revealed by the cleaning.

On the whole, once everything has been done to assure the preservation of a painting, its successful existence depends on its presentation. It will fail in its destiny to the extent to which the master's intention is marred by losses or accretions. The initial meaning will not only be obscured but often distorted. Classic examples already mentioned are a squint or a stare which can be produced by even the smallest loss in an eye (p. 226), a distant cloud made to look heavy and like a mountain by a dirty varnish, and the river which, covered by yellow varnish, had always passed as part of the green ground and was revealed only by the cleaning (on Tintoretto's 'St. George' at the National Gallery).

It is the task of the skilful and, above all, tasteful and tactful retoucher to find an appropriate solution for differing cases. He must not be hampered by merely theoretical considerations and generalizations. For examples, see plates 89–92.

The foregoing concerns only 'compensation' or filling-in of clearly defin ed major gaps. A more frequent form of damage is the so-called 'wearing', more or less severe abrasion of the paint in areas vaguely merging into well-preserved paint. The best way of avoiding deception here, and at the same time interference with the masters' modelling, is, as I said, to keep the 'stippling-in' a shade lighter than the surrounding colour.

'Neutral' Retouching

Retouching in a 'neutral tone' is frequently recommended. This may appear to be a good idea, but is in practice impossible; for, however grey a tinge may be in itself, the neighbouring or surrounding colour will give it, by contrast, a more colourful hue; and the most important rule is not to introduce any alien shade into a painting; if there is no grey in it, none must be added.

In the various galleries which have adopted the policy of visible retouching I have seen very few satisfactory examples of it, but innumerable offensive ones. It needs much more talent, skill and taste to produce a good compromise, than a good matching reconstruction. For this reason several museums in Germany have gone back to the latter. An all too visible compromise retouching foils the main aim of the purist : not to violate the integrity of the original.

I have nevertheless seen supremely well done reconstructions which were both very far-reaching and complete and yet easily visible from close by. Many were executed by Signor and Signora Paolo Mora at the Istituto Centrale del Restauro in Rome, on a number of highly important early Italian paintings, in the ingenious technique called *rigattino*, first mentioned in Doerner's book (1922) and promoted by Professor Cesare Brandi.[1]

Rigattino

This consists in completely reconstructing the missing parts, perfectly matching form and colour, but in fine separate stripes or 'hatching', which blend into a coherent effect when seen from a normal viewing distance, but are readily discerned on approaching the picture more closely. This method is extremely difficult to carry out and very few will be able to learn it, but it seems to me an almost ideal solution which ought to satisfy both purists and those who love old masters' works not as objects of study but as aesthetic manifestations which they want to enjoy undisturbed.

It remains to be seen whether this system, which is so effective on the comparatively unnaturalistic Italian 'primitives' and frescoes, where brushwork or sfumato play a small part, can be adapted to later and more three-dimensional styles and to small size paintings. I cannot very well imagine a Titian, a Rubens, a Rembrandt or a Gerard Dou retouched in that way; but this may be less important than it sounds : I do not know a single work of any of these masters that would need a major reconstruction. There are, however, several northern primitives with large losses that would not lend themselves readily to 'hatched' retouching.

Insight gained through Retouching

Apart from this I can see only one minor objection to the *rigattino* system. It does not afford anything like the same opportunities for getting to know the 'secrets' of the great masters as 'deceptive' retouching does. This, as I explained earlier, to be any good at all, must be done in close imitation of the several semi-

---

[1] C. Brandi, 'Il restauro e l'interpretazione dell'opera d'arte', in *Atti del Seminario di Storia dell'Arte*, I–XVI (1953). See also Bibliography, *Section* 7 (34).

88. National Gallery No. 1093, Leonardo da Vinci, 'The Virgin of the Rocks', 189·5 × 120 cm. Detail showing the Virgin's right hand, overpainted at a later period. Only the unfinished thumb is original. In a small diagonal band across the fingertips the overpainting has been removed to reveal lighter original paint. See p. 231.

89. National Gallery No. 1330, Duccio, 'The Transfiguration', 44 × 46 cm. Before the cleaning in 1951–2. The varnish was so dark that Christ's blue mantle appeared green-brown. The large loss between head and legs of the kneeling saint, lower centre, had been filled in with a muddy brown.

90. A case of 'non-deceptive' retouching. The same picture after cleaning and restoring. The missing part of the saint has been reconstructed in monochrome brown line drawing, neck and hand in the green underpaint colour. No attempt at matching the colour of the garment was made; the pink of the ground around the figure was approximately matched. See pp. 257 and 267.

91. National Gallery No. 908, Piero della Francesca, 'The Nativity', 124·5 × 123 cm. Important badly damaged parts, the faces of the two Shepherds, are left unretouched. Another damage across the Child's thighs is retouched, but left lighter than the original part and no artificial craquelure has been applied. See pp. 256 and 267.

92. Detail of the same picture showing the damaged and unretouched faces.

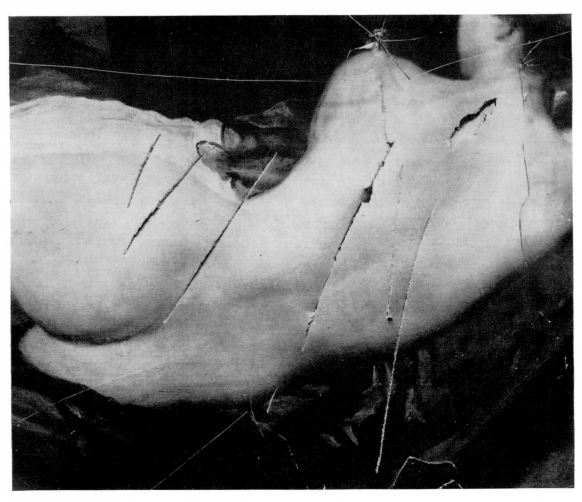

93. National Gallery No. 2057, Velázquez, 'The Toilet of Venus' ('The Rokeby Venus') *ca.* 122·5 × *ca.* 177 cm. Detail showing the slashes made by a suffragette in 1914. The fine breaks near the top of the photograph are in the glass only. Compare with plates 94 and 95 (pp. 299–300).

transparent layers of the originals. It is in trying to do this that we have learned many things which have, willy-nilly, made us connoisseurs of a kind.

The discipline of matching retouchings has been the foundation of a practical and factual probing of the masters' techniques. Several wrong guesses published in text books will be disproved by this new kind of investigation, which has been complemented by the physicists and chemists specializing in research on paintings.

Many mistakes made in earlier restorations would have been avoided if this knowledge of the masters' methods and intentions, acquired through restoration, had been known and taught. I, for one, could have avoided the mistakes mentioned before if I had known then what complete retouching and complete cleaning have taught me. It was not the slipping of a scalpel or too strong a solvent that caused those mistakes, but the lack of understanding of the masters' methods. If well-matched retouching were to go out of fashion, I should not be surprised if the connoisseur-restorer disappeared at the same time.

'More-or-less'-matched retouching encourages an attitude of being easily satisfied with imperfection. It can be carried out by craftsmen who are not sensitive artists by nature; there is certainly no more exacting way of testing a prospective restorer's general capacity for living up to the old masters' standards than closely matched retouching, which includes first-rate *rigattino*.

Seventeen 'Visible' or 'Compromise' Solutions

For teaching purposes I carried out a complete reconstruction, in the following seventeen different kinds of compromise retouching, on a painting by Hans Eworth: 'Sir John Luttrell's Wedding in a Rough Sea' (dated 1550) at the Courtauld Institute.

Visible Retouching

1. Complete reconstruction without artificial cracks   visible at 2 × magn.
2. Complete reconstruction at lower level
3. Complete reconstruction with grooves made in the finished retouching
4. Complete reconstruction but lighter and dimmer than the original

} visible with naked eye, from nearby

5. Form, in grey
6. Form, in brown
7. Colour without modelling
8. Outlines on grey putty
9. Grey putty, plain   } all easily visible
10. White putty
11. Wood left uncovered
12. Worn area stippled-in a little too light[1]
13. Worn area left unretouched

14. A hair-net pattern pressed into finished well matched
    retouching
15. A hair-net pressed in and left (as used at the Verona
    Museum)   } completely matched reconstruction visible only from nearby
16. Net pattern printed on retouching (as used at Florence)
17. Executed in 'hatching', mostly perpendicular rigattino
    (as at the Istituto Centrale del Restauro, Rome.

No doubt many more variations could be devised; the most suitable must be chosen for each individual case. The hatching system seems to me, if executed with exceptional skill, at present the most desirable one for the majority of badly damaged paintings.

Some restorers delude themselves by saying: it is all to the good that my retouchings are not well enough matched to deceive people. But apart from inducing renewed cleaning, inadequate retouching, even if comparatively small, has a curious way of degrading the entire picture. The converse never seems to happen: the higher quality of the untouched original part cannot raise the inferior retouching to its own level. An Italian proverb says: 'a rotten apple will contaminate the sound ones but a sound one will not purify the rotten'.

Pro and Contra complete Reconstruction

Whatever solution is decided on, it must, I repeat, be carried out with neat craftsmanship, in emulation of the quality of the original paint. No coarser, heavier, denser or dirtier '*matière*' must be introduced.

In recommending 'visible compensation' we must keep in mind that it will be difficult to win over the majority of private owners of pictures and art dealers to its application, though I have seen a few of the latter make gallant attempts to induce their clients to accept at least Italian 'primitives' with compromise retouching.

[1] To this could be added: 12*a*, worn area stippled in with brown undermodelling shade only.

Technique and Ethics of Retouching

Deterrent to Cleaning

The main advantages and disadvantages of either kind of treatment have already been discussed sufficiently with the exception of one important point: in a museum where a policy of visible retouching prevails, curators would be less willing to have any pictures with sizeable *'lacunae'* cleaned at all; perhaps quite unconsciously they would be unwilling to expose in their gallery damage previously concealed by the old retouching, and the fear of suddenly seeing an 'aged' and 'not too well preserved beauty' *en négligé* is one of the strongest deterrents to cleaning.

Now we can quite clearly see the connection between the National Gallery's policies of complete cleaning and complete retouching. However, if on a masterpiece at the National Gallery an important part is missing this is not concealed, and a visible compromise is adopted (as can be seen on the Duccio 'Transfiguration', No. 1330, the Piero della Francesca 'Nativity', No. 908, and the Bellini 'Madonna of the Meadow', No. 599. See Plates 89–90, 91–92 respectively.)

Contradictory Postulates

How can one explain the paradoxical fact that often the same art scholars who demand visible or even no retouching at all for purity's sake, out of reverence for the master, also defend incomplete cleaning, which obviously vitiates that purity? Is it because these people regard their pictures primarily as historical documents, antiques and objects of study and that their desire to enjoy them as works of art is not their first consideration? Or, being used to seeing the masters' subtleties obscured, or not seeing them at all, they are more ready to accept their disruption by damage?

Or perhaps restorers who carry out these two half-measures, are not always certain of being able either to clean a picture completely without harming it or to retouch it without degrading it.

Another conjecture suggests itself — has the growing acceptance of incompleteness in old paintings possibly something to do with the incompleteness in contemporary paintings where it is regarded as a virtue?

Having argued at length on the advantages and disadvantages of complete reconstruction of missing parts in pictures, I quote here a defence[1] of it by Albert Philippot, the great restorer at the Institut Royal du Patrimoine Artistique and his son Paul, Deputy Director, Rome Centre.

[1] In A. & P. Philippot, 'Le problème de l'intégration des lacunes dans la restauration des peintures', *Bulletin de l'Institut Royal du Patrimoine Artistique*, II (Brussels 1959), pp. 5–19. Bibliography, *Section* 7 (19).

Technique and Ethics of Restoration

'. . . It resembles a text of which certain words have disappeared or have become almost illegible. The reconstruction, no longer possible as far as the continuity of the creative process is concerned, yet remains conceivable and even clearly justifiable, if one accepts it as a critical act of interpretation, destined to re-establish an interrupted formal continuity, to the extent in which it remains latent in the mutilated work and where the reconstitution gives back to the aesthetic structure the clarity of meaning it had lost.'

In various National Gallery records there are full descriptions of work done on particular pictures which show that the official policy there conforms to Professor Philippot's theory; though it may seem old-fashioned to some of the advocates of visible lacunae, the policy of complete compensation can be pursued with absolute confidence for the first time in this century precisely owing to the documentation which modern science can provide, especially in the form of photographs, including those by different rays.

We restorers know full well that our retouchings will probably seem as imperfect to later generations of connoisseurs as some reconstructions now appear to us that were greatly admired in their time (see p. 40); but we are at least trying to do only the necessary minimum, to use non-darkening paint, to investigate and match more closely the masters' intention; above all, we are using only media that remain easily removable.

CHAPTER 9

Varnishes and Varnishing

After the cleaning and retouching of a picture a new varnish has to be applied to give full and even saturation to the colours and to protect the paint.

One fact that should be more widely known is that certain pictures must not be varnished at all; many are spoiled in appearance by too much or too shiny a varnish, for instance, certain early tempera or size paintings and particularly many modern works which are not meant to be shiny and to which artists such as Gauguin, Bonnard and Vuillard deliberately gave a mat tapestry effect. Varnish that has mistakenly been applied ought to be removed from such pictures and wax applied instead. Gauguin especially relied on his coarse absorbing canvases for dimming his sometimes garish colours. A varnish that gives them their full intensity (saturation) foils this intention and makes them look more vulgar.[1]

In Gauguin's letters[2] I found the following relevant passage which shows that Gauguin preferred wax to resin varnish because it does not darken:

'The varnish "de qualité extra" is never anything but resin and however bleached it may be it always reverts to its original yellow and goes on darkening. Everybody knows that the non-varnished Rembrandts have remained fresh and grey [cool] as on their first day.[3] To what should we attribute this difference if not to the varnish? White wax has none of these defects; as is proved by the ancient pictures painted with it. Wax protects paintings as well as wood against every kind of grime and deterioration.'

Of course wax will not have enough 'varnishing power' for the average oil painting gone mat.

---

[1] Since this was written a Paris art dealer told me that works in water-colour, distemper and gouache (water-colour with white and other opaque colours) are often turned into 'oil paintings' by varnishing them thickly, because 'oils' fetch higher prices than 'water-colours'. Burne-Jones put warnings against varnishing on the backs of his gouaches, but Gainsborough varnished many of his himself.

[2] *Lettres de Gauguin* (Grasset, 19—), pp. 264–5.

[3] Another addition to the collection of great painters' sayings.

In the same category of pictures which must not be varnished belong certain fifteenth- and sixteenth-century works, painted on fine linen, by such masters as Hugo van der Goes, Gerard David and Mantegna. They are, like Vuillard's, executed in size paint (distemper) with little or no priming. They are the fore-runners of canvases proper and some probably were originally made on this lighter material to be carried about in processions. They soon become unsightly through mould and flaking. In an attempt to protect them and to bring out the colours more effectively most of them have been later soaked with varnish and oil which has turned dark brown. Sometimes it is possible to extract this disfiguring impregnation by applying absorbent pastes saturated with appropriate solvents. I have treated two Mantegnas and a van der Goes satisfactorily in this way. Many of these size paintings do not bear even waxing, without first being protected with an insulating 'fixative' of the gum or gelatine type, which will not alter the refractive index of the original; otherwise the paint and particularly the ground which is not well covered will turn much darker. No ideal insulating fixative for these cases has yet come to our notice. Nor is there yet any perfect varnish for ordinary oil or tempera paintings.

Perhaps it will not be long before an almost ideal varnish is discovered. One of the promising synthetic resins, polybutyl methacrylate, has proved disappointing.[1] It has been found to turn gradually much less soluble and therefore unsuitable for valuable paintings. All varnishes or varnishing methods known at present have certain disadvantages, which are discussed in detail in specialized text books. None of the varnishes known at present offers sufficient protection against humidity, except in combination with wax.[2]

Main Properties of an Ideal Picture Varnish

1. The liquid varnish must be colourless (water-clear, transparent).

2. It must be easy to apply by brush or spray (convenient degree of viscosity; some varnishes form droplets or threads in spraying).

3. It must wet the surface well, filling the pores of the paint sufficiently (suitable 'surface tension' or 'wetting power').

4. It must dry rapidly (not remain sticky long enough to allow dust to adhere).

5. The dry film must always remain removable with mild solvents without endangering the paint (not get too hard with time, not *cross-link*).

[1] Arthur Lucas and Norman Brommelle, 'Failure of synthetic materials in picture conservation', *Museums Journal*, LIII (1953), pp. 149–55; Garry Thomson, 'Some Picture Varnishes', *Studies in Conservation*, III (1957), pp. 64–79. Bibliography, *Section 18* (9) and *Section 16* (16) respectively.

[2] M. C. Bradley, *The Treatment of Pictures*, recommends a wax application on top of polyvinyl acetate varnish: paragraphs 3.083 to 3.084 and 3.21. Bibliography, *Section 4* (41).

6. It must, applied in a thin layer, bring out the full depth and transparency of the colours without being excessively shiny (suitable index of refraction etc.).

7. It must be durable, remaining transparent, colourless, resilient (not bloom, crack, wrinkle, darken in light or darkness — keep its adhesion to the surface of the paint so as not to make frequent renewal necessary).

8. It must offer protection against moisture and gases (i.e. act as a 'moisture barrier').

9. It must protect the paint surface from direct touch and minor scratches, etc.

At the present moment it appears that MS2B promises to fulfil best most of these conditions. Its strong gloss and insufficient toughness and its permeability to humidity can easily be obviated by admixture of wax or by applying a wax rubbing (see p. 317) over it.

For further historical and scientific details, refer to (p. 274), and also to the papers by Norman Brommelle and Garry Thomson.[1]

More difficult reading for the layman is the report I have already mentioned several times, on the first seminar of its kind held in Oberlin, Ohio in 1959, *On Picture Varnishes and their Solvents*. This work was written by three leading experts on varnishes in North America, Dr. Robert Feller of The Mellon Institute, Pittsburgh, Miss Elizabeth Jones of The Fogg Museum, Harvard University, and Dr. Nathan Stolow of the National Gallery of Canada. They have earned the lasting gratitude of everybody interested in conservation matters, as has Richard Buck who engineered and organized the meeting and the free distribution of this pioneer publication to all members of I.I.C.

Oils and resins may serve as the film-forming components of both varnishes and paint media, although the properties of the resultant films will vary considerably with the type and proportion of resin. It is also likely that beeswax was in the past used as a protective coating to some extent. A very early form of varnish was pure oil thinly rubbed into the dry surface of the picture.[2] Later, between the twelfth and sixteenth centuries, literary sources indicate that a commonly-used type of varnish for pictures was composed of a resin (usually sandarac, amber or

[1] Arthur Lucas and Norman Brommelle, loc. cit., and Garry Thomson, loc. cit.

R. L. Feller, 'New Solvent-Type Varnishes', *Recent Advances in Conservation* (Butterworth, London, 1963), pp. 171–175. Bibliography, *Section 4* (69).

G. Thomson, 'New Picture Varnishes', *ibid.*, pp. 176–184. Bibliography, *Section 4* (69).

[2] Aetius Amadeus, a Greek writer of the fifth or sixth century A.D., mentions nut oil as a varnish for gilding. See Eastlake, *Materials for a History of Oil Painting* (London, 1847), I, p. 19. Bibliography, *Section 3* (40).

copal) dissolved in a drying oil (such as linseed oil) with the aid of strong heat. Oil varnishes of this sort would not only have darkened with time but also become insoluble (in all but powerful and disruptive solvents like strong alkalis). Fortunately the present-day restorer is only rarely called upon to remove varnishes of this type, the reason being that they will generally have been removed in earlier cleaning operations. These 'hard-resin'/oil varnishes were valued for their ability to withstand abrasion and washing with water. During the same period there are often mentions of one varnish of the 'spirit varnish' type, namely gum benzoin dissolved in alcohol. It was easier to make and to apply as a thin film than the oil varnishes mentioned above and probably yellowed less, but it produces such a brittle, fragile film that its use was restricted to pictures and objects not subject to much handling or surface cleaning. By the mid-sixteenth century varnishes composed of 'soft resins' (such as rosin or mastic) dissolved in volatile solvents (naphtha or distilled turpentine) appear to have been current. They also yellow with age, but, unlike the oil varnishes, are then easily removable by means of the usual neutral organic solvents employed in picture cleaning.[1] Their ease of preparation and application makes it likely that to a large extent they displaced the earlier oil/resin varnishes for pictures. However, even up to the present century oil varnishes unfortunately had some limited use, mainly on the grounds of their protective quality. In the nineteenth century dam(m)ar resin, very similar in properties to mastic, found favour as a picture varnish, otherwise the range of materials did not substantially change over several hundred years until the introduction of synthetic resin varnishes in the middle of this century.

In 1930, at the first international conference of picture conservators in Rome, a committee of about 15 leading restorers was set up under the able chairmanship of Professor W. G. Constable, in order to establish and recommend the best varnish so far known.

It was generally agreed that no ideal picture varnish existed and eventually I suggested the following method, which was unanimously accepted and later[2] officially recommended to all museums by the International Museums Office, as the best solution of the problem for the time being.[3]

---

[1] However, recent research seems to show that they become less soluble than generally surmised. Samples twenty years old are no longer soluble in comparatively mild solvents such as toluene. Such resistance to solvents used to be attributed to admixture of oil. See Oberlin Paper just mentioned and my experiments (pp. 306–8).

[2] *Les Dossiers de l'Office International des Musées*, Paris, 1933. Bibliography, *Section 4* (22).

[3] A similar method is mentioned in the English edition of Doerner of 1935, but not in the original one of 1922. Bibliography, *Section 4* (8).

Method

Apply by means of an electric spray gun a very thin layer of mastic or damar varnish (AW2 and MS2B were not yet known), just sufficient to bring out the full depth and saturation of the colours. Protection against the atmosphere is mostly left to the subsequent application. A thin varnish film is more lasting than a thick one.

When the resin film is dry it must be covered for further protection of the painting and the varnish against humidity, gases etc. with an extremely thin application of beeswax, spread on by means of a silk-hat brush or the like. This has the additional advantage of reducing excessive shine and the disturbing haze on varnishes called 'bloom'. Spraying-on the diluted wax, as practised by some restorers, results in far too thick an application and has discredited this method in certain quarters.

This procedure was acknowledged to be preferable to mixing wax into the resin varnish, because to do so reduces the virtues of the resin, its varnishing power and also those of the wax as a moisture and gas barrier.[1] Wax-resin mixtures can be applied evenly only by spraying. Less darkening was to be expected in this double film than in a resin film.

The one serious shortcoming of this method, that the wax film collected dust in hot weather, was dealt with by incorporating about 10 per cent carnauba wax, a very hard natural wax, to the wax paste, an idea of Mr. Rosen's.[2]

The formula has since been improved still further by the invention of synthetic waxes, for instance Cosmolloid, obtainable in different degrees of hardness.

Today (1966) the wax-finish method recommended by the 1930 Rome Committee has not been superseded but I hope it soon will be, for it is still far from ideal. It is in wide use in the U.S.A. even on the synthetic varnish films which are more permeable to humidity than damar but more stable otherwise.

Another slight disadvantage of the wax finish must be mentioned. It reduces a little the transparency of the underlying varnish film; this may be disturbing, especially on dark surfaces with deep cracks and irregularities.

Great care must be taken to apply as little wax paste as possible — only a trace spread on the palm of the hand and the brush — and to polish it thoroughly when dry, first with a clean, soft brush (of the type used for polishing silver) and then with velvet or the like. At any rate the very slight turbidness is usually far

[1] Mastic and damar, the varnishes most in use in the early twentieth century, moreover take weeks to harden with admixture of wax.

[2] David Rosen, 'A Wax Formula', *Technical Studies in the Field of the Fine Arts*, III (1934), pp. 114–15. Bibliography, *Section 16* (6).

less than that which a mastic, dammar, or MS2B film will nearly always show in a few days or weeks if left without wax protection.

We recently (1960) had an opportunity of checking how effective and lasting this method is. The 'Chapeau de Paille' by Rubens which I cleaned and then varnished with this method in 1946 seemed to have darkened slightly. Some colleagues believed that dust and soot had stuck in the wax finish. After a small test all the grime was removed with cotton wool very slightly moistened in water with a trace of ammonia. The grime lay on top of the wax finish which reappeared clean and flawless.[1] The thin varnish had not darkened sufficiently in fourteen years for this to be noticeable, as was ascertained by cleaning a small light spot (see plate 69).

Many people dislike wax finish because its comparative matness is disturbing when viewed at certain angles. In a similar way the shinier surface of ordinary varnish can also be disturbing by its stronger reflections, seen at other angles.

The same Varnish Committee in Rome assumed truly historic importance when George Stout (then Head of the Laboratories of the Fogg Museum, Harvard, and now Director of the Isabella Stewart Gardner Museum, Boston, Mass.) showed us a small piece of a substance that looked like clear glass. To our amazement he bent it and said : 'This is probably the varnish of the future'. His prophecy was correct; Polyvinylacetate was the first and most useful synthetic resin for picture varnish. It has enormous advantages over the natural resins; it neither darkens nor cracks nor blooms. Its drawbacks are that it can only be dissolved in solvents as strong as toluene, both during application and removal, which may endanger certain types of picture painted with resin admixture; and it is difficult to handle, because of its rubber-like consistency, on paintings needing extensive retouching. As with B72 (pp. 137 and 254) the removal of a little fluff is a major operation.

It has been pointed out by some scientists that the synthetic resins are even less effective filters of the destructive ultra-violet rays of daylight and fluorescent light than the natural resins. My belief is that this problem should not, at least in museums, be solved by varnishes but by suitable filters on or near the windows or lamps.

A few historical notes may here be of interest. In 1949 when it had become clear that the intrinsic shortcomings of these two synthetic resins, polyvinylacetate and iso-amylmethacrylate, could not be modified, I submitted a memor-

---

[1] Even if, perhaps in a warmer climate, a little surface dirt should have stuck in the wax finish, the wax with the dirt could always be removed with white spirit or turpentine without affecting an old varnish film underneath it. A fresh wax finish could then be applied to prevent dust etc., adhering to the varnish.

andum to the Conservation and Scientific Department of the National Gallery, suggesting that one should concentrate rather on trying to improve the natural resins, and pointing out that, should this be unsuccessful, another and more suitable resin would probably be found sooner or later. At the National Gallery Laboratory highly instructive experiments have been carried out along these lines.[1]

Earlier, in 1935, in a compilation of 'Problems of Possible Interest to a Laboratory for Picture Research' (never published) I suggested a three layer varnishing system: (1) mastic or dammar varnish. (2) an insulating (water soluble) layer. (3) A wax finish which could at any time be removed if it had got dirty, without disturbing layers (1) and (2). Garry Thomson had the same idea, but no satisfactory insulating substance has yet been found.[2] Since we now know that neither the natural resin varnishes nor any of the synthetic ones will after a few years be removable with white spirit, this insulating layer, soluble only in water, may not be necessary after all. At present it seems that wax, either beeswax or Cosmolloid, is the only surface coating for paintings which will remain removable by turpentine or white spirit indefinitely.

The Best Varnish so far

In 1952 I saw in New York the good results achieved by William Suhr with 'Talen's Rembrandt Varnish' on the pictures of the Frick Gallery.

The National Gallery laboratory ascertained that it consisted of polycyclohexanone, a resin invented in Germany and marketed as 'AW2'.

We experimented with it for several years and found that AW2 films tended to turn mat in places (due to microscopic wrinkling)[3] and were not resilient enough. After talks with the National Gallery Laboratory, Howards Ltd. at Ilford introduced experimentally a modified more stable form of AW2, named MS2A[4], which was at the time the most promising of varnish resins. In varnishing and handling properties it was extraordinarily like damar, though chemically

---

[1] J. S. Mills and A. E. A. Werner, 'The Chemistry of Dammar Resin', *Journal of the Chemical Society* (September 1955), pp. 3132–40: J. S. Mills, 'The Constitution of the Neutral, Tetracyclic Triterpenes of Dammar Resin', *Journal of the Chemical Society* (July 1956), pp. 2196–202. Bibliography, *Section 27* (61) and (64) respectively.

[2] Two or three layers of different natural and synthetic varnishes have been used in the States by a number of leading restorers since about 1945.

[3] N. Brommelle, 'Bloom in Varnished Paintings', *Museums Journal*, LV (1956), pp. 263–6. Bibliography, *Section 16* (13).

[4] But see pp. 246 and 271. The manufacture of MS2A was temporarily discontinued when it was replaced by MS2B, a very similar synthetic varnish of which almost everything that had been said of MS2A held good, including the wax admixture. MS2A is now again in production.

it is different. An admixture of two to three per cent wax or a wax finish over it seems to improve the resilience of all these polycyclohexanone films sufficiently. Thus they can be recommended for wide use — until a still more nearly perfect varnish is discovered — and this we may now have in MS2B. It darkens much more slowly than mastic or damar, and, we hope, less. At any rate it is the easiest of all known varnishes to remove over a long time with the mildest solvents (white spirit or turpentine) and by attrition (dry removal). It dries within an hour and is a good retouching medium for glazing.

A striking improvement has been made by Herbert Lank.[1] He has suggested plasticizing MS2A by admixing cosmolloid wax to it. His formula holds good also for MS2B:

1. Dissolve MS2A resin in an equal weight of rectified paraffin (naphtha or white spirit).
2. Dilute 18 ccm of this solution with 150 ccm paraffin, add 7 gram cosmolloid wax, grade 80H, to the warm solution. Stir until cold. This results in an excellent matt varnish for 'primitives' etc., remarkably transparent.
3. To obtain a perfectly transparent and amply shiny varnish take one part of the matt varnish (No. 2) and mix with three parts of No. 1 (concentrated shiny varnish).

In about four years of testing under severe conditions no case of blooming or any other shortcoming has been observed.

This varnish is far less vulnerable to scratching etc. than pure MS2A, but for a very damp climate a wax finish (as described on p. 273) may still be advisable even over the wax-resin varnish.

This wax-resin varnish must be melted in a water bath every time before use, until it is perfectly clear. It is difficult to apply evenly with a brush. For MS2B Lank recommends an addition of 5 per cent Shellsol to keep the wax in solution.

The Application of Varnish

To achieve a satisfactory finish on a painting is almost as difficult as to clean and retouch it well. A different degree of gloss is suited to different types of pictures. Irregularly 'parched' areas of the surface may need varying thicknesses or repeated applications of varnish. The Lank mixture is highly suitable for such modifications (one can change the proportion of wax). On some canvases the varnish keeps on sinking in, and great experience is needed to deal with all contingencies.

[1] Published in *I.I.C. News*, Autumn 1963.

Varnishes and Varnishing

Dust and fluff floating in the air are a great worry to the varnisher.[1] One or two scraps of fluff settling in the fresh film can spoil all his efforts. In despair my predecessor at the Berlin State Gallery invented an original way of avoiding this : he varnished the pictures on a boat in the middle of a lake. Modern museums have instead special varnishing rooms with filtered air, but even there one or two wisps tend to leave one's clothes and settle on the freshly varnished picture. As long as the varnish is quite fresh, for two or three minutes, the fluff can be removed with a pointed brush. Later, after drying, one can only scrape it off with a scalpel. The tiny scratch can usually be 'regenerated' with a touch of a fine brush moistened with ethyl alcohol or, for MS2B, white spirit (paraffin) and for B72, toluene. The wax finish will usually hide all traces of it.

In the nineteenth and at the beginning of the twentieth century the varnish was usually floated on thickly by means of a wide brush. The aim was to obtain an even, glossy surface. At that time it did not seem to matter if the impasto brushwork of the master was submerged. Often most of it had already been flattened by the lining iron. Only when pictures began to be cleaned did the subtleties of surface texture and colour become matters for consideration (a thicker varnish also meant of course more yellowing).

The skilful restorer can achieve beautifully thin and semi-glossy surfaces by rubbing in the varnish with a brush or by dabbing it with a clothes brush while it is getting sticky, and many who use oil or water-colour glazes in their retouching (which get hard quickly enough to resist the wiping of the brush, as B72 also will) still prefer the brush to the spray gun. This reducing of the gloss by rubbing or dabbing the varnish with a brush while it is drying can be continued with mastic or damar varnish with impunity till the wanted effect is achieved, but must be stopped when using B72 or MS2B varnish before it gets tacky.

The application of varnishes by means of a 'spray gun' instead of a brush[2] came when industry had harnessed compressed air and later electric compressors to the spraying of paint and lacquers. The chief advantages of this process are that it allows one to use easily removable retouchings which the varnish brush would efface, it leaves a thinner and more even film than does the brush and it also saves much time. The spray gun has assumed unforeseen importance through the reforming method for varnish removal (pp. 204–6).

Several comparatively small spraying units exist which do not make much more noise than a vacuum cleaner, and improved models appear every few years.

[1] Fluff from the cotton swabs caught on the sharp edges of cracks during cleaning can be removed before re-varnishing by wiping with chamois leather dipped in white spirit.
[2] H. Ruhemann, 'La technique de la conservation des tableaux', *Mouseion*, XV, 3 (1931), pp. 14–22. Bibliography, *Section 4* (17).

Some, such as Chiron (a German invention), reduce to a minimum the mist that spreads: the varnish jet (which is fan-shaped) leaves the gun enveloped in a sheath of air. This unit is light enough to be easily transportable.

Reducing Gloss

Spraying also permits thicker application on individual 'sunk-in' patches, without an 'edge', which is almost impossible with a brush. Dulling of too glossy patches by dabbing the wet varnish with a special brush is as easy on the sprayed application as on the brushed one. A pleasant 'eggshell finish' appropriate for certain pictures, can be produced by spraying on two thin films of varnish, one only a few minutes after the other, reducing the flow of varnish. (All modern guns have a special regulating screw for reducing the flow of varnish); it will reach the surface of the picture in minute drops and result in a mat finish, which can be varied according to need. Subsequent waxing will of course reduce this effect a little. A second coat applied like this will not produce a shinier, but a still duller effect.

I have used a particularly effective dulling method for Italian 'primitives', e.g. on the 'Portrait of a Lady in Yellow' by Baldovinetti in the National Gallery (No. 758): after spraying on a comparatively thick varnish (MS2A) I removed much of it when it was dry, by rubbing it down, powderizing it with a crushed mastic grain (dry removal method, p. 202) then waxing it immediately.

The old habit of warming everything before varnishing, picture, varnish, brush or gun, is important. That the drying of the fresh varnish in warmth (but not heat) improves the film, has been proved by experiments made by Garry Thomson at the National Gallery. It reduces the tendency to blooming and 'reticulation' (a microscopic wrinkling).

After drying the picture overnight in a warm room one should lay it on a table and check for dull patches, by examining it against the light, a window or a lamp, reflecting in the surface. Varnishing of individual places and then of the whole surface can if necessary be repeated.

During spraying, all open fires, including electric ones, must of course be out of use.

Varnishing without first removing the surface dirt should be discouraged. The layman is well advised to use C.R.P. or R.P.F. wax[1] for this purpose, removing all the wax with a dry cotton wool swab while it is still wet. After polishing, the picture can be immediately sprayed with MS2B if necessary, but C.R.P. will often make re-varnishing unnecessary, at least for a long time.

[1] See p. 206 and Appendix C, p. 318; both marketed by Robersons, 71 Parkway, London, N.W.1.

Varnishes and Varnishing

A new varnish applied over an old deteriorated one will improve the appearance of a picture for a few months, but eventually the cracks of the old film will impart themselves to the new one. Therefore — and for many other reasons — I must conclude with : do *not* 'do it yourself'.

The varnishes we find on old pictures may show various forms of imperfection and deterioration. The layman will just say that the painting has become dull, or 'milky', or 'brown', not realizing that these changes are nearly always confined to the varnish layer which does not form part of the painting itself.

Disturbing dullness, mattness all over or in patches can be due to a lack of varnish. When a painting is very porous or has an irregularly rough surface the varnish will 'sink in' in some areas; a thick application of varnish will sometimes help; if the roughness is excessive only submerging of the texture in an extremely thick coating of shiny varnish would achieve an even gloss; but this is not desirable and the irregularity of the surface, which may consist of a too marked canvas grain or rough brushwork, has to be accepted. It will be disturbing only when looking at the picture from certain angles.

Most varnishes begin to disintegrate soon after they are applied, at first imperceptibly, but after about twenty years they often become riddled with a network of fine fissures, covering the whole surface and resulting in a general cloudiness. The only remedy is the removal of the varnish and replacement with a new and, if possible, better one.

A frequent and very disturbing phenomenon is the so-called 'bloom'[1] on the natural resin varnish film and, to a lesser degree, polycyclohexanone resins (AW2 etc.); it affects newly applied varnishes more than old ones and seems partly due to a deposit of ammonium sulphate from the air, though moisture is also part of the cause. It can be removed with a swab of cotton wool very slightly moistened with distilled water. Brushing on a thin wax finish[2] will prevent recurrence of the bloom. At the same time this will remove any excessive shine, and will give a longer life to the varnish and thus to the picture.

This brief survey shows how important a part even the varnishing of a painting plays in the restorer's task: to preserve and show to its best advantage everything that remains of a work of art.

[1] Norman Brommelle, 'Bloom in Varnished Paintings', *Museums Journal*, LV (1956). pp. 263–6. Bibliography, *Section 16* (13).
[2] H. Ruhemann, *Mouseion*, p. 114. Bibliography, *Section 4* (17).

Conclusion

These descriptions of restoring practices may have been tedious to read for the layman, but without them it would not have been possible to show — as I hope to have done — that in the hands of a properly trained restorer the cleaning of paintings is a careful, conscientious and safe procedure, and no longer the dangerous and slapdash affair it is still sometimes assumed to be; although I would repeat here what I have said earlier — far more damage has probably been done by enthusiastic amateur cleaners than by professional restorers.

Though a number of important technical issues connected with picture cleaning still remain to be clarified, many of the problems which seemed formidable forty years ago have by now been largely solved, through the experience accumulated in this last half century and thanks to the scientists who have come to the restorer's aid and have taken a hand in his training.

Every new large exhibition of old masters' works with their recently cleaned exhibits confirms that problems, be they of policy or technique, no longer seem seriously to impede the practice of scrupulous and thorough cleaning. It is now steadily prevailing in numerous countries, where fellow restorers are working with methods similar to our own and in a kindred spirit, so that its full potentialities are being realized in ever-widening circles.

Perhaps the evidence put forward in this book will help to foster this healthy trend and to spread the realization that the total cleaning of paintings, bearing in mind of course the exceptionally vulnerable cases mentioned earlier, such as some paintings by Reynolds, is imperative for aesthetic, ethical and historical reasons apart from often helping to prolong the life of the pictures.

However, the words and photographs in this book are only second-hand evidence and we wish that everyone would see the only first-hand evidence we have, and the strongest of all our arguments, the thousands of radiant master-pieces themselves which can now be enjoyed unblemished and unblurred in many parts of the world.

APPENDICES AND BIBLIOGRAPHY

o

Introduction to the Appendices and Bibliography

As many readers are in the habit of skipping appendices and bibliographies, I should like to draw attention especially of artists, art teachers and art historians to these sections of my book. Apart from the detailed cleaning reports, already mentioned in the text, the appendices are mostly from other writers' pens, and are not easily accessible elsewhere. The frank criticism of Professor Max Doerner's classic handbook was, I think, long overdue.

In the footnotes to the text, which I hope will also prove useful, we have mentioned most of the relevant articles that appeared in *Technical Studies in the Field of the Fine Arts* and *Studies in Conservation* but the earlier issues of *Technische Mitteilungen für Malerei* and its successor *Maltechnik* are also a treasure of information on both cleaning and the technique of painting for the student who can read German. Indeed their perusal may well be worth the trouble to those who have a continuation of sound craftsmanship at heart.

H. Ruhemann

Introduction to the Experience and Ethnography

Institutions

PROFESSIONAL ASSOCIATIONS

The following are the most important organizations from the point of view of picture restorers in this country :

International Council of Museums (ICOM), UNESCO House, 6 rue Franklin, Paris XVIᵉ.

Founded in 1946, the aims of ICOM are: 'To establish an international organization representing museums and the museum profession; develop international cooperation between them; direct their efforts at the international level, in cooperation with international educational, scientific and cultural organizations, towards a preservation, advancement and diffusion of knowledge, popular education and the spread of culture and mutual knowledge and understanding among all peoples'. There are National Committees in about 50 countries, a General Assembly being held every three years. ICOM as a whole is concerned with every type of museum activity, and not merely of art galleries. Its activities are carried on by means of working committees and sub-committees, and from the point of view of picture restoration the most important of these is the ICOM Commission on the Care of Paintings. This Commission was inaugurated in 1948, the first meeting being held in the National Gallery, London, with Mr. (now Sir) Philip Hendy, Director of the National Gallery, elected as its first President. Subsequently a Museum Laboratories Committee was formed to consider some of the more scientific aspects of art objects. It was inevitable that these two committees should eventually merge since it is impossible to dissociate the scientific aspects of conservation from the aesthetic and curatorial aspects. This amalgamation has been in the process of evolution in recent years. Since 1948 meetings of the Commission for the Care of Paintings have taken place every two years at different international centres, members preparing reports on particular aspects of picture restoration or conservation, and these reports are discussed. In final and agreed version they are published eventually in ICOM's journal, *Museum*. A second periodical publication of ICOM is *ICOM News*. For details see Bibliography, Section 1, *List of Periodicals*, p. 371.

Appendix A

The International Institute for Conservation of Historic and Artistic Works (IIC);
c/o The National Gallery, Trafalgar Square, London W.C.2.

IIC was founded in 1950 'to provide a permanent organization to co-ordinate and improve the knowledge, methods and working standards needed to protect and preserve precious materials of all kinds' and 'to give information on research in all processes connected with conservation, both scientific and technical, and on the development of those processes.' There are now well over a thousand members in over 40 countries. There are four grades of members — Honorary Fellows, Fellows, Associates and Institutional Members. Honorary Fellows (of which so far only three have been created) are persons who have rendered, or are rendering, outstanding service to the world of conservation. Fellows are persons professionally engaged in conservation and have satisfied the Institute of a high standard of professional competence. Associates: Associateship is open to anyone who is interested in the aims of the Institute or wishes to receive its publications and take part in its activities. Associateship is not a professional qualification. Institutional membership is open to any corporate body, e.g. a museum, library, school, university or business) interested in the aims of the Institute and wishing to receive its publications.

The Institute maintains a register of the technical specialisations of all its professional members so is able to put any enquirer in touch with the appropriate conservation expert in almost any part of the world.

Regional Groups of IIC have also been formed in several countries with the purpose of promoting local activities, meetings and conferences. The United Kingdom Group of IIC holds monthly meetings and discussions.

IIC promotes international conferences on topics connected with conservation. The first of these was held in Rome in 1961 on the subject of 'Recent Advances in Conservation' (see Bibliography, *Section 4* (69)). A second conference, on the conservation of textiles, was held in Delft in 1964, and a third conference, on 'Museum Climatology' was held in London in the autumn of 1967.

Probably the most important of IIC's activities is its publications. These comprise: *Studies in Conservation, Abstracts of the Technical Literature on Archaeology and the Fine Arts* and *IIC News*. In addition the United Kingdom Group and the American Group of IIC also circulate their own bulletins to members. For details of periodicals see Bibliography, *Section 1*, pp. 369–70.

The Association of British Picture Restorers. 43–44 Albemarle Street, London W.1.

Founded in 1944 as a professional association for picture restorers of British nationality. Publication: Annual Report.

Appendix A

The Museums Association. 87 Charlotte Street, London W.C.1.

Founded in 1889, the Museums Association is an organization comprising and representing museums and art galleries and those who work in them both in Great Britain and overseas. Membership is also open to persons connected with or interested in museums, though not professionally employed in them. The principal aims are to promote the establishment and better administration of museums and art galleries and to improve the qualifications and status of members of museum staffs.

The Association awards a Diploma by examination, and this is a professional qualification of graduate status. A Technical Certificate is also awarded to those engaged in technical activities in museums, such as conservation, but so far the Technical Certificate has not been extended to cover the work of picture restorers.

The Museums Association Conference is held annually to discuss relevant topics.

Publications are: *Museums Journal, Museums Association Monthly Bulletin, Museums Calendar,* and a number of handbooks for the use of candidates studying for the Museums Association Diploma. See Bibliography, *Section 1,* p. 371.

TRAINING AND RESEARCH INSTITUTES; OTHER INSTITUTIONS CONNECTED WITH CONSERVATION

Space does not permit listing those conservation departments of museums and art galleries in which research or training or both are carried out. The following include those few institutes which specifically offer training courses or carry out training and research independent of a particular museum:

BRUSSELS

Institut Royal du Patrimoine Artistique, 1 Parc Cinquantenaire (4).

Established in 1934 under the Ministère de l'Instruction Publique. A centre of conservation for all public collections in Belgium, including those of churches. Training courses in conservation and restoration, including that of paintings. Research is carried out on conservation and technique, particularly that of Flemish Primitive paintings. Publication: *Bulletin de l'Institut Royal du Patrimoine Artistique,* an annual report. For details see Bibliography, *Section 1,* p. 370.

LONDON

Courtauld Institute of Art (University of London), 20 Portman Square, London W.1.

Founded in 1932. A university institute for the study and teaching of history of art. The Department of the Technology of Art comprises a laboratory for investigation and research into problems connected with physical condition, conservation and restoration of works of art and the materials used in the arts. Although teaching is given on the technical aspects of works of art, there is no professional training for picture restorers as such, although such a course was given under the author of the present book from 1946 up till his retirement from the Institute in 1951.

MUNICH

The Doerner Institute (Laboratorium für naturwissenschaftliche Gemäldeuntersuchung), Meiserstrasse 10, München 2.

Established in 1937 under the Direktion der Bayerischen Staatsgemäldesammlungen. Picture restoration is carried out and research on related topics such as painting materials and techniques. Training in picture restoration is given.

NEW YORK

Conservation Center of the Institute of Fine Arts (New York University), 1 East 78th Street, New York, N.Y. 10021.

The Center, established in 1963, gives a complete post-graduate training course in conservation of art objects, including paintings. Some research is also carried out on relevant subjects.

ROME

Istituto Centrale del Restauro, Piazza S. Francesco di Paolo, 9.

A central institute for conservation for the whole of Italy, established in 1939 under the Ministero della Pubblica Istruzione. There is a conservation and restoration department, together with a laboratory for research. Both are concerned with objects of art in general (painting, sculpture, mosaic, applied arts). A training course on restoration is available, the specialization of this particular institute being the treatment of frescoes.

Publication : *Bollettino dell'Istituto Centrale del Restauro*, for details of which see under Bibliography, *Section 1*, p. 370.

The Rome Centre (International Centre for the Study of the Preservation and the Restoration of Cultural Property), 256, Via Cavour.

This centre, established in 1959 by the General Conference of UNESCO, is designed to strengthen relations between all who are interested in the preservation of cultural traditions. It is intended as a centre for documentation and exchange of information and does not carry on original research. The Rome

Appendix A

Centre has published several valuable handbooks on aspects of conservation, authors being recruited from specialists all over the world. (See Bibliography: *Section 10* (17), *Section 11* (20), *Section 18* (14), *Section 19* (10), *Section 21* (16)).

STUTTGART

Staatliche Akademie der bildenden Künste. Am Weissenhof 1.

A school of art, this incorporates the Institut für Technologie der Malerei, and was established in 1949 under the Minister of Culture of Baden-Württemberg. There is a department for restoration of paintings (including easel paintings) and a laboratory for research. Training courses in picture restoration are given. Published work from the Institute often appears in *Maltechnik* (see Bibliography, *Section 1*, p. 371, also *Section 8* (12) for details of training courses).

VIENNA

Akademie der Bildenden Künste. Schillerplatz 3, Wien 1.

Established under the Bundesministerium für Unterricht. Restoration of works of art, particularly paintings, is carried out. Training in restoration is given, and some technical investigations carried out in the Akademie's Meisterschule für Konservierung und Technologie.

WARSAW

Central Laboratory, Conservation Studios of Historical Monuments, Senatorska 14, Warsaw.

Established in 1951 under the Ministry of Culture and Fine Arts. The laboratory is concerned with works of artistic or historical interest throughout Poland. There are facilities for carrying out scientific and technical research. See also Bibliography, *Section 8* (10).   (J. P.)

APPENDIX B

Concerning Cleaning

1. CLEANING REPORT I

This example of a routine report dating from thirty years ago may serve for a comparison with the one made in April 1965 on the Velázquez Venus.

It shows the similarities and differences between condition and treatment of a nineteenth- and a seventeenth-century painting and in addition such differences as have occurred in materials and methods of picture conservation in the past thirty years or so.

Renoir, 'Place Clichy'
('Young Girl Crossing the Road')
Belonging to Mr. Samuel Courtauld

REPORT ON WORK DONE ON THE PICTURE

Cleaning. No particles of paint being loose, the cleaning could be safely done before the relining.

The weakest possible and least dangerous solvent had first to be established. A mixture of one part ethyl alcohol (absolute) and 20 parts of highly rectified paraffin, ('white spirit') 160° C.b.p.[1] proved sufficient to remove slowly the dirty and discoloured varnish in the little test area.

Range of Safety. A counter-test was then made to ascertain the strongest solvent that would still not dissolve any of the original paint : a mixture of 5 parts ethyl alcohol to 20 parts of white spirit did not produce the slightest stain on the small cotton-wool swab even after continued wiping on different pigments (on the edge of the picture). A solution of 6 to 20 left a slight stain from the more delicate pigments only after wiping for more than a minute.

Cleaning Solvent. The *range of safety* thus established, a mixture of *1 part of ethyl alcohol to 10 parts of paraffin* was adopted for the removal of the varnish. The

[1] 160° Boiling point.

290

weakest possible solvent 1 to 20 would have involved more friction, which is better avoided. This solution of 1 to 10 could not possibly endanger the paint because a solvent about $2\frac{1}{2}$ times stronger (1 to 4) was unable to attack the paint. As the varnish yields to a mild solvent it is probably made of mastic or dammar without oil. It seems to be naturally darkened and yellowed with time.

Where the varnish was removed the colours of the picture came to light in surprising brilliance and purity, they look as if they had suffered no appreciable change since they were put on the canvas by the master. Even the whites hardly show any sign of yellowing.

Colour photograph. For the purpose of recording the difference between the appearance of the picture before and after the cleaning a few rectangular areas were left uncleaned and a *colour photograph* (Lumière autochrome) was taken of the painting in this stage. The photograph does not do complete justice to the luminosity of the picture's colours, but it does render fairly accurately the contrast in tone between the parts covered by darkened varnish and the cleaned portions.

One of the main charms of Renoir's style, the glittering of light rendered by practically pure white patches gleaming up softly here and there on his pictures, had been made almost invisible by the dark varnish layer. The blues and violets which play a great part in his pictures were much reduced and distorted. Some delicate lavender tones looked like a dirty grey-brown, because the varnish had fairly exactly the complementary (opposite) colour and neutralized the underlying tone.

Patches left uncleaned. The cleaning was then completed, except for a little rectangular patch in the upper left hand corner, a narrow strip on the upper end of the right hand edge and a shorter strip at the bottom edge (on the shoulder of the girl). These patches, which will be almost covered by the frame, are *left untouched* to allow for later comparisons or tests.

The dirty varnish accumulated in the furrows of the impasto came off easily by wiping a little longer without using a stronger solvent or a hard brush.

The only *retouching revealed during the cleaning* was around the *tear* (mentioned in my previous report on the condition of the picture), in the middle of the top border. The retouching showed after removal of the varnish as a dark and dirty patch of about 2 to 1 inches. It was evidently executed in some kind of tempera or water colour: it dissolved in water. Underneath the retouching dark putty came to light and under this some well preserved original paint, that had been carelessly covered up. The actual *damage* amounts to a tear of $1\frac{1}{2}$ inches length and about $\frac{1}{16}$th of an inch width.

The *two scratches* mentioned in my previous report are no longer disturbing as they are now free from dirt and hardly visible, they have evidently been produced in the still wet priming before the paint was put on.

The canvas is taken off the stretcher, and laid down on a clean paper underlaid with felt, face downwards. The edges are bent straight. The back of the canvas is now brushed clean and filed even with sandpaper.

The new canvas, similar in grain and quality to the original one, is stretched on a stretcher of larger dimensions than the original.

Relining mixture. On the back of the original canvas the relining mixture : *bees wax, colophonium, venetian turpentine, 3¼ to 2 to 1,* is now evenly and thinly spread on the reverse of the original canvas. The loose threads around the tear are carefully put into place. The new canvas is soaked with the same mixture by ironing it. The new canvas is carefully laid onto the back of the original one, pressed down flat working outwards from the centre. The whole is now turned upside down. We have now on top the felt (about a finger thick) then the sheet of paper (parchment paper) then the picture, now face up, and underneath the new canvas already sticking to the original one. The whole is lying on a perfectly even slate table. Now a fairly heavy *iron* kept by means of a resistance at a constant temperature of about 80° C. is slowly and repeatedly passed over the felt. Care is taken that the whole of the picture surface is getting hot enough to make the adhesive mixture melt and penetrate through the old canvas and through the paint where it is fissured by cracks. The felt and the paper will reduce the temperature of the iron to about 60° C. which will just suffice and not endanger the paint. The insulating paper has not been stuck onto the painting (because no paint was loose) and can be lifted during the process for checking its effect on the surface of the painting. The ironing is done from the *front* in order to be sure to get the adhesive to melt through to the surface. The *felt* avoids completely any flattening down of the impasto. The bigger and more raised cracks (mentioned in the first report) are ironed down separately from the front, using a thin paper for isolation. After cooling and drying over night the picture is again nailed back onto its original stretcher, which has in the meantime been cleaned and disinfected.

Stopping of tear. The little *tear* is filled up with a *putty* consisting of chalk, zinc white, gelatine, venice turpentine and a trace of wax. After drying this stopping is evened out by careful scraping. With a bit of the original canvas (taken from the turned-over edge) the canvas texture is pressed into the still soft putty.

The putty has the colour of the original preparation (ground) of the picture.

Thin varnish is rubbed on the stopping. The missing colour is then replaced first by a semi opaque layer of egg *tempera* paint. This contains a bit of bees wax so as to keep it for ever easily soluble in case one should wish to remove the retouching at a later date. The surrounding tone is not matched exactly in this layer but kept a tone lighter and cooler. With a thin final glaze of *wax-resin colour* the correct tone is now matched. This glazing paint as well could always be removed by mild solvents that could not attack the original paint.

Isolation of retouching. As the picture might need cleaning again in the future when the varnish has become dirty or perhaps slightly discoloured or disintegrated, the retouching is covered with a thin application of *gum arabic* solution, containing a drop of glycerine. This will protect the retouching from being washed away during the cleaning unless a solvent containing water is being used.

Varnishing. Finally the painting is varnished by means of a spray gun with a varnish consisting of *Dammar resin* dissolved in turpentine and white spirit. A few drops of *stand oil* are added to the solution in order to prevent the varnish film from becoming brittle too soon, or from blooming in a wet atmosphere.

The same purpose is served by the *final protection layer* now applied : *beeswax* thinned with turpentine is thinly brushed over the dry varnish, and then polished with soft wool.

This produces at the same time a convenient semi-mat surface and protects the varnish somewhat against moisture and noxious gases.

2. CLEANING REPORT II

AN EXAMPLE FROM A NATIONAL GALLERY DOSSIER

Velázquez, 'The Toilet of Venus', National Gallery No. 2057 (often called 'The Rokeby Venus')
21.4.65

CLEANING TESTS
(carried out on small areas of different colours)

65 cc. white spirit 30 cc. ethanol (ethyl alcohol)	Removes varnish with prolonged wiping
130 cc. white spirit 30 cc. ethanol	Removes varnish with prolonged wiping
100 cc. white spirit 10 cc. ethanol	Much too weak

70 cc. white spirit	}	Removes top varnish layers but not older
10 cc. ethanol		ingrained varnish or retouchings
50 cc. white spirit	}	Removes most of the varnish and some of
10 cc. ethanol		the retouching with prolonged rubbing.

Some hard retouchings and ingrained dirty varnish had to be removed with pure ethanol by means of a bristle brush. Any 'milder' solvent would have involved too much friction. Other very hard retouchings had to be scraped off. A few retouchings had first to be softened by brief dabbing with dimethylformalde-hyde.

The following detailed list of individual flaws may give the impression to a layman reader that the picture is badly damaged; but for a painting of its age it is on the whole remarkably well preserved.

The seventy photographs, most of them full size, taken before during and after the cleaning and before the retouching, give a clear idea of the picture's condition. Some of the photographs were taken with infra-red or X-rays and some were in colour. Only four of them are reproduced in this book, but the dossier is accessible to serious students on appointment.

In the dossier, this working report is preceded by a brief history of the painting since it came to the Gallery in 1906. The most important date was 1914, when the picture was seriously damaged by attack (see plate 93); it was relined and repaired in the same year.

OLD RETOUCHINGS AND DAMAGE

PHOTOS
1
(*Seam*
15)

The majority of the retouchings were unnecessarily wide, covering sizeable areas of original paint, particularly along the upper edge of the picture in the curtain and along the *horizontal seam* running through the head of Cupid (photo 1). There is considerable wearing along this seam in the grey background (photo 2) (less in the curtain), perhaps due to some attempt at ironing the raised seam down.

Red Curtain. The *curtain* between the seam (and in many places up to $1\frac{1}{2}$ inches beyond it), and the edge of the picture ($5\frac{1}{2}$ inches or 14 cm) was widely overpainted probably to hide fairly extensive wearing.

Though the very thick areas of overpainting near the top edge were easy to split off, cleaning tests showed that I could not succeed in removing the overpainting everywhere in the red area without at the same time removing traces of original paint.

It was therefore decided to remove the overpainting only in a few

F. National Gallery No. 2057, Velázquez, 'The Toilet of Venus' ('The Rokeby Venus'), 122·5 × 177 cm. Several large areas have been cleaned; others have been left untouched. Here the dark yellowish varnish hides the delicate colours, the luminosity, much of the three-dimensional effect and the bold brushwork of the painting.

key patches, just sufficiently to ascertain what the original colour was, and then to improve the overpainting where necessary.

26–31   For the condition after this partial cleaning see Joyce Plesters'
and 69 report on micro samples.

The Grey Background shows, apart from the obvious damages probably
32 caused by accidents, numerous small flake losses and slight wearing
33 here and there. Presumably it was painted very thinly in the first place. Along the edges of the canvas there are a number of losses between ¼ and 1 inch diameter; a small triangle of red (curtain?) was uncovered in the right upper corner.

Pentimenti. An earlier outline of Venus's head in profile shows dis-
23 turbingly. The area has been worn. It does not show well in I/R. An earlier broad dark outline shows about 4 inches above the present contour of Venus' arm. The figure of Cupid also has many *pentimenti* (see below).

The Frame of the Mirror is well preserved apart from 3 negligible small
36, 37 losses and the pentimento, bottom right, where an earlier lay-out of
43 the white sheet is now showing through the dark paint of frame and background.

The Mirror Image is well preserved apart from worn patches at the root
14, 16 of the nose and within the left (from onlooker) eye socket. The shadowed areas between eyebrows and mouth show a fairly wide area of slightly disturbing light craquelure.

Cupid. His left foot and the lower part of his leg show many small
41 flake losses and extensive wearing, extending into the sheet. He is
42 painted sketchily and possibly unfinished. There are worn patches in the half shadow of his stomach, thigh, calf and ankle. Brown or red lines connected with mottled patches run parallel with the outlines of his arm, stomach and thigh — these presumably conceal pentimenti but may have been strengthened in an earlier restoration.

45, 46 *Venus.* The back of Venus shows 5 recent slashes; approx. 4, 6½, 10, 13½
51–3 (two joined), 1, 7¾, 13 and 3½ (irregular) inches long, (see 1931 re-
57–8 port on p. 9, Vol. 1). Other larger damages caused through *accidents*,
46–7 not mentioned in this earlier report are: three older tears on her thigh, back and arm and approx. 15 small losses, recorded in ph. nos. 51–53. There is slight light *wearing* in the shadow between Venus' *buttocks*,
51 and at the small of her back, but the figure is otherwise well preserved.
55 Her *left foot* is very sketchy; her big toe was overpainted black and
1 reappeared during cleaning.

44   *White sheet and blue-green scarf above Venus.* Three of the slashes extend
52   into this area. The blue-green of the scarf is slightly worn and shows
wide, light cracks.

59   *Dark grey bedspread.* This has one small and one long slash (already
68   mentioned), 8–9 larger older lesions between 1 and $4\frac{3}{4}$ inches long and
two approx. 1 inch wide. There are worn areas in a few shadows and
along the lower right edge of the bedspread. The right lower corner
of the picture up to about 8 inches from the corner is much worn and
perhaps entirely overpainted.

Here again, instead of trying to remove the overpainting and revealing the wearing and several pentimenti (e.g. traces of dark violet on
the left of the lower sheet in a higher position on the right), it was
thought preferable to keep the overpainting and only improve it where
necessary.

62   The left bottom angle up to about 6 to 7 inches from the corner was
overpainted in black (removable with solvent) and now shows the
lower parts of the bed, and two or three original alterations of colour
after removal of a modern black overpainting, (of which a square is
left in the corner).

62   *Lower part of sheet.* Many small losses and much wearing along bottom
70   edge up to 2 to 3 inches from edge.

Sept.–Nov. 1965

RETOUCHING

After the cleaning, the gaps in the paint were filled with a putty of gilder's
whiting, a little stand oil and glue; some burnt umber pigment was added to match
the tone of the original ground.

The retouching was carried out with Paraloid B72 as a medium with powder
pigments, xylene as a diluent and Shellsole E as a retarder.

VARNISH

MSB2 was used for preliminary, intermediate and final varnish . . . 3 per cent
wax was added to the final (sprayed-on) application.

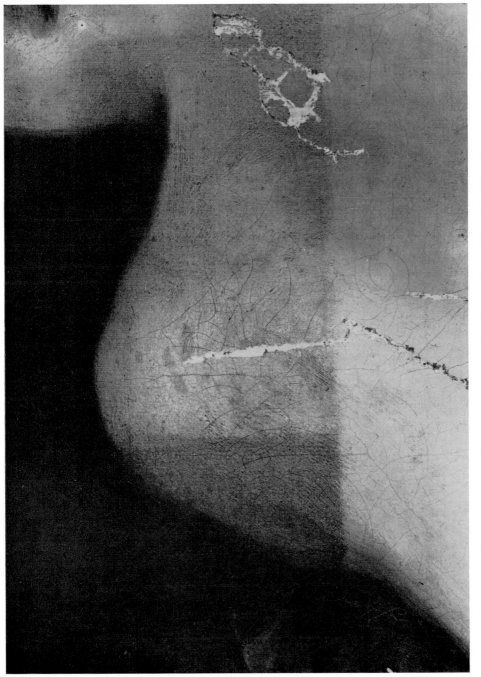

94. Detail, during cleaning. The dark rectangle on the left hand side of the shoulder shows, untouched, a tinted varnish applied over the retouchings made in 1914. The retouchings yielded, together with this varnish, but an older, harder yellow varnish remained, which covered darkened retouchings. This is shown in the dirty rectangle across the upper part of the shoulder. In the band along the lower edge of the photograph all varnish and practically all the retouchings have been removed. This photograph shows why any attempt at 'leaving a thin even layer of the old varnish' on a picture will nearly always fail.

95. 'The Rokeby Venus' after cleaning, before retouching. Five small rectangles are left uncleaned. See Appendix B, p. 298.

Appendix B

3. NOTES ON VARNISH REMOVAL

Comparative rates of *Evaporation* of the most widely used cleaning solvents.

White Spirit 0·2 (Petroleum Spirit)   Slow

Xylene 0·7

Ethyl alcohol (ethanol) 2·1

Toluene 2·6 (slightly poisonous)

Methanol 3·5 (poisonous)

Acetone 20·0 (less poisonous)   Fast

This list shows how much faster acetone evaporates than all the other usual solvents.

DILUTION OF SOLVENTS WITH 'WHITE SPIRIT'

(Other terms for white spirit are: rectified paraffin or petroleum, naphtha, petroleum spirit, turpentine substitute and sangajol)

To dissolve the same old varnish films the following proportions are approximately equivalent:

ACETONE	ETHANOL	ISOPROPYL ALCOHOL
	diluted with white spirit:	undiluted:
$\left\{ \begin{array}{l} \text{Acetone 1 part:} \\ \text{white spirit 3} \end{array} \right\} = \left\{ \begin{array}{l} \text{ethanol 1 part:} \\ \text{white spirit 12} \end{array} \right.$		I.P.A. = acetone — white spirit 1 : 1
$\left\{ \begin{array}{l} \text{Acetone 1 part:} \\ \text{white spirit 2} \end{array} \right\} = \left\{ \begin{array}{l} \text{ethanol 1 part:} \\ \text{white spirit 8} \end{array} \right.$		

A PIONEER EXPERIMENT

In 1936 George Stout compared in a systematic experiment the gelling and solving effect of different solvents on dried films of different oils and resins. As a result of his experiment, which he arranged to be as similar as possible to the actual conditions prevailing in picture cleaning, he gave figures of effectiveness to each of the solvents.

I have picked out the figures allotted to acetone and alcohol, probably now the two most often used cleaning solvents; among the films tested I have chosen copal as a characteristic hard varnish and the linseed oil film to represent the paint. The conclusion to be drawn from this paper seems to be clearly in favour of acetone.

If alcohol has 3 points of effectiveness in dissolving the varnish it would have the same effectiveness also on the paint; thus if one tried to reduce the effect on the paint (by diluting the alcohol, say, with white spirit) to nil, the same dilution would have no effect on the varnish either.

In contrast acetone, which has an effectiveness rate of 3, on the oil film, could be reduced by dilution to a point where it would have no effect on the oil film, but the same dilution of the acetone ($19:3=6$) would still have an effect of 6 points on the varnish.

Stout himself does not draw this conclusion and he is aware that several variables prevailing during actual picture cleaning are not taken into account in his paper, but his results tally with my experience with hundreds of paintings of different periods. At any rate Stout showed us the direction in which future tests may be developed.

On the following pages are some notes on tests made, not on comparatively young films applied on glass in the laboratory and containing no pigment, but made on actual old paintings of known age. In these tests naturally all the variables of conditions were operative though only the more obvious were observed, for instance the unique brevity of contact with the paint of acetone, due to its fast evaporation, at least three times faster than that of any alcohols or any other solvent useful for picture cleaning.

Rembrandt, 'An Old Man in an Armchair' (N.G. 6274)

CLEANING TESTS

1 part acetone to 3 parts white spirit : safe.

1 part alcohol to 5 parts white spirit : safe, slow.

All colours impervious[1] to pure alcohol or pure acetone except vermilion red.

1 part ethanol to 3 parts white spirit was eventually used for the cleaning. To avoid unnecessarily prolonged rubbing, some of the retouchings are dabbed with pure ethyl alcohol and then wiped off with the 1 to 3 mixture.

A TYPICAL ROUTINE CLEANING TEST

Rembrandt, 'An Old Man in an Armchair' (N.G. 6274)

Test on rectangular remnant of old varnish : on vermilion red[2] sleeve and white cuff (see photograph and macros p. 221), rolling with *ethyl alcohol* 20 times

---

[1] 'Impervious' or 'safe' indicates that after removing the varnish (avoiding friction) no trace of pigment is visible on a fresh swab (see p. 192).

[2] This red spot was chosen for the test, because it is often the most vulnerable colour in paintings.

removes practically all of the varnish; 5 times further wiping finishes the varnish removal, leaving the last swab white.

Rolling 12 times with *acetone* removes nearly all varnish.

Further 3 times wiping removes the rest, the last swab remaining white.

This test showed that both *ethyl alcohol* and *acetone* were effective and safe and that acetone worked considerably faster and involved less rolling.

'Wearing' often interpreted as a sin of the cleaner may at times be a virtue of the master. Indeed much of what makes good painting is the individual way in which the great painters leave here and there the ground or lower layer of their paint only slightly covered or even bare. This intuitive trick of handling is often done with esprit or wit as in Bonnard's, Manet's and Dufy's case.

There are many instances in Rembrandt's work.

A restorer who is not a painter and has not much experience might be tempted to retouch and 'finish' such passages which sometimes resemble abraded or 'over-cleaned' ones.

Giorgione Fragment from 'The Adulteress brought before Christ' at the Glasgow
   Gallery; now in private ownership, on loan to the National Gallery.
   Acetone does not remove all retouchings and does not attack original paint.
   Dimethylformamide briefly dabbed on: more effective, does not attack leaves, hat, flesh, except after too prolonged wiping.

Dimethylformamide slowly attacks original black. Pure acetone does not attack the black.

Pure acetone removes retouching from black.

Alcohol attacks slowly brown imprimatura under black.

Acetone also attacks. Therefore special care has to be taken where imprimatura lies bare (rolling instead of wiping).

Derain, signed; Park scenery, bought Dec. 62 at Sotheby's, owner: Lord
   Plowden.
   The yellow varnish does not yield to *toluene*.
   Paint yields to toluene (a 'mild' solvent).
   It thus seems impossible to remove the varnish in the ordinary way.
   Quick rolling with pure *acetone* (4 times) removes all varnish and no paint.
   Quick rolling with pure *alcohol* (ethyl) 3 times removes *little* varnish and, at the third time, paint: green, red; less black, as was ascertained on small spots at the edge of the painting.

After rolling with alcohol, acetone rolling still removes some varnish.

An example, where rolling (to avoid friction) with undiluted acetone seemed the best solution for a difficult problem (varnish harder than paint). Undiluted ethanol did not work.

Pittoni, Church House.

For comparison with acetone undiluted *isopropyl alcohol* was tried (after surface dirt had been removed with saliva).

90 times wiping removes all varnish (except from deepest grooves).

Pure acetone: removes all varnish with 8 to 9 times wiping, also from grooves, involving 10 times less wiping than isopropyl alcohol. Pure ethyl alcohol removes all varnish with 10 to 12 times wiping.

Neither acetone nor alcohol attacks any paint.

Rolling with pure acetone or pure ethyl alcohol removed all varnish from Pittoni with ca. 5 times *rolling*.

Conclusion. In this case isopropyl alcohol offers no advantage over acetone, which removes the varnish with 10 times less wiping or with rolling which avoids friction. The rolling method is much less effective with isopropyl alcohol, which attacks the varnish more slowly and evaporates more slowly than acetone; there is thus a greater risk of the solvent (isopropyl alcohol) diffusing into the paint and affecting it.

Solvent test

Solvent test on *Molenaer*[1] (seventeenth century) (regular solvent used: ethyl alcohol, 1 to 4 in white spirit). Pure acetone: 9 times wiping removes all varnish; 2 parts acetone to 1 part white spirit, ca. 40 times wiping removes all varnish and no paint.

Thus in this case the theory that acetone (or other 'strong' solvents) can act more readily on varnish or paint with a small addition of diluent than it can undiluted, does not seem to apply.

In comparing my notes on the comparative effectiveness of solvents with the results of Stolow's parameter experiments it seems to me as if, among the many variables prevailing in varnish removal, he has chosen one of the less operative in the actual process of varnish removal from pictures.

For instance, though it is true that isopropyl alcohol is a useful slow cleaning solvent for certain cases, the solvents Stolow lists as producing the highest degree of swelling: benzene, chloroform, carbon tetrachloride trichlorethylene etc. are in practice too fast evaporating to swell noticeably, in normal cleaning procedure, a varnish, let alone an old paint film. Our difference of opinion is probably sufficiently explained by the fact that the scientists in their forced

[1] Private collection.

304

Appendix B

immersion tests altogether forego the greatest safety factor, the fast evaporation of the solvent, and that they experiment on young mostly unpigmented oil films instead of old paint.

Before we can begin to judge the relative importance of the danger of leaching to which these two pioneers have drawn attention, we would have to see graphs showing the comparative amount of swelling and leaching of old paint films at different lengths of contact with fast evaporating solvents, also somehow taking into account the fact (which Elizabeth Jones has proved [*ibid*, pp. 166–197]) that most of the solvent is absorbed by the varnish film before reaching the paint surface.

Until then we must ask whether the scientists have not considerably overrated the danger of leaching, misled by their own unrealistic experiments.

The following questions come to mind :

Cannot the risk of leaching be almost eliminated by skilful rolling with acetone ?

Will not the maximum leaching have already occurred in most old pictures during the many and harsh cleanings they have undergone in the past ?[1]

Will not therefore most varnish removals be carried out nowadays without risk of further leaching ?

Will not this risk perhaps in the long run turn out to be negligible, negligible at least in comparison with what was hidden before the varnish removal ?[1]

At any rate cleaners must be grateful to the scientists, who have tackled this new field of research, for increasing our understanding of what happens during the cleaning of a picture and for suggesting new solvents or combinations of solvents and above all for their — at first a little too alarming — altogether wholesome warnings.

REFERENCES

Feller, Jones and Stolow, *On Picture Varnishes & their Solvents*, Oberlin, Ohio, 1959, pp. 60–91.
Rees Jones (in German) Editor R. G. Straub *Ueber die Erhaltung von Gemälden & Skulpturen*, Zürich-Stuttgart, 1963, pp. 49–57. See Bibliography, *Section 16* (20) and *Section 14* (11) respectively.

[1] P. L. Jones, in his article in *Conservation*, X, 3, August 1965 'The leaching of linseed oil films in isopropyl alcohol' has contributed new data which seem to support my less pessimistic attitude to the question of leaching.

He found that the leaching consisted in the removal of 'oxidation products'. The question arises whether these are not parts of the film unessential to its structure. The percentage of soluble matter in stand oil films, which he ascertained to be so much lower than that in raw oil films, may be significant because most old masters' pictures were probably painted with oils much more like stand oil than like raw oil. Bibliography, Section 27 (104).

Appendix B

4. CLEANING TESTS MADE ON COPIES AT THE DOERNER INSTITUTE, MUNICH

	VARNISH	DATE	YELLOWED	TEST SOLVENT	TIMES WIPING	REACTION
I	Dammar	19.LX.1941	Slightly	Turpentine	40	None.
				Toluene	40	Varnish not quite removed.
II	Dammar and ⅓ Wax.	(dates reported by Ostenrieder: over 20 years old.)	Slightly	Turpentine	40	None.
				Toluene	10	Wax admixt: readily soluble, removes varnish partly.
III	Mastic pure.	at least 20 years old.	Noticeably yellowed	Turpentine	50	None ⎱ (Varnish
				Toluene	100	None ⎰ less soluble than paint.)
IV	Mastic and 'a little' wax.	over 20 years old.	Noticeably yellowed.	Turpentine	60	None.
				Toluene	100	Removes varnish (wax admixture keeps varnish soluble).
V	Dammar and thickened linseed oil.	over 20 years old.	Noticeably yellowed.	Turpentine	100	None.
				Toluene	80	Partly.
					90	Removes varnish.
VI	Dammar and linseed oil and Venetian turpentine.	over 20 years old.	Noticeably yellowed.	Turpentine	80	None.
				Toluene	56	Removes varnish. (Venetian turpentine keeps film more readily soluble.)

Conclusion: None of the six 20-year-old varnish films yields to turpentine.

Pure mastic does not yield to toluene (even after 100 times wiping).

Dammar or mastic with wax or Venetian turpentine admixture yield slowly to toluene (60–100 times).

Admixture of a little wax or Venetian turpentine to mastic or dammar varnish seems advisable to facilitate later removal.

These results may serve as a rough guide to what may be expected in cleaning paintings of similar techniques and age, but many more tests on paintings of more accurately recorded techniques will have to be carried out before definite conclusions can be drawn.

As soon as one of the non-yellowing synthetic resins, perhaps B72, has been developed into a satisfactory varnish one could visualize paintings in the Doerner technique or other techniques which would never need varnish removal.

It would however be questionable whether admixture of considerable proportions of resin to oil paint and layers of oil-resin (or pure resin) paint alternating with tempera coatings would offer enough technical or optical advantages over straightforward oil paint (perhaps with small additions of resin) to offset the disadvantage of reduced stability.

5. TESTS CARRIED OUT ON STUDENTS' PAINTINGS, MORE THAN 20 YEARS OLD, AT THE DOERNER INSTITUTE, IN MUNICH.

In August 1962 I tested four paintings, *more than twenty years old*, for their resistance to cleaning solvents. They were painted by students of the *Doerner Institute*; they bore on their reverse dates and notes on the technique used: Dr. Wolters very kindly put them at my disposal and delegated a student of the Institute (Mrs. Silvia Shapiro) to witness and take down my observations.

PICTURE I. *Copy after Rubens* by Toni Roth, dated 10 May 1940. Media used: Linseed oil, resin, Venetian turpentine, beeswax and egg tempera mixed together. Unfortunately the proportions of the ingredients are never stated clearly enough, but in every case the proportion of resin seems to have been considerable.

This picture was never varnished, the others were covered with a film of mastic or dammar.

Special tests on varnish films follow. Each painting was first tested with turpentine and then with toluene, one of the mildest solvents for old varnish films. Small areas were wiped without pressure in a circular movement with cotton wool swabs dipped in the solvent. The swabs were continuously watched for traces of colour; the number of wipings was recorded.

PICTURE I. 8 times wiping with turpentine: no effect; 8 times wiping with toluene began to dissolve the yellow imprimatura (ground toning), probably carried out in resin and Venetian turpentine or dammar. The ninth wiping produced red traces on the swab, the fifteenth blue colour.

Conclusion: this unvarnished picture needed only surface dirt removal, but the removal of a 20 years old mastic film would have entailed loss of paint.

PICTURE II. *Copy after H. v. Habermann* by Toni Roth, dated 12 October 1939. Media: $\frac{2}{3}$ dammar and $\frac{1}{3}$ linseed oil added to oil colours; Imprimatura in dammar only. 8 times wiping with turpentine : no effect; 8 times with toluene removed some red, 10 times : green, and yellow imprimatura.

Conclusion : all colours yielded readily to toluene before all the varnish was removed. Varnish removal dangerous.

PICTURE III. *Copy after Dürer*, made before 1936 (date reported to me by Mr. Ostenrieder) Medium : oil-resin paint added to egg tempera. Varnished with mastic or dammar. (All pictures are noticeably yellowed.) 20 times wiping with turpentine : no effect; 10 times with toluene : attacked red, 20 times : black and imprimatura.

Conclusion : the same as on picture II.

PICTURE IV. Fruit still-life, dated 3 August 1938. Medium : 2 parts dammar and 1 part linseed oil added to Fiedler oil colours. Turpentine : no effect; toluene : 10 times : attacked (burnt green earth) imprimatura, 15 times : attacked red, 20 times : yellow, 40 times : green-brown.

Conclusion : all colours quickly yielding to toluene (40 times wiping). As the 20 years' old varnish would not yield completely to 10 times wiping, its removal would not be feasible.

PICTURE V. I made similar cleaning tests on a *copy after el Greco* which I made in 1918 with Blockx oil colours to which I added Blockx amber-oil medium.

Toluene removed some of the varnish comparatively quickly, but eventually attacked the paint.

However the more interesting result was that turpentine removed from the protruding canvas grain the red ground which I had applied with oil-mastic paint.

General Conclusion

These tests prove that Professor Doerner's advice to painters to admix high proportions of mastic or dammar resin with their oil paint is unsound.

So is the advice to paint the 'imprimatura' (the yellow toning of the ground) in dammar varnish as medium. This layer, though the lowest, is easily attacked by cleaning solvents which 'undermine' the paint layers, wherever the solvent penetrates them (through pores and cracks).

6. FORMS FOR RECORDING TESTS ON VARNISH REMOVAL

The following forms show the results of cleaning tests carried out on various paintings with the purpose of establishing the safety margin (see p. 192). The tests were all carried out with acetone either undiluted or in dilution with white spirit (rectified paraffin). 'Safe' here means that no trace of colour appeared on the cleaning swabs. Where the difference between the concentration of the solvent used for the cleaning (column 3) and the maximum 'safe' concentration was 10 per cent or less, it was considered that a safety margin had *not* been established. In these cases, the success of the varnish removal depended largely on skilful handling or, as for instance on certain Reynolds' portraits, had to be given up.

The bottom strip was added to these forms for speedier reference. I have reproduced the whole form in the first few instances, and thereafter shown only the bottom strip, which provides a summary of the information obtained. The cross in the last panel means that a definite safety margin was established.

In the following cases a definite safety margin was established :

ARTIST OR SCHOOL Italian, type Pier Francesco Fiorentino		OWNER Col. Lord Southesk		DATE OF TESTS July 1948		
PERIOD Fifteenth century				EXAMINED BY H.R.		
TITLE OR SUBJECT Madonna and Child		PREVIOUS CLEANING		PHOTOGRAPHS		
CONDITION Panel, very much over-painted		CLEANING TESTS All safe at 100% acetone		CLEANING CARRIED OUT WITH Varnish and most retouchings came off at 20%		
PERIOD OR DATE Italian, 15th century	MEDIUM Tempera?	IMPERVIOUS TO pure acetone	SAFE 100%	CLEANED 20%	SAFETY MARGIN +	

ARTIST OR SCHOOL Piero di Cosimo (1462–1521)		OWNER Berstl		DATE OF TESTS 1947–1948 EXAMINED BY H.R.		
TITLE OR SUBJECT Portrait of a young man		PREVIOUS CLEANING		PHOTOGRAPHS Photographs (H.R.) X-ray (Courtauld Institute) Ultra-violet (Courtauld Institute)		
CONDITION Panel see separate report on condition and technique (H.R. 23/8/47)		CLEANING TESTS All safe at 100% acetone		CLEANING The picture was cleaned at 52% acetone in white spirit		
PERIOD OR DATE Florentine 16th century	MEDIUM Tempera? or oil?	IMPERVIOUS TO acetone	SAFE AT 100%	CLEANED 52%	SAFETY MARGIN +	

Appendix B

| ARTIST OR SCHOOL
Rogier School | OWNER
Vincent Korda | DATE OF TESTS |
| PERIOD
16th century | | EXAMINED BY
H.R. |

| TITLE OR SUBJECT
Portrait of a Lady | PREVIOUS CLEANING | PHOTOGRAPHS
Infra-red (Courtauld Institute)
X-ray (Courtauld Institute) |
| CONDITION
Panel
Poor preservation | CLEANING TESTS
All parts safe at 100%
acetone | CLEANING CARRIED OUT WITH
The picture was cleaned at 33%
acetone with white spirit |

PERIOD OR DATE	MEDIUM	IMPERVIOUS TO	SAFE AT	CLEANED	SAFETY MARGIN +
Northern 16th century	oil?	acetone	100%	33%	

PERIOD OR DATE	MEDIUM	IMPERVIOUS TO	SAFE AT	CLEANED	SAFETY MARGIN +
Italian, sixteenth century	oil	acetone	100%	22%	
Italian, sixteenth century	oil	acetone except green on sash: safe at 36%		50% sash cleaned separately	+
Northern, seventeenth century	oil	acetone	100%	36%	+
French, seventeenth century	oil		50%	33%	+
Dutch, seventeenth century	oil	acetone	100%	1 vol isopropyl-alcohol: 1 vol white spirit	+

Appendix B

PERIOD OR DATE	MEDIUM	IMPERVIOUS TO	CLEANED WITH	SAFETY MARGIN
Spanish, middle seventeenth century	oil	pure acetone	pure acetone	+
		(Note: as all colours were completely impervious to undiluted acetone, no weaker solvent was tried.)		
French, eighteenth century	probably oil	pure acetone	1 vol acetone 3 vols white spirit	+
British, late eighteenth or early nineteenth century	oil	pure acetone	acetone wiping	+ (large)
German (?) middle nineteenth century	oil & resin ?		acetone rolling	+
English, nineteenth century	oil	pure acetone	30%	+
English, nineteenth century	oil	pure acetone	20%	+
English, 1881	oil	pure acetone	acetone wiping	+

In the following cases *no* safety margin was established :

ARTIST OR SCHOOL Cranach	OWNER Lord Southesk	DATE OF TESTS July 1948
PERIOD 1472–1553		EXAMINED BY H.R.
TITLE OR SUBJECT	PREVIOUS CLEANING	PHOTOGRAPHS X-ray (Courtauld Institute)
CONDITION Panel See separate report on technique (H.R. 28/8/48)	CLEANING TESTS Safe at 100% *except:* red, safe at 50% black and grey-black safe for cleaning at 40% but not under test conditions	CLEANING The varnish was tinted yellow The picture was cleaned at 36%

PERIOD OR DATE	MEDIUM	IMPERVIOUS TO	SAFE	CLEANED	SAFETY MARGIN
Northern, sixteenth century	oil ?	acetone *except* reds, black and grey	40%	36%	negligible

Appendix B

ARTIST OR SCHOOL 'RD' or 'DR' PERIOD 1601	OWNER Lord Southesk		DATE OF TESTS June 1948 EXAMINED BY H.R.		
TITLE OR SUBJECT The Garden of Eden	PREVIOUS CLEANING		PHOTOGRAPHS Photograph (Courtauld Institute)		
CONDITION Panel, signed RD or DR, 1601 The picture is very well preserved except in sky	CLEANING TESTS Not entirely impervious to pure acetone All safe at 50%		CLEANING Varnish turbid but not very yellowed. Action below 36% slow The picture was cleaned at 40%		
PERIOD OR DATE Netherlands, 1601	MEDIUM oil	IMPERVIOUS TO	SAFE AT 50%	CLEANED 40%	SAFETY MARGIN negligible

ARTIST OR SCHOOL Guardi school PERIOD Eighteenth century	OWNER Vincent Korda		DATE OF TESTS October 1948 EXAMINED BY H.R.		
TITLE OR SUBJECT Piazza San Marco	PREVIOUS CLEANING		PHOTOGRAPHS		
CONDITION Poor preservation	CLEANING TESTS Blue sky only safe at 100% acetone. All safe at 50%		CLEANING The picture was cleaned at 40%		
PERIOD OR DATE Italian, eighteenth century	MEDIUM oil	IMPERVIOUS TO	SAFE AT 50%	CLEANED 40%	SAFETY MARGIN negligible

PERIOD OR SCHOOL	MEDIUM	IMPERVIOUS TO	SAFE AT	CLEANED	SAFETY MARGIN
Italian, eighteenth century	oil		40%	40%	Nil
British, middle nineteenth century	oil-resin			acetone rolling	none

(An example where no safety margin could be established, paint and varnish being equally vulnerable. However, by rolling with acetone (undiluted) the picture was safely cleaned. The fast evaporating acetone was absorbed by the varnish first before it could attack the paint layer.)

PERIOD OR SCHOOL	MEDIUM	IMPERVIOUS TO	SAFE AT	CLEANED	SAFETY MARGIN
French, nineteenth century	oil		36%	27%	negligible
English, 1874	oil-resin?	toluene		with toluene	pure acetone too strong. 1 vol acetone : 3 white spirit safe; 1 : 2 not safe on browns
British 1894	oil-resin?	— (browns yield to varnish solvent)		rolling with undiluted acetone	none

7. SUGGESTED FORMS TO RECORD TREATMENT AND CONDITION

BRIEF RESTORATION REPORT

Number............ *Date*............ *Restorer* ....

Master or School............................ *Owner* ....

Title or Subject	*Panel Canvas*	*Medium*	*On cleaning (see special page)*	*On Master's Method (see special page)*	

Condition before cleaning
Surface dirt
Varnish, shade, thickness
   Disintegration
 	
Paint
  Scaling, etc.
  Losses (retouched)
      (puttied)
      (unretouched)
  Wearing
 	
Unnecessary retouching
  Ground
  Support
  Additions to support
	Photos	Consolidation
		  Fixing loose paint
		    Adhesive
		    Tool
		    Temperature
		Removal of old canvas
		  Impregnation
		  Adhesive
		Lining
		
		  Adhesive
		  Ironing
		  Hot table
		  Vacuum
		  Transfer
		    Putty
			Retouching
			  Layers Media
			
			Pigments
			
			Varnish
			
			sprayed?
			
			Wax finish
			Remarks
			
			Finished date:
				Photos nos.
				
				Initials

Appendix B

BRIEF NOTES ON MASTER'S METHOD

Number.............. Artist.................... Country.............. Date..............

Subject........................... Magnifier.................... Illumination..............

Place and date of examination...

Discoloration, etc Layers (1–9 from top downwards)	Medium	Hue	Consistency	Pigment	Remarks
0. Varnish VIII					
1. Final modelling VII					
2. Local colour, lights, shadows VIA					
3. Local colour, main tone VI					
4. Underpaint B, lights, shadows VA					
5. Underpaint A, main tone V					
6. Monochrome, heighten- ing, shading IVA					
7. Monochrome modelling IV					
8. Drawing-in III					
9. Toning II					
10. Ground I					
11. Support O					
(Nos. I to VIA to be read from the bottom up)					

Signature of Examiner....................................

See pp. 110–115 on how to fill in this form.

Appendix B

8. SUGGESTED TEST PAPER FOR A RESTORER'S DIPLOMA

Answer any four questions, one of which must be No. 5 or No. 6. Time allowed, two hours.

1. Describe either (a) Rubens's panel technique or (b) the 'primitive' Italian technique with green underpaint.

2. Describe the treatment to be adopted for blisters and flaking paint.

3. Describe the safety-margin cleaning test.

4. Give an account of the technique of retouching.

5. What is the significance of the refractive index of pigment and medium?

6. Give as many examples as you can of pigments introduced since 1700. Name some historically important pigments which are now considered to be obsolete.

7. Name some typically 'heavy' and typically 'light' pigments.

8. What is the main use as an aid to restoration purposes of: (a) ultra-violet; (b) infra-red; (c) x-rays?

9. What are the ideal aims of the restorer?

10. Should losses in paintings be completely disguised by retouching or left visible? Give reasons.

11. Describe the disadvantages of cradling.

12. Describe the significance in restoring of the 'turbid medium effect'.

Appendix B

9. SPECIAL DIFFICULTIES

BLANCHING ON A MICHELANGELO (N.G. No. 809)

In 2 or 3 small places in dark greens where perhaps a corrosive liquid had run over the picture, perpendicular bands ca. 1/2 cm. wide and 3 cm. long remained whitish after cleaning with acetone or ethanol, also around a previously much retouched loss near the bottom edge. A similar effect occurred also in other places where cleaning was tried with ethanol or acetone, but to a lesser degree.

Tests: wiping with diacetone alcohol 1 : 1 gradually darkens the spots to their proper tone, but after drying (ca 10 minutes) they turn white again.

After wiping with ethanol + diacetone alcohol 1 : 1 they turn a little less white.

Wiping with ethanol and diacetone and rubbing well with dry cotton wool while still wet, when repeated a second or third time leaves the area properly dark as one would expect it to look normally without varnish.

However one thin application of MS2A varnish is not quite sufficient to make the trace of the blanching invisible.

The white deposit (precipitate) scraped from a blanched area on the Michelangelo was ascertained, by Joyce Plesters and John Mills, to be gesso (calcium sulphate). This must have been carried up through the cracks to the surface by evaporation of the solvent.

A RARE CASE

In Renaissance paintings the Virgin's mantle is usually blue; if it appears green one generally assumes that a yellowed varnish or oil has turned it green.

However, in 1964 I had a Flemish sixteenth-century picture to clean, with a *green blue* Virgin's dress and mantle. The swab of a small cleaning test was analysed by Joyce Plesters and the green (not yellow) in it was proved to be a copper carbonate. This is unlikely to have been used later than the eighteenth century, and probably original sixteenth century.

Here the blue does not seem to have turned greener with time as perhaps in 'The Virgin of the Rocks' by Leonardo, where the green is coming through from the underpaint (and probably partly intentionally); but the blue appears to have been deliberately turned into a green blue, by means of a green glaze, by the master himself.

There are two other garments of the same hue in the picture.

The blue is azurite, not ultramarine. Lapis lazuli is rare in Flemish paintings.

(J.P.).

Varnish Recipes

One cannot give a definite recipe for a varnish solution since the concentration depends very much on the preference of the restorer and on the picture being treated. However in general one uses between 40 and 50 per cent for the polycyclohexanone ketone resins N and MS2A, and between 10 and 20 per cent for the acrylic resin Paraloid B72.

Basic mat varnish solution

A very mat varnish undiluted, suitable for certain early tempera or for size paintings; slightly reduces saturation of colours, contains about 5 per cent wax by weight:

    150 ml white spirit

    18 ml varnish solution (ketone resin N or MS2A)

    7 gm Cosmolloid wax 80 H[1]

The wax is dissolved in the warmed white spirit and added to the varnish solution with vigorous stirring until nearly cold.

Dilute mat varnish solution

Only slightly mat, scarcely diminished saturation, about 1 per cent wax by weight:

    1 part basic mat varnish solution (see above)

    3 parts basic varnish solution

C/W wax for polishing pictures (prevents bloom and protects varnish films against humidity) (p. 273).

Extremely thin application and thorough brushing with a soft brush is necessary.

    100 gm Cosmolloid wax 80 H

    25 gm 'A' wax[2]

    375 ml white spirit 115°

[1] Cosmolloid wax Grade 80 H: Astor, Boisselier and Lawrence, Ltd., 9, Savoy Street, London, W.C.2.

[2] A (Polythene) wax (B.A.S.F.): Bush, Beach and Segner Bayley, Marlow House, Lloyd's Avenue, London, E.C.3.

Appendix C

The waxes are melted together and then poured into the warmed white spirit with vigorous stirring. When cool the paste is put into screw-top jars. The addition of approx. 5 ml. kerosene slows down the evaporation of solvent.

Ammonia wax paste

Based on a formula published by H. R. in *Technical Studies, III* 1934–5, p. 3–15.

    50 gm beeswax[1]

    150 ml turpentine or white spirit

    15 ml. 0·880 ammonium carbonate diluted with 30 ml. water

The beeswax is dissolved in warm turpentine. When the wax is almost cold but still liquid the diluted ammonia solution is added with vigorous stirring. A smooth paste is obtained.

This paste is used for removing retouchings or varnish not soluble in the usual varnish solvents. It is applied fairly thickly to the surface of the picture, a small area at a time, left on for about three minutes and then removed with a clean swab; it does not run, very small spots can be treated and the effect can be modified by length of application and concentration of ammonia.

The following excerpts are translated from the 'Dossiers de l'Office International des Musées', Paris 1933.

Committee of Experts for the Preparation of a *Manual on the Conservation of Paintings*, 30–31 March 1933, in Paris.

Professor Constable asks the Committee if it would not agree to abiding by the conclusions of the 'Special Commission for the restoration of paintings and the application of varnishes', of the Rome Conference (1930).

Mr. Ruhemann believes that one could agree at once upon the least bad varnish which could be recommended at the present stage of the research made in this field.

Mr. Stout concurs with this view.

Dr. Plenderleith deems it prudent to base any conclusion regarding this on laboratory tests, before formulating a process in the manual on restoration.

Nevertheless, after an exchange of opinions, the Committee recognizes that an accord can be reached from the conclusive experiments already made, with an application of resin as first layer, then covered with wax, which fulfils the role of protecting the resin.

Mr. Ruhemann explains the method of application which can be carried out with a brush or a spray gun. Polishing with a very soft brush (applying the wax thinly) follows and eventually one polishes with a flannel. The wax has the draw-

[1] Some of the synthetic waxes are unsuitable because they do not emulsify well.

Appendix C

back of collecting in the cracks, but this disadvantage counts for little in view of the effectiveness of this substance.

Professor Constable, summing up the conclusions of this discussion, believes that this is one of the most important results of the meeting.

At the request of the committee Mr. Ruhemann proposes the following text for the resolution on this subject:

At the 'Special Committee for the Restoration of Paintings' of the Rome Conference some experts recommended as varnish resins dissolved in turpentine (with a small addition of oil); others advocated beeswax.

Each of these substances answers only part of the ideal properties formulated by the Committee.

Resin varnish is relatively the best we know at present, but its protective properties are insufficient.

Wax, on the other hand, constitutes the best protective coating, but sometimes it does not fulfil so completely its task as a varnish, of giving to the painting the necessary transparency and depth of colours [saturation].

The majority of the postulations indicated by the Rome Committee could be fulfilled if one first applied a resin varnish which one would then protect by a thin coating of wax.

The resin (preferably dammar) yellows little and one can even reduce this shortcoming to a minimum; for this substance can be applied in a very thin layer, since the superimposed wax layer would complement the effect of the resin.

The resin film prevents an excessive accumulation of wax in the cracks and the depressions of the paint film, which would otherwise cause a disturbing opacity at these points.

The disadvantages of wax as a final coating are negligible compared with the advantages it offers:

1. Touching with the finger leaves a slight mark, but this is easily removed by polishing.[1]
2. Before re-varnishing or regenerating, the wax must be removed, which is easy with turpentine.[2]
3. In strong heat the wax tends to get sticky and to make dust adhere, but one must and can prevent this.[1]

[1] These three shortcomings have been almost entirely eliminated by adding carnauba wax to the mixture or using hard (synthetic) cosmolloid wax instead of beeswax. (See p. 273).

Scientific tests will have to establish whether the extremely thin application of wax used in this varnishing method is sufficient to reduce the yellowing of the underlying varnish layers. It certainly reduces considerably its tendency to blooming.

[2] This is not necessary when using polycyclohexanone varnishes, especially when wax has been added as plasticizer or for reducing gloss.

319

4. Frost can turn wax mat by crystallization. Polishing remedies this.[1]

Formulas

One part of the dammar resin, dissolved in five parts of petroleum spirit (white spirit) or rectified turpentine; add not more than 5 per cent poppy oil or 2 per cent castor oil to obtain greater elasticity.

Apply this varnish in a warm and dry atmosphere as thinly and evenly as possible. (Application by means of a spray gun is preferable). Leave to dry several days, avoiding change of temperature.

Dissolve one part of bleached beeswax in five parts of turpentine in a double boiler at 60 degrees centigrade.[2]

This ointment is applied cold by means of a very soft brush, (silk hat brush or baby's hair brush), as thinly and evenly as possible, rubbing about as little as a small pea's volume into your left palm, rubbing the brush in it, then brush evenly onto the surface, an area no bigger than a hand at a time. Anything but the thinnest application would spoil the transparency of the varnish. Leave to dry for about an hour.

Polish with even softer brush (or velvet, if greater gloss is desired).[3]

Professor Constable recalls certain general remarks which ought to figure in this chapter; particularly the observation made by Mr. Folch y Torres, regarding the protective coating on 'primitives'; this should not be varnished but waxed.

Professor Lavagnino quotes the case of the frescoes of the Saints Severino and Sosia at Naples which were waxed fifteen years ago and have since shown very disturbing darkening.[4] Thus wax is not advisable for frescoes, while certain murals executed in encaustic could be waxed.

[1] See note 1, p. 319.

[2] All these substances must be of best rectified quality.

[3] N.B. The use of dammar, turpentine, poppy and castor oils has largely been superseded by the use of materials less susceptible to discoloration. The description of the technique employed is however still extremely useful.

[4] As the darkening has not been observed directly after waxing it may have been due to dust sticking to the surface. This might have been avoided by using an addition of carnauba wax.

APPENDIX D

Useful Articles Reprinted

1. STANDARDS OF PRACTICE AND PROFESSIONAL RELATIONSHIPS FOR CONSERVATORS ADOPTED BY IIC-AG[1] JUNE 8, 1963; APPROVED FOR LEGAL SUFFICIENCY AUGUST 7, 1963

I. PREAMBLE

The following standards and procedures are approved by IIC-AG as applying to professional practice by conservators, as defined in the Articles of Association of IIC, in the examination and treatment of works of art. Such practice is considered to comprise three categories.

A. Scientific analytical study of art objects, for such purposes as identifying materials, method of construction, modifications by age or other agencies, and comparison with comparable material, but not as a preliminary to treatment.

B. Examination and treatment of works of art, whether by private or institutional operators.

C. Supplying previously developed reference data which may bear on condition, authenticity, authorship or age of specific objects. This can be either by formal publication or private communication.

II. GENERAL CONSIDERATIONS OF POLICY

These are broadly applicable to all categories.

A. *Professional attitude.* It must be axiomatic that all professional actions of a conservator be governed by unswerving respect for the integrity of works of art. Such respect is manifest not only in policies of restoration, but in selection of courses of treatment, in safeguarding against accident, pro-

---

[1] International Institute for Conservation of Historic and Artistic Works, American Group. The mimeographed typescript of this document was circulated to members of IIC in 1963. Since then a revised Final Draft has been prepared and circulated in 1967.

321

tection against loss, and strict avoidance of misinterpreting technical evidence.

B. *Contractual relationships.* A sound contractual relationship includes the need for clear understanding, written in cases of private contracts, of the exact work to be done, the basis for charges if any, the extent and substance of reports, including photographs as appropriate, responsibility for insurance coverage deemed adequate for operator, owner and object, provisions for safeguarding objects, method of delivery, and any sub-contracting or re-assignment of work. It is recommended that a lawyer be consulted.

C. *Assumption of responsibility.* It should be a conservator's responsibility to contract for investigation or treatment only to the limits of his professional competence and facilities. Should he not be trained or equipped for a full scientific study by generally accepted current technical means, any specific limitations must be stated and accepted by both parties from the beginning. Wherever further opinions seem to be required such further opinion or opinions are a necessary part of a comprehensive report. In the same manner a conservator should be held irresponsible if he undertakes to carry out a course of treatment for which he is inadequately trained or equipped.

D. *Interpretation of evidence.* It is obvious that a scientific investigator has the obligation to present *all* the evidence he has developed about an object commissioned to him for study, favourable or otherwise, and also to supply from his professional knowledge a clear exposition of the significance of each part of the evidence. It will be held improper for him to make outright formal declarations as to age, authenticity and the like (which subsequently might form the basis of a claim or legal action) when such declaration exceeds the logical development of the scientific evidence.

E. *Limitation of reconstruction.* In replacing losses or damage, a conservator can be expected to accord little or much restoration according to a firm previous understanding with the owner or custodian. It is equally clear that he cannot ethically carry this to a point of modifying the known character of the original, whatever the motives for so doing might be.

F. It shall be considered inconsistent with the professional integrity of conservators in any of the three categories of procedure to engage in the following outside activities :

    1. Issuing paid 'expertises' or authentications.

    2. Acting as paid or commissioned agent in the selling or purchasing of works of art.

    3. Engaging in such selling or purchasing for personal profit.

    4. Making monetary appraisals of works of art.

Appendix D

Whenever it becomes necessary for owners of works of art to request museum or commercial analytical laboratories or private consultants to engage in scientific study of art objects for the purpose of developing data which may bear on condition, authenticity, authorship, or age of a specific object, the following procedure shall be followed by all parties concerned.

A. *Initiating the study.* The owner of the work of art, or his qualified agent, or a qualified officer of an institution shall send to the examining agency a written request with statements covering the following points as required :

1. The purpose of the study listing any specific questions which, if possible, are in need of answer.

2. Whether (a) the whole object, or (b) samples from the object are to be made available for study. If samples only are to be sent to the laboratory, the exact location of the samples on the object and the name of the person who took the samples are to be given.

3. If the whole object is to be sent to the analyst, (a) the legal owner, (b) its value, (c) to what extent it is covered by insurance, (d) by what carrier it is to be sent to the laboratory and returned to the owner, and (e) that the object is to be sent to the investigating laboratory at the owner's risk and expense.

4. Explicit permission to take samples from the object during examination.

5. Whether the investigator (a) is merely to report facts and observations, or (b) if the investigator is expected to draw conclusions from the facts.

6. Whether the laboratory findings are (a) to be kept in strict confidence, or (b) whether the findings, regardless of their nature, can be used by the investigator in formal publications and in oral declarations.

7. Whether any of the evidence produced is intended for use in legal proceedings.

B. *Conducting the study.* The analyst or laboratory official on receiving the object shall :

1. Supply a written receipt to the owner verifying its condition and inform the owner how the object will be stored and guarded.

2. Inform the owner what fees, if any, are to be charged for the analytical

services. If there is to be no charge, state that fact explicitly. State also what other charges may be made for photographs, X-rays, spectrograms, and for outside analytical services, and others.

3. Make a photographic record of the condition of the object.

4. Keep a careful and detailed written record of all observations and findings, giving dates.

C. *Preparing and submitting the report.* On completion of the investigation the investigator shall:

1. Render to the owner a typewritten report of his findings with conclusions, if conclusions have been requested. The report shall cover methods of test, kind and type of instruments and equipment used, and analytical procedures employed in sufficient detail so that, if the owner wishes, the tests can be repeated and checked on the same object by an independent investigator in another laboratory. If it has been necessary, with the owner's permission, to take samples from the object, give location and amount of each sample.

2. List all other persons who assisted or co-operated in the scientific investigation.

3. List what published works or authorities he has consulted in the course of the study.

4. State what limitations, if any, he may wish to place on the use of the findings. That is, whether or not the findings may be used voluntarily in legal proceedings; whether or not they may be quoted in formal publications or in oral declarations.

IV. PROCEDURE FOR ENGAGING IN AND REPORTING OF EXAMINATION AND TREATMENT OF WORKS OF ART BY PROFESSIONAL EMPLOYEES OF INSTITUTIONS.

A. *Report of examination.* Such reports shall include, in writing, the following information.

1. Date of examination and name of examiner.

2. Identification of objects with that in report. This may be done by photographs, word descriptions, measurements and accession numbers.

3. Descriptions of materials, structure and method of fabrication. Physical, chemical and biological identification of materials composing the object. Statement of method of determination employed or reference to published standard method.

4. Record of alteration and deterioration. Locations and extent of

physical defects, chemical alteration and its products, previous repairs and compensation. Statement of method of determination sufficiently detailed to permit duplication by another examiner.

5. Deductions or interpretations of observations and analyses. Comments relative to the degree of alteration.

6. Where evidence indicates forgery, every available test which can supply information on materials and structure shall be employed. After thoroughly checking his results the examiner shall recommend consultation with one or two disinterested individuals qualified by scientific or art historical training to review the evidence.

B. *Proposal for treatment.* Before any treatment is undertaken a summary or copy of the examination record shall be supplied to the responsible custodian of the object. This shall be accompanied by :

1. An outline of the proposed treatment.
2. A statement of the results to be expected.
3. An estimate of the probable time required for the treatment.

The official custodian's written approval shall be secured before treatment is begun.

C. *Report of treatment.* Such report shall include :

1. A statement of the procedures followed in the current treatment with exact descriptions of materials and methods, including :
   (a) The method by which accretion or deterioration products were removed.
   (b) Method and materials used in correcting distortion in form and shape and in reinforcing, consolidating, stabilizing and protecting structure and surface.
   (c) Kind, extent and location of compensation employed.

2. Photographs as follows :
   (a) Condition before treatment with date.
   (b) Photograph in 'actual state' without compensation.
   (c) Photograph after treatment with date.
   (d) Photographs as required to supply data about structure, method of fabrication and state of object as revealed during process of treatment. Photographs or diagrams which clarify method of reconstruction or compensation.

V. PROCEDURES SPECIFICALLY APPLYING TO EXAMINATION AND TREATMENT OF WORKS OF ART BY SELF-EMPLOYED PROFESSIONAL CONSERVATORS.

These do not differ from those applying to institutional employees except in the fields of contractual relations and assumption of responsibility. Procedures in these fields shall include :

A. Written proposals stating :
   1. Work to be done, estimated charges, and estimated date of completion.
   2. Arrangements for insurance and its specific coverage, method of delivery, and provisions for safeguarding objects.
   3. Any sub-contract or re-assignment of work proposed.
B. A signed contract by the owner or his authorized agent, which may be a signed copy of the letter of proposal.
C. It is recommended that a lawyer be consulted as to the adequacy of the contract until such a time as a standard form be adopted.

VI. OPERATING SAFETY PROCEDURES FOR CONSERVATORS.

The following considerations apply to all who are engaged in art conservation, regardless of category of employment.

A. *Safety of personnel.*
   1. *Radiation.* X-ray installation and operating procedures should conform to approved specifications as described in Eastman Kodak's book, *Radiography in Industry.* Most state labour departments will supply an inspection service to determine the operating safety of radiographic installations.
   2. *Toxic vapours.* Adequate exhaust and ventilation should be a part of all laboratory installations where volatile solvents are habitually used. The National Association of Mutual Casualty Companies' *Handbook of Organic Industrial Solvents* covers these requirements in detail. Suitable respirators should be available for special requirements.
   3. *Mechanical equipment.* Power tools of all kinds should be provided with adequate light, operating space, and safety guards. Their use should be restricted to properly qualified and authorized persons. Cleanliness should be rigidly enforced. Instruments producing dust, abrasive powders and the like should be equipped with positive exhaust systems, and provided with appropriate respirators for operators.
   4. *Corrosive liquids.* Standard laboratory requirements for quantity storage and operating containers of acids, alkalis, and other reagents should be rigidly followed. Only authorized personnel should have access to them.

5. *Fire Hazards.* The building housing the studio or laboratory should conform to Underwriters' requirements in construction. Uses to which other parts of the building may be put should not be of a hazardous nature. Working and storage areas should be of fireproof construction, and equipped with adequate extinguishing apparatus.

B. *Safety of art objects.*

1. *Vapours.* The same requirements that apply to personnel should be observed.

2. *Protection against theft.* Working and storage areas should be of adequate construction, and capable of systematic locking routine. Only authorized personnel should have access.

3. *Protection against accidental damage.* Working and storage areas should be adequate for safe handling and storage of objects. Individual storage racks for paintings and shelves for three-dimensional objects should be available. Working equipment should include sturdy, well-designed furniture such as tables, easels, horses. Objects should be removed or handled only by experienced persons.

Secondary personnel should be of responsible character and adequate training in the handling of works of art. They should not engage in activities for which they have inadequate professional training.

Objects should not be removed from the operating or storage building except on due notice and authorization by the owner or custodial institution.

Transportation and packing of objects should be by approved agencies and according to established methods.

2. CONTROVERSY IN 1846[1]

by NORMAN BROMMELLE[2]

Mr. Brommelle, who was Restorer at the National Gallery, describes some aspects of the controversy which broke out in 1846 over the cleaning of pictures at the National Gallery, in which the chief protagonists were the art dealer, Morris Moore, and Sir Charles Eastlake, then Keeper of the Gallery

TO THE EDITOR OF THE TIMES

Sir, — I beg to represent to you that, should the present pernicious system with regard to our national pictures be continued, in a very few years those noble works of great masters, which we have collected at so much expense, will be utterly destroyed.

[1] Reprinted from *Museums Journal*, LVI (London 1967), pp. 257–62.
[2] Now Keeper of the Department of Conservation at the Victoria and Albert Museum, London.

Appendix D

I visited the National Gallery yesterday morning on its reopening, and to my great surprise and indignation I found the finest Rubens we possess, viz. *Peace and War*, completely flayed. — I know no more appropriate word to designate the shameful manner in which this splendid work has been treated during the last holidays.

To close the gallery for so long a period is very bad management, but that, in addition to being deprived of the study of our pictures annually six consecutive weeks, there should be during that time persons actively labouring to deprive us of them altogether, is a question which demands strict and public enquiry. If the gallery were always kept open, as under proper management it would be, the public would be better enabled to watch the proceedings of the persons entrusted with the care of the pictures, and the work of destruction might perhaps be prevented from being carried on wholesale as at present. To return, however, from this digression.

The *Peace and War*, so preeminently rich and harmonious in colour, is now almost as remarkably crude and discordant. With characteristic ignorance the fine rich glazings have been scoured off without the slightest regard to, or perception of proportion, so that we now have the distant objects most offensively confusing themselves with those in the foreground.

The fine Cuyp has been treated in a similar manner, and such is the rage for destruction that the Velazquez, one of the new purchases, has also been subjected to the dreadful ordeal of the cleaner's hands. This picture was as remarkable for its fine preservation as for its noble qualities as a work of art. Those who were well acquainted with this picture before its recent misfortune will find, instead of its pure and solemn tone, a chalky film spread over it. . . .

I am acquainted with most of the finest pictures in Europe, and I have seen the dreadful havoc committed on many of them, but I never saw a more flagrant case than that of the *Peace and War* nor one that more urgently called for interference. It will, however, be fortunate if this strong case prove the means of saving other great works from a similar fate.

Yours obediently

VERAX

It was this letter by 'Verax' published in *The Times* of 29th October 1846 which began the first and most protracted of the controversies on the cleaning of pictures at the National Gallery. It was to end with the publication, more than six years later, of the Report of a Parliamentary Committee of Enquiry which ran to 1,000 pages and weighed $7\frac{1}{2}$ lb. The present writer has discussed elsewhere the light which this Report and other documents of the period throw on the restoration methods of the time, and this article will describe some aspects of the controversy itself, and the conditions in which it took place.

The National Gallery, founded in 1824, was not transferred to its present building till 1838, where, during the period considered here, it occupied only five rooms to the left of the main entrance, the remainder being given over to the Royal Academy. In this small area, a fraction of the present space, there were as many visitors in the peak year of 1851 as in 1949, the year of the Munich exhibition. In bad weather and after the Changing of the Guard and especially on Mondays, the scene (described in 1850 by the Keeper, Thomas Uwins) can only be visualized now by visiting Paddington Station towards the end of a Bank Holiday. The Gallery was regarded as a place 'in which children of all ages may recreate and play . . . where food and refreshment may conveniently be taken . . . On frequent occasions, I have perceived a quantity of orange peel in different corners of the place . . . a man and a woman had got their child, teaching it its first steps; they were making it run from one place to another, backwards and forwards'. On one occasion the Keeper, remonstrating with a group of country folk who had drawn their chairs round to begin a picnic, was offered a glass of gin and invited to join the meal. In this confusion it is surprising that the pictures, hung closely together, and mostly without glass, suffered no more actual harm than an occasional childish finger print in a patch of bloom, though on one occasion a man 'in a moment of very furious moral rage, took up his crutch and struck a picture and destroyed it entirely; it might be put together again if it were worth while'.

To the frowsy atmosphere of dense crowds was added a black smoke from chimneys of the nearby parish wash houses and the steam engine used to work the fountains in Trafalgar Square. The effect on the paintings appalled those who had known the nucleus of the collection in Angerstein's house earlier in the century. Increasing obscurity from a glutinous dark deposit which gradually settled on the pictures was accelerated by the treatment that William Seguier, the first Keeper of the Gallery, devised to ameliorate it. This consisted in applications of linseed oil, and of the notorious Gallery Varnish — a megilp of mastic and boiled oil. On William's death in 1843 this treatment was continued by his brother John, a restorer. In 1846 Charles Eastlake, who had followed William Seguier as Keeper, had four pictures cleaned; these were Rubens, *Peace and War* (No. 46), Titian, *Bacchus and Ariadne* (No. 35), Cuyp, *Cattle and Figures* (No. 53) and Velazquez, *Philip IV Hunting Wild Boar* (No. 197). A few pictures had been cleaned on acquisition in 1844 without arousing, at the time, any public comment (a letter from Verax had been turned down by *The Times*). Verax (Morris Moore) whose first letter in 1846 is quoted above, was not only the first but the chief protagonist of the attacks which followed. Moore, who was still a young man, had shared a studio with Alfred Stevens in Rome, and had since become an active and successful art dealer, in London. His character emerges clearly from his eloquent and passionate evidence before the 1853 Committee, and from the tigerish pamphlets which he published from time to time. His chief target appears to have been Eastlake, Keeper from 1844 to 1847, who later became P.R.A. and was clearly destined to be the first Director (with increased powers and salary) when the Gallery was reconstituted, a post that Morris Moore may well have coveted himself.

On 19th November 1846 in a second letter to *The Times*, Moore described Titian's *Bacchus and Ariadne* as having been 'scraped raw' in some parts and 'repainted' in others, 'the former process especially, has the effect of altering the apparent position of some of the objects'. This, wrote Moore, 'ought to be the last of a series of barbarisms'. Besides criticizing the purchasing policy of the Gallery and the hanging of the pictures, Moore later went on to assert that the Velazquez *Boar Hunt* (one of the cleaned pictures) had been purchased hurriedly by Sir Robert Peel for the Nation at an enhanced price, by a trick practised by Farrar, the dealer, who was alleged to have represented that the picture was about to be exported to Holland for the King's collection, whereas in fact it had just returned from there after being turned down. When, in 1853, Moore returned to this accusation before the Committee of Enquiry, his furious interchanges with Farrar caused the Committee to clear the room and retire into secret session.

Among other critics at this period was John Ruskin (then aged 29) who said that *Peace and War* was 'for the present utterly, and for ever partially, destroyed. . . . Time may, perhaps, restore something of the glow, but never the subordination; and the more delicate portion of the flesh tints . . . are destroyed for ever'. Ruskin thought the Cuyp 'nearly uninjured', the *Bacchus and Ariadne* had 'escaped scot-free' and that he had never seen a Velazquez which gave him more delight or which he believed to be in more genuine and perfect condition. Ruskin admitted that dirt must be removed, but it should be done by patient friction and without removing varnish.

In January 1847 Eastlake presented a report to the Trustees defending the cleaning of the disputed pictures. This report became the subject of a long and characteristic lampoon by Morris Moore of which the following two extracts might convey some of the flavour: 'The "Report" begins with the hackneyed lament "the absence of spacious and well-lighted rooms for conveniently carrying on the operations of cleaning pictures on a more extensive scale" . . . he then has the assurance to tell us that in consequence of the "operations having been unavoidably limited to a small number at a time the pictures which *are* cleaned present a temporary contrast in their appearance to the mass of the collection''. Temporary contrast! Had he said that *flayed* pictures must inevitably present a hideous and *irremediable* contrast to those which have not undergone that process, he would have accurately described the state of the *cleaned* pictures.'

'After these . . . follow the letters of the five Royal Academicians which Mr. Eastlake begged the Trustees to "permit" him "to subjoin to this report in his own vindication and that of Mr. Seguier" but as they have received from the public the contempt they deserve, and are only remarkable for imbecility tinged with something worse, I shall not condescend to notice them further than by observing that with true academical wiliness they try their utmost to make the *picture-cleaner* their comrade's scapegoat; and that it is grievous to reflect that the silly person who signs himself "Thomas Uwins" and who says in his letter that "nothing can exceed the beauty which the Cuyp and the Velazquez present as the effect of the *picture-cleaner's* skill" is curator (!) of the pictures in Her Majesty's possession.'

By the time that the Enquiry of 1853 was held, interest in the four pictures, cleaned in 1846, had cooled, and no doubt John Seguier's varnish had mellowed in the interval. There were newly cleaned pictures to excite fresh horror or admiration. It is a characteristic of picture cleaning controversies that though the expressions of vituperation which are used are transmitted almost unchanged through the years from one controversy to another, it is the most recent operations which are the subject of the controversies. It is unlikely that any critic in 1946 would have thought it worth while to waste emotion on the deeds of John Seguier. Witnesses in 1853 considered that the Cuyp had mellowed in tone. On the Velazquez *Boar Hunt*, Eastlake explained that it had been very much injured in relining with an overheated iron, long before its acquisition by the Gallery. He had not been aware of this in 1846. According to George Lance, the restorer became so much affected by the accident that he saw the figures of the picture passing over his bed in procession, and eventually fancied that he saw a skeleton in it. The picture after being offered successively to Wilkie and Landseer for 'repair' was finally partially repainted by Lance, from whose detailed evidence it appears that John Seguier had removed some of the repaints and left others. At the time of this cleaning, Lance, from motives of prudence, had not revealed the part he had played in restoring the picture to the perfect state in which everybody, including Ruskin, had supposed it to be. The rest of Lance's repainting, which was extensive and somewhat inventive, was not removed until the recent cleaning in 1950. Seguier said that he had 'a good deal of trouble to make it satisfactory'. Opinion was divided about Rubens's *Peace and War*, but not vociferous. Eastlake, with some caution and a surprising amount of circumlocution, revealed that, as with the Velazquez, the state of the picture was rather more complex than he had thought in 1846. He had then believed that it had not been previously restored, though in 1848 details of considerable previous restorations of damages, and a reglazing of the colours, came to light. Seguier was certainly aware of this, and probably removed some at least of the previous restorer's work, apparently without Eastlake's realizing it, though he was said to follow the cleaning work closely. Eastlake's evidence in 1853 on the cleanings of 1846 was somewhat ambivalent. While defending Seguier's work, which he had proposed and supervised, he had at the same time to dissociate himself from it sufficiently for his reputation not to suffer.

We return now to the year 1847 when Eastlake resigned the Keepership. His place was taken by his friend Thomas Uwins, R.A., who was nine years his senior. Uwins was a vague and rather timid man, the son of a bank clerk, who had, however, progressed from designing fashions for Ackermann's 'Repository' to Surveyorship of Pictures to the Queen. In William Seguier's time the Keeper's actual power, as a result of the ineffectiveness of the Trustees, was considerable. During Eastlake's term of office the Trustees gradually assumed more responsibility. With Thomas Uwins, the power of the Keepership became almost nominal; at Board meetings he appears scarcely to have offered his opinions at all. A few pictures were cleaned in 1850–51, without causing any fuss. In 1852 the Trustees asked John Seguier, without consulting Uwins, to submit a list of pictures needing attention. As a result Seguier cleaned nine pictures in the six weeks' vacation of 1852. When the Gallery was reopened, a new and virulent phase of the controversy began and continued intermittently until it was summed up with judicious moderation in a *Times* leader of 28th December. *The Times*, while on the whole regarding the matter as 'in some degree an artists' quarrel' suggested that there were grounds for dispute on the question of pronouncing between 'certain coats of paint or glaze some of which, as not ascribable to the original artist, should be removed from the picture'. *The Times* proposed the formation of a Royal Commission to examine the matter, and suggested that further work should be held up for the time being. The siting of the Gallery, its constitution and the selection of pictures had also been subjects for active public discussion, and the Parliamentary Committee, when it finally began work in April 1853, was empowered to consider all these matters.

The pictures most criticized of the nine were Canaletto, *Stonemason's Yard* (No. 127), Veronese, *Consecration of St. Nicholas* (No. 26), Claude, *The Queen of Sheba* (No. 14), and Rubens, *Conversion of St. Bavo* (No. 57). On the Canaletto (*see Plate XXIX*) Morris Moore was in characteristic form: 'That picture has been literally flayed; the transparent colour on the shadowed side of the beams nailed diagonally on the mason's shed to give it support, has been nearly rubbed off. ... The like may be said of the fragments in the mason's yard; the effacement of half-tints and shadows has reduced them to unmeaning reliefless surfaces, similar in effect to the detached portions of a theatrical scene. ... This picture may be quoted as a sad instance of the passion now so fatally prevalent for reducing old pictures to as white an appearance as possible. The various white objects in it have been scoured, utterly regardless of the position in which they are placed, to an almost uniform whiteness. The consequence is that near and distant objects are jumbled together in unmeaning confusion, and that the linear perspective is forced into direct antagonism with the aerial. I will here remark, that the chalky, veiled appearance of the immediate foreground is owing to the solvent having disturbed some portion of the body pigment. ... The sky has a smudged appearance, such as I know, from experience, to be the result of an improper action of some strong solvent. ... There is an absence of that freshness and sharpness of execution which, until the late cleaning, characterized this picture.' Similar though more moderate views were expressed by other witnesses. John Seguier said that the picture was in a very fine and perfect state, except for a damage in the sky, which he imagined Sir George Beaumont, the former owner, had repaired. This picture was cleaned again in 1955 so that the present writer had an opportunity to study it at all stages of the work, for lengthy periods. The conclusion was drawn that Morris Moore's observations, though expressed immoderately, were not wholly unjust; it was the interpretations which he placed upon them that were faulty. The shadows were indeed slightly rubbed, and there was considerable overpaint over a large portion of the sky covering sound original paint as well as damage. It is more than likely that both damage and overpaint were done when the picture was owned by Sir George Beaumont or earlier, and that before the cleaning by Seguier these damages could not be seen under the varnish or were not remembered by Morris Moore. It is probable that Seguier under- rather than overcleaned the picture. Seguier was a busy man with a great many clients and his general practice was to avoid reaching the stage when so much old retouching came away that extensive restoration was needed. Undercleaning would account for the veiled appearance in the foreground which Morris Moore attributed to smearing of body pigment.

Criticism of the other pictures followed the same pattern, with a spirited attack by Morris Moore, echoed by his supporters, and a stolid, stonewalling defence by Seguier. According to Morris Moore, the Claude *Queen of Sheba* had had an inscription made illegible (this had also been stated by *The Times*, and authoritatively refuted the next day by Ralph Wornum); in Rubens's *St. Bavo* an eye had been knocked out, and much else besides; Claude's *Marriage of Isaac and Rebecca* was now hard and flat 'like a tea board', the sky had been 'tormented'; glazings had been removed from all the pictures.

The word 'glazing' was explained at length in different ways by the principal witnesses, since it was, after all, the focal point of the controversy. In this the hapless Uwins started badly by saying that the best painters of every school used very little glazing, that it was 'quite a modern quackery' and that it was called *'la velatura Inglese'* because only the English used it. Morris Moore declared that it was a disgrace to the country that the man who uttered this view should be at the head of the National Gallery. It needed a great deal of patience and persistence on the part of the Committee to extract from the witnesses their understanding of the term 'glazing'. Some took it to mean an all-over glazing or toning and one asserted that Rubens finished his pictures with a toning consisting of black and yellow ochre mixed with megilp. Morris Moore said that glazes of different colours were used over all the opaque colours even the lights, by the Old Masters, especially the Venetians, but that they were 'graduated' in different areas, to produce the maximum effect. Uwins, who had been generally attacked for his remarks, said that he was painting before Morris Moore was born and that the latter's childish ignorance of art startled him because he thought that a man who wrote in newspapers must be a very learned man on the subject. The views of Eastlake, whose treatise on the history of oil painting still remains a standard work, were perhaps more concordant with modern opinion. He said that the general principle was to use either transparent or opaque colours in thin washes over other colours for modifying the basic opaque layer, and that the Italians, using the terms *velare* and *velatura* for both transparent glazes and thin opaque scumbles, did not, in principle, distinguish between them.

On the central point of whether any of this *velatura* had been removed by John Seguier, the Committee did not finally commit themselves. They noted that although 'Sir C. Eastlake did not state his views very definitely' he thought that too much old varnish had been removed and that some pictures had been unequally cleaned, but that 'in no case had the original work of the Master been disturbed. The crudeness and want of harmony resulting from unequal cleaning would soon be remedied by the discolouration of varnish and the film of dirt which would again spread over the painting. . . .'

Uwins remained as Keeper until 1855, when the Gallery was reorganized with Eastlake as the first Director. It appears that Morris Moore continued to be active, since the National Gallery has in its archives a pamphlet dated 1856 written by him and published by an organization described as 'The National Gallery Reform Association'.

Appendix D

REFERENCES

Report from the Select Committee on the National Gallery, together with the Minutes of Evidence. The House of Commons, 25th July, 1850. Ditto, 4th August, 1853.

Hendy, P. *Catalogue of Cleaned Pictures*. National Gallery, London, 1947.

Brommelle, N., Material for a History of Conservation.' *Studies in Conservation*, II (1956), p. 176.

3. THE IMPREGNATION AND LINING OF PAINTINGS ON A HOT TABLE[1]

by H. RUHEMANN

Much of the content of this article has been made obsolete by Rees Jones' and Straub's invention of the vacuum method (Bibliography, *Section 11* (14) *and* (16)), *but it may be of historical interest.*

INTRODUCTION

The drawbacks of ironing in lining paintings have long been realized, and several reliners are reported to be using instead hot presses much like those employed in veneer work.

During 1947–48 the makeshift arrangement described in the report[2] on the treatment of 'La Haie : Landscape near Arles' (66 × 82 cms) had to serve, but in 1948 Mr. Rees Jones, the Courtauld Institute of Art, University of London, constructed on my suggestion an electrically heated and controlled metal table specially designed for impregnation and lining. His detailed description of it follows below. It has worked most satisfactorily with a minimum of drawbacks.[3]

For lining with aqueous compounds the hot table will perhaps prove less convenient, because it may dry the adhesives too quickly during the work; but in wax-resin lining the hot table seems to overcome to a great extent the disadvantages of ironing.

It is well known how difficult it is to apply a reasonably even layer of adhesive, and just enough of it, on a canvas that is cool or not uniformly warm. Formerly the general practice was to apply a little too much adhesive and to squeeze out the surplus during the lining beyond the edges of the picture. This involved repeated and prolonged ironing with much heat and pressure for remelting the adhesive between the two canvases wherever it was desired to get rid of the surplus. Often it was impossible to avoid wrinkling and uneven stresses in the lining canvas and at times even in the original canvas.

[1] Reprinted from *Studies in Conservation*, I (1953), pp. 73–6.

[2] See below, pp. 340–44.

[3] On the suggestion of the author, a firm has recently produced an electrically heated rubber blanket, which provides a convenient and readily portable alternative to the hot table. The principle of the operation described in the text remains unchanged.

Appendix D

In nineteenth-century paintings containing a soft resin the risk of melting it was considerable. Pictures with high impasto needed an elaborate bedding which made the necessary ironing on the front of the paintings at least very awkward. Where the lining was undertaken mainly to ensure the fixing of all loose or 'chalking' particles, it was impossible to achieve sufficient and uniform impregnation of the paint without prolonged ironing. Furthermore, it was impossible to control the distribution of heat, and to avoid the accumulation of heat in some areas that had to be touched repeatedly.

Two large and important paintings have recently been impregnated and lined on the hot table at the Courtauld Institute: namely a portrait by Renoir in oil-paint, which presented no special difficulties, and a landscape by Constable. The latter seemed to contain some soft resin admixture in the paint, since it softened a little at a comparatively low temperature and with 50 per cent acetone in rectified paraffin. Ironing in the traditional way would therefore have involved unnecessary risks.

As should always be done in all restoration work on important pictures, the substances and methods to be used in every case were tested on small trial pictures and on small areas of the painting to be treated. A portrait of no value which was obviously painted with a resinous medium melted in places on the hot table and acquired the wrinkles which the heat had caused in the insulating paper. This served as a warning, and after ascertaining in a corner of the Constable that the paint could be 'modelled' with an electric spatula heated to about 65° C., the treatment was carried out on the hot table, keeping it at the minimum heat necessary to melt the lining adhesive, namely, about 55° C. Very brief heating was sufficient to achieve ample cohesion between the two canvases. There was no curling or flaking, nor was the paint brittle, so that impregnation was not required. The main reason for the lining was that the original canvas had become brittle and had torn along the edges.

On the Renoir, on the other hand, minute particles of paint were flaking off in many places along the weave, and impregnation was necessary.

Whenever the main purpose of lining is to fix loose paint, it is preferable first to finish the impregnation separately and then to apply the new canvas. In this way it is easier to ensure the maximum penetration while using less heat. The sticking together of the two canvases can then be done at a much lower temperature than was needed for the impregnation.

As our hot table was not large enough for either of the two pictures mentioned, they were each heated in two or three sections, while the rest of the painting was supported by a table of the same height as the hot table, the edge of which was covered with a band of linoleum.

Appendix D

1. Removal of surface dirt with detergent.[1]
2. (*a*) Removal of varnish, unless it is sound.[1]
   (*b*) If the paint is too loose for devarnishing, the old varnish can be regenerated either by the Pettenkofer or the spraying method.
3. Application of a new varnish, containing a little alcohol, soon after the regeneration.
4. Facing with several layers of mulberry paper, and fabric, if much scraping etc. has to done on the back. (Varnish or paste adhesive, according to the case.)
5. Removal from stretcher.
6. Removal of old relining, dry wherever possible.
7. Stretching on a large stretcher by means of wide packing-paper bands.
8. Sandpapering of the reverse.
9. Bad curling must be ironed down at this stage, using damp blotting-paper (and a felt if impasto is present).
10. Stretching of the lining canvas on a stretcher wide enough to contain the other stretcher.
11. Heat table to approx. 65° C. Maintain at this temperature, and check for half an hour.
12. Test on a corner of the painting with a hot spatula what temperature the paint will bear. Reduce hot-table temperature accordingly.
13. Put insulating (parchment) paper[2] on the hot table. Lay the new canvas on it and paint the new canvas (no matter which side) uniformly and thinly with the hot adhesive by means of a very wide brush. (If not quite successful, the canvas can be quickly cooled a little by inserting a piece of asbestos board between the hot plate and the insulating paper, and when in a buttery consistency the adhesive can be evened out and the surplus removed with a spatula or a clothes-brush.) Put the new canvas away on insulating paper.
14. Lay the picture on the hot table over insulating paper, *face down* (no felt is necessary except on very resinous paint with high impasto, because very little pressure will be applied). When the picture is hot, paint plenty of adhesive on the back, brush it with a clothes-brush and repeat until the picture is well permeated (and the adhesive shows on the facing).
15. Brush off surplus adhesive and even out. There should be on both canvases only just enough adhesive to produce a slight sheen.
16. Reduce the temperature of the hot table to about 45° C.

[1] This can of course only be done if the paint is firm enough.
[2] This has been superseded by Melinex.

17. Put the two canvases together on a cold table.
18. Put them on the hot table over insulating paper, picture face down. When the adhesive on the back is just showing signs of melting, insert a piece of cardboard between the plate and insulating paper and switch off the current from the table.
19. Press the canvases together by brushing radially from the centre with a clothes-brush, squeezing out all air bubbles while the canvases are cooling.
20. When necessary the picture can be pressed (on the cooling table) with boards and weights.

NOTE. — No part of the painting should be kept hot longer than strictly necessary for the desired effect. Large pictures or canvases likely to shrink through prolonged heating should therefore be treated in strips.

DESCRIPTION OF THE TABLE

I am indebted to Mr. S. Rees Jones for the following description of the mechanical and electrical construction of the hot table. The construction is laminar, consisting of the aluminium top, an asbestos-cement sheet which carries the heating element and a further sheet of the same material as a base. These three components are held together by a channel-sectioned brass rim, allowance being made for thermal expansion in length and breadth of the aluminium top but not in thickness, which is negligible. The dimensions of the aluminium and the asbestos-cement sheets are $54'' \times 36''$, and the total thickness of all these makes up the internal gap of the brass channel which is $1''$; the aluminium is $\frac{1}{8}''$ thick.

The heating element

The heating element is made of asbestos-sleeved nichrome wire, resistance $0 \cdot 43$ ohms per foot, inserted in parallel channels $\frac{3}{16}''$ wide between thirty-one rows of abestos-cement spacing-pieces which are screwed to the upper asbestos-cement sheet as shown in the diagram. The spacing-pieces in twenty-nine of the rows are $1''$ wide while the two outer rows are $\frac{1}{2}''$ wide, an arrangement which insures an increased heat input per unit area along two of the edges. The purpose of this arrangement is to offset the additional radiation of heat at the edge.

It will be seen that the winding is double, with a centre tapping; there are approximately $74'$ in each half, giving two resistances of 32 ohms.

Temperature-control

The heating element is designed to operate on 240 volts A.C., one half being directly connected and the other fed through an energy controller. Any type of controller such as a resistance or variable transformer may be used, but in the present instance a variable on-off ratio device was found to be most convenient. By this means the mean input can be controlled over the range 1·7 kW to 3·4 kW.

CONCLUSION

Some experience will of course be needed for obtaining satisfactory results with the method here described, and much will depend on finding in each case the temperatures required for the different operations. As the table takes a long time to heat up and to cool off, careful timing and checking is imperative. No doubt suggestions for improvements, for which there is still much scope, will be forthcoming.

It is hoped that the trouble and expense of constructing an electric hot table will be offset by the advantages of the method, which, in using brushes instead of irons, reduces risks by eliminating the unnecessary pressure of the iron and its irregular and partly superfluous application of heat. Thus bedding becomes almost obsolete. The ease and speed of working afforded should also prove welcome. In special cases it is conceivable that an electrically heated rubber roller would be preferable to the table. Such an apparatus should present no particular difficulties in construction.

TABLE CHAUFFANTE POUR L'IMPRÉGNATION ET LE RENTOILAGE DES PEINTURES

Sommaire

Il y a longtemps qu'on s'est rendu compte des inconvénients du repassage des tableaux. On peut aujourd'hui les pallier grâce à la méthode de la table chauffante.

Elle vaut notamment pour le rentoilage à la cire, au dosage si difficile sur une surface froide. De même on élude le repassage prolongé et irrégulier, nécessaire pour éliminer l'excédent d'adhésif.

Désormais le fer à repasser sera presque superflu puisqu'une simple brosse suffit à assurer l'adhérence des deux toiles.

On évite ainsi le danger d'écraser les empâtements sans devoir recourir à l'usage d'un feutre ou à d'autres artifices.

H. R.

Appendix D

4. RESTORATION OF 'LA HAIE: LANDSCAPE NEAR ARLES' BY VAN GOGH[1]

by H. RUHEMANN

INTRODUCTION

In connexion with the preceding article on relining-work by means of a hot table the following detailed report on the treatment of a modern painting may be of interest.

At the time when this work was done no electrically heated and regulated table was available, only a makeshift arrangement: but some of the advantages of circumventing the use of laundry-irons came out clearly in this case, which offered particular difficulties. Here we shall follow our workshop notes, believing that the reader will appreciate a direct approach.

CONDITION BEFORE RESTORATION, AND RECORDS

Photographs

Black-and-white photographs of most of the fruit-tree area, approximately original size, were taken in raking light to record the impasto. For comparison before and after treatment see Figs. 1 and 2, which show examples.

As some of the blemishes mentioned below would not show well on a photograph, they were marked on a tracing made from a large reproduction of the picture.

Damages

In about seven minute areas the paint and the priming are missing, and the dark grey-brown canvas lies bare. In about thirty small spots the paint only is missing and the white priming underneath is visible. The sharply broken edges distinguish these damages from the many small areas that had never been covered by paint. There are about thirty places where the paint is partly detached from the ground. In some, only the top impasto-strokes are missing and a certain amount of paint underneath is preserved. In a few areas the tops of the impasto are flattened and here and there marked with the weaving pattern of a canvas put on the still soft paint. This is a well-known feature of many paintings by Van Gogh. He stacked them one on top of another, before the paint was hardened.

The picture is covered with grey house-dirt, much of it accumulated in the hollows of the texture.

It seems that the painting had never been varnished. There is a lining stuck to the back with some water-soluble adhesive, which has become brittle, and there

[1] Reprinted from *Studies in Conservation*, I (1953), pp. 77–81.

Appendix D

are several raised areas in the sky, apparently caused by accumulations of relining-adhesive between the two canvases.

In the areas noted as flaking there are either deep cracks going right through the whole thickness of the paint, or fine cracks in the upper layer only.

TESTS

Preliminary cleaning tests made on the edge of the picture

Some yellow and yellow-green passages were susceptible even to wiping with dry cotton wool, almost like pastel. The other colours were firm and did not rub off with turpentine, rectified paraffin (B.P., approx. 160° C.), or benzene. The bare priming yielded to water and to alkaline wax paste.

Benzene removed much of the surface dirt, but not all.

To secure the paint for transport, where it was loose, drops of pale relining-mixture were melted on to it. See formula below.

Impregnation tests

A trial in a corner showed that the molten wax adhesive mixture readily permeated through both canvases; the old deteriorated relining-adhesive did not present any obstacle. The wax adhesive does not darken the bare priming noticeably.

Further cleaning tests

Benzene gradually removed not only the wax mixture but also practically all the surface dirt from an area impregnated for testing. Probably the hot solutions helped to loosen the dirt. Even the vulnerable yellows did not stain the cotton wool, if friction was avoided; high-quality absorbent cotton wool soaked up both the wax and the dirt when gently dabbed on the hot surface, previously wetted with benzene. Heating with a lamp helped.

IMPREGNATION

The relining-canvas proved strong enough. To prevent needless disturbance of the brittle paint the old lining was retained, and thus a new relining was avoided.

A special pale mixture, largely dammar instead of the usual rosin, and gum elemi instead of Venice turpentine, was prepared according to the following formula:

> 6 parts bleached beeswax
> 3 parts gum dammar
> 1 part pale colophonium
> 1 part gum elemi.

Appendix D

In place of an electrically heated table, which was not then available, a copper tank, larger than the picture, was heated to about 65° C. by two large paraffin stoves. After a few hours it was found that the temperature on the copper surface remained sufficiently even and steady. The molten wax compound was freely applied with a brush to the tank. The picture was laid on it, face upwards. The wax mixture slowly seeped through to the surface where the paint was thin or cracked, and, of course, more quickly where there was no paint. Where the picture was not quite touching the tank, it was pressed down with a painting-brush.

For inspection the picture was lifted up, and patches on the back that were found to be too dry were painted with additional wax mixture.

Where the surface was not sufficiently flooded with the adhesive a further quantity was sprinkled on by grating it (in cold condition) with a cheese grater. A photographic lamp was used for additional heating of the surface, to ensure that the mixture penetrated as completely as possible from the back to the surface. The picture was kept on the hot tank, which was maintained at about 60° C., to soak for two or three hours under constant observation; then it was left to cool completely. A test made beforehand on a corner of the painting showed that some of the paint softened slightly at this temperature, but did not melt; nor did the areas change in shape. Even slight pressure in the warm condition would have injured the impasto.

FIXING OF LOOSE SCALES

The paint was now firm everywhere, but where it was detached from the ground — curling upwards — it was still standing up separated from the canvas by a layer of wax mixture. From these areas the surplus wax was soaked off (as described under 'Cleaning Tests'), after which tissue-paper was stuck over them with 'Gloy' (flour paste) containing a drop of oxgall to improve adhesion. As the picture was not going to be exposed to the stress entailed in the removal of relining or to ironing, it had been considered unnecessary and inconvenient to cover the whole surface with a facing.

When dried the paper was made transparent by wetting with rectified paraffin oil; a very small thick iron plate was heated, covered with insulating parchment-paper and laid under the area being treated. As soon as it was melted the surplus wax was pressed out sideways from underneath the paint with the finger and along the grooves of the brushmarks with fine dental instruments. During the cooling this local downward pressure was continued where necessary. When the area was cool again the remainder of the wax was removed from the tissue-paper with benzene; the paper was then wetted and pulled off.

During the cooling the raised areas in the sky were pressed even with the palm of the hand while the picture was lying face up on a felt, insulated by parchment-paper. The raised areas now stood out slightly on the back.

REMOVAL OF SURPLUS WAX AND DIRT

Small areas at a time were wetted with benzene; as soon as the wax was soft enough the bulk of it was gently wiped off with a semi-soft paint-brush (badger-hair); benzene was applied and dabbed off alternately with best absorbent cotton wool. This removed wax residues and surface dirt alike in most places. Where such dirt was accumulated in the deeper grooves and recesses of the texture it was necessary, in order to remove it, first to soften it with benzene, then quickly to heat it with an electric lamp, and finally to pick it out by means of a quill cut to a point; since the quill was more resilient than the paint scratching could not occur.

In a few places where a plane of the impasto faces upwards the dirt did not yield to benzene; it had probably become engrained there before the paint was dry. Much of this black dirt was removed with a wax paste emulsified with a drop of ammonia, wherever it was very disturbing, and where it lay on solid paint containing much white. Here and there the paint forms a kind of bridge with thin fragile points. Underneath some of these the hardened wax mixture was left as a support.

In the past I have relined three other Van Goghs, without a hot table, by ironing. The eventual results were perhaps as satisfactory as in the case here described, but they were achieved with incomparably greater risk and trouble. An elaborate insulation with tin foil and a sawdust bedding was necessary to protect the high impasto. During the prolonged and laborious ironing it was extremely difficult to judge whether or not heat had been applied evenly enough to ensure everywhere uniform and sufficient penetration of the adhesives to impregnate and secure completely all the lower paint-particles.

'La Haie' was a particularly vulnerable painting: the advantages afforded by the hot-table method proved most valuable — above all, the fact that it was possible to watch the actual surface unhindered by facing or bedding, and to observe the effect of the treatment at every stage.

SURFACE-PROTECTION

After a few days when the benzene had thoroughly evaporated and the wax-resin mixture well hardened, a wax finish (1 part bleached beeswax, 1 part rectified French turpentine, 3 parts rectified paraffin 160° C. B.P. and ⅓ part carnauba wax) was very sparingly applied with a badger-hair brush. After a few hours the surface was gradually polished with another badger brush in small sections at a time.

Appendix D

SUMMARY

By using a heated table and soft brushes instead of laundry-irons it was possible to impregnate this picture safely. It is painted with unusually high and fragile impasto. Through a fortunate combination of circumstances it was also relatively easy to clean it with impunity. The adhesive and solvent employed to remove the excess removed at the same time most of the surface dirt without any friction. The rest could be safely removed with a quill. There was no varnish present on the painting.

After the impregnation had secured all the loose and chalking paint, the unsuccessful old lining could perhaps have been removed without undue risk. A new one could easily have been affixed at a comparatively low temperature, and by dabbing with brushes. As, however, the lining-canvas was sufficiently strong, it was decided to leave it in order to avoid even the slightest unnecessary hazard.

RESTAURATION DE " LA HAIE: PAYSAGE DES ENVIRONS D'ARLES "
DE VAN GOGH
Sommaire

Il s'agissait de solidifier un tableau de van Gogh, dont la peinture s'était détachée de la toile en plusieurs endroits. Il fallait le saturer d'un mélange de cire et de résine. D'habitude cela se fait au moyen d'un fer à repasser.

Dans ce cas on s'est servi d'une table chauffée pour éviter le repassage des empâtements extrêmement hauts et fragiles. Pour la pression nécessaire des brosses suffisaient. On pouvait les employer directement sur la peinture sans aucune protection.

Quoique la peinture fût très vulnérable des circonstances favorables permettaient de la nettoyer sans causer de dégâts. Le solvant qui servait pour enlever le surplus de cire enlevait en même temps, sans aucune friction, presque toute la crasse de la surface.

5. EXPERIENCES WITH THE ARTIFICIAL LIGHTING OF PAINTINGS[1]

by HELMUT RUHEMANN

After studying the scientific articles by Crawford and Thomson in this issue, the reader might like to hear in contrast a restorer's point of view. The problem of artificial lighting is becoming more urgent every day. Many offices, workshops, shops, and picture galleries all over the world have little or no daylight. It is

[1] Reprinted from *Studies in Conservation*, VI (1961), pp. 83–5.

Appendix D

obvious that the pictures and the public must get the appropriate lighting.[1] But are such subtleties of colour as the two authors discuss really important? Does it really matter so much that a picture appears a little yellower or a little colder? Let me answer this question with a few examples from my experience.

During forty years of picture restoration I have done little else but 'colour matching', often under inadequate artificial light. In about 1945 I learnt from one of the managers of G.E.C. that new fluorescent lamps were being developed which would render daylight correctly. I felt relieved, and since then I have been eagerly following the steady improvement of fluorescent lamps. When the English 'Northlight' and 'Colour Matching' (high colour temperature) lamps appeared, the problem seemed almost to be solved. Very soon the National Gallery, London, and other galleries in other countries had installed these or similar fluorescent tubes. When, during a dark spell, this illumination was switched on to supplement daylight, it would pass unnoticed. The lighting in the first of the new rooms at the National Gallery came from Colour Matching fluorescent tubes supplemented with a small proportion of tungsten filament lamps to add a little warmth. All the details are to be found in Messrs. W. E. Rawson Bottom's and J. B. Harris's extremely useful article, 'Artificial Lighting as Applied to Museums and Art Galleries' (*Trans. Illuminating Engineering Society*, 23, no. 1 (1958)). I regarded all this as a success of historical importance. Unhappily, things have not gone right since then.

In 1952, after the New York Metropolitan Museum had installed a new lighting system in the picture galleries, I saw there one of the finest Cézanne exhibitions ever to be brought together. The great impression I had anticipated never materialized. Only after some time did I realize the cause of my disappointment: spotlights of a warm sunset hue illuminated the pictures. They killed the delicate blues and cool greens so characteristic of Cézanne and thereby robbed the paintings of much of their distinction. After a brief and friendly argument, the Director in charge of the pictures agreed with my criticism of the lighting. But has it been changed since then? One is naturally reluctant to spend another large sum for a new installation while experiments are still in progress — as they always will be.

My experience at the Metropolitan repeated itself almost exactly at the Tate Gallery exhibition of the Whitney Collection. Three friends of mine, sensitive connoisseurs, were like myself disappointed that the famous pictures left them unmoved, and agreed that the lighting was to blame. In this case, warm fluorescent lamps of a sulphurous hue had turned the Impressionists' subtle blues to an

[1] About the harmful effect of the Ultra-Violet in artificial lighting see *Conservation*, VI, No. 2–3 (1961), pp. 49–70. [See Bibliography, *Section 22* (30).]

inky hue, and had slightly distorted many other colours. The pictures looked curiously jaundiced, like some colour reproductions.

Such lighting still lingers in a few rooms at the National Gallery, London, where, for instance, a hand of Rembrandt's 'Margareta Trip', as colourful as a Monet in real daylight, appears almost monochrome brown under the inferior fluorescent light. In the 'English' room a grim gale scene by Turner is made pleasant and gay by one of those sunset-coloured floodlights, which moreover illuminate large pictures unevenly.

Another most telling illustration of my argument is one of Pissarro's master-pieces, 'The Louvre in Snow', at the Tate Gallery. This I admire and love particularly because it fulfils, to a higher degree than any other picture I know, the Impressionists' great aim of *la juste nuance* (the precise hue). It is therefore an ideal test case for our purpose. I had known the picture, still comparatively fresh and clear, in Paris, and was for many years distressed to see much of its unique subtlety disappear under a yellowing varnish and accumulating dirt at the Tate Gallery. At last, it was beautifully cleaned by Stefan Slabczynski, and all its delicacy and brilliance were recovered unimpaired. And now the artificial light-ing has nullified Slabczynski's efforts. This and other great Impressionist paintings have had their vitality sadly impaired by fluorescent lighting of inferior colour rendering.

Why all this confusion, when almost perfectly satisfactory lighting is available? What happened may often have been something like this. Viewing the new 'cool' fluorescent lamps, many people must have said 'This is good. But is it not a little too cool?' For it is certainly true that a cool artificial light appears un-pleasant if it is much less strong than its natural counterpart. Manufacturers obligingly supplied, from their large ranges, warmer lamps, but with less good colour-rendering characteristics. The colour-rendering properties of illuminants have not until recently been closely examined, either by scientists or conservators. Thus the use in museums of warmer tubes (lamps of a colour temperature of around 2800–4000° K.) gained in popularity. In England these are often called 'white' or 'warm white' — though they are far from it.

I am happy to see that Dr. Crawford has, with his painstaking tests, confirmed that the cool fluorescent lamps are very much better at colour rendering than the warm ones.

The other method of making fluorescent light warmer by the addition of tungsten lamps frequently seems to lead to unpleasant results. I would have preferred that Dr. Crawford had not made any recommendations for this kind of thing, since the haphazard mixing of fluorescent and tungsten lamps seems to be spreading like an epidemic.

346

Appendix D

Though Dr. Crawford's results reinforce the opinions of colour-conscious conservators, many of us who attended his tests at the National Gallery and the Victoria and Albert Museum felt that his method did not allow us to use our discrimination in the happiest way. What I would like to see is a method whereby a painting can be seen under two kinds of light simultaneously, in the same way that half of a painting can be cleaned of a discoloured varnish, though I realize that adaptation of the eye must be allowed for. Yet however much time is allowed for adaptation, the nuances of a Pissarro or Sisley, the sparkle of a Renoir, the mother-of-pearl charm of a Rubens never return under a faulty light. The danger is that the public may become so used to deficient lighting that they may forget or never become aware of these subtler pleasures.

Four centuries of darkened varnish, several decades of the black-and-white photograph, and the very variable success of the colour print may have induced a kind of colour-blindness. The successes of the Impressionists and of the later campaign for the removal of discoloured varnish are both in danger of being partly nullified by inferior lighting. For a dark varnish distorts just one picture, but bad lighting affects a whole room. It is the task of the scientists and lighting consultants to advocate nothing but the best available, and to scorn compromises such as mixtures and lamps of poor colour rendering. Most galleries would gladly accept such advice, once the advantages had been explained.

Perhaps a standing committee, composed of a curator, a lighting engineer, a scientist, an architect, and a restorer, all with special experience in lighting, could be formed to prepare a pamphlet or series of pamphlets for the guidance of museums.

In summary of my own views, I do not advocate any but the coolest types of fluorescent lamps (such as the U.K. Northlight or Colour Matching). Lamps of intermediate colour temperature (about 4200° K.)[1] may be even better in certain circumstances, provided they are in the top rank for colour rendering. The Philips 34 (3700° K.) seems to be the most successful in this warmer category. It is now being installed in several London museums and galleries. In my opinion the warmest kind of lamps, especially the warm fluorescent lamps (below 3700° K.), but also tungsten itself, are not good enough for particularly subtle masterpieces of colourism.

EXPÉRIENCES AVEC L'ÉCLAIRAGE ARTIFICIEL DES PEINTURES
Résumé

L'article exprime le point de vue d'un restaurateur concernant les propriétés

[1] For retouching and for especially delicate cases I recommend the 'whitest' light e.g. Atlas Northlight 6300° K. colour temperature.

du rendu des couleurs au moyen des sources de lumière artificielle. Il trouve que certaines lampes à incandescence falsifient les couleurs de beaucoup de tableaux, parce qu'elles amortissent les bleus et d'autres variations délicates de couleurs. Il mentionne comme exemple certaines peintures de Cézanne et de Pissarro. Les tubes fluorescents qui possèdent un bon rendu des couleurs sont recommandés quand la lumière artificielle est nécessaire.

6. THE MASTERS' METHODS AND COLOUR REPRODUCTION[1]

Address to Process Engravers Club by H. RUHEMANN

On the whole the quality of colour reproduction, in all the different processes from letterpress to collotype, has lately improved so rapidly in Britain that it seems fast approaching perfection. This is not only gratifying but immensely important, because the colour printers' task is becoming as relevant to the life of mankind as wireless broadcasting.

Mr. H. Ruhemann, consultant restorer to the National Gallery and lecturer-in-charge of the Technology Department, Courtauld Institute of Art, London University, gave a talk on 'The Masters' Methods and Colour Reproduction' at the monthly dinner meeting of the Process Engravers Club on March 29th at the Cafe Royal, London. Mr. Leslie Holt, president, presided. Mr. Ruhemann illustrated his main points with excellent Ektachrome slides showing details of paintings by famous old and modern masters; a few of these slides also showed paintings which he had made himself to illustrate the methods used by the masters. We are publishing the bulk of Mr. Ruhemann's address, but unfortunately it is not possible to reproduce the pictures he described. From his clear description, however, readers will have little difficulty in following the substance of the talk. Mr. Ruhemann said:

PROCESS ENGRAVERS' PATIENCE

'During my contact with process engravers in the production of my book *The Artist at Work* (which Penguin Books are soon bringing out) I was much impressed with the immense care and patience they devote to their work. This applies both to the heads of firms and the engravers or etchers. At first I thought the quality attained depended on the individual firm or their retouchers, but eventually all the different firms working for the book achieved equally admirable results — if one only made clear what one wanted brought out and if they were not too much hampered by considerations of time and costs.

[1] Reprinted from *The British and Colonial Printer*, CXLVIII (London, 1951), pp. 542–3, 546.

'I am afraid my experience is not only brief but also limited to the field of so-called "fine art". Nevertheless I hope some of the points I am going to make may hold good as well for the much wider and therefore in a way more important field of commercial art reproduction.

'As you all know, nature is so rich and manifold that no painter can render all her aspects, such as form, colour, tone and atmosphere at the same time. He cannot hope to give the "total visual effect". He must select those facets of the visual world that delight him most and must omit others.

'Then again there is so much in the painting of a great master that the person who sees it can never take in everything at the same time. He too has to choose and to sacrifice.

'More so still the colour printer. He knows only too well how little chance he has of ever reproducing exactly everything there is in a painting. He has to leave out all that he cannot hope to render with his limited process. But he must strive to give all the important aspects of a painting. Now, what is important? I shall try and show what I myself find important in some masters' work. But the decision of what to stress and what to neglect will of course depend much on the purpose for which a picture is being reproduced. For instance in my book I wanted to underline some of the different artists' characteristics which are mentioned in the text.

'Incidentally, I shall be frequently using the technical terms "warm" and "cool", which simply mean yellowish or orangey on the one side and blueish on the other.

RUBENS' FLESH TONES

'Here is my first example, an allegory by Rubens with several female nudes. You could never reproduce this successfully if you overlooked the subtle cool middle tones, which can get lost so easily and yet are the essential thing that makes Rubens' flesh paint superior to that of any other painter. He often creates them in a most ingenious way, not by admixing greyer or bluer pigment to his flesh colour, but by exploiting this phenomenon: if you have a canvas or a panel, white on one half and dark brown on the other and then paint plain flesh colour evenly over both halves the paint will look warm over the white and cool over the dark; orange pink on one side, where the light from the white ground shows through, blueish pink where the dark tone of the brown ground shows through.

IMPORTANT OPTICAL LAW

'This is due to a little-known optical law of great importance in painting. I shall illustrate it by an experiment: a small pack of white tissue paper is held over the lens of the projection lantern. Every sheet of paper is a little shorter than the one underneath so that the light shines through thicknesses gradually increasing from the top to the bottom.

'The effect is striking : the light appears white at the top, yellow a little lower down, then orange and eventually deep red; this is exactly what happens to the sun : it is made to look red by something like the tissue paper, something semi-transparent, translucent, misty : the turbid atmosphere that surrounds the earth. When you see the sun high up in the sky it shines perpendicularly through a comparatively thin layer of atmosphere but in going down it has to pass at an increasingly oblique angle through more and more turbid atmosphere, which just like the thickest part of the tissue paper pad on the lantern, eventually makes the white light appear deep red.

'This is explained by that important optical law I mentioned. It says : "Light seen through a turbid medium appears warm; darkness seen through a turbid medium appears cool". An instance of this other side of the law are distant woods that appear blueish; in the same way the dark red veins in our hands are made to look blue through the turbid medium of the skin.

LIGHT AND DARKNESS

'Most paint is an excellent turbid medium — it is rarely quite opaque. You will now believe me if I tell you that Rubens conjured up those peculiar blue middle-tones, without really painting them, just by making light and darkness mingle, as in nature; the light of his light flesh paint and the darkness of a brown monochrome under-modelling which he painted underneath.

'Unfortunately the colour engraver cannot proceed in the same way with his inks, but as soon as he knows that he has to look out for it he can arrive at a very near approximation of this important effect which plays a great part in the paintings of the great colourists of all ages. As I can show you by many examples of pictures by ancient and modern masters they did not model their figures and objects just with darker paint of the same hue, but almost consistently observed an alternation of cool highlights, warm general light, cool middle tones and warm shadows. Once this is clearly understood, colour reproductions need no longer be impaired by faces that are equally pink all over or garments that have no variation in hue, but only in degree of darkness. By a deliberate accentuation of warmth or coolness in the right place the printer can simulate much of the intricate effects of the painting.

TRICK OF THE 'PRIMITIVES'

'The early Italian masters, called 'Primitives', obtained in their flesh parts a similar variegation (that is a modulation in hue of one given field of colour) by a different trick which is anything but primitive. It is, in fact, the most scientific device ever invented in painting.

'I am showing a detail from an early 16th century work which fortunately, some 19th century predecessor of mine seems to have overcleaned, so that you can now see how the master — like most painters in Italy from the 12th to the 16th century — under-painted the flesh with green. The pure pink of the upper paint is neutralized to a reasonable half tone where the green which is the opposite or complementary of the pink shines through the thinning strokes, and a far less muddy effect is achieved than could be got by admixture of black or brown. The shadows are, just as in the Rubens, painted on top with a transparent brown.

EQUIVALENT OF THE KEY PLATE

'You will have realized how closely this sequence of translucent layers resembles your printing methods. My slide of a reconstruction I painted after a Botticelli shows the brown undermodelling which establishes the form everywhere on the picture, before the colour is put on in a separate stage; this kind of separate monochrome form stage was a widespread practice among old masters and your equivalent of it, the key plate, is still in general use. This slide also shows how the colours of the garment are variegated in subtle ways, the greens by letting the brown underpaint shine through in places, the blues, by under-painting them in green, which is irregularly covered, etc.

'In this original there are about six different pinks, each "built up" in a different way; one of them was done by scumbling plain white over a dry vermilion, another by underpainting with red ochre and scumbling white and black in different shades and thicknesses over it. This deliberate irregularity which gives the colours their character and charm might be easily taken for a flaw by an inexperienced etcher who might be tempted to reduce them instead of carefully stressing them.

MOTTLED OR 'SHOT' EFFECTS

'This insistence on giving pulsating life, character and richness to, say, a sky or a garment by mottled or "shot" effects goes through all periods; Bellini, Titian, Renoir, Van Gogh, Cézanne and Rouault are only a few examples, where uniformity in one field of colour must be avoided in a good reproduction.

'Modern colour printing has achieved miracles in rendering the different textures of the various painting media, such as watercolour, pastel, tempera and oil. As you know oil paint was introduced into fine "easel" painting by the Van Eycks in about 1420. I am showing slides of the hands from one and the same early 16th century painting, one of them executed in the earlier egg tempera technique, the other in oil. A good colour etcher can easily bring out these delicate but important differences — if his attention is drawn to them. The tempera hand is harder, more linear and painted in separate streaks, the oil hand is softer, rounder, smoothly merged, more naturalistic, but has less style than the other one.

'A detail from a Van Eyck shows still more clearly the smoothness and softness of modelling which this refined oil technique had made possible; it also shows how delicately the flesh colour alternates between warm and cool tones. Van Eyck, like most masters, achieves the cool tones partly by the turbid medium effect, partly by actual mixing.

BOSCH ASSERTS PERSONALITY

'Hieronymus Bosch (1460–1516) paints his very blue-green half tones by admixture of blue. He is one of the first to give up the smooth handling of the earlier masters, which was probably an expression of their objective and self effacing attitude — they effaced every stroke of their brush — whereas Bosch asserts his vigorous personality and deliberately leaves the traces of a most expressive "handwriting" crisp and unblurred.

'Vermeer (17th century), much like the Italian "primitives" uses a grey green underpaint for the flesh portions; Goya (around 1800) a grey one; the strongly magnified slide shows grains here and there, which again could easily be taken for flaws, but Goya purposely left coarsely ground white in his paint in order to render the porousness of the skin. Tiepolo and Guardi (18th century) use coarse grain paint everywhere, probably to help them give the illusion of atmosphere. They have another peculiarity; they first paint everything softly and finish off with black lines. Dufy, the contemporary French master, also first paints broadly, often carrying the "local colour" of things beyond their confines, and then he defines them again with drawn details and outlines not in black but in the different colours of the objects themselves.

IMPRESSIONISTS AND POST-IMPRESSIONISTS

'The linear style of an Italian primitive like Paolo di Giovanni will come naturally to an etcher used to commercial designs but if he got too much precision and hardness in retouching a block of an "impressionist" he would spoil the main point of the painting. The impressionists, like Turner, strove to render sparkling light and colour, and atmospheric softness at the expense of form.

'Some Post-impressionist masters such as Bonnard and Chagall have a kind of powder puff softness in their touches which must not be lost in the etching. It often proves impossible to reproduce the luminosity of an impressionist and other modern paintings unless the black or grey key block is discarded. On the other hand nothing could be more mistaken than to over emphasize the strong colours of a modern painting to the point of vulgarity, as is so often done in cheap prints. If for instance the strength of the hues were stressed in reproducing this view of the Mont Blanc by Kokoschka at the expense of the extremely delicate and precise reduction of saturation, the main theme of this picture, the uncanny and menacing aspect of the glaciers, even in sunshine, would be missed.

LIGHTING FOR TEXTURE EFFECTS

'To render actual texture effects, the skilled colour separation photographer will of course use an extra light at a suitable angle, for instance to make the tooled gold background in an early altar-painting sparkle and tell in the reproduction.

'For a Chardin a particularly sharp angle of lighting is needed to bring out the subtle rough touch with which — as one of the first — he imitates the iridescence of the atmosphere.

'In photographing extreme "impasto" (thick brushwork) in, say, a Rembrandt or a Van Gogh, it is imperative to have the light falling onto the painting from the same side and angle as the master had it in painting the picture. Another most important thing is not to print the shadows cast by the ridges of paint too black, but rather in a faint purple. I know an otherwise superb reproduction which was much impaired by not observing these two points.

FAST APPROACHING PERFECTION

'However, on the whole the quality of colour reproduction, in all the different processes from letterpress to collotype, has lately improved so rapidly in this country that it seems fast approaching perfection. This is not only gratifying but immensely important, because the colour printer's task is now becoming about as relevant to the life of mankind as wireless broadcasting.'

At the end of the talk the audience were asked to make suggestions for possible improvements in colour printing and in fact several interesting points were raised in the discussion.

USE OF STANDARD INKS

Mr. Ruhemann was asked whether he thought that the adoption of the British Standards Institution of standard letterpress three- and four-coloured inks was a wise one.

He replied that on the whole he thought it was, and that for his book amazingly accurate results were obtained with standard inks, but in two or three cases of larger reproductions which he had come across, certain pure carmine hues did come out far too weak or too purple because the standard magenta ink was used; or a special light blue or a greener hue of yellow had to be introduced as extra blocks.

Mr. Leslie Holt defended the standard inks very convincingly.

WHEN ETCHER DOES NOT SEE ORIGINAL

Mr. Ruhemann pointed out that he had several times found colours beautifully matched, but covering either too large or too small an area. He believed that it was because small *colour transparencies* had to be used as a guide by the etcher instead of the original painting, and it was impossible to see the extent of a colour patch accurately in a small scale reduction. As a remedy he suggested the introduction of small enlarging projection lanterns with a standard cool daylight lamp. Another speaker suggested that the galleries should be urged to allow more colour reproduction work to be done on their premises.

During the discussion Mr. Ruhemann asked if the following regrettable kind of experience was unavoidable in future:

At the National Gallery a colour print of an important picture during cleaning was needed. One of the leading firms undertook the job. First a photographer came, then a colour separation photographer, thirdly an etcher who had never seen the picture came with pulls, then another foreman etcher who was new to the job with more pulls (which were hopelessly inaccurate) and finally, after months, the first man let them know that they had to give up. Could not at least the etcher see the picture always *before* he started the retouching, if the picture was in London?

SUBTLETIES HIDDEN BY VARNISHES

When one member of the Club asked why he wasn't taught all that the lecturer had said and showed, 30 years ago, Mr. Holt replied that one of the reasons was that the subtleties mentioned were until recently hidden by dark yellow varnishes. Mr. Ruhemann agreed and said colour printers could do a lot by suggesting that dirty pictures they were asked to reproduce should first be cleaned.

Mr. Cartwright (of Bolt Court) said that some elementary optics were taught in his school, but nothing quite like the refinements Mr. Ruhemann had pointed out. It was agreed that this kind of information would be beneficial for both staff and etchers.

7. BOOK REVIEW[1]

by H. RUHEMANN

MAX DOERNER, *Malmaterial und seine Behandlung im Bilde*, Munich, 1922, and *The Materials of the Artist and their Use in Painting*, London, 1955. G. Harrap & Co. Ltd.

In a period of decline, Professor Doerner rekindled painters' interest in sound craftsmanship, and his book is still widely regarded as the standard treatise on artists' materials and methods. In 1955, an English edition entitled *The Materials of the Artist and their Use in Painting* was published by G. Harrap & Co. Ltd, London. Of this I am reviewing those passages which directly or indirectly bear on picture cleaning and restoring. Those concerning the techniques of the masters will be discussed in my projected book on 'The Masters' Methods and the Forgers' Devices'.

The more recent German editions revised by Professor Toni Rothe after Doerner's death contain valuable amendments and additions (e.g. warnings against over-rating Pettenkofer's regenerating method and against the use of copaiva balsam for restoring and as a paint ingredient), but, unfortunately, he sometimes further complicates the already complicated and lengthy original, and it is not always clear where Rothe's extensive additions begin and end. (See also G. L. Stout's review of Doerner's book in *Technical Studies*, 4 (1935), pp. 44–50.)

Doerner's chapters on materials and methods, which form the bulk of the book, are full of very valuable advice and recipes for painters. However, these last forty years have yielded enough new experience to make a new annotated edition desirable, considering the continued popularity of the book.

It is tragic that the same great teacher who strove to reintroduce lasting and luminous painting techniques, must be blamed for the fact that museums of modern art are now full of unsound and darkened paintings which cannot be brightened by cleaning because they are painted with large proportions of natural resins or balsams (mastic, dammar, Venetian turpentine, etc.), which Doerner recommended, not knowing that they darken as much as oil or more, and are less durable. He, like almost every expert of his time, believed that all or most of the brown that stained the cleaning swabs of restorers who tried to remove the varnish from, say, a Rembrandt, was original paint. He correctly argued that pure oil paint would not come off so easily and, taking the brown varnish in the swabs for original paint, drew the wrong conclusion : that Rembrandt painted with a great deal of soft resin. Consequently, Doerner encouraged young painters to use as a

[1] Reprinted from *Studies in Conservation*, IX (1964), pp. 170–2.

painting medium mastic or dammar and Venetian turpentine *with oil as an addition* (these are the original words in the German edition).

The story he tells on p. 377 of a Rembrandt painting (of which the authenticity had been doubted) that was destroyed by cleaning trials is possibly true (though it seems more likely to me that the picture was a fake), but the conclusion he draws is utterly false. Doerner: 'The resin and balsam he [Rembrandt] and his school use are precisely the kind which dissolve rapidly in alcohol.' The old masters either did not use these ingredients at all, or else such small proportions of them that in their combination with drying oil they have become sufficiently hard with time to be insoluble even in undiluted alcohol or acetone. I have myself cleaned seven Rembrandts and witnessed four being cleaned, as well as several Rembrandt school pictures. If ever a Rembrandt were found where original paint 'comes off down to the ground' by cleaning tests with alcohol, it would certainly be an exception and would have to be carefully tested for authenticity by other means.

Doerner makes several categorical statements about Rembrandt's unmistakable and 'large' use of resins and writes: 'There is no colour easier to regenerate than just this resin paint. I have never seen a Rembrandt where anything but the varnish needed regenerating [but removal was always safer and indicated — H.R.], the paint itself showed no signs of decomposition except a marked craquelure here and there.' On p. 320 of the German edition of 1922, Doerner writes: '[Rembrandt's] self portrait in the Uffizi used to be covered with layers of varnish of a strong yellow which gave the picture an inexpressible charm and something mysterious [I am translating literally]. When after decades I saw the pictures again these charms had disappeared.' When I myself [H.R.] saw the Rembrandts at the Uffizi in 1958, they were still dark yellow, though they had only recently been semi-cleaned for an exhibition in Amsterdam. This error of Doerner's is all the more surprising since other remarks of his show that he was well aware of the deceptive effect of 'yellow varnishes' and (p. 360, English edition) that 'probably later-applied oil [!] varnishes may have given rise to the assertion that Rubens applied final yellow glazes over his shadows'. Again, on p. 404: 'The delusion that the old masters possessed a "gold tone" (which in reality was chiefly the result of yellowed varnishes containing oil!) enticed many restorers in the second half of the past century into creating such gold tones artificially with colours such as *stil de grain*, etc. Today these paintings appear hot and even burnt'; on p. 379: 'oil varnishes by browning or becoming opaque may ruin the effect of a painting in the worst possible manner.' All this is in contradiction to what Doerner had said on p. 325: 'All the varnishes had a warm reddish tone which gave a certain warmth to the relatively cool tempera pictures.' Later: 'coloured varnishes are often mentioned in early books on painting; their effect must have been that of a glaze.' The warm reddish tone showed only in the thick bottle;[1] not in the rubbed-in utterly thin application Cennini prescribed. To produce any appreciable yellowness or warmth the brown transparent oil or varnish would have to be floated on very thickly indeed. The fact that Doerner repeatedly blames the darkening of varnish on its oil content is significant. In the 1940s, I covered, for comparative tests, a panel with applications of most materials used in painting and restoring. The linseed oil samples were, after a few years, among the least yellowed. (That drying oils properly prepared and used yellow very little is now common knowledge.) The innumerable old masters' paintings doubtlessly painted (at least predominantly) with oil[2] which still show bright cool whites belie Doerner's recurring assertions that the paintings of Van Dyck, Rubens, Rembrandt, Vermeer and others would have darkened much more had they been painted predominantly with oil.

A further assessment of Doerner's chapters on the 'Techniques of the old Masters' (pp. 135 ff.) is reserved for my book on a similar topic, but I have to mention here briefly certain passages that have a close bearing on cleaning and restoration.

On p. 315: 'Thus the technique of the Florentines serves to illustrate the tempera technique; the technique of the Van Eycks, the *mixed technique*[3] a combination of, [or rather an alternation of] tempera and oil colours.' This is Doerner's main wrong guess, and has caused a great deal of confusion.

Doerner based his suppositions regarding the techniques of the masters chiefly on the methods he himself and his pupils used in their copies; when they obtained effects which they found similar to *the originals*, they concluded *that they had hit on the actual* material and process used by the master. Scientific methods of verification were, in Doerner's days, not sufficiently developed, and experience in cleaning very limited.

The copy test is naturally highly unreliable, if only because the imitation is rarely quite so close to the original as it may appear to the copyist. Doerner naively affirms that with his *Mischtechnik* the modern painter can achieve works 'equal in merit to those of the old masters'. One characteristic attribute of a very old painting, the glass-like transparency which oil paint only acquires with time, Doerner and his followers tried to imitate directly by admixture of increasing quantities of resin to their paint. The kind of transparency this produces is very different from the real thing and, after a few months, turns into an unpleasant

[1] Joyce Plesters, 'Dark Varnishes — Some Further Comments', *Burlington Magazine*, Vol. 104 (1962), p. 453.

[2] Coremans, Gettens and Thissen, 'La Technique des Primitifs Flamands', *Conservation*, I, No. 1, pp. 1–29 and pp. 145–61.

[3] On mixed technique, cf. G. L. Stout, 'One Aspect of the so-called Mischtechnik, *Technical Studies*, 7 (October 1938), No. 2, p. 59.

sliminess. As for the merit of luminosity and durability, when I examined at Munich in 1948 some of the copies made by Doerner's pupils, I was shocked to see how badly they had lasted.

Naturally the erroneous picture Doerner had formed of the method of 'Those early schools' (p. 339) prompted a false idea regarding the possibility of safe varnish removal. 'The white body (underpaint) was the basis which was merely coloured (*gefärbt* = tinted or dyed) in layers of pure shades. . . .' (I give a more literal translation from the German than in the English edition.) This was certainly not a widespread method. The colour layers are usually comparatively thick and contain a great deal of mixed ('not pure', p. 336) pigments. On p. 337 : 'At the very last (moment) tones as thin as a breath were spread over the glazes, for instance, white over lights to modify excessive warmth and other tones to strengthen dark accents or emphasize the form. . . . . These last technical refinements are naturally of a very delicate nature and are only very rarely seen today on old pictures.' This is one of Doerner's unsubstantiated guesses. The English edition adds : 'Being very susceptible to injury, they have frequently been lost in the process of restoration.' Many of Doerner's descriptions sound rather like the fumblings of an inexperienced copyist.[1] The only cases of actual paintings I know which correspond to this tinting method imagined by Doerner are Monticelli's (1829–1886). I have seen paintings by Monticelli where only isolated traces of colour had resisted cleaning. Everywhere else the plain grey and white underpaint had been laid bare. Monticelli's technique seems also to resemble the process Doerner vaguely ascribed to all old masters in general, and particularly to van Eyck, Dürer, Grünewald and Baldung Green in so far as he must have used soft resins for his colour glazes, for the reason that it has been found possible to remove them so easily and completely. Norman Brommelle tells me that, in cleaning paintings by Monticelli, he found the colour glazes exceptionally vulnerable.

Similar unfounded surmises recur repeatedly, e.g. on p. 364 where Doerner writes : 'It is obvious that there is Venice turpentine in Vermeer's paint. This is evident . . . also in the susceptibility of his paint to damage by inappropriate cleansing media'. Quite apart from the fact that all paintings are 'susceptible to damage by *inappropriate* cleansing media', would this not apply to a higher degree in Rubens's works which, according to Doerner, contain such large proportions of resins and Venice turpentine (the latter a balsam softer than solid resins) ? Tests on many of Rubens's paintings which I have cleaned proved that

[1] On p. 170 Doerner himself says : 'The attempt to create harmony by means of a final glaze gives the least satisfactory results.' . . . 'The dilettante in particular all too frequently confuses painting with tinting'; and on p. 204 : 'glazes, to repeat this once more, as a final effect spoil the picture.' All this contradicts what he says elsewhere in the book.

all his colours withstood very strong solvents such as undiluted alcohol or acetone as well as considerable heat.

Doerner's chapter on restoring in general contains sound traditional advice and a few very useful contributions, e.g. the use of kneading rubber for removing surface dirt from paintings; solvents in paste form made up with chalk, wax, or the like for softening stubborn repaint and — an important suggestion anticipating Cesare Brandi — retouching, correctly colour-matched, but made visible by hatching (p. 407). However, some obsolete or unsound advice must also be mentioned. The formula (p. 397) of a mixture for cleaning gold ground is rather dangerous. Turpentine or lavender oil with copaiva (which yellows considerably) or castor oil (which never dries) to combat blooming of varnishes has been made obsolete by wax finish. Modern varnishes have much less tendency to bloom than mastic, dammar or copal. On p. 403, for fixing loose paint, Doerner recommends 'ironing with dammar and wax and glue *until the iron is cold'*. This is very dangerous: one must never lift the iron (or rather the spatula used nowadays) when it has cooled below the melting point of the adhesive being used, otherwise there is a risk that the loose paint particles will stick to the spatula and be torn off. Instead of using the emulsion formula given it is preferable first to treat the flaking areas with some thin glue followed by wax if this is indicated. On p. 408 he says: 'Pure oil retouches afterwards change colour to a great extent. One can often observe such places on old paintings, from which one might be tempted to conclude that the restorer had been colour-blind, so black have bright tones often become.' Doerner rightly warns against pure oil as a retouching medium (p. 408); but he recommends instead a mixture which would darken even more: 'mastic or dammar varnish[1] 1 : 3 in turpentine and up to half the amount of fatty oil', pp. 406–10. As a retouching method he says; 'put one colour over another (in glazes) without resorting to mixing', believing erroneously that this is how most old masters worked. On the other hand he does not mention that reconstructions ought to be made in the same sequence of all the main layers found in the original. Of course, he never had a chance of studying these sequences seriously because in his time most pictures were still veiled by dirt and dark varnishes, otherwise he would not have made so many erroneous statements on the masters' methods, particularly those of Rembrandt and Rubens which he only half understood. To summarize briefly the main points:

Rembrandt did not paint over a *grisaille* with white highlights, and Rubens did not underpaint his transition tones with a blue-grey. The colour reproduction in the German edition of a copy made after a Rubens under Doerner's guidance bears little likeness to the real thing. None of the originals, after which his pupils'

[1] He probably meant resin.

copies (which I saw in Munich) were made, are done in *Mischtechnik*: 'painting with tempera into wet resin-oil paint' and repeating this in alternating layers; and if ever any old master used this not very sound and optically quite unsatisfactory method, it must have been a rare exception.

However, on p. 242, Doerner presents painters with an invaluable gift which makes up for all his small errors, an actual *mixing technique* of great practical use: he suggests mixing a thickly ground oil white (containing relatively little oil) with up to an equal volume of tempera white (white pigment ground in egg or casein or both). This mixed white can be used in the same way as pure oil paint and mixed with the other colours. It sets quickly and may be over-painted with impunity before it is quite dry. It will also yellow less than pure oil paint. Most of Martin Bloch's works were painted with this 'Misch-Weiss' and have lasted perfectly since the 1920s. It also gives a pleasant mat surface to the paintings.

BIBLIOGRAPHY

Notes on the Arrangement of the Bibliography

During the past fifty years the literature of conservation of works of art, like that of every technical subject, has grown at an astonishing rate. The mass of published material presents difficulties to a compiler of a bibliography. For easy reference the present bibliography has been divided under thirty-one separate subject headings.

A considerable amount of information, particularly in recent years, has appeared not in books but in periodicals, so that *Section 1* is a list of those journals and periodicals in which articles on picture conservation, restoration and examination most often occur. *Section 6* is a list of exhibitions relating to these same subjects and for which published catalogues exist; it is arranged alphabetically by place names. The 31 sections of the bibliography are listed on pp. 367–8. With the exception of *Sections 1* and *6*, they are each arranged *chronologically* under the subject heading of that particular section (though if in any particular section more than one work has been published in any one year, the several works are given in alphabetical order of author for that particular year). Within each of the sections (*Section 1, List of journals and periodicals*, excepted) the references are numbered. Hence any item can be referred to by the number of the section followed by the number of the particular item within that section, e.g. *10* (15) indicates the 15th reference in *Section 10, Treatment of panel supports*. This system of reference to the bibliography is used in the text and footnotes of the main part of the book and in the Index on pp. 482–508.

The above arrangement has the advantage that a reader who wishes to trace the development over the years of any particular aspect of picture conservation may do so by reading straight through from beginning to end the relevant section of the bibliography, whereas a reader seeking up-to-date developments in a particular field need only turn to the end of the section in question. The arrangement in chronological order under subject headings will also enable any reader who wishes to do so to bring the bibliography up to date as new works are published. A disadvantage of the arrangement is the inevitable difficulty in classifying some works according to subject matter since they may cover a number of the subjects listed in the various Sections of the bibliography. Some of the more important works may be found listed in more than one section and in addition a certain amount of cross-referencing has been given at the end of each section. It should be borne in mind when using the bibliography that some of the more substantial works listed in *Section 4, Works on, or containing sections on restoration, post 1900,* may include as full and valuable information on any particular topic, e.g. the treatment of canvas supports, as some of the articles in *Section 11* specifically on that subject. The same is true of *Section 27, Technical and scientific examination, general,* where there are to be found works on general scientific examination which contain valuable information on, say, application of X-radiography.

Although extensive, this bibliography cannot claim to be wholly comprehensive. Like the main text of the book it is limited to the subject of European easel paintings (i.e. pictures painted on panel or canvas), so that wall-paintings, water-colours, drawings and oriental painting are excluded. A small number of books on painting materials are included in so far as these have bearing on picture restoration, but the main volume of literature on artists' materials and techniques, together with that concerned with authentication and forgery, has been reserved for the bibliography of a second book by the author now in preparation. Another limitation of the bibliography is that it includes only those books and articles concerned with conservation and restoration of pictures or with the direct application of science and technology to the conservation or technical examination of paintings. Hence an article describing the behaviour of panel paintings with changes in atmospheric humidity will be included, but an article in a journal of wood technology describing the behaviour of wood as such with similar changes in atmospheric humidity will not be included. In fact the modern conservator may find much useful information in the literature of, for example, paint, wood, plastics, heating and ventilating technology, but this is beyond the scope of the present book and its bibliography. Fortunately, the technical and scientific literature is regularly abstracted in *Art and Archaeology Technical Abstracts*, the abstract journal of the International Institute for Conservation of Historic and Artistic Works (I.I.C.), for details of which see *Section 1*, p. 370.

A serious restriction in compiling this bibliography has been the language barrier. An attempt has been made to cover the relevant literature published in English, French, German and Italian, but that of our Dutch and Belgian colleagues (when published in Dutch or Flemish) has been under-represented, likewise the Scandinavian literature. The most serious omissions are of the Polish, Russian and Yugoslavian literature of conservation. Unfortunately full translations are rarely accessible to us. Short French summaries are sometimes given but it is not always easy to assess a written work from such a summary. Specific references to works

Bibliography

in these languages have been given only if a full translation was available or if either author or bibliographer was personally acquainted with the author in question or his role in conservation. Because of these linguistic limitations it has not been possible to include some books on restoration in the Russian language nor what appears to be a useful and interesting Polish journal of conservation, *Ochrona zabytków* (Cracow). But again, *Art and Archaeology Technical Abstracts* (see above) does provide abstracts of books and articles published in what are to us the less familiar languages.

In a limited sense this is a critical bibliography. For reasons of space full critical reviews could only be given for a few of the most important or the most controversial works. A few lines of critical appraisal had to suffice for many more, whilst the vast majority are merely cited by author and title. Where the title of a book or article does not seem to indicate adequately its content or scope a brief description has been added. The more important books or articles are reviewed by the author and are signed with his initials (H.R.). The remaining reviews and comments are those of the bibliographer who must take responsibility for the accuracy and completeness (or otherwise) of the entries. One or two instances occurred of books or articles which appeared from their reviews or abstracts to be of some importance but which, at the time, were not available to either author or bibliographer. These have been noted, and if possible the appropriate review or abstract cited. All the remaining works listed are those which over the years have seemed to either author or bibliographer to have contributed to our knowledge of the conservation, restoration or scientific examination of paintings, or, by arousing our critical faculty have stimulated our interest in the subject.

JOYCE PLESTERS

Scientific Department,
The National Gallery,
London W.C.1

Bibliography

LIST OF CONTENTS

Bibliography

Bibliography

List of Journals and Periodicals

It will be seen from the bibliography which follows that information about the conservation and restoration of paintings is scattered widely through periodical publications. There are and were, however, a few periodicals wholly or largely devoted to the subject of conservation (including that of paintings) and a few more which less often, but still fairly regularly include relevant articles. The following are the most important, and the current journals if regularly read will probably give a good idea of modern conservation and restoration and new developments:

A. JOURNALS WHICH HAVE NOW CEASED PUBLICATION

Mouseion (Bulletin de l'Office International des Musées), Paris. 1927–1946 inclusive, quarterly. Illus.

Mainly museology, but important early articles on conservation and restoration of paintings, including papers read at the Rome conference on picture restoration held in 1930. Its function is now taken over by *Museum* (see below).

Technical Studies in the Field of the Fine Arts. Published for the Fogg Art Museum, Harvard University. 1932–42 inclusive, quarterly. Illus.

Articles on conservation and restoration, scientific and technical examination and techniques of works of art and archaeology, including many important contributions on picture restoration. There are also abstracts of books and articles relating to these subjects.

Technische Mitteilungen für Malerei und Bildpflege (The journal of the Deutsche Gesellschaft für rationelle Malverfahren), Munich, 1886–1944 inclusive. Fortnightly.

Largely technical information for practising painters, but articles on the technique of the old masters, also probably the earliest periodical regularly to publish articles on restoration and technical examination of old paintings. It ceased publication in 1944 and was continued in 1955 as *Maltechnik* (see below). For further information as to contents see *Section 4 (2)*, p. 371.

B. CURRENT JOURNALS

Publications of the International Institute for Conservation of Historic and Artistic Works (I.I.C.) (see Appendix A, *Institutions*, pp. 286–7).

(i) *Studies in Conservation* Vol. I (1952)–Vol. III (1957–58) published twice yearly; Vol. IV (1959) onwards published quarterly. Illus.

Entirely devoted to the conservation, restoration, scientific and technical examination and research connected with historic and artistic works, including easel paintings. Articles are published in either English and French with French or English summary, and, in recent years, summaries in German and Italian. Book reviews. Many new developments in conservation are published in this journal.

Bibliography

(ii) *Art and Archaeology Technical Abstracts*. Vol. VI (1966) No. 1 onwards is published at the Institute of Fine Arts, New York University, for I.I.C. and with the collaboration of the two institutes. Previously, from Vol. I (1955) onwards these abstracts appeared as *I.I.C. Abstracts* and were published from the London office of I.I.C. Twice yearly.

The above abstracts are not merely of articles and books dealing directly with the subjects of conservation, restoration and technical examination, but cover the whole field of the technical literature concerned with, for example, paint, wood, textiles, synthetic resins, methods of analysis, lighting, air conditioning.

(iii) *I.I.C. News Letter*. Published twice yearly, Jan. 1960 onwards. General news of Institute activities and membership throughout the world, and occasional technical information about processes and materials of restoration, etc.

(iv) *Bulletin of the American Group, I.I.C.* Editorial Office (Editor R. L. Feller) : National Gallery of Art Research Project, Mellon Institute, Pittsburgh, Pa., U.S.A. Twice yearly.

American members of I.I.C. meet annually as a regional group of the Institute and publish this Bulletin which has general news of the group's activities but also a good many useful articles on topics relating to conservation and restoration.

(v) *United Kingdom Group, I.I.C. Reports* of meetings.

Members of I.I.C. in Great Britain have also formed a regional group which meets each month (except for the summer vacation). Mimeographed reports of lectures and discussions are circulated to members of the group, but are available to other I.I.C. members on request.

Some current foreign periodicals largely concerned with conservation and restoration of paintings.

Bollettino dell' Istituto Centrale del Restauro, Rome. Published at somewhat irregular intervals but generally appearing one or more times per year, by the Libreria dello Stato, Istituto Poligrafico dello Stato, Rome. Illus.

Reports of restoration and investigation carried out at the Istituto Centrale del Restauro in Rome. From time to time very detailed accounts of the investigation and restoration of major pictures appear. An interesting feature is that entitled 'Schede di Restauro', reporting on the various restorations of paintings currently carried out at the institute.

Bulletin de l'Institut Royal du Patrimoine Artistique, Brussels. Published for the Institut Royal du Patrimoine Artistique (Koninklijk Instituut voor Het Kunstpatrimonium), Brussels, at 1 Parc du Cinquantenaire, Brussels 4, Belgium. Annually from 1958 onwards. Illus.

Reports of restoration and research, a high proportion of which concerns easel paintings, carried out at the Institute. Frequently detailed and very valuable information is given concerning pictures of major importance.

Bulletin du Laboratoire du Musée du Louvre. Published at 38 Quai du Louvre, Paris 1er, annually from 1956 onwards. Illus.

Mainly confined to articles on the technical examination of works of art, in particular those physical methods, such as the use of special radiations, in which the laboratory of the Louvre specializes.

Intermuseum Conservation Association Bulletin, Oberlin, Ohio. A bulletin issued for members of the Intermuseum Conservation Association, the laboratory for which is at Oberlin, Ohio (for details see *Section 19*, 4). Although brief, these bulletins have some interesting and useful information. Once every two or three years, 1952 onwards.

Maltechnik. Published by Verlag Georg D. W. Callwey, Munich, quarterly, 1955 onwards. Illus.

This journal is really a continuation, modernized in format, of *Technische Mitteilungen für Malerei und Bildpflege* (see above), and like the latter is partly concerned with techniques and materials for contemporary painting, partly with restoration and study of technique of old masters. A special feature are the pages given over to answering readers' questions on technical matters.

Some journals of museology which from time to time contain articles relevant to picture restoration and conservation.

Museum. Published by UNESCO (United Nations Educational, Scientific and Cultural Organization), Place de Fontenoy, Paris 7ᵉ. Vol. I, 1945 onwards, quarterly. Illus.

Although mainly featuring museology in a general sense, this journal does from time to time publish important articles on air-conditioning and lighting, also reports of the ICOM sub-committee on the Care of Paintings (see Appendix A, p. 285). It is the successor to *Mouseion* (see above).

Museums Journal (formerly *The Museums Journal*). Published by the Museums Association, 87 Charlotte Street, London W.1. Monthly from 1901–1961 (Vols. I–LX), thereafter quarterly.

General museology, but some articles on lighting, air-conditioning, premises for restoration, etc. and the occasional article on picture restoration.

Museum News. Journal of the American Association of Museums, published by the American Association of Museums, 2306 Massachusetts Avenue, N.W., Washington 8, D.C., from 1921 onwards, monthly. Illus.

Mainly general museology, but since 1964 has also published some Technical Supplements which are of interest and use to the conservator of paintings.

Museumskunde. The journal of the Deutscher Museumsbund (German Museums Association). Published by Verlag Walter de Gruyter & Co., Berlin, twice-yearly. Illus.

General museology with the occasional article on aspects of picture conservation.

Journals of art-historical research.

As will be seen from the bibliography itself the occasional article on picture restoration is to be found in a number of periodicals devoted in general to the history of art. Of these, the following two have given appreciable attention to topics of picture cleaning and restoration and of technical examination:

Bollettino d'Arte. Published by the Libreria dello Stato, Istituto Poligraphico dello Stato, Rome. 1921 onwards (with a break between 1938 and 1948), quarterly. Illus.

Bibliography

The Burlington Magazine. Published by the Burlington Magazine Publications Limited, 258–268 Gray's Inn Road, London W.C.1. From 1903 onwards, monthly. Illus.

A. RESTORATION AND CONSERVATION

SECTION 2

History of Picture Restoration and Conservation

1849

(1) MERRIFIELD, Mary P. *Original treatises, dating from the XIIth to the XVIIIth centuries, on the arts of painting.* . . . London, 1849. In 2 volumes.

Although primarily of value for the history of technique of painting, as derived from early manuscript sources, Mrs. Merrifield's work has a great deal of material of interest to the restorer. Specifically concerned with the history of restoration is the translation of a manuscript by Sig. Giovanni O'Kelly Edwards on the history of the restoration of the public pictures at Venice. Signor Pietro Edwards, O'Kelly Edwards's father, was employed by the Venetian government to organize restoration of pictures in the public collections at Venice during the late 18th and early 19th centuries. Some details of the condition of pictures at that time and methods of restoration are given. Mrs. Merrifield's introduction and notes are also illuminating.

1910

(2) BREDIUS, A. 'Drie Schilders-restaurators in 1685 te Amsterdam' ('Three painter-restorers in 1685 in Amsterdam'). *Oud-Holland* (Amsterdam), XXVIII (1910), pp. 189–191.

Details of early Dutch restorers, their work, contracts, signatures, etc.

(3) STÜBEL, M. 'Gemälderestaurierung im 18 Jahrhundert' ('Picture restoration in the 18th century'). *Cicerone* (Leipzig), XVIII (1926), No. 4, pp. 122–135.

An interesting account of the history of picture restoration in Italy, France, England and Germany, with detailed information concerning restoration in Germany (particularly in the Dresden Gallery) in the late 18th and early 19th centuries. Unfortunately no precise literary references.

(4) BREDIUS, A. 'Hoe er vroeger reeds gecopieerd en gerestaureerd werd' ('How early works were copied and restored'). *Oud-Holland* (Amsterdam), XLVII (1930), pp. 157–158.

Information on Dutch restorers and copyists of the 17th century.

(5) JONI, I. F. *Le memorie di un pittore di quadri antichi, con alcune descrizioni sulla pittura a tempera e sul modo di fare invecchiare i dipinti e le dorature* (The memoirs of a

painter of old pictures, with some description of painting in tempera and the method of ageing paintings and gilding). Florence, c. 1931, pp. 284.

A rather sensationally written autobiographical account of scurrilous practices in forgeries and restorations. Of particular interest for indicating the type of maltreatment a picture may have undergone before entering a collection or being treated by a responsible restorer.

(6) RINNEBACH, Helmut. 'Gemälderestaurierung und ihre Geschichte' ('Picture restoration and its history'). *Technische Mitteilungen für Malerei* (Munich), LIII (1937).

(7) STÜBEL, Moritz. 'Gemälderestauration und ihre Geschichte' ('Picture restoration and its history'). *Museumskunde*, IX (1937), pp. 51–60.

A short history of restoration from the 16th century onwards and its relation to the art trade and connoisseurship, with a warning against overpainting.

1940

(8) VAN SCHENDEL, A. and MERTENS, H. H. 'De restauraties van Rembrandt's 'Nachtwacht' ('The restoration of Rembrandt's "Night Watch"'). *Oud-Holland* (Amsterdam), LXII (1947), pp. 1–52 (with English summary).

As well as giving an account of its most recent restoration, condition and treatment, the authors trace the history of the conservation and restoration of the picture.

(9) FRISON, E. 'Apotheker François Mathieu Verbert (1769–1854) en de restauratie de meesterwerken van de Vlaamse Schildershool te Antwerpen in 1816' ('Apothecary François Mathieu Verbert (1769–1854) and the restoration of masterpieces of the Flemish school of painting at Antwerp in 1816'). *Pharmaceutisch Tijdschrift voor Belgie*, 36ste Jaarang Nummer 4 (April 1959). See also 38ste Jaarang, Nummer 2 (February, 1961).

Biographical notes on the chemist-pharmacist Verbert who was entrusted with the repair and restoration of Flemish paintings which were returned from France in 1816.

1950

(10) BORELLI-VLAD, Licia. 'Restauro e restauratori di dipinti in Francia dal 1750 al 1860' ('Restoration and restorers of paintings in France from 1750 to 1860'). *Bollettino dell'Istituto del Restauro* (Rome), III–IV (1950), pp. 71–84.

This account includes the introduction of transfer techniques in France in the mid-18th century.

(11) CAGIONO de AZEVEDO, Michelangelo. 'Provvidenze del Senato Veneziano per le opere d'arte' ('The sponsoring of works of art by the Venetian Senate'). *Bollettino dell'Istituto Centrale del Restauro* (Rome), III–IV (1950), pp. 121–131.

The founding of a restoration workshop in Venice by P. Edwards at the end of the 18th century.

Bibliography

(12) MAROT, Pierre. 'Recherches sur les origines de la transposition de la peinture en France' ('Researches on the origins of transfer of paintings in France'). *Annales de l'Est*, Université, Faculté des Lettres, Nancy, France, 1950. 44 pp.

A history of transfer of paintings (from panel to canvas or from old canvas to new canvas), a process which appears to have originated in France in the 18th century.

(13) THOMSON, G. Scott. 'The restoration of the (fourth) Duke of Bedford's pictures (during the eighteenth century). *The Burlington Magazine*, XCII (1950), pp. 320–1.

Not a great deal of technical detail but some information as to prices, agreements, etc.

(14) *L'Agneau Mystique au Laboratoire — examen et traitement. Les Primitifs Flamands III. Contributions à l'étude des Primitifs Flamands* (The 'Mystic Lamb' in the laboratory — examination and treatment. Flemish Primitives III. Contributions to the Study of Flemish Primitives). De Sikkel, Antwerp, 1953. 130 pp.

In addition to a description of recent examination and treatment of the picture, the entire history of conservation, as far as it is known, is summarized, and photographs of some early overpaints and restorations are included.

(15) PROCACCI, Ugo. 'Di un scritto di Giovanni Bottari sulla conservazione e il restauro delle opere d'arte' ('A letter by Giovanni Bottari on the conservation and restoration of works of art'). *Bollettino dell'Istituto Centrale del Restauro* (Rome), XXIII–XXIV (1955), pp. 131–145.

The author discusses a letter written by Bottari as a preface to the reprint of 1730 of Borghini's 'Il Riposo' and compares it with passages in dialogues by Bottari which deal with the neglect and ill-treatment of old paintings. Interesting sidelights on early restoration.

(16) BROMMELLE, N. 'Material for a History of conservation.' *Studies in Conservation*, II (1956), pp. 176–188.

A description of restoration and conservation practice in the National Gallery, London, during the 19th century, particularly as revealed in the 1850 and 1853 reports of the Select Committees of Inquiry on the National Gallery appointed by the House of Commons (see *Section 3*, Nos. (44), (45)).

(17) BROMMELLE, N. S. 'Controversy in 1846.' *Museums Journal* (London), LVI (1957), pp. 257–262.

The controversy is that which raged over the cleaning of certain pictures in the National Gallery, London, in 1846. Of particular interest for comparison with more recent controversies on the same subject.

(18) PARS, H. H. (pseudonym of Hans Diebow and Hans Schwarz van Berle). *Pictures in peril*. Translated from the German by Katharine Talbot. Oxford University Press, London, 1957.

The various hazards to which pictures may be subjected — war, fire, mutilation, repainting, incompetent or dishonest restoration — are classified and illustrated by notable cases. An interesting but rather popularized account.

1960

(19) COREMANS, Paul. 'La recherche scientifique et la restauration des tableaux.'

Bibliography

('Scientific research and the restoration of pictures'). *Bulletin de l'Institut Royal du Patrimoine Artistique* (Brussels), IV (1961), pp. 109–116.

The author traces the influence of science on restoration of paintings from the early nineteenth century until the present day.

(20) 'La Descente de Croix de Rubens. Étude préalable au traitement' ('Rubens's "Descent from the Cross". A preliminary study before treatment'). *Bulletin de l'Institut Royal du Patrimoine Artistique* (Brussels), V (1962).

In this, the first of two issues of the Bulletin largely devoted to the recent restoration of the Rubens altarpiece from Antwerp Cathedral, there is a chronological account of the condition and past restorations of the altarpiece, compiled from archives by J. van den NIEUWENHUIZEN. It is interesting to note that there is a record of the altarpiece having been cleaned (though in what way and to what extent seems not to have been recorded) as early as 1623.

(21) MURARO, Michelangelo. 'Notes on traditional methods of cleaning pictures in Venice and Florence.' *The Burlington Magazine*, CIV (1962), pp. 475–477.

By means of extracts from contemporary documents in Venetian archives, the author illustrates the attitude to picture restoration in 18th and 19th century Venice, as well as its organization and practice. The period covered is that during which the restoration of pictures in state collections was in the charge of Signor Pietro Edwards. The author whets the appetite of his reader by producing short extracts from unpublished documents to which he has access. The only lengthy extracts from these sources so far published were those transcribed and translated by M. Merrifield (see No. (1) above) in her book of 1849.

(22) EMILE-MÂLE, Gilberte. 'Le séjour à Paris de 1794 à 1815 de célèbres tableaux de Rubens. Quelques documents inédits.' (The sojourn in Paris between 1794 and 1815 of celebrated pictures of Rubens. Some unpublished documents.'), VII (1964), pp. 153–171. *Bulletin de l'Institut Royal du Patrimoine Artistique* (Brussels).

Contains interesting material concerning 18th and early 19th century restoration and conservation, including references to names of particular restorers of that period.

(23) GUILLERME, J. *L'atelier du temps* (Time's studio). Publ. Hermann, Paris, 1964. 246 pp., illus.

This book classifies the types and causes of changes which may occur in paintings with the passage of time, e.g. physical decay, vandalism, accident, overpainting, deliberate alterations, incompetent or misguided restorations. The work seems to have been compiled entirely from literary sources rather than from personal observation of such changes by the author himself. In view of this limitation, it is to be regretted that the references and bibliography suffer from certain inaccuracies and inadequacies, particularly in view of the considerable interest of the subject matter covered.

(24) STOUT, George L. 'Thirty years of conservation in the arts.' *Studies in Conservation*, IX (1964), pp. 126–128.

A summary of remarks to the American Group of I.I.C. in New York, June 1963, outlining the development of conservation from the early 1930s up to the present day.

See also *Section 3* (14), (20), (25); *Section 4* (5).

Bibliography

Works on, or containing Sections on Restoration, pre-1900

Few works exist dating before the mid-nineteenth century which deal solely with restoration and conservation of paintings. Before that time information about restoring practice usually has to be sought in the odd chapter or paragraph included in handbooks on painting. The following are references which the present bibliographer has come across in random reading. The earliest sources are described in full not so much for their relative importance but because they are rare or inaccessible books. The earliest written sources are often only of interest to us as examples of malpractices in the past which may serve to explain the imperfect condition of many old master paintings. In view of some early descriptions of treatment it is only surprising that so many pictures have survived, often in good condition. Many later books have little more to commend them, but it is interesting to note, among the more progressive authors, the gradual dropping of dangerous and dishonest practices and the development of modern methods and viewpoints.

Of uncertain but possibly early date

(1) *The Mount Athos manuscript.*

This is a handbook of painting prepared by and for the guidance of the monks of the monastery of Mt. Athos. It is written in Greek and our knowledge of it comes mainly from an edition and French translation by A. Didron and P. Durand, published in Paris in 1845 as *Manuel d'Iconographie Chrétienne*. The content is reputed to date from as early as the 12th century, though Victor Hugo in his introduction to Didron and Durand's edition remarks that the manuscript from which they worked was in fact a copy no more than 300 years old. The present bibliographer finds difficulty in accepting that some of the contents, as given by Didron and Durand, for example some of the varnish recipes, can date from as early as the 12th century, but we are, of course, hindered in our assessment by lack of first-hand knowledge of the manuscript.

For what it is worth, there occurs on p. 43 of Didron and Durand's book a paragraph entitled 'Comment il faut nettoyer les vieilles images' ('How to clean old pictures'). The method described is to place the picture in, or rather over, a bath of water and pour onto its surface 'eau forte' (presumably nitric acid), aided by friction with a brush. At the required stage the action of the nitric acid is halted by submerging the picture in water. Needless to say, nitric acid would be capable of destroying entirely some components of paintings (e.g. a chalk ground, lead white and other pigments) and of damaging severely most others. It is not surprising therefore to find that the author of this passage, while claiming success with the method for some pictures, admits failure in the case of one painting, being left only with the bare panel! The recipes given for varnish are numerous and varied, including turpentine resin (rosin) dissolved in turpentine essence, sandarac in alcohol and sandarac in solvent naphtha, but directions and ingredients are by no means easy to interpret.

Bibliography

(2) *Paduan Manuscript*

This manuscript was transcribed and translated by M. MERRIFIELD in the mid-nineteenth century and is published in her book *Original treatises . . . on the arts of painting* (see *Section 2* (1), p. 372), Vol. II. pp. 643–720.

The manuscript was judged by Mrs. Merrifield to be late 16th century. On pp. 672–673 is to be found a section entitled 'How to wash old pictures previous to varnishing them.' The method described is to wash with black soap, 'alume di feccia' (probably tartar) or, rather inexplicably, 'that amalgam which is used for the backs of mirrors.' Afterwards revarnishing is to be carried out with a varnish of mastic resin dissolved in linseed or nut oil and spike oil (essential oil of lavender).

(3) SANDERSON, William. *Graphice*. London, 1658.

A general handbook on painting but on p. 86 is a paragraph headed 'To make clean a foul, or old Picture, in Oyle.' Warm beer applied with a sponge is recommended for cleaning, then the application of a solution of *Gum-dragon* (the present bibliographer interprets this as Gum tragacanth) to give a gloss and serve as a sort of varnish. The writer warns against the use of *blew starch* (by which is probably meant the blue ground-glass pigment smalt, which was used as laundry blue at the time, and as seen below was sometimes recommended as an abrasive for cleaning paintings), glare of eggs (i.e. white of egg, presumably as a varnish), 'or other such trash, as is very common, it will take off the *heightening* and spoil the grace of the work.' On p. 85 is given a recipe for a varnish of mastic dissolved in oil of spike.

(4) ANON. *The excellency of the pen and pencil*. London, 1662.

Included is a mention of the use of a mixture of wood ashes and water (equivalent to a solution of potash, a strong alkali), or of smalt (a blue pigment composed of ground glass) for cleaning. Both would have been likely to damage the picture. For revarnishing the use of gum-water, white of egg, 'common varnish' or 'distilled varnish' is recommended.

(5) SMITH, John. *The art of painting in oyl*. London, 1676, with several subsequent editions, the latest of 1723.

The edition available to us is that of 1687 and contains somewhat horrifying instructions to scour the picture with water and smalt (see above), remarking that this process should not be carried out too often since it 'must needs wear off a little of the Colours'. An awareness is shown of the tendency for oil paintings to yellow if kept in the dark and the possibility of reversing this change by exposing the picture for a time to sunlight.

(6) *The Volpato manuscript*.

This is another of the manuscripts transcribed and translated by M. MERRIFIELD, and published in her *Original treatises . . . on the arts of painting* (see *Section 2* (1), p. 372), Vol. II, pp. 721–758.

The manuscript is thought to be Venetian and late 17th century (post 1670). It is in the form of a dialogue between two painter's apprentices. On pp. 750–751 of M. Merrifield's transcription and translation, the junior of the apprentices remarks that his master has some pictures soiled by smoke and wishes him to wash them and he does not know how. The senior apprentice remarks that this must be a trick which the master wishes to play on a friend or patron because 'good pictures either never are washed or the owners perform this operation themselves' (!). He mentions, though, that pictures are easily spoiled by careless washing and has even seen pictures which after being washed have scaled off because the gesso beneath was affected by moisture. He then goes on to advise, however, that such pictures should be cleaned with a paste of water and fine wood ash (this would give an alkaline solution). The senior apprentice warns against rubbing oil into the surface of pictures, and also against the injurious effect of dust. Also mentioned is the practice, continued in Italy even in the late 19th century, of applying to the backs of flaking canvas paintings a preparation commonly known at a later date as 'beverone', or an oily mixture made of scrapings of palettes and pressings from dirty brushes boiled up with oil of turpentine, the purpose being to re-attach the flaking paint on the front of the picture. This preparation would be expected to discolour with age.

(7) d'EMERY. *Nouveau recueil de curiositez* (New collection of curiosities). Paris, 1688.

This is a small manual of practical information on almost every subject, with one chapter (Chapter XIV) on painting. P. 251 has instructions for washing old pictures and giving them a beautiful lustre. A drastic method for cleaning is given, namely rubbing with a warm solution of soda mixed with sand. A varnish is recommended based on Venice turpentine dissolved in essence of turpentine.

1700

(8) SALMON, William. *Polygraphice*. In 2 volumes. London, 1701.

Pp. 172–173 of Vol. I, Chap. XII: 'Of the cleansing of any old painting', suggests sponging with wood ash and water or with smalt (see comments above, Nos. (3), (5)). Revarnishing with either white of egg or 'common varnish' (sandarac in linseed oil) is described. Again awareness is shown of the bleaching by sunlight of oil paintings yellowed by being kept in the dark.

(9) WATIN, M. *L'Art du peintre, doreur et vernisseur* (The art of the painter, gilder and varnisher). 1st edition Paris 1744. New editions in French up to 1823, and German translations of 1784 and 1834.

The 4th edn. of 1785 was available to us. P. 105: 'Manière de nettoyer les tableaux', warns against the use of potash, abrasives, urine, etc. for cleaning, suggesting the moderate use of 'black soap' with water. Mastic varnish in turpentine is recommended for revarnishing, or egg white for newly-painted pictures. P. 250 gives a remarkably clear and enlightened definition of the requirements of a picture varnish, pointing out that such a varnish should be thin and colourless, its purpose being only to bring out the colours in the picture and conserve them, not to impart a colour of its own. Nor should it give such brilliance to the surface that the viewing of the subject matter of the picture is hindered. Varnishes with a tendency to discolouration should be avoided.

(10) ANON. *London Magazine*, April 1758, pp. 180–183.

This is a reprint of part of Dossie's *'The Handmaid to the Arts'* (see below, No. 11), 'for the Benefit of such of our Readers as may have an Inclination to clean their own pictures. . . .' Water is used for removing dirt and coatings of gum arabic, white of egg, honey etc., while olive oil and butter are dubious recommendations for the removal of patches and stains. Wood ashes are considered efficacious but dangerous. Spirits of wine (ethyl alcohol) is to be used for removal of resin varnishes, avoiding friction. This seems to be one of the first descriptions of picture cleaning in which removal of discoloured varnish is clearly distinguished from removal of surface dirt. A rather dangerous practice of flooding the whole picture with alcohol is described, then subsequently flooding with water to remove the alcohol and dissolved varnish. Essential oils, such as essence of lemon, are also mentioned as possible cleaning solvents.

(11) DOSSIE, R. *The handmaid to the arts*. In 2 volumes, London, 1758. Also editions of 1767 and 1796.

The reprint from Volume I on cleaning of paintings is given above (10). In Vol. II, Appendix, pp. 381–387 the transfer of paintings is described under the heading 'Method of taking off paintings in oil, from the cloths or wood on which they were originally done; and transferring them intire, and without damage to new pieces.' The operations described sound extremely dangerous. The picture is laid face downwards on paper (though not at this stage faced) and the reverse soaked with boiling water 'till it appears perfectly soft and pliable'. It is then turned over and the front faced with fine linen using glue as the adhesive. It is again placed face downwards, a raised border of wax formed round the edge to make a shallow trough, the bottom of which is the reverse of the canvas of the painting, and 'a proper corroding fluid', e.g. oil of vitriol (sulphuric acid), aquafortis (nitric acid) or spirit of salt (hydrochloric acid) poured in 'to eat and destroy the threads of the original canvas'. The acid is let out and the surface washed with water, the 'weakened' canvas threads then picked out. A new canvas is then laid on the back of the paint surface with hot glue and pressed with lead plates. The linen facing on the front of the picture is then to be removed by a similar use of acids, and the glue removed with hot water, after which the picture may be varnished. It is hardly necessary to say that the use of concentrated acids on a painting is likely to destroy a chalk or lead white ground as well as a number of other pigments and do serious damage besides. (Compare also No. (1) above). The manner described for the transfer of panel paintings is a little more in accordance with modern practice, the wood of the panel being planed off in the usual way, but the canvas facing applied to the front previous to this process is again removed with acid. The author remarks rather lightly '. . . in the case of pictures greatly decayed, or paintings on wood taken from buildings . . . there can be no great loss if a failure should happen'.

(12) MAUCLERC, M. *Traité des couleurs*. Paris, 1773.

Pp. 115–120 is a dissertation on the cleaning of paintings, but not in much practical detail. There is a brief description of relining. The desirability of a varnish which will neither darken nor crack is expressed. On pp. 93–95 there is noted a picture varnish composed of Venice turpentine, mastic and turpentine essence. The author remarks that though this varnish may yellow with time it is easy to remove. White of egg varnish is also mentioned.

(13) PILES, Roger de. *Élémens de peinture pratique. Nouvelle édition entièrement refondue, et augmentée considérablement par Charles-Antoine* JOMBERT (Elements of practical

painting. New edition entirely remodelled, and considerably enlarged by Charles-Antoine JOMBERT). Amsterdam, Leipzig, Paris, 1776.

Nominally derived from de Piles' *Les premiers éléments de la peinture pratique* of 1684, the text has been greatly modified. The section on pp. 171–179 dealing with cleaning and restoration appears to be the work of Jombert. Crude methods of 'brightening' and cleaning old pictures are described including the use of water, urine, soda and soap boiled together, abrasion with stiff brushes. The curious method of a compress of sorrel leaves also mentioned in No. (14) below also occurs. Rubbing with linseed oil after washing is recommended, though mastic varnish and white of egg beaten with wine are also listed as varnishes. An unusual type of varnish is a mixture of nut oil diluted with alcohol (the effect would be of applying an oil film to the painting, since the alcohol would evaporate in a comparatively short time).

(14) *Encyclopédie méthodique. Beaux-arts.* (Systematic encyclopoedia. Fine arts). In two volumes, 1791 and later editions.

The edition available to us was that of 1791. Entries concerning picture restoration are to be found under: *Nettoyer* (To clean). Under this heading there is a warning that cleaning of paintings must be done intelligently and with care. *Raccommoder* (To repair): The vast increase in the number of picture repairers at this time is remarked on and it is lamented that much of the work is bad or dishonest. *Restauration* (Restoration): the difficulty of well-matched retouchings subsequently changing is discussed, and the desirability of inpainting losses only, not overpainting. Puttying of losses is described. After cleaning and retouching, a new varnish which must be colourless and drying is applied, though varnish removal is a subject rather skirted round, the view seeming to be that usually washing with water before applying a new coat of varnish will suffice. There is some rudimentary but sensible advice on conservation, e.g. not to expose paintings to the sun, to smoke from candles or lamps, or place them close to stoves. Although there is some sense in the idea that fog is not good for pictures, the author is probably not wholly correct in saying that the sea air of Venice is responsible for darkening Venetian School pictures there. *Tableau*, nettoyage des tableaux (Picture. Cleaning of pictures): The main part of this entry lists the crude methods of cleaning already mentioned in earlier items of the present Bibliography, e.g. black soap, soda, potash, and an old method of rubbing the surface of the dirty picture with crushed leaves of sorrel (see (13) above). However, a further note, by M. Robin, does discuss the possibility of varnish removal using alcohol but more or less dismisses it as too dangerous, preferring surface cleaning followed by revarnishing. *Toile* (canvas): Relining is described in detail, including a preliminary facing of the front surface with paper. The relining adhesive is at this date glue. Ironing of the relining canvas is also mentioned. Mention is made at the same time of transfers from panel to canvas carried out in France earlier in the century by Hacquin and Picault. The transfers carried out by Picault of the Raphael 'S. Michael' and Andrea del Sarto's 'Charity' are cited as early examples of the process of which Picault is said to have been the inventor.

(15) ANON. *A compendium of colours and other materials used in the arts.* London, 1797.

A section on cleaning (involving the use of water, wood ashes, olive oil, butter and other unsuitable materials. Alcohol or turpentine is also suggested for varnish removal, but the idea of mixing the two seems not to have arisen. When a picture is covered with a varnish which does not yield to either alcohol or essential oils or water, then the use of ley (a solution of wood ashes) is resorted to. The method of flooding the picture surface first with alcohol then with water as described in No. (10) above is also included. The section entitled 'Of transferring pictures' is lifted bodily from Dossie's *The Handmaid of the Arts* (see above, No. (11)). A number of recipes for varnishes are given, some for use in painting media, others specifically for final surface coating. The latter include an innocuous mastic-in-turpentine varnish said to be recommended by the painter Mengs, another varnish consisting of what seems to be an inordinately large variety of different resins dissolved in alcohol, and it is also seen that copal/oil coach varnish was accepted as sometimes being used on paintings. From other parts of the book concerned with the practice of painting it can be seen that at this period, the late 18th century, soft resins seem often to have been incorporated in painting media, hence special care must be exercised in cleaning pictures of this period.

(16) HACKERT, Philipp. *Lettera sull'uso della vernice nella pittura* (A letter concerning the use of varnish in painting). Perugia, 1788. Also in German translation as: *Ueber den Gebrauch des Firniss in der Malerey*. Dresden, 1800.

In this small book the author, a landscape painter, puts forward the view that paintings must be properly protected with a coat of varnish from the effects of dust and atmosphere. He does not object to the cleaning of old pictures provided that proper revarnishing is carried out afterwards.

1800

(17) ANON. *The artist's assistant or school of science*. London, 1803.

The main item of note is 'Method and Process for Transferring Paintings' by Mr. Robert Salmon (pp. 151–160). For this invention he was apparently awarded the Great Silver Pallet by the Society for the Encouragement of Arts, Manufactures and Commerce in 1796. It is mainly a method for transfer of wall-paintings to canvas or panel but is also mentioned as of use for transfer from wood panel. A facing canvas then a facing board are first stuck to the front of the painting with paste. When the original support has been detached, and if necessary removed, a new canvas support is applied to the back with an adhesive of oil/copal varnish and lead white. The front facing is then removed. The process is, in essentials, similar to modern methods of transfer, though nowadays oil/copal/lead white adhesive would be unlikely to be used.

(18) TINGRY, P. F. *Traité théorique et pratique sur l'art de faire et appliquer les vernis* (Theoretical and practical treatise on the art of making and applying varnishes). Geneva, 1803. Translated into English and published as: *The painter's and varnisher's guide*, London, 1804.

Older and inadvisable methods, described in many of the works listed above, are repeated, for example flooding of the picture surface first with alcohol then with water. Olive oil and butter are suggested for removal of 'foreign bodies' and stains which resist the application of soap and water, also ether for removal of stubborn stains and ox-gall for cleaning off surface grime. Caution is advised in the use of alkalis. An innovation in this book is that of cleaning tests to be made in corners of the painting. White of egg is mentioned for a temporary varnish, while the recipe for 'Varnish No. IV. For valuable

Bibliography

paintings' consists of mastic in turpentine, with minor additions of frankincense and camphor (the latter presumably as a plasticizer). The same methods and recipes are repeated in later editions of the same work, and in the same author's *Painter's and Colour-man's Complete Guide* of 1830.

(19) IBBETSON, Julius Caesar. *An accidence or gamut of painting in oil and water colours.* London, 1803.

Written in rather a satirical vein, but on pp. 7–9 there is an interesting account of the malpractices of some picture restorers of the time (e.g. the method of cleaning the surface of a picture by rubbing with a brick and water). Recipes for mastic varnish and for drying oils are also included.

(20) MILLIN, A. L. *Dictionnaire des Beaux-arts.* Paris, 1806. In 3 volumes. See entry under 'Restaurer' (To restore), Vol. III, pp. 431–440.

The author is to a large extent concerned with restoration of monuments, but there are interesting sidelights on principles of restoration, and a favourable mention of picture restoration of the time, of Signor Pietro Edwards' responsibility for the restoration of paintings in Venice in the late 18th—early 19th century, and in Paris of a commission nominated by the Institut (and including the well-known scientists Berthollet and Guyton) to investigate projects for picture restoration. There is also an account of early transfers from panel to canvas effected by Hacquin in France in the 18th century. Not very many practical details.

(21) BURTIN, François-Xavier de Burtin. *Traité théorique et pratique des connoissances qui sont nécessaires à tout Amateur de Tableaux* (Theoretical and practical treatise of knowledge necessary to every patron of paintings). In 2 volumes, Paris, 1808.

The two volumes are concerned mainly with topics of connoisseurship, but Chapter XV, Vol. I deals with the different methods used for cleaning pictures and precautions to be taken in relining and restoration. The author urges the collector to learn how to clean and restore his pictures, in order to be able to keep them under his eye and on his own premises, so avoiding subjecting them to hazards of transport or treatment by dishonest or incompetent restorers. He is one of the first authors to point out that methods and materials used in cleaning pictures must be chosen according to the particular picture in question and its peculiar condition; what may be safe for one work may be dangerous for another. He then goes on to treat of cleaning according to the type of discolouration which has to be removed (this is excellent in theory, but in practice it is not, of course, usually known beforehand, or at any rate before cleaning tests have been carried out, what nature of discoloured film covers the picture). For ordinary mastic varnish, dry removal is recommended in the case of smooth-surfaced pictures but a mixture of alcohol and turpentine for removal by solvent when the dry method of rubbing is not possible. The possibility of varying the proportion of alcohol to turpentine according to the type of picture and the varnish film to be removed from it is discussed, perhaps for the first time in the literature, and it is mentioned that the solvent is to be applied by morsels of cotton or on smooth linen rags which must be changed as soon as they become charged with dissolved varnish. Late 18th—early 19th century taste creeps in with the proviso that the connoisseur must decide how much varnish to remove in any case, since the picture must not be rendered 'too cold and thin by the force of clarity'! Warning is given against the practice of rubbing drying oils into the surface of paintings since in time a crust of dried oil and dirt will build up. In the paragraphs concerning the removal of 'un mauvais vernis' (i.e. a wrong type of varnish), such as copal or amber varnish, from a painting, certain radical misconceptions occur, such as the conviction that if a material is soluble in a particular solvent at a certain time it will always remain soluble in that same solvent. (We now know that this is not the case with natural resins which undergo chemical changes with age and exposure which may entirely change their solubilities.) In the case of removal of water-soluble varnishes such as white of egg, or glue, the author's experience is that these are by no means as easy to remove or as harmless as they are generally supposed to be and would not recommend their use. For removal of smoke and surface dirt without removal of varnish, soap and alkalis are suggested and even the drastic remedy (included in the earlier works cited above) of rubbing the surface with fine sand. There is also a dissertation on the types of 'mildew' — or as we now term it, 'bloom' — which occur on the surface of paintings. The whole of the subject matter on conservation is a mixture of enlightened views and comparatively modern methods with some misconceptions and crude and incorrect practices. Although he includes the barbarous method of scrubbing with sand, cited above, the author produces the, for its time, very shrewd observation that glazes although they may *look* very transparent and delicate to the eye are often in fact not at all easily damaged, but he recommends close attention to the layer structure of the picture before cleaning is commenced. The process of relining is described with a warning not to use irons too hot, glue being, of course, the adhesive used at this time. An interesting list is given of prices charged in Paris for relining pictures of various sizes at the time. Chapter XVI (Vol. I, pp. 428–445) is on the varnishes which are employed on pictures and divides them into bad varnishes (including white of egg, fish-glue, oil, copal and amber, and all varnishes in alcohol solvent) and good varnishes (particularly mastic in turpentine or less costly oliban, also known as frankincense, in turpentine).

(22) Mazzares, Giuseppe. *Saggio pittorico* (An essay on painting). Trapani, 1825.

A brief essay, but in that it mentions by name Niccolò Franchini, a Sienese, as living in 1761 and being employed in the repair of canvases, replacement of paint losses, etc. is of some interest.

(23) Bouvier, Pierre Louis. *Manuel des jeunes artistes et amateurs en peinture* (Manual for young artists and amateur painters). Original French edition, Paris, 1827.

This handbook went into numerous editions and translations, some with supplements on restoration by co-authors. An English version was published in New York in 1845. The third edition, Paris, 1844, has a supplement by C. F. Prange: 'L'art de restaurer et de conserver les vieux tableaux.' There were five German editions and that of Leipzig of 1910, *Handbuch der Oelmalerei für Künstler und Kunstfreunde,* has an appendix 'Anhang über Conservierung, Regeneration und Restauration alter Gemälde' ('Appendix on the conservation, regeneration and restoration of old paintings) by A. Erhardt and is edited by E. Berger.

In general, varnish removal is effected by alcohol as a solvent. The method of dry removal by rubbing is not recommended for old paintings or weakened canvases. It is noted that varnish removal is only easy if the varnish is a resin/voltatile solvent type, not an oil/resin varnish. Mastic in turpentine is the generally accepted varnish. The 3rd French edition suggests that on matters of restoration F. X. de Burtin (see above,

No. (21)) should be consulted. (J.P.). In general the sections on restoration are vague and amateurish. (H.R.).

(24) KÖSTER, C. *Ueber Restauration alter Oelgemälde* (On the restoration of old oil paintings). Heidelberg, 1827.

A wordy period piece. The following extract may suffice to judge its quality: 'Since the restorer must at the same time be a painter, it will not be difficult for him by glazes to adjust those areas that have lost their patina (during the cleaning) to those parts which have kept their patina. . . . A restorer who is conscious of his capability as a painter may, in desparate cases, dare more than one who is not.' Köster does advocate the founding of a training institute for restorers. (H.R.).

(25) MONTABERT, J. de. *Traité complet de la peinture* (Complete treatise on painting). In 9 volumes. Paris, 1829.

Volume IX, Chapter 692, 'De l'art de nettoyer et réparer les peintures' ('The art of cleaning and repairing paintings'). The author remarks aptly that '. . . what forces one to remove varnishes and repaints and so almost constantly to torment the pictures' is largely 'the habit of varnishing with resins which yellow and the badly understood usage of retouching the damaged paintings with oil colours'. Like several authors of the late 18th and 19th centuries, de Montabert's despair with the discolouration of oil paintings with age had reached such a pitch that he advocates encaustic painting instead. He also recommends varnishing the surface of pictures with wax so that they may be washed with water without harm. He also believes that some types of wide cracks may have been caused by the bad habit of applying a temporary varnish (e.g. egg white) over the paint before it is thoroughly dry. Advice on transfer and relining (derived from Hacquin) and on cleaning (mainly quoted from Bouvier) are fairly sensible for the time. His formula for putty is based on whiting mixed with parchment glue and a little yolk of egg. He strongly discourages uneven cleaning of different parts of a painting, and observes: 'The taste, the ideas or the manner of the repairer must not appear at all.' (H.R.).

1830

(26) AN ARTIST. *Advice to proprietors on the care of valuable pictures*. London, 1835.

The practical advice on conservation and restoration is not very sound, but the booklet is interesting for the history of restoration and the condition of some old master paintings at the time.

(27) MÉRIMÉE, J. F. L. *De la peinture à l'huile* (Oil painting). Paris, 1830. Translated into English by W. B. Sarsfield Taylor, as *The art of Painting in oil*. London, 1839.

Chapter VI (of both editions): 'De la conservation des tableaux et de leur restauration' ('The conservation of pictures and their restoration'). In this chapter a certain amount of sound advice on conservation is given. There is warning not to expose pictures to sunlight for long periods since alterations may occur not only in the pigments but also in media and varnishes. The author strongly expresses the opinion that varnishes which have become yellow or lost their transparency ought to be removed, and this is quite easy to do because the only varnish usually encountered is mastic in turpentine (this observation is also true of present-day practice). He warns that if oil/copal

Bibliography

varnishes have to be removed care must be taken not to attack original glazes. The dry, abrasive method is again recommended for removing simple mastic varnishes. For removal with solvent a mixture of alcohol, distilled turpentine and oil (linseed oil?) is recommended; the last two ingredients presumably have the role of restrainer or diluent. He describes the use of alternate cotton wool swabs, one impregnated with alcohol, the other with oil, for alternate use in initiating and restraining solvent action. There is a discussion of the relining and transfer of canvas paintings (involving the careful preliminary facing of the fronts), a glue/flour-paste adhesive mixture being in use at this date. The transfer of wood-panel paintings to canvas (apparently introduced in the first half of the 18th century) is described, and the application of cradles to panel paintings, glued on but with movable horizontals. The rather old-fashioned mixture of white lead, red lead and drying oil as an adhesive in relining and transfer is mentioned. The dubious practice of 'nourishing' paint surfaces which have gone dry, using a mixture of oil and turpentine is described. There is a healthy stress on the need for practical experience in dealing with all types of pictures.

In Sarsfield Taylor's preface to the English translation of 1839, he remarks, '. . . it is by the process of restoring, that discoveries are made of the various methods of the schools, as well as the particular method of the master.'

(28) ARSENNE, L. C. *Manuel du peintre et du sculpteur* (The painter's and sculptor's handbook). In 2 volumes. Paris, 1833.

In Volume II there is a dictionary of art terms, and on p. 388 is to be found an entry for *RESTAURATION des tableaux* (Restoration of pictures). Some iniquitous practices are recommended, such as the cradling of panels, the pricking of blisters before laying with glue, and the impregnation of dried-out pictures with oil and turpentine (the surplus being removed with potash). Interesting ideas include wax as an adhesive for patching tears in canvas (a forerunner of the modern wax relining), and the method of pressing a piece of canvas of similar grain into the still-soft putty of an area of loss so as to give it an appropriate texture. A method of cleaning is suggested by which the old varnish is treated with alcohol, left for 24 hours then rubbed off dry, a method which seems to lose the advantages both of the dry and solvent modes of cleaning. However, cleaning with swabs and alcohol and/or turpentine is also described, a sensible warning being given that dark areas of paintings may be more vulnerable to solvent action or friction than are light areas. An account of transfer mentions that the reverse side of the painting with the underpainting may often be observed when the original support and ground is removed, but then goes on to recommend the removal of these original underlayers since they are probably cracked!

(29) WELSCH, Fr. *Vollständige Anweisung zur Restauration der Gemälde* (Complete instruction on the restoration of paintings). Quedlinburg and Leipzig, 1834.

A compilation of recipes, manipulations etc. Cleaning agents include such old and unsuitable ones as beer, sand, soda, raw potato, pumice, butter, vinegar, ammonia, acids, alkalis and urine, with an excessive reliance on the cleansing properties of both water and oil. Several of the methods, especially for relining and transfer, are still in use. Much of the text is identical with that of Lucanus (see below, No. (35)). (H.R.).

(30) FIELD, George. *Chromatography or a treatise on colours and pigments*. London, 1835.

Bibliography

(N.B. The term chromatography is here loosely applied to the study and measurement of colour, whereas in present-day scientific terminology it specifically indicates the separation and identification of substances by means of their particular rates of flow through a chosen medium.)

Chapter V: 'On the durability and fugacity of colours', discusses the fading of some pigments and the darkening of others from the effect of light — a comparatively early rationalization and organization of previously observed but unrelated phenomena. The author notes that the only recently-discovered lead chromate pigments suffer blackening in a polluted atmosphere. In contrast to his forward-thinking views on effects of light and atmosphere on paintings and their components, the author then goes on warmly to recommend such unsuitable surface coatings as copal varnish and shellac. There is also a somewhat disturbing assumption that darkening of oil paintings is often caused by the rising to the surface of a crust of excess oil medium which may with impunity be removed. Chapter XXV, 'On picture cleaning and restoration' again looks forward to present-day practice. For example it is advised that before removal of varnish is carried out, surface dirt should be removed or it will impede the former operation. Again, the dry removal of soft-resin varnishes, such as mastic, by the dry, rubbing method is recommended. Alkalis are to be used only as a last resort for stubborn stains or repaints. Cleaning is described as carried out with alcohol diluted with turpentine, the solvent action being stopped when necessary by the application of linseed oil. An early version of the 're-forming technique' of cleaning is also described (see below (52) and *Section 16* (19)), by revarnishing the picture then removing simultaneously the newly-applied varnish and the old varnish into which it will have sunk.

(31) BEDOTTI, Jean. *De la restauration des tableaux* (The restoration of pictures). Paris, 1837.

A rather simplified account of early 19th century practices of relining, cleaning and retouching. It includes alarming instructions for the repainting of worn areas, particularly in the case of worn paint of skies done on a dark ground, to be followed by 'patination' of the entire area with soot.

(32) STÖCKLER, J. K. *Praktisches Hülfsbuch der Kunstfreundes* (The practical handbook for the art lover). Pesth and Leipzig, 1838.

The customary varnish for pictures is again described as mastic dissolved in turpentine. Of special interest are descriptions of current methods for the transfer of paintings from wood or stone to canvas: 1. Hacquin's method. 2. Barezzi's method. 3. Salmon's method.

(33) FIELDING, J. M. *On painting in oil and water colour*. London, 1839.

Chapter X: 'On picture cleaning.' Methods of cleaning include that of dry abrasion (the finger first dipped into 'impalpable' pumice-stone powder), and using mixtures of alcohol with turpentine. Olive oil is suggested as a suitable substance to check solvent action. There is the usual account of glue/paste relinings and transfers of the time. The danger of the use of alkalis in cleaning is touched upon.

1840

(34) SCHULZE, A. *Praktische Anweisung zur Lackirkunst und zum Oelfarben Anstrich*

(Practical guide to the art of varnishing and to painting in oil). Quedlinburg and Leipzig, 1840.

Chapter X on varnishes for paintings, includes the traditional instructions for cleaning pictures, yet a difference is stressed between the all-over varnish as a protective coating and the use of 'varnish' (i.e. solutions of resins) for grinding colours and as a component of painting media.

(35) LUCANUS, Fr. G. H. *Vollständige Anleitung zur Erhaltung, Reinigung und Wiederherstellung der Gemälde, zur Bereitung der Firnisse, u.s.w.* (Complete guide to the preservation, cleaning and restoration of paintings, the preparation of varnish, etc.) Halberstadt, 1842.

An authoritative little treatise, knowledgeable by the standards of the time. The author laments the lack of training institutes for restorers. On the practical side, he recommends shellac as a retouching medium and a varnish (it darkens and also becomes insoluble with age), but also claims to have discovered copaiva balsam and dammar resin as media and varnishes. He warns, quite rightly, against excess addition of resin to paint, noting that if this is used 'the eminent clarity of fresh paintings does not last long'. He is also opposed to the use of white of egg as a temporary varnish. There is a good chapter on varnishes, though many obsolete recipes are included. Complicated and obsolete recipes for surface cleaning and varnish removal are also given, including such harsh treatment as hot water, coarse sand, hot alcohol with alkalis. He describes, though discourages, the partial removal of the browned surface from copper resinate greens (e.g. on pictures by Cranach), but is at least aware of this problem. A few of the formulae given appear sound, and might be worth a trial. Among these are the application of a mixture of flour paste, chalk, glue and venice turpentine and wax between the two canvases during relining or transfer. A warning against overpainting is given. The usual misunderstanding concerning 'patina' occurs. Asphalt or mummy is described as being added to mastic varnish 'in order to give to new paintings, especially copies, the appearance of older ones', perhaps also to cover up new retouchings and defects and thus deceive the art collector. Lucanus sums up: 'Only he who is capable of creating works of art of some importance and who is familiar not only with the technical side in painting in general, but also is capable of penetrating completely into the spirit of the work, should restore; only he will recognize and revere every peculiarity of the painting, and only to such a person can one entrust the most important work of art with good conscience.' (H.R.).

(36) AMERICAN ARTIST, An. *Handbook of young artists and amateurs in oil painting.* New York (Wiley & Putnam), 1845.

Seventh Part (pp. 281–291), 'The varnishing, cleaning, repairing and lining of pictures'.

Mastic turpentine varnish is again recommended as being the most suitable and most usual for pictures. Removal of old mastic varnish by the dry method is described, and mentioned as suitable for removing varnish from new paintings, whereas alcohol is thought to be more suitable for cleaning old paintings, The hazards of cleaning operations seem rather over-rated, but probably because comparatively newly-painted pictures seem to be uppermost in the author's thoughts. Egg white is again included as a suitable temporary varnish for newly painted pictures, but there is some erroneous second-hand information about the ability of egg white to dissolve varnishes. Disorders of canvases, mending of tears, relining, are also considered, the relining adhesive used being a rye-flour paste. On the whole the book has a rather amateurish approach to restoration.

(37) MOGFORD, Henry. *Handbook for the preservation of pictures.* Publ. by Winsor and Newton, London, 1845.

This small (23 pp.) booklet contains remarkably concise, and, for its period, sensible instruction on relining, cleaning, retouching and varnishing of oil paintings.

(38) TRIPIER-DEVEAUX, A. M. *Traité théorique et pratique sur l'art de faire les vernis* (Theoretical and practical treatise on the art of varnish making). Paris, 1845.

A handbook for the commercial preparation of varnishes and lacquers for every purpose, but pp. 274–279 repeat Tingry's recipes and instructions for varnishing pictures (see above, No. (18)), and pp. 279–285 give alternative varnishes for paintings, including one composed of dammar in turpentine. The author of the work is anxious that picture varnishes even before application should be as colourless and clear as possible, even urging that colourless turpentine should be sought out.

(39) HAMPEL, J. C. G. *Die Restauration alter und schadhaft gewordene Gemälde* (The restoration of old and damaged paintings). Weimar, 1846.

Many of the recipes which are given are similar to those in Welsch and Lucanus (see above Nos. (29) and (35)). Unsuitable or dangerous processes include the use of a mixture of vitriol and alcohol with wire brushes for the purpose of cleaning. The application of a dough consisting of flour mixed with alcohol for the purpose of softening tough old varnishes anticipates the method of Robert van Eyck (see p. 204 of the present book). On p. 44 the author praises '. . . The most beautiful brown glaze . . . consists of diluted asphalt (bitumen) . . . it suffers no change at all either through time or temperature.' On pp. 55–56 he quotes a number of formulae for emulsion media of Punic wax with soap, cream etc., which were popular at the time. On pp. 60–64 there is an interesting paragraph 'On falsified pictures or signatures.' (H.R.).

(40) EASTLAKE, Charles Lock. *Materials for a history of oil painting.* In 2 volumes. Vol. I, London, 1847. Vol. II, published posthumously, London, 1869. Reprinted by Dover Publications, Inc., in 2 volumes, New York, 1960, under the title: *Methods and materials of the great schools and masters.*

Eastlake seems to have extracted from the most important sources available, in several languages, every piece of information of interest concerning the methods and materials of the great schools and masters. He was not only an outstanding scholar, but also had wide practical experience as a painter and (after he had written this work) as Director of the National Gallery. Much of his writing has a bearing on picture restoration. Although he stresses that the only documented deliberately-pigmented varnishes used by the old masters were for the purpose of making transparent pictures on tinfoil, his own ideas of the masters' intentions were still largely coloured by the darkened varnishes which covered nearly all pictures in his time. On pp. 362–364 he writes: 'The toning brown should be used everywhere to mitigate crudeness, even in partial tints (that may be too vivid).' On pp. 370–373 he seems to confuse darkened original varnishes or later deliberately tinted varnishes with original glazes; on pp. 255–256 there is some contradition on the same count, and he speaks of 'the good effect of Time on pictures'. On pp. 506–507 (Volume I) he produces complicated explanations for Rembrandt's 'uniform tawny colour'. We now know that this was confined to the removable discoloured varnish which concealed beautifully preserved whites and cool nuances. (H.R.).

(41) FIELDING, Theodore H. *The knowledge and restoration of old paintings*. London, 1847.

Ideas on cleaning are fairly sensible for the time. Surface cleaning is carried out using water or ox-gall before varnish removal is embarked upon. The usual methods of varnish removal, i.e. dry friction or dissolving in a mixture of alcohol and turpentine, are recommended. Unfortunately, advice as to revarnishing is unsound. The author dismisses mastic because it does not keep its colour and 'chills', and recommends copal/oil varnish, stipulating that the latter should be colourless or very pale. It has long been known that copal/oil varnishes become insoluble with age and difficult, if not impossible to remove safely, and the same applies to shellac which the author suggests as a suitable medium for retouching.

(42) HUNDERTPFUND, Liberal. *Die Malerei auf ihre einfachsten und sichersten Grundsätze zurückgeführt* (Painting reduced to its simplest and safest principles). Augsburg, 1847.

Not concerned with restoration, but it is interesting to note, in view of the date, that in the section on varnish preparation the author expresses the view that only mastic or dammar in turpentine are safe and suitable varnishes for paintings.

1850

(43) DÉON, Horsin. *De la conservation et de la restauration des tableaux* (The conservation and restoration of pictures). Paris, 1851.

Noteworthy is the author's gallant and forceful plea for cleaning pictures at the Louvre. It remained unheeded for a century. He fulminates against charlatanism and secrecy. His chapters on woodwork, lining, transfer, etc. are as sound as could be expected, given the limited knowledge of his time. (H.R.).

(44) *Report from the Select Committee on the National Gallery; together with the minutes of evidence, appendix and index*. Ordered to be printed, by the House of Commons, London, 25 July 1850. viii + 110 pp.

(45) *Report from the Select Committee on the National Gallery; together with the proceedings of the Committee, minutes of evidence, appendix and index*. Ordered to be printed, by the House of Commons, London, 4 August 1853. 1 + 965 pp.

These are reports of two Select Committees appointed by the House of Commons to enquire into the management of the National Gallery, London. They are two of the most revealing documents of all time concerning the practice of, prejudices against, enthusiasm for, and misconceptions about picture restoration. The Committees interrogated officials of the National Gallery, leading artists of the day, connoisseurs and collectors, restorers and other specialists, and a verbatim report is given of the daily proceedings of the Committees. Among matters discussed are: climatic conditions in the National Gallery at the time; the policy and practice of cleaning, including exhaustive discussion of the nine pictures cleaned in the vacation of 1852, the appearance of which after cleaning

Bibliography

provoked fierce controversy; types of varnish, including the notorious 'Gallery varnish', a mastic/turpentine varnish to which a proportion of drying oil was added in a vain attempt to prevent 'bloom', so prevalent at the time because of the impure atmosphere; relining and transfer; training of restorers.

(46) MERRITT, Henry. *Dirt and pictures separated, in the works of the old masters.* London, 1854.

Chapter 1 debunks the delight shown by some connoisseurs in 'a dark invisible, but very fine old picture'. Chapter 2 deals with the relative durability of paintings in oil. Chapter 3 shows antipathy towards picture restoration in general (an attitude which seems to stem from the cleaned pictures controversy of 1853). Chapter 4 concerns picture cleaning, including the history of the use of varnish. The similarity is pointed out between the optical effect and the protective function of a varnish with those of a piece of glass placed in front of the painting. Chapter 5 attempts, rather unsuccessfully to sort out the confusion between final glazes and the varnish layer. Chapter 6 introduces the concept of the 'Standard picture'. While recognizing the prime importance of treating each picture as an individual case, the author points out the utility for the restorer of building up a stock of information on the materials, technique, probable condition and peculiar vulnerability of paintings of particular artists, schools or periods. He goes on to classify the technique and condition of various types of pictures. Chapter 12 describes the activities of incompetent or dishonest picture restorers under the title of 'Picture destroyers'. Chapter 13 is devoted to 'The Restorer' and Chapter 14 to 'Devotion of the Restorer', in which the concepts of integrity and honesty are stipulated as desirable attributes for the picture restorer.

(47) HERTEL, A. W. *Die Oelmalerei in umfassender technischer Beziehung* (Oil painting — a comprehensive technical approach). Weimar, 1857.

Mostly concerned with the practice of oil painting, but Chapter XXVIII is on varnish removal (i.e. of mastic or dammar varnishes). Appendix II is devoted to the subject of restoration of oil paintings. A brief, intelligent treatment of restoration is given, quoting largely from Horsin Déon (see No. (43) above) and for relining, etc. from Lucans (see No. (35) above). On p. 309 the author states 'A proper respect for old masters consists by no means of careful preservation of the dirt that covers their works and veils their qualities, but it does involve careful removal of this grime so that it does not influence the colours. . . . It is a very relative honour, befitting only the antiquary, to boast of the ancient rust and of the wrinkles of a varnish. This unfounded pride is best left to the collectors and dealers.' On p. 310 he points out that old varnish must be removed before applying new. 'Nourishing' of picture surfaces with diluted drying oils is advocated, but this occurs in most other treatises of the period. (H.R.).

(48) GOUPIL FESQUET, F. A. A. *Manuel complet et simplifié de la peinture à l'huile, suivi du traité de la restauration des tableaux* (Complete and simplified manual on oil painting, followed by a treatise on the restoration of pictures). Paris, 1858.

1870

(49) SECCO-SUARDO, G. *Il restauratore dei dipinti* (The restorer of paintings). Part I, Milan 1866. Part II completed 1873 and published posthumously in 1894, with an intro-

duction by the author's son. Both parts as a third edition, Milan, 1918, considerably re-edited.

A classic handbook dealing with all aspects of restoration in great detail. Much of the material remains still valid, but much has been made obsolete by later developments. The author condemns all other writers on the subject, including Eastlake, Mérimée, Montabert, etc. as of little use, only Cennini shedding a 'ray of light', and he criticizes at tedious length both early and contemporary authors. It should be mentioned that the term 'restauro' he uses in the sense of retouching (also sometimes 'restauro pittorico'). With regard to retouching he remarks that neither exact imitation nor lastingness is possible, whatever the restorer may affirm. He warns against 'covering the very parts which should serve as a model', but takes it for granted that after finishing the cleaning and retouching a tinted varnish or 'artificial patina' will be applied. He speaks in the same sentence of the desirability of complete cleaning and of preserving 'that sort of most precious patina, the fruit of time and the characteristic of age and authenticity ('originalità')', observing that 'Dirt helps the picture by reducing excessive luminosity'. In his favour, he criticizes : curators who are more interested in the labels under their pictures than in making detailed examinations or technical researches on them; 'paintings made to look too new with excess of shiny varnish'; retouchings in oil, since they will go on darkening (he recommends water-colour or tempera for retouching). Some of the methods of panel treatment illustrated are still useful, but he nevertheless advocates reinforcement of deteriorated panels (after thinning down to 8–10 mm.) by sticking on a thick panel *across the grain*, a very unsound practice. (H.R.).

(50) FORNI, Ulisse. *Manuale del pittore restauratore* (Manual for the painter-restorer). Florence, 1866.

Positive contributions made by the author are : praise for the writings of Mérimée, Déon (see above, Nos. (27), (43)); Oil retouchings are condemned, together with too-glossy varnishes and excessive retouching. Retouchings (whether 'neutral' or matching) are recommended to be carried out in tempera or water colour. The necessity for training schools for restorers is stressed. Complete cleaning is advocated, also the necessity for abolishing 'trade secrets' in restoration practice. A novel suggestion, adopted independently by the author of the present book, is the use of adhesive tape or plaster in the lifting of loose flakes of paint so that they may be reattached (transparent 'scotch tape' can nowadays be used). Forni anticipates the 're-forming method'; in commenting on the Pettenkofer process (see below, No. (52)), he remarks that the greatest advantage of the use of alcohol vapour is not that it regenerates the old varnish, but that it makes it easy to remove merely with turpentine and without damage to the picture. Advice which is either unwise or else obsolete includes : the use of shellac (which both darkens and becomes insoluble with time) as a retouching medium; the use for the same purpose of dammar and copaiva balsam (in modern practice these have been replaced by synthetic resins, which though not perfect, are an improvement on the natural resins). 'Moderate cleaning' only is recommended, and the preservation of 'patina' commended. There are also detailed recipes for 'artificial patina' to be applied to pictures, ingredients including liquorice, infusions of tobacco ash or cigar ends, and coffee. (H.R.).

Bibliography

1870

(51) HOLYOAKE, Manfred. *The conservation of pictures.* London, 1870.

One of the most interesting features of this small book is the use of the term 'conservation' rather than 'restoration' in its title. Serious consideration is given to the question of environment, e.g. the importance of proper atmospheric conditions, the damaging effects of damp, sunlight, or of hanging pictures over a fireplace or exposed to lamp or candle smoke. Protection, as distinct from restoration, of pictures is emphasised throughout. Excessive retouching is condemned. Cleaning (i.e. varnish removal) is defined, and praise is given to the cleaned Claudes in the National Gallery. There is also a discussion of mastic as a picture varnish.

(52) PETTENKOFER, Max V. *Über Ölfarbe und Konservierung der Gemälde-Gallerien durch das Regenerations-Verfahren* (On oil painting and conservation for picture galleries by means of the regeneration process). Braunschweig, 1870.

In the 1860s Pettenkofer was granted two patents for his invention of regenerating pictures by exposure to alcohol-saturated air and the application of copaiva balsam, for re-establishing lost 'molecular cohesion' of varnish and paint. The Bavarian State Collections acquired the right to apply this treatment to their pictures. A violent controversy ensued. Pettenkofer in his book claims that 'The Regeneration Method should for all times avoid and make obsolete varnish removal from pictures (p. 34), but if a varnish is too thick and yellow it can be reduced and partly removed, since it can never be removed entirely without damaging the paint. . . . Only charlatans can contend that a resin varnish can be wholly removed without damaging the colours of glazes, for the resin varnish is being used precisely because it penetrates into the paint and does not just lie over it. . . .' For present-day knowledge see pp. 170–208 of the present book. Pettenkofer half realized the limitations of his method (p. 48) : 'The alcohol-saturated air will again and again for a considerable time re-establish the cohesion (of the paint) . . . repeated application of copaiva oil will protect the paint from excessive brittleness.' It is, however, understandable that he overrated the virtues of his patent when one considers its spectacular effect on deteriorated resin varnishes. Unfortunately the effect proved to be only temporary, and in addition the copaiva balsam applied yellows considerably with time.

For varnish removal, Pettenkofer recommends 'absolute spirits of wine' (i.e. ethyl alcohol) and copaiva balsam mixed in equal parts, but considers that as a rule removal by dry rubbing is advisable. For removing surface dirt he recommends water and then turpentine (both of which are comparatively ineffective for this purpose). He regards the main cause of clouding (i.e. decomposition) of varnish (and paint) as condensed water from the air. In addition to his regeneration of resin varnishes, he seems to have obtained some success in regenerating so-called ultramarine sickness and a visually similar phenomenon which occurs in the greens of 17th century paintings (see p. 25). (H.R.).

(53) FÖRSTER, Carl. *Ueber den Verfall der Restauration alter Gemälde in Deutschland und Protest gegen das v. Pettenkofer'sche Regenerations-Verfahren* (The decline of restoration of 'old masters' in Germany and a protest against the Pettenkofer regeneration process.) Munich, 1870. (See No. (52), above.)

Bibliography

(54) Ludwig, H. *Ueber die Grundsätze der Oelmalerei* (The principles of oil painting).

Leipzig, 1876. Ludwig's little book on painting methods shows a profound understanding of the potentialities of oil paint and deserves a thorough appreciation, though it only touches on the present topic. Some of his remarks show great insight into the condition and conservation of pictures : p. 212; 'The art history of an epoch can be really brought to life only by someone who knows the inmost motives of its art practice and who can give us a true concept of the masters' working methods.' Footnote, p. 117 : 'What Goethe admired as the Venetians' golden tone, and after him so many amateurish connoisseurs, is as a rule nothing but the work of clumsy retouchers, who made their ill-matched retouchings disappear below an all-merging ('all-reconciling') yellow varnish. The genuine dominant tone does not appear yellow but all colours are completely clear and saturated ('feurig schon farbig').' Page 210 (speaking of copying old masters) : 'Since nearly all gallery pictures are covered with a varnish one must know how to discount its colour from the appearance of the actual painting.' Page 212 (at the end of a detailed description of the layers constituting a sky (e.g. in a picture by Ghirlandaio); he nevertheless includes 'the uniting allover varnish' ('Verbindender Generalfirniss'), also on p. 257, after another analysis of the building up of the paint of a sky : 'warming general glaze'. In these cases it was most probably the yellowed varnish which he was unwittingly describing. (H.R.).

(55) Blockx, Jacques. *Compendium à l'usage des artistes peintres et des amateurs de tableaux* (Compendium for the use of artist-painters and lovers of art). Antwerp, 1881 1st edn.

The edition available to us was that of 1904. Causes of alterations in paintings and methods for averting them are discussed, including the possibly harmful effect of fumes from gas-lighting. Varnishes should be applied only in very thin coats to oil paintings for the dual purpose of bringing out 'relief' in the picture and protecting the paint surface from air. Resin varnishes are condemned as ingredients of painting media since the brilliance they give will prove ephemeral. A considerable awareness is shown of conservation proper, i.e. avoiding exposure of the picture to bright light, which, the author remarks, will not only change some pigments but will also accelerate oxidation of oils and varnishes. It is recommended that panel paintings should be coated on the back for protection and the author is well aware of the sensitivity of wood panels to changes in atmospheric humidity, so that at this early date he recommends the installation of hygrographs and thermometers in museums. He is averse to relining and transfer of paintings, perhaps on grounds of economy. He advocates an amber-in-oil medium manufactured by his firm.

1890

(56) Church, A. H. *The chemistry of paints and painting*. First published 1890. Third edition, revised and enlarged, London, 1901.

Mainly concerned with the chemical constitution and properties of painting materials, but the author has a strong sense of the importance of proper conservation. Chapter XXIV, 'The study of old paintings and drawings', deals with changes and deterioration in these works with age. Chapter XXV, 'Conservation of pictures and drawings' concentrates not so much on restoration as on preservation, while Chapter XXVI describes experiments (advanced for their time) on the fading of various pigments with exposure to light. Altogether, an enlightened work of its period, much of the content even now not superseded.

(57) RIS-PAQUOT, O. E. *Guide pratique du restaurateur-amateur de tableaux* (Practical guide for the restorer-amateur of pictures. Paris, 1890.

A rather poor and out-of-date work for this late period. Possibly the only thing to be said in the author's favour is that he does distinguish between dirt on the varnish, discolouration within the varnish, and dirt which may be beneath the varnish. However, he has praise for 'that patina which only time can give to pictures' but is willing to admit that sometimes artificial patina is applied (such as the practice of smoking pictures) to fakes and modern copies. The use of alkalis for cleaning is condemned as is that of soap and water, though urine is recommended, as in some much older works, as a surface cleaning agent. Varnish removal is effected not by solvent mixtures but by the older process of swabs dipped in alcohol followed by swabs dipped in poppy oil (see No. (27), above).

(58) KEIM, A. W. 'Das Aufkleben von Leinwandgemälden' ('The sticking-down of canvas paintings'). *Technische Mitteilungen für Malerei*, XII (1895), No. 4, p. 5.

For its time, a sensible article on relining.

(59) DALBON, Charles. *Traité technique et raisonné de la restauration des tableaux. Précedé d'une étude sur leur conservation.* (Technical and rational treatise on the restoration of pictures. Preceded by a study on their conservation.) Paris, 1898.

The author is very conscious of the importance of atmospheric conditions. With regard to cleaning, he remarks that there are some people who will not hear of it and 'prefer to keep their pictures covered with old, yellowed, opaque and cracked varnish, which they style "patina"'. He recommends the usual methods of removal, either by dry rubbing or alcohol/turpentine mixtures, but is the first writer (known to the present bibliographer), to mention the very useful technique of rolling, rather than rubbing, a swab over the picture. Unfortunately, he admits, despite his previous censures, to preferring in some cases a little of the old varnish left and 'evened out' over the picture, but is strongly opposed in principle to the application of artificial 'patina', which renders the picture itself heavy and dull and is generally used to conceal either the defects of the picture or the clumsiness of the restorations. It is recommended that retouchings should be done over an intermediate varnish (seemingly a comparatively modern practice), and if the retouching is to be done in oil colours, excess oil should be removed from tube colours by spreading them first on paper. The method of relining described still uses a glue adhesive. There is also some information about the history of transfer.

(60) FISCHER, Ludwig H. *Die Technik der Oelmalerei* (The technique of oil painting). Vienna, 1898.

Mainly concerned with the practice of oil painting, but two chapters are of interest: 'Varnishes for oil painting' — the dual purpose of the varnish as a protective coating against air and damp, and in order to bring out the colours of the painting, is emphasized; also that the varnish must be clear, colourless and free-flowing, as well as drying within 24 hours. Mastic-turpentine varnish is recommended rather than copal (or dammar) because it is readily obtainable in solution from colour merchants, or can easily be prepared. The use of a special broad, soft varnish brush (illustrated) is specified. Emphasis is laid on keeping the varnish layer thin and not revarnishing except when absolutely necessary. A temporary varnish of egg white mixed with sugar is still recommended for newly-painted pictures. A chapter on the conservation of oil paintings is contributed largely by a restorer of the Royal Collections, who recommends conditions for the display and storage of paintings. Quite sensibly, he points out the unsuitability for paintings of premises where the heating is only on for part of the time (e.g. many churches) and suggests, correctly, that it would be more advantageous from the point of view of the welfare of the pictures not to have heat at all, rather than sporadic heat. The defects which may arise from variations in temperature and humidity of the surroundings are pointed out. The author discusses the reaction between damp and acid pollutants in the air and the effect on some pigments, hence varnishing of the front and protection of the back surface of the picture are desirable. With regard to cleaning, the author regards ordinary removal of varnish by solvent as rather dangerous and prefers the — at the time — fashionable Pettenkofer process (see No. (52) above). It is emphasized that in any case varnish removal is generally a task for the professional. There is also appreciation of the importance for good puttying as a preliminary to inpainting. Salutary advice is given to painters as to lasting methods and materials.

(61) Voss, Eugen (Portrait painter). *Bilderpflege* (The care of paintings). Leipzig, 1899.

A largely obsolete small handbook intended for the use of owners of pictures, characteristic of the period. The author recommends enthusiastically 'Phoebus A' for refreshing and 'nourishing' paintings. This preparation contained vaseline — a non-drying grease — and was, unfortunately, in use for a number of years. Also typical of the attitude of the period: (p. 36) 'If the darkening (on some parts of the painting) is disturbing, it is advisable to remove the varnish; if it is not disturbing it is preferable to slightly tone the areas which stand out too light — and in this way bring them into harmony with the whole.' A sensible suggestion is the removal of surface dirt (with a nearly dry chamois leather) before revarnishing, and another is to apply wax dissolved in turpentine to the reverse of the picture before washing the front. (H.R.).

Section 4

Works on, or containing sections on restoration, post-1900

1900

(1) Schäfer, H. T. *Notes on the cleaning, restoration and preservation of paintings*, London, 1901. 30 pp.

(2) Keim, Adolf W. *Ueber Mal-Technik, ein Beitrag zur Beförderung rationeller Malverfahren* (On painting technique, a contribution to the furthering of Rational Painting Procedure). Leipzig, 1903. 449 pp.

Chapter V concerns restoration and conservation of paintings; the author criticizes the use of harmful agents on pictures, such as vaseline, sugar of lead etc., and also the Pettenkofer process (see *Section 3* (52), above). The main interest of the book lies, however, in a description of the aims and activities of the association for Rationelle Malverfahren, which its author was largely responsible for founding, the object being to promote sound techniques and materials in modern paintings and good conservation of old, and involved testing of materials and methods. Pages 439–449 gives a useful list of the more important articles published over the years in the associations journal, *Technische Mitteilungen für Malerei* . . . (see *Section 1*, p. 369).

1910

(3) KAINZBAUER, S. *Ars, Behandlung und Wiederherstellung der Öl-, Tempera- und Fresko-Gemälde* (The art, treatment and restoration of oil, tempera and fresco paintings). Vienna, 1910.

Kainzbauer makes at a surprisingly early date a few very useful suggestions for which one might easily credit later restorers.

He argues well against leaving yellowed varnishes and 'dirt patina' but later partly contradicts himself: 'Pictures must keep their antique character and must not look like newly finished, therefore leave some of the varnish.' — 'Dark areas need often not be devarnished.' I have dealt with these fallacies on pp. 236–237.

That old panels have to be reduced to almost 1 mm. thickness before being backed by a new panel, must have been known to carpenters long before this time. His idea of strengthening very thin panels by applying on the back a 'putty' made up of very fine sawdust and dextrin (a vegetable glue much in vogue in the early 20th century, but long obsolete) is a kind of forerunner of the wax cement now in use. Rubber solution as back protection and for patching up tears was not bad — while it lasted. To soften flakes and cupping on canvas pictures by regenerating with alcohol and ironing the adhesive in from the back is a sensible suggestion. To prick blisters with a cold needle and stick them down with copaiva balsam is less ingenious, so is ironing without a bedding: 'pastosities must not be ironed lest they would be flattened'. Glue or dextrin for lining is quite the wrong thing. Again, 5 parts water with 1 part ammonia (probably a weak water solution is meant) for removing surface dirt is excellent if used with almost dry swabs. Kainzbauer's plea not to encroach on original paint in retouching is praiseworthy but he naturally takes oil-resin as a retouching medium for granted.

Two further useful inventions from this booklet: 'For pressing texture into the (wet) putty take a plaster cast of the back of the canvas (which must be greased). The mould must also be greased before pressing it on to the putty'. (Talcum powder is better than grease for this purpose. If a little wax has been incorporated in the putty it need not be wetted — H.R.). 'When retouchings darken: scrape off the surface with a sharp knife. They will then stay right'. My experiments for testing this are not concluded, but they were satisfactory on one or two occasions.

How original these contributions are I do not know. When one flatters oneself for having found some little novel improvement in our field one usually sooner or later realizes that one has been anticipated by some more advanced fellow restorer by a matter of fifty or a hundred years.

Kainzbauer's little book is typical for many of that period that I have read, in German, Italian, French and English; but most of them are much less useful'. (H.R.).

(4) MOREAU-VAUTHIER, C. *La peinture* (Painting). Paris, 1913. Pages 213–293 are concerned with restoration. An English translation under the title *The technique of painting*, with a preface by E. DINET, London, 1923.

1920

(5) FRIMMEL, Theodor. *Gemäldekunde* (Knowledge of painting). Leipzig, 1920.

A handbook for art historians with a basically technical approach; a treasury of information and useful references, many on early restorations of paintings from 1500 onwards (pp. 138–159), relining from 1729, transfer from 1800, and transfer from copper by a galvanic process carried out by Dr. Buettner Pfaenner zu Thal in 1894. There is a sensible, but now partly obsolete chapter on restoring, including some of the common fallacies of the period. Pettenkofer's regeneration process is much over-rated. The author insists that 'the last layers of varnish must not be removed for reasons of safety', but he exposes the practice of 'smearing a tinted varnish over the cleaned picture', and advocates retouching which is visible on close inspection. (H.R.).

(6) BASCH-BORDONE, J. *Handbuch der Konservierung und Restaurierung Alter Gemälde* (Handbook of conservation and restoration of old paintings). Munich, 1921.

(7) DOVER, Henry T. 'The restoration of paintings.' *The Burlington Magazine*, XXXIX (part II, 1921), pp. 184–188, 221–223.

Now out of date, recommending practices which would be no longer approved, e.g. glue relining, cradling of panels, pricking of blisters. It is also mentioned that at this time some owners still insisted on a toned varnish being applied.

(8) DOERNER, Max. *Malmaterial und seine Verwendung im Bilde*. Berlin, 1922. Numerous subsequent German editions, e.g. 11th edn. Stuttgart, 1960. English translation by E. Heuhaus: *The materials of the artist and their use in painting*. London, 1935; most recent English edition, with some revisions, London, 1955.

See H. R.'s critical review, reprinted in Appendix D, pp. 355–360.

(9) GUNN, Maurice J. *Painting restoration and picture cleaning*. London, 1922.

This book is primarily devoted to works on paper, with only one chapter on cleaning and repairing of oil paintings.

(10) LAURIE, A. P. 'The preservation and cleaning of pictures.' *The Connoisseur*, Sept.–Dec. 1925, pp. 131–137.

(11) LAURIE, A. P. *The painter's methods and materials*. London, 1926. 250 pp., illus. Chapter XIX, 'Preservation and cleaning of pictures.'

On p. 227 Laurie writes: 'Washing with turpentine or even with soap and water removes some superficial dirt, but does not remove the ingrained tarry particles which seem to have eaten their way into the oil surface. They can only be removed with a solvent which at the same time removes some of the paint of the picture; if the picture has not been protected by a varnish, injury to the picture itself is inevitable if an attempt is made to clean it.' There may be rare cases in which a painting in slow drying before varnishing has gathered an inordinate amount of surface dust, but the situation described by Laurie does not tally with my experience of cleaning paintings.

Laurie, though he often broke new ground in his many publications (some of which repeat, however, much of the content of the work cited), did not always draw valid conclusions from his experimental findings. As an example I quote a remark (*Mouseion*, 1934, see No. (26) below) : 'Velázquez' translucent final shadows seem to consist of a very dark brown varnish, easily soluble in alcohol.' Laurie told me that he was present when cleaning tests were made on the 'Rokeby Venus' after the picture had been slashed (see pp. 293–300 of the present book) and he found that the brown pigment, which he surmised to be bitumen, came off with the varnish. I have had occasion to verify on two works of Velázquez that the original shadows could be cleaned safely with undiluted alcohol or acetone, in either of which the paint was insoluble, though on the other hand the varnish could still be removed safely with a diluted mixture of either solvent, and together with any dirt or soot which might have been trapped in it. (H.R.).

(12) BEAUFORT, Thomas Richard. *Pictures and how to clean them.* London, 1926.

Mostly concerned with cleaning prints, but a useful list (illustrated) of tools. Methods now rather old-fashioned, e.g. for varnishing recommends mastic plasticized with gum elemi or Canada balsam.

(13) EIBNER, Alexander. *Entwicklung und Werkstoffe der Tafelmalerei* (Processes and working materials of the panel painter). Munich, 1928.

As no English translation exists, this work is here reviewed in some detail.

This, one of the most important books in our field, would be well worth an English translation, even today.

Prof. Eibner's principal aim is, as he explains in his introduction, to put the practice of painting on a basis of scientific knowledge of the materials, in order to assure the durability of future work.

Eibner's book is mainly of interest for the practising painter but contains much that is fundamentally important for the restorer and conservator of paintings. Chapter I 'Changes in the layers of oil paintings' contains (a) a thorough research into the causes of cracking (pp. 15–51) well illustrated by 27 plates and (b) into those of the yellowing and darkening of oil paintings.

He explains the important difference between *early or shrinkage cracks* (arising mostly through inadequate technique) during the drying and hardening of the oil film and on the other hand the *late cracks* in dried oil paint films, which have no longer any movement of their own. The latter are caused by the expansion and contraction of the support and are finer and deeper than early cracks. They occur predominantly at right angles, those running against the direction of the wood grain being shorter.

Eibner blames reticulation, 'bark' formation, (crocodile skin texture) on slow drying lacquer character of dark colours, also on turpentine balsam (Venetian Turpentine) aided by artificial drying by warmth and re-softening of poppy oil paint through heat.

Eibner draws attention to the fact that young oil paint films can easily be saponified or swelled, less and less easily with increasing age. 'The reason for this phenomenon' he continues 'is the maturing of the oil film into an irreversible colloid'. He considers the possibility that resins also may, in the ageing oilpaint, go through a maturing process

Bibliography

which turns them into irreversible colloids, as the now practically insoluble resins amber and copal must have been soluble thousands of years ago.

'If it is right to add resins to oil paint, then the technical aim must be to make them turn insoluble. Whether it is attainable must be proved by the examination of resinous oilpaint films removed from old oilpaintings. The fact that they can be removed at all does not seem to point to those resins having already become irreversible (see pp. 306–308 on my tests on 20 years old paintings containing resin, varnished with mastic). (H.R.).

In his excellent report on the rise and fall of Pettenkofer's regenerating method Eibner mentions its main shortcoming, that it makes blind varnishes clearer, but does not remove their yellow or brown colour; he continues (p. 164): '*That this, i.e. the yellowed varnish must be removed so as to recover, as far as still possible, the original colour values of the picture, is not open to doubt* (unterliegt keinem Zweifel)'.

Naturally the removal must be carried out in such a way that no overcleaning occurs, which frequently happened in the past'. Eibner also condemns the use of copaiva balsam (recommended by Pettenkofer and Doerner) because it can swell old paint films making them soluble and hygroscopic (p. 168) [moreover it is very yellow and yellows further considerably with time as I have ascertained by experiments. H.R.].

Eibner also draws attention to the misguided practice of mixing copaiva balsam to oil colours and media.

On p. 175 Eibner says 'The yellowing of varnish films arises earlier than that of the oil film and is eventually more pronounced than the latter.'

Page 176: 'Ochres, siena earths and iron reds may *darken Back protection*: (moisture barrier) postulated by Pettenkofer, Keim, Ostwald, Laurie, Täuber und Steppes: tinfoil, wax-resin.

Even Pettenkofer knew the yellowing of resin, otherwise he would have developed his method in a different way.'

Experiments published in Eibner's Appendix show . . . '*proof that resin films may yellow more than lean thin linseed oil paint and that this yellowing and browning of oil painting was caused principally by surface coatings.*'

Warning against *oil-resin paint*, danger worsened — the copaiva balsam turns picture brown in a few weeks.

'The least of the causes of yellowing and browning and darkening: linseed oil; the stronger: Yellowing and browning of varnishes, the very strongest: Oil-resin-balsam paint.'

Other causes for darkening: siccatives and 'growing through' of burnt umber, asphalt etc.

Stand oil yellows less: (linolein — acid glycerine made inactive) but dries slowly. Eibner does not mention one cause of the darkening of pictures: Surface dirt, (soot, and nicotine on top of the varnish or fixed by it), which is often browner than the darkened varnish itself.

Eibner, p. 53:

Yellowing of oil must be distinguished from yellowing of resins.

I. Humidity factor. In completely dry air: no yellowing of oil during same spell. Liquid oils: no yellowing but bleaching in light (see also p. 62) only linked to drying, begins as soon as it is sticky. *Primary*, reversible yellowing: in 4 weeks, on *covered* samples.

Bibliography

II. Only (in the dark) white lead — linseed maximum, zinc white and lead less, poppy oil still unyellowed. Re-bleached in daylight, in 8 days.

III. Secondary, *age* yellowing : if excess of oil and thickness of application is avoided : *no disturbing yellowing occurs in centuries*; proof : old masters *after removal of varnish*. Page 54 : Golden 'Gallery tone' explicable if *oil lacquers* used. 56, 57 : 'Frans Hals Haarlem varnish removal : no yellowing in paint itself — all yellowing in varnish, proves that yellowing was for a long time blamed on the wrong cause, the oil, whilst strongly yellowing *surface coatings* were the cause.' — 'Thus linseed oil is neither the only nor the strongest cause of yellowing but it is the best if paint not excessively fat or thick or does not contain yellowing additions.'

Several of the theories published by even the most eminent pioneers in our field in the 19th and early 20th centuries have had to be revised in the light of recent experience gained during the cleaning of the old masters' paintings. Eastlake, Laurie, Doerner and Maroger are cases in point. On the other hand Eibner bases his theories on his own rather conclusive experiments. His publications are largely as valid today as when they were first published in the 1920s and 30s. (H.R.)

1930

(14) VALLEY, Amédée. *La restauration des tableaux* (The restoration of pictures). Paris, 1930, 40 pp.

No original contribution worth mentioning, except perhaps a useful paragraph on restoration of pastels. (H.R.).

(15) *International Conference on the Examination and Preservation of Works of Art, Rome, Oct. 1930.*

A useful summary of the proceedings and conclusions of the Committee on the Restoration of Paintings and the Use of Varnish is given in the *Museums Journal* (London), XXX (July 1930–March 1930), pp. 221–223.

(16) PAPARI, T. V. '*Méthodes de conservation des peintures anciennes*' ('Methods of conservation for old paintings'). *Mouseion*, XVI (1930), No. 4, pp. 8–17.

(17) RUHEMANN, H. 'La technique de la conservation des tableaux' ('The technique of picture conservation'). *Mouseion*, XV (1931), No. 3, pp. 14–23.

(18) TOCH, Maximilian. *Paints, painting and restoration*. New York, 1931.

Even taking into account its comparatively early date, this book contains a considerable amount of mistaken advice, amateurish ideas about 'glazing' and 'restoration'. Confusion also arises with an X-radiograph printed in the negative (i.e. areas of greater absorption, notably lead white, appearing black) without explaining this fact. Valuable, however, is a detailed list of pigments and of twenty-eight solvents, with useful comments. (H.R.).

(19) TUDOR-HART, P. 'Nettoyage, rentoilage et vernissage des peintures' ('Cleaning, relining and varnishing of paintings'). *Mouseion*, XV (1931), No. 3. pp. 23–41.

(20) WIESE, Erich. 'La conservation des tableaux contemporains' ('The conservation of contemporary pictures'). *Mouseion*, XX (1932), No. 4, pp. 23–26.

(21) BAUER-BOLTON, Victor. 'La conservation des peintures de chevalet — les supports

Bibliography

et les fonds' ('The conservation of easel paintings — the supports and the grounds'). *Mouseion*, XXIII–XXIV (1933), pp. 68–91.

(22) LEAGUE OF NATIONS, Office International des Musées. *Les Dossiers de l'Office International des Musées, 2. Documents sur la conservation des peintures.* (Dossiers of the International Museums Office, 2. Documents on the conservation of paintings). 56 pp. Paris, 1933.

Chapter I, an account of the International Conference for the Study of Scientific Methods applied to the Examination and Conservation of Works of Art, held in Rome in 1930; general conclusions of the Conference. Chapter II, the work of a committee of experts set up to enable the preparation of a manual of conservation of paintings (see No. (15), Nos. (27), (28)), among members of which are included W. G. Constable, H. J. Plenderleith, G. L. Stout and H. Ruhemann. Chapter III comprises a circular issued separately in 1933 as *Mouseion — Information Mensuelles, (August)*. The preservation of paintings in museum collections.

Although some of the practical procedures advocated would now be considered out-of-date, the principles enunciated still remain sound. Chapter II contains a list of desirable properties for a picture varnish which still remains an ideal standard even now being striven for in the development of modern synthetic resins. In Chapter III there is sound advice on climatology.

(23) PLENDERLEITH, H. J. 'The examination and preservation of paintings. A digest.' *Museums Journal* (London), XXXII (April 1932–March 1933), pp. 308–310, 349–351, 388–389.

A useful summary of the content of papers read at the Rome Conference (see above, Nos. (15), (22)) of 1930.

(24) BUSCH, Harold. 'Vom richtigen und falschen Restaurieren' ('Good and bad restorations'). *Die Kunst*, XXXV (1934), pp. 185–188.

(25) HILER, Hilaire. *Notes on the technique of painting*. London, 1934. 2nd ed. 1954.

Written for painters, with ease and charm. Good introduction stressing the importance of technique, method and beautiful 'matière' and speaking of '. . . Those pedants who prefer to look at their favourite masterpieces through one or several coats of brown varnish . . . the sort of people who prefer age and other considerations which would alone interest the commercially minded collector. . . .'

Chapter I on Painting Technique and not relevant to my topic (to be reviewed in a forthcoming book).

Chapter II on Colour and Pigment, p. 297 very useful table 'Pigments at a Glance'.

Chapter III on Vehicles and Media (including varnishes) enumerates uncritically many substances and recipes, confuses 'petrol' with 'petroleum' (see p. 194). On p. 162 the usual wrong guess regarding van Eyck's technique, which is *not* on a base of tempera or an emulsion; recommends as varnish: wax, which has not enough varnishing power except for light modern pictures, excellent on top of a resin varnish, 'Ceronis' remains sticky, p. 167. Hiler rightly condemns Soehne's varnish: incompatible with oil, darkens and becomes too hard because it is made of Shellac.

Chapter IV : The Ideal Studio : for my own views see pp. 69–71.

Chapter V : Conservation of Paintings. Only an experienced restorer could pick out the few really useful suggestions. Hiler credits Henley instead of Pettenkofer with the invention of the Regenerating Method. Water as diluent for alcohol introduces water into the paint which is inadvisable. Pure turpentine is after a short time no longer sufficient to dissolve mastic or dammar films (p. 288). The list of solvents contains a few useful substances but omits toluene and acetone. No preliminary cleaning tests are mentioned. *Rentoilage* or rebacking of canvases is not virtually transferring a rotten canvas to a new one; transferring implies the removal of the old canvas, which is rarely done. Glue alone for relining is to be strongly discouraged (see pp. 150, 153), and casein glue because of its strong tension and shrinking is the worst for repairing 'rips and holes' or for putty. On p. 291 Hiler mentions as 'the only disadvantage of retouching in tempera that it does not change with time and therefore may become apparent with the passage of years as the rest of the picture gradually changes'. In reality most paintings more than, say, 150 years old have probably reached about the maximum of possible change in tone and we restorers are very happy to have at least this one retouching medium, tempera, which will usually not change noticeably and will not stand out as a dark patch eventually.

The extensive bibliography is useful but contains few comments.

The index is incomplete and the glossary partly faulty. (H.R.)

(26) LAURIE, A. P. 'Le dévernissage des tableaux anciens et la suppression des repeints' ('The removal of varnish from old pictures and the eradication of repaints'). *Mouseion*, XXV–XXVI (1934), Nos. I–II, pp. 216–220.

See H.R.'s review of No. (11), above.

(27) ANON. 'La conservation des peintures' ('The conservation of paintings'). *Mouseion*, XLI–XLII (1938), pp. 1–272 (entire volume).

See below, No. (28).

(28) ANON. *Manuel de la conservation et de la restauration des peintures* (Manual of the conservation and restoration of paintings). Office International des Musées, Paris, 1939. 310 pp., illus.

This manual is a reprint of No. (27), see above, with the addition of a table of pigments and their properties (in French, English, German and Italian) together with a brief dictionary of technical terms in French, English and German.

This handbook was the direct outcome of the International Conference on picture conservation and restoration held in Rome in 1930 (see above, Nos. (15), (22), (23)). It was written by an international group of specialists including G. L. STOUT, H. J. PLENDERLEITH and H. RUHEMANN. With its emphasis on the importance of proper environment and on systematic examination of condition before treatment, it is perhaps the first modern textbook on the subject to be published. Part I lays down the general principles of conservation, then follows a description of methods of examination (by special illumination, microscopy, X-radiography, etc.). Conservation in the sense of physical environment and safety precautions is next dealt with. Although advances have been made since in, for example, air conditioning techniques, the advice as to general principles is still sound. Part II comprises picture restoration, in the sense of treatment: general principles of restoration; disorders and treatment of the protective coating, the paint layer, the ground and support. The appendix 'Recommendations Pratiques', is reprinted from the circular mentioned above, No. (22).

Bibliography

(29) MAYER, Ralph. *The artist's handbook of materials and techniques*. 1st edn. New York, 1938. The most recent English edition (considerably revised), Faber and Faber, London, 1965.

Chapter 13 : The Conservation of Pictures.

Though the author modestly disclaims it he gives in these thirty pages a nearly comprehensive little manual which is useful not only to the amateur but even to the professional picture restorer.

Mr. Mayer repeats the traditional fallacy that turpentine, mineral spirit and naphtha remove the grime from the surface of a varnish film. In fact they remove little more than does a dry cotton wool swab. In my opinion it is essential to remove the grime because it forms an insulating layer which is not readily broken up by the usual solvents and if left would often induce the cleaner to use unnecessarily 'strong' solvents (see p. 190). The cleaning mixture suggested : 5 parts alcohol, 3 parts turpentine and 1 part ethyl acetate seems to me rather powerful for an amateur or beginner. Like the rather unnecessary castor oil which Mr. Mayer mentions as retarder, turpentine can under certain circumstances actually make the mixture more effective rather than 'weaken' it, (see p. 190). Against blooming (synthetic varnishes hardly do bloom) a thin rubbing with wax (see p. 279) is surely sounder than machine oil. It seems a pity that the recent revision does not include a mention of the vacuum lining method or of Coremans, Gettens and Thissen's research into the media of the van Eycks' school; they found that no tempera paint was used in their technique. Mayer writes on p. 34 : 'The fifteenth and sixteenth century paintings *innovated* [sic] by the Flemish artists soon after the year 1400 and referred to by Vasari and other older writers as oil paintings were, for the most part, precisely the sort of works we call tempera paintings today when referring to tempera in the highest stage of development, and some were produced by employing alternate coats of tempera and oily or resinous mediums as in the accepted tempera variations'. Here Mr. Mayer merely quotes Doerner's unsubstantiated guesses; or has he any new evidence to offer? (H.R.)

1940

(30) BUCK, R. D. and STOUT, G. L. 'Original and later paint in pictures'. *Technical Studies in the Field of the Fine Arts*, Vol. VIII (1940), pp. 123–150.

Systematic methods for distinguishing retouching and repaint from original paint.

(31) CONSTABLE, W. G. 'Cleaning and care of the National Gallery pictures.' *Nature*, London, CLXII (1948), pp. 166–167.

An assessment of the findings of the Weaver Committee (see below, (36) and (43)).

(32) KECK, Sheldon. 'On the conservation of early American paintings.' *Antiques* (Boston, New York), LIII (Jan. 1948), pp. 52–54.

(33) STOUT, George L. *The care of pictures*. Columbia University Press, New York, 1948 (see pp. 99–103 of present book).

(34) MAROGER, Jacques. *The secret formulas and techniques of the masters*. Publ. by Studio, New York, 1948.

Although not directly concerned with picture restoration, this book is of relevance because if the author's theories on technique and materials of the masters were correct it would be impossible to clean many pictures. Maroger does not keep his initial promise to confine himself to facts. His many complicated recipes for oil and wax media and what he terms 'black oils' are based on guesses, some of them 100 years old, and most of them wrong, as has since been proved by research and experience. See the review by Ralph Mayer, *Magazine of Art*, Nov. 1949, p. 273. (H.R.).

(35) MAYER, Ralph. *The painter's craft*. Van Nostrand Co. Inc., 1948. Most of the contents appear in (29), see above.

(36) WEAVER, J. R. H. 'The National Gallery. Report of Expert Inquiry on cleaning pictures.' *The Times*, 8th May, 1948.

An account by the author of the report of the Weaver Committee, set up to inquire into the cleaning of pictures at the National Gallery, London. The author was also chairman of the Committee. (See also No. (31) above, No. (43) below).

(37) AUGUSTI, Selim. *Tecnica e restauro* (Technique and restoration). Miccoli, Naples, 1949. 5 pp. Not available to author or bibliographer.

(38) KECK, Sheldon. 'The care and cleaning of your pictures.' *Brooklyn Museum Bulletin*, X (1949), No. 3, pp. 1–12.

Sensible advice to the curator and private collector.

(39) THIÈLE, G. Van. *La restauration des tableaux*. H. Laurens, Paris, 1949. Not available to author or bibliographer.

(40) WEHLTE, Kurt. 'Probleme der Gemäldeerhaltung' (Problems of picture conservation'). *Zeitschrift für Kunstgeschichte* (Munich–Berlin) XII (1949), pp. 90–104.

1950

(41) BRADLEY, Morton C. *The treatment of pictures*. Art Technology, Cambridge, Mass., 1950.

In his preface and introduction Bradley describes and confines clearly and modestly the purpose and scope of his treatise. 'It is useful . . . only as a handbook for competent conservators (American for 'restorers') and curators and for students working under their direction; for others it is likely to be useless, certain to be dangerous'.

This is to my mind easily the most useful, most highly professional and most systematic and exhaustive handbook of its kind.

For each process there are paragraphs on: definition, purpose, danger, precautions, material and equipment needed and method; often alternative methods are mentioned and from four to twenty manipulations enumerated in list form.

The book is brought out in the form of a ring folder with loose leaves so that the reader can insert his comments on new pages.

The unfamiliar decimal numbering system instead of page numbers, necessary for this scheme makes it difficult to find one's way through the book, particularly as the index is very incomplete.

I should think it well worth while to produce a cheaper English edition, brought up to date, with the index and glossary extended and improved by including English equivalents for a few American terms.

The often excessive terseness could then perhaps be amended and some minor points added; for instance the drawback of using glue size for fixing cleavage could be mentioned and the danger pointed out of blanching that heat and moisture at times cause not only in the varnish, but also in the paint film; this is not always entirely reversible, even with the excellent remedies Bradley recommends.

The brief chapter No. 1. 31 'Attaching a Composite Wooden Support' (of balsa wood), a method which R. D. Buck showed to the restorers and craftsmen at the National Gallery in 1948 is important, so is the next No. 1. 32 'Channelling a Wooden Panel'. The chapter on retouching (which should not be called 'restoring') is less thorough and useful. 'In-painting' with oil paint (No. 23. 1) is recommended, which is by now well superseded.

Apart from such minor details this model handbook would be difficult to emulate, let alone improve upon, except perhaps by carrying out Bradley's initial idea of gradually expanding it with new pages by other restorers.

I should like to add here an appeal to all leading colleagues to get together and put this into practice. (H.R.)

(42) CERCLE DES ALUMNI DES FONDATIONS UNIVERSITAIRES. Art et Science. *Alumni* XIX (June 1950), pp. 246–387.

This issue of the journal is devoted to the relationship of art, science and conservation, and a number of articles are concerned with picture restoration: Le nettoyage et la restauration des peintures anciennes: Position du problème (The cleaning and restoration of old pictures: the presentation of the problem) by René Huyghe; Le point de vue du critique d'art, by Paul Fierens; Het standpunt von de museumdirecteur (The standpoint of the Museum Director), by Waltger Vanbeselaere; Le point de vue du laboratoire (The point of view of the laboratory) by René Sneyers; The viewpoint of the conservator by George L. Stout; L'introduction d'un nouveau critère dans l'appréciation des oeuvres d'art: Les sciences naturelles, by Paul Coremans, pp. 292–301; The philosophy of science and art, by F. I. G. Rawlins.

Papers of considerable interest with a philosophical rather than practical approach to restoration.

(43) 'Cleaning of pictures. Part one.' *Museum* (UNESCO, Paris), III (1950), No. 2. Foreword. Introduction by Theodore Rousseau, pp. 110–111. The Weaver Report on the cleaning of pictures in the National Gallery, pp. 112–176.

The Weaver Report (see above, No. (36)), is printed in full and illustrated with numerous photographs.

(44) 'Cleaning of pictures. Part two.'
Museum (UNESCO, Paris), III (1950), No. 3. In English and French. Illus. 'The Louvre Museum and the problem of cleaning old pictures,' by René HUYGHE, pp. 190–206. 'The restoration of the "Pietà" of Sebastiano del Piombo,' by Cesare BRANDI, pp. 207–219. 'Some comments on the cleaning of the "Night Watch",' by Arthur van SCHENDEL, pp. 220–226. 'Cleaning and restoration of old paintings — the point of view of a physical and chemical laboratory', by Paul COREMANS, pp. 227–232. 'The future of museum conservation', by Murray PEASE, pp. 233–242. 'Cleaning of pictures at the National Gallery, London' (the National Gallery's reply to an ICOM questionnaire on the removal of varnish), pp. 243–251.

The contents of the above two numbers of *Museum* comprising 'Cleaning of pictures.

Bibliography

Part one' and 'Cleaning of pictures. Part two', have been reprinted as :

The care of paintings. UNESCO Publication No. 778, in English and French, Paris, 1951.

(45) GOULINAT, Jean G. and AUBERT, Lucien. *Technique de la peinture; détérioration et restauration* ('The technique of painting; deterioration and restoration'). Paris, 1950.

The authors at the time of writing occupied the posts of Head and Secretary respectively of the restoration department at the Louvre museum.

(46) COUTO, João. *The present position of the problem of treating paintings.* Edições Excelsior, 1952, 31 pp. + illustrations.

A discussion on conservation of paintings and a description of the premises, facilities, and work of the restoration department of the National Museum of Art at Lisbon.

(47) FELLER, Robert L. 'The conservation of paintings.' *Carnegie Magazine* (Pittsburgh, Pa.), XXVI (1952), pp. 370–373.

A brief review of principles, practice, and the role of science.

(48) KECK, Sheldon. 'The care of paintings.' *New York History* (Journal of the New York State Historical Association, Cooperstown, N.Y.), Jan. 1953, pp. 105–120.

(49) CONSTABLE, W. G. *The Painters' Workshop.* Oxford University Press, London, 1954.

See Chapter 9, 'The restorer's contribution.' The author, best known as an art historian, gives a lucid though brief description of deterioration of paintings, its prevention and repair.

(50) KECK, Caroline K. *How to take care of your pictures.* Published by the Museum of Modern Art and the Brooklyn Museum, New York, 1954. 54pp., illus.

Practical information and instruction on conservation and restoration presented in simple straightforward terms for the private collector or museum curator.

(51) SAVAGE, George. *The art and antique restorer's handbook.* Philosophical Society Library, New York, 1954. 140 pp.

The restoration of antiques and *objets d'art* is dealt with in much more detail than that of paintings concerning which the text is of small amount and scattered throughout the encyclopedia format of the book. Most of the information is sound, though a few old-fashioned and unsound practices are recommended, e.g. the use of castor oil as a restrainer, the application of copaiva balsam to 'nourish' the picture after cleaning. A certain inconsistency appears here and there. Under the entry for 'patina' the author distinguishes between changes in the original surface produced by age in furniture and metals and the false patina of dirt or discoloured varnish. He says that he does not object to the removal of this from pictures. Yet in his entry on 'Oil paintings, cleaning and preservation' he maintains that the aim is to leave a thin layer of varnish to avoid a 'skinned' appearance. There is a healthy warning to antique dealers that the inexperienced should not tackle cleaning or restoration of paintings.

(52) BRACHERT, Thomas. *Gemäldepflege* (Picture conservation). Otto Maier Verlag, Ravensburg, 1955. 103 pp., illus.

An excellent, admirably concise handbook, well illustrated, containing a detailed and useful list of pigments and solvents. The chapters on woodwork and lining reveal extensive practical experience. The same cannot be said of the section on cleaning; though it also contains much useful advice it seems mostly based on earlier publications.

Turpentine on its own for varnish removal is advocated in one book after another, but I have never seen any worthwhile effect. Benzol, unless added to alcohol, is not a powerful solvent. Madder (Krapplack) in old oil paintings is not at all 'easily soluble' but remarkably tough.

Mr. Brachert asks (in 1955) on page 9: 'Did Rembrandt really paint brown — in brown?' and: 'Who can answer where the final glaze (Schlusslazur) begins? Here modern technique must provide the aids.' This claim and his belated questions have been answered 45 years ago when de Wild senior first cleaned the Frans Hals pictures in Haarlem and the chemist van der Sleen published his scientific tests carried out on the pictures during the varnish removal. It became clear that the imaginary 'Schlusslazur' was not in the paint but only in the darkened varnish and could be removed without risk to the paint. A considerable number of Rembrandts have since been cleaned totally and with complete success in Holland, the United States and Great Britain, so that it is no longer necessary to use the words 'totally cleaned' in a pejorative sense. Had the restorers gone on with their less conscientious and less complete cleaning they would to this day not be able to answer Mr. Brachert's questions, because they would never have grasped the very considerable difference between 'the yellowed varnish coatings and a final glaze'. The timid, groping cleaner would never have got any wiser; but now Mr. Brachert can convince himself, even at the Louvre where one or two Rembrandts have recently been almost totally cleaned, that Rembrandt did not paint brown in brown but with a wealth of colourful nuances, warm and cool, and without a 'Schlusslazur'.

May I correct the quotation of my recipe for CRP? It does not contain any alcohol which would defeat its main object, i.e. not to attack any varnish film, but it does contain 10 per cent carnauba wax, which ensures a hard, non-sticky surface. (H.R.).

(53) RUHEMANN, H. 'The care of paintings.' *House and Garden* (London), May 1955, pp. 69, 101, 110.
    Advice to the private collector.

(54) SCHAFER, J. 'Das Restaurieren von Gemälden' ('The restoration of paintings'). *Weltkunst* (Berlin), XXV, pp. 27–12.

(55) PLENDERLEITH, H. J. *The conservation of antiquities and works of art.* Oxford University Press, London, 1956 (French translation published 1966, Eyrolles, Paris).
    Chapter VII, 'Easel paintings', is a brief but useful description of the disorders, diagnosis and treatment of easel paintings, intended mainly as a guide to the museum curator, rather than as detailed instruction for the practising restorer. The Introduction 'The influence of environment' is a useful summary of the destructive agents which attack works of art.

(56) LOHE, Hermann. 'Ueber die Schäden am "Höllensturz" con P. P. Rubens' ('The damage to the "Fall of the Damned" by P. P. Rubens'). *Kunstchronik* (Nürnberg), 1959, No. 4, p. 89.

(57) ROTH, Toni. 'Zur Konservierung und Restaurierung von Gemälden' ('The conservation and restoration of pictures'), *Weltkunst* (Berlin), VIII (1959), pp. 7–8.

(58) CLARK, Carl Damle. *Pictures, their preservation and restoration.* The Standard Arts Press, Butler Maryland, 1959. 270 pp., illus.

Bibliography

This work has not, unfortunately been available to either the author of the present book or the compiler of the bibliography, so it is not possible to assess its merit. However, a list of contents will be found in *I.I.C. Abstracts*, III (1960), No. 1. Abstract No. 2353.

1960

(59) ALTHÖFER, Heinz. 'Einige Probleme der Restaurierung moderner Kunst' ('Some problems in the restoration of modern art'). *Das Kunstwerk* (Baden-Baden), XIV (1960), Heft 5–6, pp. 51–59.

(60) ALTHÖFER, Heinz. 'Wiener Methoden der Gemälderestaurierung' ('Viennese methods of picture restoration'). *Maltechnik*, LXII (1960), pp. 50–55.
A description of methods used in the restoration studios of the Harrach gallery in Vienna.

(61) DEKVAR, V. L. and DROWN, F. E. 'Restoration of pictures at Baroda.' *Museums Journal* (London), LX (1960), pp. 95–98.
The treatment of a large collection of European oil paintings in poor condition.

(62) KECK, Caroline K. 'Conservation of contemporary art.' *Museum News* (Washington, D.C.), XXXVIII (1960), No. 5, pp. 34–37.

(63) WEHLTE, K. 'Infrarot-Strahler' ('Infra-red radiator'). *Maltechnik*, LXVI (1960), pp. 75–81.
Mainly concerned with the use of infra-red sources of heat in restoration processes such as wax-relining.

(64) WILLEMSEN, E. 'Katalog der restaurierten Werke' ('Catalogues of restored works'). *Jahrbuch der Rheinischen Denkmalpflege* (Düsseldorf), XXIII (1960), pp. 327–460.
Processes described include the use of insecticides and wood preservatives, treatment of wood panels, retouching with synthetic resin media, protective wax surface coatings.

(65) COREMANS, Paul. 'The conservation of paintings.' *Museums Journal* (London), LXI (1961), pp. 105–109.

(66) POMERANTZ, Louis. *Is your contemporary painting more temporary than you think?* Chicago, 1962.
Warning and advice as to the problems of conservation likely to arise in connection with modern paintings.

(67) AMERICAN FEDERATION OF ARTS. 'Preserve your pictures.' *A.F.A. Quarterly* (New York), I (1963), No. 4, 26 pp.
Particularly concerned with environment, storage, packing etc.

(68) BOISSONNAS, Alain G. 'The treatment of fire-blistered oil paintings.' *Studies in Conservation*, VIII (1963), pp. 55–63.

(69) *Recent advances in conservation*, edited by G. THOMSON. (Papers given at the I.I.C. Rome Conference, 1959), Butterworth, London, 1963.
Contributions relevant to the subject of picture conservation comprise: Evaluation of spectral radiation hazards in window-lighted galleries, by Laurence S. Harrison;

Bibliography

The influence of light on museum objects by J. Lodewijks; Some studies on the protection of works of art during travel, by Nathan Stolow; Relative humidity in a closed package, by Kenzo Toishi; Les méthodes d'analyse appliquées aux oeuvres d'art et aux antiquités, by Selim Augusti; Proposal for a handbook on analysis of materials of paintings, by Rutherford J. Gettens; Methods of analysis (physical and microchemical) applied to paintings and antiquities, by E. T. Hall; Application of the electron microbeam probe and micro X-rays in non-destructive analysis, by W. J. Young; The conservation of works of art in tropical and sub-tropical zones, by W. Boustead; The effect of ageing and re-forming on the ease of solubility of certain resins, by Elizabeth H. Jones; Application of science to cleaning methods: solvent action studies on pigmented and unpigmented linseed oil films, by Nathan Stolow; Some applications of mechanics to the treatment of panel paintings, by Richard D. Buck; Treatment of warped wood panels by plastic deformation, moisture barriers and elastic support, by Christian Wolters; The transfer of easel paintings, by A. W. Lucas; La conservation des peintures sur panneaux, by G. Urbani; New solvent-type varnishes, by Robert L. Feller; New picture varnishes, by Garry Thomson; La formation des conservateurs et des restaurateurs, by P. Rotondi; Training for engineers in conservation, by Sheldon Keck; The training of restorers, by Helmut Ruhemann; Programme of the faculty of conservation at the Academy of Fine Arts in Warsaw, by Bohdan Marconi. Summaries also appear in *Studies in Conservation*, VI (1961), No. 4.

(70) *Über die Erhaltung von Gemälden und Skulpturen* (On the preservation of paintings and sculpture), edited by Rolf E. STRAUB. Zürich and Stuttgart, 1963.

Contributions concerned with picture restoration are: Einige Wissenschaftliche Gesichtspunkte zum Problem der Konservierung von Kunstwerken (A scientific viewpoint of the problem of conservation of works of art) by A. E. A. Werner, Ein technischer Beitrag zum Problem der Firnisabnahme (A technical approach to the problem of varnish removal), by Stephen Rees Jones; Ein neues Verfahren zur Übertragung von Tafelmalereien bei teilweiser Beibehaltung des Bildträgers (A new process of semitransfer for paintings on panel), by Peter F. J. M. Hermesdorf; Ein Verfahren zur Übertragung italienischer Tafelbilder des 13 bis 15 Jahrhunderts (A process of transferring Italian panel pictures of the 13th to 15th centuries), the method of Augusto Vermehren, described by Edgar Denninger; Über die Erhaltung von Holztafelbildern (The preservation of pictures on wood panel), by Rolf E. Straub.

This publication is a 'Festschrift' and shows the advantages of high level variety and internationality (5 countries) and at the same time the inevitable disadvantages of a Festschrift: incompleteness and a certain unevenness in quality.

Straub writes in his introduction: 'it is quite possible to conserve a painting or a sculpture in an exemplary manner, and at the same time to impair its artistic substance. ... The restorer must not neglect craftsmanship, and,' he continues, 'connoisseurship in the good old-fashioned sense, in close co-operation with the art historians.'

Straub condemns severely the removal of old paint from antique wood sculptures, the waxing and varnishing of frescoes and the separating of the two faces of panels painted on both sides. (H.R.)

Bibliography

(I) *A. Werner — 'Some Scientific Aspects of Conservation'*

I quote Werner's own succinct English summary:

'In this article, recent progress in the treatment of documents, prints and drawings and *easel paintings* is briefly surveyed. Attention is drawn to the need for the deacidification of paper and the Barrow process of lamination is discussed. In the bleaching of prints and drawings the advantages of the sodium chloride method are considered in some detail. Some of the new synthetic materials used in the consolidation of wooden antiquities are described.

He uses as a starting point Plenderleith's book, 'a milestone on the progress scientific methods have made *in the past 3 decades in the service of the arts*'; he adds some of his own experiments and experiences; for bleaching of mould spots he suggests the use of sodium chlorite as safer than Chloramin T (Gettens, *Museum 5*, 1952), as a back protection for panel paintings in transit: a cover of polyethylene; for impregnation of wooden objects: epoxyd or epichlorhydrin resins as well as immersion in wax (Straub deals in more detail with resin in his article). Werner mentions as superior replacements for natural rubber, glue, starch or wax, synthetic substances such as carboxymethylcellulose, polyvinyl alcohol, 'Maranyl' Nylon C109/P (I.C.I. Limited), particularly useful where an elastic non-aqueous adhesive is indicated, and as a protective application over a crumbling surface where the passing of moisture must not be prevented. Synthetic waxes show a great number of properties not found in natural waxes; polyethylene waxes are recommended and polyethyleneglycol waxes for certain purposes.

III. Professor *Kurt Wehlte's* fully illustrated report on the salvage operations and the Uncovering of Wall Paintings in the Cemetery-Church at Balsthal contains much valuable technical information. The work consisted mainly in the removal of up to 11 layers of whitewash and the uncovering and fixing of a disintegrating original 'chalk-secco' mural. A wetting agent and injection, by means of a syringe, of a calcium casein glue and special 'fresco presses' with a screwing device were used. The retouching was carries out in 'tratteggio' (hatching method). The medium used is not mentioned.

During the work a niche with 3 valuable well preserved murals of the 15th century was discovered. It had been walled in shortly after they were finished.

IV. *Varnish Removal: A Technical Approach* — Stephen Rees Jones. I quote:

'Two aspects of the process of cleaning paintings are considered: (1) The action of the solvent on the varnish and on the paint and (2) the means by which the softened varnish is removed. The hazards resulting from (2) are as great as those from (1), which is normally considered to be the chief source of danger. The action of wiping the dissolved varnish off the surface may cause prominences such as the ridges of the impasto and the raised edges of cupped paint in the surface of the painting to be worn away and in general result in a mat chalky film. Rolling cotton with swabs over the surface of the paint causes less damage than a wiping action. An experiment in which cotton wool swabs are eliminated altogether is described.' (Robert van Eyck's Method).

'Elementary ideas of solvent action can be misleading: for example, that it is possible to neutralise the action by means of a restrainer, or to so dilute the solvent that a "safe" strength is being used. Any solvent which is used will diffuse into the paint and cause some degree of swelling and softening: the discrimination between paint and varnish depends entirely on the difference in the degree of swelling. The swelling with a particular solvent will depend on the ratio of pigment to medium, on the age, on the proportion of resin added to the medium, among other things.'

'Volatility of the solvent is an effective control of the process. Investigations have shown that the maximum degree of swelling produced by a given solvent depends on a constant termed the solvent parameter which can be derived from thermo-dynamic data. In this way it is possible to choose from the many solvents which act on resin those which have the least action on oil paint. The solvent parameter is not the only factor governing the choice for solvent because volatility is equally important. Obviously a very active solvent of low volatility is extremely dangerous whilst a very volatile inactive solvent can serve no purpose. Any highly active solvent used should for safety's sake be volatile. It sometimes occurs that an active volatile solvent removes the more soluble constituent of the varnish film leaving behind an insoluble residue. This undesirable result can be avoided by using a solvent mixture that contains a small proportion of a solvent of low volatility which will keep the varnish film soft until it is removed in its entirety.'

We have been quoting Rees Jones's excellent English summary.

In it he does not mention an important assertion made in the German text:

. . . 'It can however be assumed with certainty that these effects [leaching], observed on artificially aged oil films, are far less strongly pronounced than on the old films with which the restorer has to deal generally'.

This may give the impression that varnish removal does in general result in a mat chalky film and in up to 40 per cent of loss of substance.

Together with Laurie, Stout and Stolow, Rees Jones has to be regarded as a pioneer in the scientific research on the behaviour of varnish and paint films during the process of picture cleaning. His potentially very valuable contributions, including the present one, lose a little in accuracy and value because the distinction between forced laboratory tests and what happens in the actual varnish removal is not clearly enough drawn. This is apt to cause unnecessary alarm and confusion among readers who are not scientists.

In order to fulfil the beneficent task of enlightening the cleaner on the forces and variables involved, the scientist has to produce in his forced laboratory tests the maximum effect, for instance of leaching, in order to be at all able to measure the expected effect on the paint film, and to prove it, whereas in contrast the restorer tries to avoid this effect altogether, or as far as it is possible. Rees Jones rightly emphasises that the idea is misleading, that the resin of the varnish is simply dissolved by the solvent, and the paint layer remains quite unaffected (p. 49). But he omits to mention that an old paint film is cross-linked and fundamentally different from a varnish film in structure and reaction to solvents. He also legitimately warns against 'cumulative effect' and wearing during the various removals of varnish carried out in the course of time by the friction with the cotton wool swab. This friction has an unfavourable effect, because it disturbs the paint layer too much, to a degree which is below the demarcation of safety. Erosion of the surface by the solvent can occur, though only to a miscroscopic degree. On page 53 he says 'when the solvent evaporates relatively slowly, and is very active, a dangerous and uncontrollable situation is created'; he slightly contradicts this by continuing later, 'the safety of the process entirely depends on ascertaining whether the highest concentration (of the solvent) on the paint surface is not so high that it produces a swelling which would allow the paint to yield to the wiping of the swab.'

Bibliography

On p. 51 Rees Jones mentions Bradley's important suggestion to apply a rolling, instead of a wiping movement in cleaning, and above all, he publishes for the first time Robert van Eyck's ingenious experiments carried out at the Courtauld Institute of Art in 1952 with the aim of excluding entirely cotton wool swabs and friction. I quote : 'the most effective of the many experiments was undertaken with a commercial polyvinyl chloride paste to which acetone was added. In applying this thin paste to a picture surface, the acetone penetrated and with that part of the varnish film which was thus put into a state of sol mixed with the paste and was so incorporated into the rubber-like film which formed in the course of several hours. This film did not adhere to the surface and could easily be pulled off, as it were as a complete mould of the paint surface film, with pastosities, craquelure etc. Where retouchings existed in the varnish layer they can be observed embedded in the film. The process being simultaneously applied to the whole surface has the serious disadvantage that it does not allow the restorer the necessary divergent treatment of technically different portions of the paint film. Where such exist resin glazes would obviously suffer and the effect on the paint layer containing resin would not be slight.

'On the other hand paint layers consisting of pure drying oils or of egg tempera can be completely de-varnished with this method without impairing protruding parts, however high the impasto or however strong the cupping of the paint may be. The fine surface texture will be better preserved, since no attrition or abrasion happens during the swelling. It is, however, regrettable that the many-fold composition of the paintings excludes the general adoption of such an automatic method. Probably the cotton wool swab will remain in the skilled hand of the restorer and satisfactory results may thus be expected, under the condition that it will be handled in complete comprehension of the relevant physical data.'

Rees Jones explains why the traditional conception that the use of turpentine can stop the effect of a stronger solvent is erroneous as well as the idea of the restorer that in diluting his strong solvent to a certain point it will then no longer attack the paint. However, it does so in reality, as countless restorers have proved many a time, because precisely as Rees Jones says, the cleaner can vary the time factor by exploiting the fast evaporation of acetone (see pp. 201 and 203).

Rees Jones concludes that one has to take into account 'that the time factor is far safer as a guiding thought for the restorer than the misleading idea that in a certain solvent the paint is insoluble.' (H.R.)

(71) CORNELIUS, F. du Pont. 'Further developments in the treatment of fire-blistered oil paintings.' *Studies in Conservation*, XI (1966), pp. 31–36.

SECTION 5
Accounts of particular restorations

This list is necessarily limited. More examples can be found in the relevant journals. Of these the *Bulletin* of the Institut Royal du Patrimoine Artistique, Brussels, gives exceptionally detailed accounts of certain important restorations, as also does the

Bibliography

Bollettino of the Istituto Centrale del Restauro, Rome, which in addition has a section entitled 'Schede di Restauro' describing recent restorations carried out at the Istituto. The other most important sources are the year books, annual reports or periodical bulletins of art galleries and museums. The *Annual Report* of the National Gallery, London, must be singled out for special mention in this respect, for it gives not only detailed descriptions of the most important restorations carried out, but also short accounts of every picture treated during the year in question.

1920

(1) VAN DER SLEEN, G. *Quelques recherches à propos du nettoyage des tableaux de Frans Hals à Haarlem* ('Some researches in connection with the cleaning of the pictures by Frans Hals at Haarlem'). Archives du Musée Teyler, Series III, V Haarlem, 1922.

A pioneer work on the subject, establishing that the darkening of these paintings was almost entirely confined to the varnish which could be safely removed. (H.R.)

1930

(2) GRAU MAS, Manuel. 'La restauration d'une toile du Greco' ('The restoration of a canvas painting by El Greco'). *Mouseion*, XXVII–XXVIII (1934), No. III–IV, pp. 223–227.

(3) RUHEMANN, H. 'A record of restoration.' *Technical Studies in the Field of the Fine Arts*, III (1934), pp. 3–15.

An account of the restoration of Roger van der Weyden's 'St. Luke making a portrait of the Virgin' in the Museum of Fine Arts, Boston (see pp. 43–44 of present book).

(4) PROCACCI, Ugo. 'Quelques récentes restaurations de peintures de la Toscane' ('Some recent restorations of Tuscan paintings'). *Mouseion*, XXXIII–XXXIV (1936), Nos. I–II, pp. 227–247.

(5) RINALDI, A. de. 'La restauration du tableau no. 371 de la Galerie Borghese' ('The restoration of picture No. 371 in the Borghesi Gallery'). *Mouseion*, XXXVII–XXXVIII (1937), Nos. I–II, pp. 211–223.

A Raphael 'S. Catherine' becomes after cleaning a 'Lady holding a unicorn.'

1940

(6) 'A restoration with plastics.' *Paint, Oil and Chemical Review* (Chicago), CIII (1941), No. 9, p. 40.

An account of the transfer and restoration, by Sheldon Keck, of a 17th century panel painting to a sheet of polyvinyl acetate resin — an early use of plastics in restoration.

(7) BUCK, Richard D. 'Reclaiming a Flemish painting.' *Bulletin of the Fogg Museum of Art*, X (1947), pp. 193–209.

(8) GERSON, H. 'Cleaning the "Night Watch". ' *The Burlington Magazine*, LXXXIX (1947), p. 345.

An account of the cleaning of Rembrandt's portrait group.

Bibliography

(9) MOSCHINI, Vittorio. 'Recent restoration in Venice.' *The Burlington Magazine*, LXXXIX (1947), pp. 31–34.

Cleaning and restoration of paintings by Tintoretto, Carpaccio, Tiepolo, Giusto de' Menabuoi.

(10) VAN SCHENDEL, A. and MERTENS, H. H. 'De restauraties van Rembrandt's Nachtwacht' ('The restoration of Rembrandt's Night Watch'). *Oud-Holland*, LXII (1947), pp. 1–52 (with English summary).

History and documentation of previous restorations, account of recent condition and treatment.

(11) PROCACCI, Ugo. 'Recent restoration in Florence. I. Masaccio's "Madonna with St. Ann"; II. Fra Angelico, Sassetta and others.' *The Burlington Magazine*, LXXXIX (1947), pp. 309–316, 330–335.

A description of restoration work at the Gabinetto del Restauro of the Uffizi.

(12) ROUSSEAU, Theodore. 'Report on an early Rembrandt', with technical notes by Murray PEASE. *Bulletin of the Metropolitan Museum of Art* (New York), VI (1947), pp. 49–53. Report of condition, cleaning and restoration.

(13) COREMANS, Paul. 'The recent cleaning of Rubens' "Chapeau de Paille"', *The Burlington Magazine*, XC (1948), pp. 257–261.

An article which provides answers, based on scientific observations, to some criticisms of the cleaning of the picture at the National Gallery, London.

(14) ORTOLANI, Sergio. 'Restauro d'un Tiziano' ('Restoration of a Titian'). *Bollettino d'Arte*, Anno, XXXIII (1948), pp. 44–53.

The cleaning and restoration of Titian's portrait of Pope Paul III in the Pinacoteca, Naples.

(15) SORRENTINO, A. and GNUDI, C. 'Restauro delle ante d'organo di Cosmè Tura della Cattedrale di Ferrara (The restoration of an organ front by Cosimo Tura in the Cathedral of Ferrara'). Bolletino d'Arte, Anno, XXXIII (1948), pp. 262–265.

1950

(16) COREMANS, Paul. 'Treatment of the polyptych of the Adoration of the Lamb.' *Museum* (UNESCO, Paris), IV (1951), pp. 67–72.

An account of the restoration of the van Eyck polyptych.

(17) KECK, Sheldon, 'A case of artistic face-lifting.' *Bulletin of the Brooklyn Museum*, New York, XII (1951), pp. 17–21.

Cleaning showed that an 18th century English portrait had been overpainted to resemble one of Hoppner's known sitters.

(18) URBANI, G. 'Restauri Caravaggeschi per la Sicilia' ('Restoration of Caravaggios for Sicily'). *Bollettino dell' Istituto Centrale del Restauro*, Rome, V–VI (1951), pp. 61–91.

An account of the cleaning and restoration at the Istituto Centrale of several pictures by Caravaggio and Caravaggiesque painters from Sicily, including Caravaggio's *Resurrection of Lazarus and Adoration of the Shepherds* from the Museo Nazionale, Messina.

Bibliography

(19) URBANI, Giovanni. 'Recupero di un Tiziano' ('The recovery of a Titian'). *Bollettino dell' Istituto Centrale del Restauro* (Rome), VII–VIII (1951), pp. 17–24.

The restoration of a much-damaged 'Stigmatization of S. Francis' from the Museo Provinciale, Ascoli Piceno, and its subsequent re-attribution to Titian.

(20) *L'Agneau Mystique au Laboratoire*. Part of the series *Les Primitifs Flamands*, being Number 2 of Part III, *Contributions à l'Étude des Primitifs Flamands*. De Sikkel, Antwerp, 1953. 130 pp., 71 plates.

A comprehensive account of the history of restoration, recent examination, technique, materials, condition and treatment of Van Eyck's polyptych. Under the direction of P. Coremans, with contributions by P. Coremans, R. Lefève, L. Loose, A. and P. Philippot, R. Sneyers, J. Thissen.

(21) COUTO, João. 'Restoration of the polyptych of the chancel of the cathedral of Évora.' *Studies in Conservation*, III (1957), pp. 30–39.

The treatment of an altarpiece on wood, Netherlandish School c. 1500.

(22) FASTNEDGE, R. 'A restored work by Signorelli at Liverpool.' *The Burlington Magazine*, XCV (1953), pp. 273–274.

An unusual feature of this picture was the wide margin, previously concealed by an early frame, of paint free from all later accretions or from effects of exposure to light.

(23) PROCACCI, Ugo. 'Distacco di tempere ducentesche sovrapposte' ('The detachment of overpainted 13th century tempera'). *Bollettino d'Arte*, I (1953), pp. 31–37.

An account of the separation of an early 13th century crucifix in tempera from the late 13th century painting done over it. Both paintings were retrieved intact.

(24) RUHEMANN, H. 'Restoration of *La Haie: Landscape near Arles* by Van Gogh.' *Studies in Conservation*, I (1953), pp. 77–81.

Cleaning and restoration involving the impregnation and re-adhesion of loose paint with high impasto. See also Appendix D, pp. 340–344 of present book.

(25) BALDINI, Umberto. 'Restauri di dipinti fiorentini' ('Restoration of Florentine paintings'). *Bollettino d'Arte*, Anno XXXIX (1954), pp. 221–240.

In connection with an exhibition of Four Masters of the Early Renaissance (Palazzo Strozzi, 1954), the recent restoration is described of a few of the works, notably the 'Madonna and Child with St. Ann' by Masaccio and Masolino, and Uccello's 'Battle of S. Romano', both in the Uffizi Gallery. Fully illustrated with interesting photomacrographs and photographs by raking light.

(26) BRANDI, Cesare. 'Restauri a Piero della Francesca.' ('Restorations to Piero della Francesca'). *Bollettino d'Arte*, Anno XXXIX (1954), pp. 241–258.

A description of panel treatment, cleaning and restoration of important works by Piero: the 'Flagellation' (Galleria Nazionale, Urbino), the *Madonna di Senigallia* (Galleria Nazionale, Urbino), and the polyptych in the Galleria Nazionale, Perugia. The last mentioned is notable for the detection and subsequent removal of a grey artificial 'patina' under later repaints and puttying.

(27) RUHEMANN, H. ' "The Adulteress brought before Christ", by Giorgione.' *Scottish Art Review* (Glasgow), V (1954), No. 1, pp. 13–18.

An account of the cleaning and restoration.

Bibliography

(28) RUHEMANN, H. 'The cleaning and restoration of the Glasgow Giorgione.' *The Burlington Magazine*, XCVII (1955), pp. 278–282.

(29) WOLTERS, Christian. 'A Tuscan Madonna of c. 1260 : technique and conservation.' *Studies in Conservation*, II (1955), pp. 87–96.

(30) BERTELLI, Carlo. 'Il restauro di un quadro di Tiziano' ('The restoration of a picture by Titian'). *Bollettino dell'Istituto Centrale del Restauro*, Vol. XXX–XXXII (1957), pp. 129–143.

An account of the technical examination, condition, cleaning and restoration of the version of Titian's 'La Religione' in the Doria Pamphili Gallery, Rome.

A novel type of stretcher was used for the canvas.

(31) BUCK, R. D. 'Oberlin's Ribera : a case history.' *Bulletin of the Allen Memorial Museum* (Oberlin, Ohio), XIV (1957), pp. 69–72.

A record of the examination and treatment of Ribera's *The Blind Old Beggar*.

(32) CARITÀ, Roberto. 'Il restauro dei dipinti Caravaggeschi della Cathedral di Malta' ('The restoration of Caravaggiesque paintings in the cathedral of Malta'). *Bollettino dell'Istituto Centrale del Restauro*, XXIX–XXX (1957), pp. 41–82.

The transportation of the pictures from Malta to Rome and the restoration and photographic documentation carried out at Rome.

(33) MAZZINI, F. 'Il restauro del cosidetto trittico di S. Michele del Bramantino (Pinacoteca Ambrosiana, Milan') ('The restoration of the so-called triptych by Bramantino [Pinacoteca Ambrosiana, Milan]'). *Bollettino d'Arte*, XLII (1957), pp. 83–87.

During treatment it was discovered that the 'triptych' had originally been a single canvas, a 'Pala' or banner, and it was reconstructed as such.

(34) MOSCHINI, Vittorio. 'Nuovo allestimenti e restauri alle Gallerie de Venezia' ('New arrangements and restorations in the galleries of Venice'). *Bollettino d'Arte*, Anno XLII (1957), pp. 74–83.

Pictures cleaned and restored include works by Palma Vecchio, Moretto and Titian.

(35) SUHR, William. 'The restoration of the Merode altarpiece.' *The Metropolitan Museum of Art Bulletin*, New York, XVI (1957), pp. 140–144.

The treatment of the altarpiece by Robert Campin in the Cloisters Museum, New York.

(36) BUSCH, G. and BELLSTEDT-LANGE, L. 'Ein ungewöhnlicher Restaurierungsfall' ('An unusual case of restoration'). *Maltechnik*, II (1958), pp. 35–38.

A painting by Caspar David Friedrich at the Kunsthalle, Bremen, had lost a fifth of its canvas by damage during the war. The missing passage was replaced by an enlarged photograph of the picture before it was damaged.

(37) CELLINI, Pico. 'Il restauro del S. Luca di Raffaello' ('The restoration of Raphael's "S. Luke" '). *Bollettino d'Arte*, Anno XLIII (1958), pp. 250–262.

An account of the cleaning and restoration carried out by A. Vermehren of a damaged painting of S. Luke painting the Virgin (collection of the Accademia di S. Luca).

(38) 'La Justice d'Othon de Thierry Bouts' ('The Justice of Othon by Dieric Bouts'). *Bulletin de l'Institut Royal du Patrimoine Artistique*, I (1958), pp. 7–69.

Includes : articles on the stylistic and technical examination by A. and P. Philippot,

Bibliography

the laboratory examination by R. Sneyers and J. Thissen, and the treatment, by A. Philippot and R. Sneyers.

(39) GOULD, Cecil. 'A famous Titian restored.' *The Burlington Magazine*, C (1958), pp. 44–55.

An account of the cleaning and restoration of Titian's 'Noli Me Tangere' in the National Gallery, London. Restoration by N. S. Brommelle.

(40) BROMMELLE, Norman. 'St. George and the Dragon,' *Museums Journal*, London, LIX (1959), pp. 87–95.

An account of the cleaning, restoration, materials and technique of Uccello's 'St. George and the Dragon' in the National Gallery, London.

(41) COREMANS, P., SNEYERS, R. and THISSEN, J. 'Memlinc's Mystiek Huwelijk van de H. Katharina onderzoeken behendlung' ('Memlinc's "Mystic Marriage of S. Catherine, examination and treatment'). *Bulletin de l'Institut Royal du Patrimoine Artistique*, II (1959), pp. 83–96. (French summary).

Interesting for the decision taken — unusual at the Institut Royal — to reconstruct some missing areas of the pictures.

(42) 'Il restauro della "Maestà" di Duccio' ('The restoration of Duccio's Maestà'). *Bollettino dell' Istituto Centrale*, Rome, XXXVII–XL (1959).

This issue is devoted to a detailed account of the examination, condition and treatment of Duccio's great altarpiece from Siena Cathedral.

(43) MARCONI, Bohdan. 'The conservation of the painting "The relief of Vienna",' 1683, by Joseph Brandt. *Muzealnictwo Wojskowe* (Military Museology), Warsaw, I (1959), pp. 139–147. Restoration of a large picture, seriously damaged in wartime, particularly by effects of water.

(44) PLUMMER, Pauline. 'Restoration of a retable in Norwich Cathedral'. *Studies in Conservation*, IV (1959), pp. 106–115.

Cleaning, technical examination and restoration of a late 14th century retable composed of several panels.

(45) QUANDT, Russell, 'Restoring Van Dyck's masterwork, "Rinaldo and Armida".' *The Baltimore Museum of Art News*, XXIII (1959), No. 1, pp. 5–8, illus.

(46) ROUSSEAU, Theodore. 'El Greco's "Vision of Saint John".' *Bulletin of the Metropolitan Museum* (New York), XVII (1959), pp. 241–262.

1960

(47) MOSCHINI, Vittorio. 'Altri restauri alle gallerie di Venezia' ('Some more restorations at the Venetian galleries'). *Bollettino d'Arte*, XLV (1960), pp. 353–365.

Accounts and restorations of pictures including works by Gentile Bellini, Giovanni Mansueti, Carpaccio and Tintoretto.

(48) NICOLSON, Benedict. 'The recovery of a Degas race course scene.' *The Burlington Magazine*, CII (1960), pp. 536–537.

An account of the cleaning by H. Ruhemann of a picture by Degas which had been overpainted on several occasions by the artist himself in his last and declining years. See p. 207 of present book.

Bibliography

(49) PACKARD, Elizabeth G. 'A problem in technical research; the Walters "St. Francis" — a contribution to El Greco studies.' *Journal of the Walters Art Gallery*, XXIII (1960), pp. 49–71.

A description of the technical examination, materials and technique, cleaning and restoration, of the Walters Art Gallery El Greco, 'Saint Francis receiving the Stigmata.'

(50) GROSS-ANDERS, Hertha. 'Dürers "Dresdner-Altar" und seine Rettung' ('Dürer's Dresden altar and its rescue'). *Maltechnik*, LXVII (1960), pp. 68–81.

The recovery and restoration of a war-damaged triptych.

(51) GOULD, Cecil. 'New light on Titian's "Schiavona" portrait.' *The Burlington Magazine*, CIII (1961), pp. 335–340.

A description of results of recent cleaning (by H. Ruhemann) revealing new details of composition and information on technique.

(52) 'Het Calvarie-Drieluik toegeschreven aan Justus van Gent en de bihorende Predella' ('The Calvary triptych attributed to Justus of Ghent and the related predella'). *Bulletin de l'Institut Royal du Patrimoine Artistique*, Brussels, IV (1961), pp. 7–43. (French summary).

A detailed account of the condition, technique, materials, scientific examination and treatment, with contributions by N. Verhaegen, A. de Schryver, R. Marijnissen, R. Sneyers, P. Coremans, J. Thissen, A. Philippot.

(53) MEZZETTI, A. 'Restauri ferraresi: notizie e problemi.' (Ferrarese restorations: reports and problems'). *Bollettino d'Arte*, XLVII (1962), pp. 272–283, with further technical notes by H. Paganini and O. Caprara.

Recent restorations of pictures mainly in Ferrarese galleries, with interesting accounts of their problematic conditions and their treatment.

(54) STOLOW, Nathan. 'From the Laboratory of the National Gallery — Le pont de Narni by Corot.' *The National Gallery of Canada Bulletin*, II (December 1963), pp. 1–4.

The relining, cleaning and restoration is described, with interesting use of modern synthetic resins for retouching medium and surface coating.

(55) STOLOW, Nathan. 'The Toilet of Venus by Boucher.' Loc. cit. above, pp. 8–11.

Investigation of conditions, materials and technique; cleaning and restoration.

(56) Rubens, *'Descent from the Cross.'* Two numbers of the *Bulletin de l'Institut Royal du Patrimoine Artistique*, Brussels, are largely devoted to this altarpiece from the cathedral of Antwerp. V (1962) includes a description of the problem of conservation, a history of previous conservation and restorations, a description of condition before the recent cleaning and restoration, composition and structure of the paint layers, the nature of the supports and the ground, the atmospheric conditions in the cathedral, framing and presentation in the cathedral. VI (1963) gives descriptions of the painting technique, the treatment, and the analysis of some of the painting materials present.

(57) QUINTAVALLE, Augusta. 'Parmigianino ritrovato' ('Parmagianino rediscovered'). *Paragone*, Milan, CLXXIX (Nuova Serie), Nov. 1964, pp. 19–31.

Includes an account of the cleaning and restoration of Parmagianino's 'La schiava turca,' in the National Gallery of Parma.

(58) 'Il restauro della Madonna della Clemenza.' *Bollettino dell'Istituto Centrale del Restauro*, Rome, XLI–XLIV (1964).

Bibliography

This issue is devoted to a detailed description of the condition, technical examination, materials, technique and treatment of an early (6th–7th century A.D.?) altarpiece in Santa Maria in Trastevere).

(59) BLUNT, Anthony. 'Mantegna's "Triumph of Caesar" at Hampton Court: Report of work in progress.' *The Burlington Magazine*, CIV (1962), p. 322.

An interim report on restoration of the series of so-called cartoons by Mantegna at Hampton Court.

(60) HEYDENRYK, Henry, MORATZ, Frank and MORATZ, Barbara. 'The double Dali — an essay in transparent mounting.' *Museum News* (Washington, D.C.), XLI (1962), pp. 35–37.

A description of the treatment of a picture on canvas by Salvador Dali painted on both sides; it was relined with glass fibre fabric so as to enable the painting on the reverse to be visible.

(61) PAWLOWSKI, Stanislaw. 'La restauration d'une peinture de Lucas Cranach' ('The restoration of a painting by Lucas Cranach'). *Bulletin du Musée National de Varsovie*, IV (1963), pp. 13–17. In French.

In wartime storage the surface of the paint of this picture stuck to that of another picture and, in detaching the two, some of the paint of the Cranach became detached. The article describes its replacement and subsequent restoration work on the picture.

(62) HAMSIC, Mojír, 'Restaurace Madony Sebastiana del Piombo' ('Restoration of a Madonna by Sebastiano del Piombo'). *Umění* (Prague), 1964, pp. 37–45. In Czech, French Summary.

Restoration of a picture recently acquired by the National Gallery of Prague.

(63) QUINTAVALLI, A. Ghidiglia. 'La "Schiava Turca" del Parmigianino' ('The "Schiava Turca" by Parmigianino'). *Bollettino d'Arte*, XLIX (1964), pp. 251–252.

Removal of tinted varnish and overpainted background from a portrait by Parmigianino in the National Gallery of Parma.

(64) WEHLTE, Kurt. 'Tizians Zinsgroschen, ein Sorgenkind der Restauratoren.' ('Titian's "Tribute Money", a problem child for restorers'). *Maltechnik*, LXX (1964), pp. 5–10.

An account of the various methods used to treat Titian's *Tribute Money* in the Staatliche Gemäldegalerie, Dresden.

(65) NITKIEWICZ, Walter J. 'Treatment of the Gettysburg Cyclorama.' *Studies in Conservation*, X (1965), pp. 91–118.

Of interest for the handling of a canvas painting of immense size.

(66) DIX, Ursus. 'The restoration of a painting by Luca Giordano.' *The Connoisseur*, CLX (1965), pp. 80–83.

The restoration of a large, much-damaged (in some areas fragmentary) canvas painting, interesting for the use of modern materials and for the resolving of problems of repair and inpainting. See also *Section 9 (22)*.

See also *Section 4 (44)*.

Bibliography

SECTION 6

Catalogues of exhibitions of cleaned and restored pictures and of exhibitions relating to restoration or scientific examination

The following have been the most notable exhibitions. The majority of the catalogues are illustrated with photographs:

BERGAMO

(1) *Mostra di Opere Restaurate*. Palazzo della Ragione, September 1960. Pictures from the province of Bergamo.

BROOKLYN, New York.

(2) *Catalogue of an exposition of painting conservation, materials, methods, machines.* The Brooklyn Museum, New York, 1962.

Every conscientious picture restorer who reads this programme-catalogue will wish to thank Caroline Keck and her executive committee for realizing this novel exhibition. A great deal of directly applicable information and indeed many important lessons have been condensed into these papers.

Mr. David B. Eisendrath's advice for photographing paintings is invaluable. R. D. Buck's and J. W. Seiffert's scheme of using flash bulbs for U.V. photography is a bright idea. Sheldon Keck's diagrams are most useful —. By comparison Dr. Jane Sheridan's short paper on chemical analysis gives one little to bite upon. In her interesting report on enzymes an indication would have been welcomed whether they could be expected to be useful on paintings.

Mr. Feller should have added to his note on polyethyleneglycol a warning against using it on paintings and an explanation why the different ingredients, for instance two waxes, are given in the formulas for lining and in what or for what special purpose one formula is preferable to another. Under 'solubility of beeswax' he puts: 'Hot alcohol, acetone'. It is not clear whether the 'hot' applies also to 'acetone'. I have found one of the virtues of wax is that it is not easily soluble in (cold) alcohol or cold acetone; this makes it often possible to clean with impunity paintings treated with wax, even to clean a hard varnish off a painting executed in a medium containing wax, such as some works by Stubbs.

In his article on moisture barriers R. D. Buck covers the subject with exemplary brevity and clarity.

I agree with Mr. J. Roth that in transfer 'partial removal of the wood will achieve partial results . . .' but I do not quite see why the extremely high impasto would rule out the use of the transfer technique. Surely a papier mâché mould such as recommended by Stout should overcome the difficulty.

Dr. Nathan Stolow contributes a highly useful list of solvents. A footnote would have been welcome explaining in simple words to the restorer with little or no scientific training (who alas still forms the majority of the profession) in what way the knowledge of the 'density and solubility parameter' is of practical value.

Dr. Feller's paper on the main resins and varnishes used on paintings contains much valuable information. A few words on the handling properties and relative shortcomings

Bibliography

of each substance would have been helpful, for instance that mastic and dammar are less pale than MS2A and that B72 is as colourless as and less rubbery than polyvinyl acetate and methacrylate.

It seems a good idea to try to counteract the risk involved in removing a crosslinked butyl-methacrylate varnish by applying it over a layer of dammar or AW2, but perhaps B72, which seems so promising, will soon supersede these methods.

The articles on responsibilities, minimum requirements, fire extinguishers and lighting are all excellent. I should just like to add that wherever one of the two kinds of fluorescent lamps most closely approaching the hue of natural daylight (e.g. Northlight) are not adopted for some reason, it should be kept in mind that not only different objects but also different paintings require different hues and intensity of illumination. For instance on a Poussin a warmer and dimmer light may be more acceptable than on a Pissarro which needs the coolest daylight to bring out all the *'juste nuance'*, the very *raison d'être* of many impressionist pictures.

The E.P.C. programme-catalogue will be a worthy and welcome neighbour to the other American classics on our book shelves: Stout's *Care of pictures*, Gettens & Stout, Morton Bradley's book, Mayers's handbook and the Oberlin Seminar publication'. (H.R.)

FERRARA

(3) *Mostra di Opere d'Arte Restaurate.* Palazzo dei Diamanti, May–Oct. 1964. Catalogue by Amalia Mezzetti.

Works of art, including easel paintings, currently restored in Ferrarese galleries, churches and other public buildings.

FLORENCE

Since the end of the last war 10 exhibitions of restored works of art have been held, a major part of which have been devoted to the treatment of fresco paintings, but a number of easel paintings have also been included. The earliest and most recent examples of the catalogues are:

(4) *Mostra di opere d'arte restaurate*, Palazzo Strozzi, 1946. Catalogue under the care of Ugo Procacci.

(5) *Mostra di opere d'arte restaurate, Decima Esposizione*, 1959.

LIVERPOOL, *England.*

(6) *Cleaned pictures.* Catalogue of an exhibition of 41 pictures held in 1955 at the Walker Art Gallery, Liverpool. The contents include a historical and technical summary and a glossary of terms. (Reviewed by N. Brommelle, *The Burlington Magazine*, XCVII (1955), p. 354).

LONDON

(7) *An Exhibition of Cleaned Pictures.* Catalogue of the exhibition held at the National Gallery, London, in 1946–47 of pictures cleaned between 1936 and 1947. See pp. 79–95 of present book for comments.

MILAN

(8) *Mostra di Dipinti Restaurati.* Pinacoteca Ambrosiana, Oct. 1956. Easel paintings from the collection of the Pinacoteca Ambrosiana.

Bibliography

MOSCOW

(9) *Exhibition of the Restoration and Conservation of Works of Art*. Pushkin Museum, 1963.
Mostly objects of art, but some easel paintings included.

NAPLES

The following exhibitions have been held at the Museo di S. Martino :

(10) *Mostra Didattica del Restauro*. Dec. 1951–Jan. 1952.

(11) *IIa Mostra di Restauri*. Dec. 1952–Jan. 1953.

(12) *IIIa Mostra di Restauri*. Dec. 1953–Jan. 1954.

The above exhibitions relate to works of art, including pictures, from museums and churches in and around Naples.

(13) *IVa Mostra di Restauri*. Palazzo Reale, 1960.

Includes pictures by Simone Martini, Masaccio, Masolino, Botticelli, Perugino, Giovanni Bellini, Titian.

PARIS

The following exhibitions are principally concerned with scientific examination using special radiation, e.g. X-ray, infra-red or ultra-violet photography or other specialized methods of photography :

(14) *L'Oeuvre d'Art et les Meéthodes Scientifiques*. Musée de l'Orangerie, March–April, 1949. Introduction to the catalogue by René Huyghe, preface by M. Florisoone, catalogue by M. Hours.

(15) *Exposition de Quelques Documents Scientifiques d'après les Peintures de Léonard de Vinci*, compiled by M. Hours and comprising pp. 87–112 of the catalogue of the exhibition 'Hommage à Léonard de Vinci'. Editions des Musées Nationaux, Paris, 1952.

(16) *Étude Scientifique du Retable de Besançon au Laboratoire du Musée du Louvre*. Catalogue of the exhibition, Oct. 1953, with a preface by M. Hours.

(17) *Rembrandt, Étude photographique et radiographique*. Musée du Louvre, May–Sept., 1955. Catalogue by M. Hours.

PERUGIA

(18) *Mostra di dipinti restaurati*. Palazzo Donini, Aug.–Sept., 1953.

(19) *IIa Mostra di dipinti restaurati*. May–June, 1954.

(20) *IIIa Mostra di dipinti restaurati*. July–Oct. 1956.

The above exhibitions are of pictures mainly from the National Gallery of Umbria at Perugia.

ROME

A number of exhibitions of restored paintings and objects of art have been held at, or been connected with, the Istituto Centrale del Restauro, for example :

(21) *V Mostra di restauri*. Istituto Centrale del Restauro, March 1948.
A number of easel paintings were included.

(22) *Mostra di dipinti restaurati: Angelico, Piero della Francesca, Antonello da Messina*. Palazzo Venezia, March 1953.

Bibliography

(23) *Restauri di Arte in Italia, VIII Settimana dei Musei Italiani*. Palazzo Venezia, April–May, 1965.

Examples of recently restored works from museums and churches in Italy, including a number of easel paintings.

UDINE

(24) *Prima Mostra del Restauro*. Salone del Castello, June 1963.

Paintings from the Museo Civico at Udine and from elsewhere in the region.

URBINO

(25) *Antichi Dipinti Restaurati*. Palazzo Ducale del Urbino, March–April 1953.

Includes paintings by Lotto, Barocci, O. Gentileschi, Guercino, etc.

(26) *Mostra di Opere d' Arte Restaurate*. Palazzo Ducale del Urbino, April 1965.

Mostly easel paintings.

VENICE

(27) *Restauri nel Veneto*. Gallerie dell' Accademia, March–June, 1966.

Pictures restored include some by Gentile and Giovanni Bellini, Tintoretto, etc.

SECTION 7

General principles and discussion of ethics and aesthetics of picture cleaning

(It has not been possible to include under this heading the voluminous correspondence, particularly that in the daily press, which has appeared on the subject. A summary of correspondence in *The Times* concerning cleaning of pictures at the National Gallery, London, c. 1946–47 is given in the condensed version of the Weaver Report on the Cleaning of Pictures in the National Gallery which appeared in *Museum* (UNESCO, Paris), III (1950), pp. 112–176. (Bibliography. *Section 4* (43).)

1920

(1) BELL, Clive. 'Cleaning of pictures.' *The Burlington Magazine*, XL (1922), pp. 127–128.

The author remarks that those who are truly interested in pictures in the aesthetic sense wish not merely to have them, but also to see them.

(2) 'The repair of pictures,' *Journal of the Royal Society of Arts*, (London) LXXV (1926–27), Dec. 1926, p. 117.

Recommendations of the Royal Academy Committee on the Treatment of Old Pictures. The Committee conferred with the Trustees of the National Gallery, London, and the latter supported the several enlightened recommendations made.

1930

(3) PUYVELDE, Leo van. 'Le nettoyage des tableaux anciens' ('The cleaning of old pictures'). *Annuaire des Beaux-Arts* (Brussels), 1933, pp. 19–30.

423

Bibliography

A general discussion on the desirability of cleaning, with some illustrated examples.

(4) CLARK, Kenneth. 'The aesthetics of restoration.' *Proceedings of the Royal Institution of Great Britain*, XXX (1938), No. 141, pp. 382–397.

A lecture given at the Royal Institution, 20th May, 1938.

1940

(5) FRIEDLÄNDER, Max J. *On art and connoisseurship*. English edition (translated by Tancred Borenius), Bruno Cassirer, London, 1942.

See Chapter XXXVII, 'On Restorations.' A classic; unfortunately the translation does not live up to the distinguished German. (H.R.).

(6) HONEYMAN, T. J. 'The cleaning of pictures.' *The Studio*, CXXXIV (1947), pp. 180–183.

An article in support of proper cleaning and restoration on aesthetic and historical grounds.

(7) PLENDERLEITH, H. J. 'Cleaned pictures at the National Gallery.' *Nature* (London), Volume CLX (1947), p. 523.

A review of the Cleaned Pictures Exhibition held at the National Gallery, London, in 1947, an assessment of picture cleaning, restoration and preservation and of the standard of criticism levelled at the exhibition.

(8) 'The problem of cleaning.' (Editorial). *The Burlington Magazine*, LXXXIX (1947), pp. 329–330.

Editorial discussing the Cleaned Pictures Exhibition at the National Gallery, London, and also in general the aesthetic aspects of cleaning and restoration.

(9) WEAVER, J. R. H. 'The National Gallery — Report of expert inquiry on cleaning pictures.' *The Times*, Saturday, May 8, 1948.

A summary of the proceedings and conclusions of the Weaver Committee set up to inquire into the cleaning of pictures at the National Gallery, London.

(10) BRANDI, Cesare. 'The cleaning of pictures in relation to patina, varnish and glazes.' *The Burlington Magazine*, XCI (1949), pp. 183–188.

A principal claim of the author is that early varnishes were sometimes pigmented deliberately.

1950

(11) MacLAREN, Neil and WERNER, Anthony. 'Some factual observations on varnishes and glazes.' *The Burlington Magazine*, XCII (1950), pp. 189–192.

The authors, on re-examining the evidence brought forward by C. BRANDI (see above) conclude that it does not indicate the use of pigmented varnishes, as distinct from glazes, by early painters.

(12) FIERENS, Paul. 'Faut-il nettoyer les tableaux anciens?' ('Is it necessary to clean old pictures?'). *Revue Générale Belge*, XL (1949), 7 pp.

(13) CONSTABLE, W. G. 'Curators and conservation.' *Studies in Conservation*, I (1954), pp. 97–102.

Bibliography

(14) HULMER, Eric C. *The role of conservation in connoisseurship.* Thesis (Ph.D.). University of Pittsburgh, 1955. Not seen by the author or bibliographer up to the present time.

(15) WEIHS, Fritz. 'Wo sind Firnisabnahmen unerlässlich?' ('When is varnish removal indispensable?'). *Maltechnik*, LXI (1955), pp. 116–118.

(16) ALTHÖFER, Heinz. 'Grenzen und Möglichkeiten des Restaurierens' ('Limitations and possibilities of restoring'). *Oesterreichische Forschungsinstitut für Wirtschaft und Politik, Bericht und Informationen*, XIV (1954), Heft 661, pp. 13–14.

(17) STRAUB, Rolf. 'Das Technische und das Allzutechnische in der Gemälderestaurierung' ('The technical and the all-too-technical in picture restoration'). *Maltechnik*, LXII (1956), pp. 69–70.

(18) LUCAS, A. W. 'The cleaning of pictures — some reasons and reactions.' *Apollo*, LXV–LXVI (1957), pp. 138–142 and 145.

The author is now Chief Restorer at the National Gallery, London.

(19) PHILIPPOT, Albert and Paul. 'Le problème de l'intégration des lacunes dans la restauration des peintures.' *Bulletin de l'Institut Royal du Patrimoine Artistique*, Brussels, II (1959), pp. 5–19.

1960

(20) 'Réflexions sur quelques problèmes esthétiques et techniques de la retouche.' ('Reflections on some aesthetic and technical problems of retouching.' *Ibid*, III (1960), pp. 163–172.

(21) WILLEMSEN, E. 'Die Restaurierungswerkstatt — Aufgaben und Probleme' ('Restoration studios — tasks and problems'). *Jahrbuch der Rheinischen Denkmalpflege* (Düsseldorf), XXIII (1960), pp. 323–324.

Problems of taste in restoration.

(22) RUHEMANN, Helmut. 'Leonardo's use of sfumato.' *The British Journal of Aesthetics*, I (1961), pp. 231–237. A refutation of Gombrich's contention that 'Leonardo deliberately cuts down information by his sfumato which G. conceives as an all-over blurring.'

(23) GOMBRICH, E. H. 'Blurred images and the unvarnished truth.' *The British Journal of Aesthetics*, II (1962), No. 2, pp. 170–179.

A reply to H. Ruhemann's article (see above).

(24) GOMBRICH, E. H. 'Dark varnishes : variations on a theme of Pliny.' *The Burlington Magazine*, CIV (1962), pp. 51–55.

The author argues that a description by Pliny of Apelles' use of a dark liquid or 'atramentum' upon his finished pictures might have influenced later painters to use deliberately tinted varnishes.

(25) KURZ, Otto. 'Varnishes, tinted varnishes and patina.' *The Burlington Magazine*, CIV (1962), pp. 56–59.

The author produces a number of descriptions, recipes, etc. which he believes either imply the use of deliberately coloured varnishes by painters in the past, or else anticipation of discolouration of the varnish at the later date.

Bibliography

(26) MAHON, Denis. 'Miscellanea for the cleaning controversy.' *The Burlington Magazine*, CIV (1962), pp. 460–470.

The author critically reviews the historical evidence as to the nature of varnishes and the effects of age on pictures brought forward by O. Kurz and E. H. Gombrich (see above, (25) and (24) respectively).

(27) MURARO, Michelangelo. 'Notes on traditional methods of cleaning pictures in Venice and Florence.' *The Burlington Magazine*, Volume 104 (1962), pp. 475–477.

An interpretation of accounts of 18th and 19th century restoring practices in Italy, with reference to present-day practices.

(28) PLESTERS, Joyce. 'Dark varnishes — some further comments.' *The Burlington Magazine*, CIV (1962), pp. 452–460.

A critical review of historical sources relating to varnishes, varnishing practice, effects of ageing, and picture cleaning, with special reference to previous articles by O. Kurz and E. H. Gombrich (see above, (25) and (24) respectively).

(29) REES JONES, Stephen. 'Science and the art of picture cleaning.' *The Burlington Magazine*, CIV (1962), pp. 60–62.

The author expresses doubts as to the validity of the scientific evidence produced in order to demonstrate the safety of picture cleaning.

(30) THOMSON, Garry. 'Notes on Science and the art of picture cleaning.' *The Burlington Magazine*, CIV (1962), pp. 499–500.

A reply to S. Rees Jones's article in the same journal (see above, (29)).

(31) VAN DE GRAAF, J. A. 'The interpretation of old painting recipes.' *The Burlington Magazine*, CIV (1962), pp. 471–475.

The author's main aim is to give some idea of the complexities involved in the interpretation of old painting recipes, of which he gives examples, but in addition he warns against the application of wrong interpretations to arguments concerning cleaning and restoration.

(32) WITHEROP, J. Coburn. Letter concerning the National Gallery (London) cleaning controversy. *The Burlington Magazine*, CIV (1962), pp. 265–266.

An account of an interesting experiment made by the author to compare the initial colour of various types of varnish, first in the bottle and then as freshly applied on a picture surface.

(33) ZYKAN, J. 'Die Restaurierung von Kunstwerken' ('The restoration of works of art'). *Speculum Artis* (Zürich), XIV (1962), No. 4, pp. 30–31.

The extent to which retouching is desirable is discussed.

(34) BRANDI, Cesare. *Teoria del restauro* (Theory of restoration). Edizioni di Storia e Letterature, Rome, 1963.

A compilation of all the author's writings from 1931 onwards which have bearing on the subject of restoration and conservation of works of art and architecture. The author attempts to work out a comprehensive theory of restoration. This theory includes a great reverence for 'patina' — a term which for him may comprise effects of age, varnish (whether original or later) and some other accretions or additions. It is proposed that even later additions to a picture may be left if they represent a stage in the 'evolution of the object as a work of art' (the author here draws an analogy with the additions which may have been made to historic buildings through the ages).

The present writers cannot agree that a 'theory' of restoration can be enunciated, but only general principles, since each picture, or other work of art to be treated is an individual case, nor does it seem to them that the concept of 'patina' employed in such loose terminology is a useful one.

(35) GOMBRICH, E. H. 'Controversial methods and methods of controversy.' *The Burlington Magazine*, CV (1963), pp. 90–93.

An article in reply to those by J. Plesters and D. Mahon in the same journal (see above, (28) and (26) respectively).

(36) KURZ, Otto. 'Time the painter.' *The Burlington Magazine*, CV (1963), pp. 94–97.

A further article considering the effects of age and of discoloured varnishes on paintings, and the attitude of the painter to these phenomena; in reply to articles by D. Mahon and J. Plesters in the same journal (see above).

(37) JONES, P. L. 'Scientism and the art of picture cleaning.' *The Burlington Magazine*, CV (1963), pp. 98–103.

Mainly a reply to an article by Garry Thomson (see above, (30)) in the same journal, concerning scientific evidence in the cleaning and conservation of pictures.

(38) 'The Murray Pease Report', *Studies in Conservation*, IX (1964), pp. 116–121.

A report by a Committee on Professional Standards set up by the American Group of I.I.C. under the chairmanship of the late Murray Pease. It gives a useful outline of practical, ethical and legal aspects of conservation and technical examination for the professional conservator.

(39) REES JONES, Stephen. 'The cleaning controversy: further comments.' *The Burlington Magazine*, CV (1963), pp. 97–98.

A further article criticizing cleaning methods at the National Gallery, London, and in answer to articles by D. Mahon, J. Plesters, G. Thomson in the same journal (see above).

(40) *Studies in Western Art. Acts of the twentieth International Congress of the History of Art*, Volume IV, *Problems of the 19th and 20th Centuries*. Princeton University Press, Princeton, New Jersey, 1963.

Pages 137–186: *The aesthetic and historical aspects of the presentation of damaged pictures.*

Introduction by Craig Hugh SMYTH (Chairman); 'Taste and science in the presentation of damaged pictures,' by Philip HENDY; 'Il trattamento delle lacune e la Gestalt psycologie' ('The treatment of lacunae and the Gestalt philosophy') by Cesare BRANDI; 'Restoration and conservation,' by Richard OFFNER; Discussion session with contributions by: Millard Meiss, Paul B. Coremans, Sheldon Keck, José Gudio, Charles Seymour Jr., Henri Marceau, Trenchard Cox, John Coolidge, George L. Stout, John Maxon, Edward S. King. Conclusion by Craig Hugh Smyth.

The essential problem discussed was the extent and type of retouching permissible or desirable for damaged paintings. A wide range of views was expressed.

(41) KECK, Caroline K. 'History and philosophy of conservation.' *Bulletin of the American Group — I.I.C.*, V (1964), No. 1, pp. 1–3.

Bibliography

(42) LODEWIJKS, Johan E. 'Die Stellung des Restaurators im heutigen Museum und seine Beziehungen zu Fachgelehrten verschiedener Richtungen' ('The position of the restorer in the museum today and his relationship with scholars of various disciplines'). *Ergänzungsbände des Berliner Jahrbuchs für Vor- und Frügeschichte*, I (1964), pp. 71–80. Restaurierung und Konservierung. Bericht von der 5. Tagung der Arbeitsgemeinschaft des technischen Museums-personals, in Berlin, 1964.

Reflections concerning the professional relationships in museums of restorers, scientists and art historians.

SECTION 8
Training of Restorers

1920

(1) WOLTERS, A. 'Die Ausbildung von Restauratoren für die Museen' ('The education of restorers for museums'), *Kunstchronik und Kunstmarkt* (Leipzig), XLVI–XLVII (1926), pp. 697–699.

1930

(2) 'Pour une éducation professionnelle des restaurateurs d'oeuvres d'art' ('Towards a professional education for restorers of works of art'). *Mouseion*, IXX (1932), No. 3, pp. 83–86.

Proposals put forward by a group of Viennese curators; an excellent outline scheme.

1950

(3) WEHLTE, K. 'Restauratoren Ausbildung' ('The education of restorers). *Maltechnik*, LXI (1955), pp. 101–102.

(4) KECK, Sheldon. 'On education in art conservation.' *Brooklyn Museum Bulletin* (Brooklyn, New York), IXX (1958), pp. 3–9.

A plea for establishment of standards and educational facilities in conservation.

(5) PHILIPPOT, Paul. 'Réflexions sur le problème de la formation des restaurateurs de peintures et de sculptures' ('Reflections on the problem of the training of restorers of paintings and sculptures'). *Studies in Conservation*, V (1960), pp. 61–70.

The author gives an excellent summary of the present international position in the training of restorers and of practical suggestions for improvement.

His now famous phrase on the question of cleaning should be quoted here, since it has not yet, I believe, appeared in English: '. . . and this applies not only to decisions as to whether certain additions should be removed or not, but also to operations such as the cleaning, which should always take into account the general condition of the work and the danger which may exist in presenting as materially new a work or an antique object, this artificial annulment of history, introducing between the reality of the work and its appearance a contradiction which actually falsifies its authenticity.'

Is not this philosophy based on several false premises? Is it not impossible for a cleaner to remove from a painting the true visible effects of age intrinsic in it? Should no distinction be made between *objets d'art* and subtle masterpieces of colouring? Should the picture cleaner or restorer (or curator) in a museum on principle use his own taste and predilection in leaving on or adding to a masterpiece (I am here not speaking of paintings of indifferent quality whose main merit may consist in their 'oldness') a 'harmonizing' tone. Does not this falsify the authenticity of a work in a more arbitrary manner than the freeing of the original paint from later accretions? (See also pp. 170–189 of the present book.) (H.R.)

(6) GETTENS, Rutherford J. 'Teaching and research in art conservation.' *Science* (American Association for the Advancement of Science, Washington D.C.), CXXXIII (1960), pp. 1212–1216.

(7) SCHUBART, H. and BROMMELLE, N. 'Co-operation for conservation in Great Britain.' *Museums Journal* (London), LXI (1961), pp. 109–113.

(8) COREMANS, Paul. 'Un enseignement théorique et pratique sur l'examen scientifique et la conservation des biens culturels' ('A theoretical and practical course on the scientific examination and the conservation of cultural property'). *Bulletin de l'Institut Royal du Patrimoine Artistique*, Brussels, VI (1963), pp. 80–90 (also reprinted in English translation).

(9) PHILIPPOT, Paul. 'Zur Situation der Gemälde- und Plastik-Restauratoren und zum Problem ihrer Ausbildung' ('The situation of painting and sculpture restorers and the problem of their training'). *Museumskunde*, III (1963), pp. 133–136.

(10) *Recent advances in conservation*, edited by G. THOMSON, London, 1963. (Papers given at the I.I.C. Rome Conference, 1961).

Contributions on the subject of training: 'La formation des conservateurs et des restaurateurs,' by P. Rotondi; 'Training for engineers in conservation,' by Sheldon Keck; 'The training of restorers,' by Helmut Ruhemann; 'Programme of the faculty of conservation at the Academy of Fine Arts in Warsaw,' by Bohdan Marconi.

(11) KECK, Sheldon. 'First aid for art. The Conservation Center at New York University.' *Museum News* (Washington D.C.), XLIII (September, 1964), No. 1, pp. 13–17.

An account of the formation and curriculum of the Conservation Center for professional training in conservation of objects of art and archaeology, including paintings.

(12) STRAUB, Rolf E. 'Ausbildung von Restauratoren im Stuttgarter Institut.' ('The training of restorers at the Stuttgart Institute'). *Maltechnik*, Volume LXXI (1965), pp. 33–37.

A description of the course in restoration given at the Staatliche Akademie der bildenden Künste at Stuttgart.

(13) WEHLTE, K. 'Restauratorenausbildung' ('The education of restorers'). *Maltechnik*, LXI (1965), pp. 101–102.

Particular mention of training institutions in Germany.

Bibliography

SECTION 9
Documentation and recording of condition and treatment

1930

(1) AKKE, Kumlein. 'Les fiches de renseignements techniques sur les peintures contemporaines' ('Forms for technical information about contemporary paintings'). *Mouseion*, XXV–XXVI (1934), pp. 220–225.

The author describes a form, modelled on that used at the Alte Pinakothek, Munich, to be filled in with the artist's technical description of the painting, and to include date, technique, materials (e.g. type of varnish), primarily for the purpose of aiding future conservation and restoration of the work.

(2) RUHEMANN, Helmut. 'A record of restoration.' *Technical Studies in the Field of the Fine Arts*, III (1934), pp. 2–15.

An account of the full documentation of condition and treatment of a particular painting. See also pp. 103–116 and plates of the present work and *Studies in Conservation*, II (1954), pp. 17–40.

(3) STOUT, George L. 'A museum record of the condition of paintings.' *Technical Studies in the Field of the Fine Arts*, III (1935), pp. 200–216.

(4) STOUT, George L. 'General notes on the condition of paintings — a brief outline for the purposes of record.' *Technical Studies in the Field of the Fine Arts*, VII (1939), pp. 159–166.

1940

(5) RAWLINS, F. I. G. and STOUT, G. L. 'Brief methods of describing paint.' *Technical Studies in the Field of the Fine Arts*, X (1941), pp. 37–46.

Systems for classifying paint of pictures according to dispersion of pigment, particle size of pigment, proportion of medium, type of craquelure, etc.

1950

(6) BUCK, R. D. 'The inspection of collections.' *Museum News* (Washington, D.C.), XXIX, 1 October 1951, pp. 6–8.

A system for recording condition.

(7) DUDLEY, Dorothy H. and BEZOLD, Irma. *Museum registration methods*. Publ. by the American Association of Museums, Washington, D.C., 1958. 225 pp.

Covers aspects of storage, packing, registration, classification, and inspection of art objects, also a trial glossary for describing condition.

1960

(8) ALTHÖFER, Heinz. 'Zur Dokumentation in der Gemälderestaurierung' ('Documentation in the restoration of paintings'). *Oesterreichische Zeitschrift für Kunst und Denkmalpflege* (Vienna), II–III (1963), pp. 81–93.

Bibliography

SECTION 10

Treatment of panel supports

1930

(1) STILLWELL, S. T. C. and KNIGHT, R. A. C. *Investigation into the blistering and flaking of old panel paintings on wood.* Department of Scientific and Industrial Research, Forest Products Research, Project O, Investigation 53. Princes Risborough, England, 1931.

(2) SUHR, William. 'A built-up panel for blistered paintings on wood.' *Technical Studies in the Field of the Fine Arts*, I (1932), pp. 29–34.

(3) LAURIE, A. P. 'The warping of panels.' *The Museums Journal* (London), XXXII (1933), pp. 389–391.

(4) HOPLINSKI, Jean. 'Restauration d'une peinture sur bois au Musée National de Cracovie' ('Restoration of a painting on wood in the National Museum of Cracow'). *Mouseion*, XXXVII–XXXVIII (1937), pp. 87–91.

1940

(5) KECK, Sheldon. 'The transfer of a small icon to a support of vinyl resin.' *Technical Studies in the Field of the Fine Arts*, IX (1940), pp. 11–20.

(6) ROSEN, David. 'Notes on the preservation of panel pictures.' *Journal of the Walters Art Gallery, Baltimore*, IV (1941), pp. 123–127.

(7) ROSEN, David. 'Preservation versus restoration.' *Magazine of Art* (Washington, D.C.), XXXIV (1941), pp. 458–471.

(8) BUCK, Richard D. 'Treatment of paintings on wood in museums not air-conditioned.' *Museum News* (Washington, D.C.), XXV (June 1947), p. 7.
   Partial report of experiments on panels to determine the effectiveness of moisture barriers in preventing movement and warping of panels.

(9) PACKARD, E. and KIRBY, J. C. 'The structure of some South German panel paintings — a problem in conservation.' *Journal of the Walters Art Gallery, Baltimore*, X (1947), pp. 91–97.

(10) PEASE, Murray. 'A treatment for panel paintings.' *Metropolitan Museum of Art Bulletin* (New York), III (1948), pp. 119–124.

1950

(11) STEVENS, W. C. and JOHNSTON, D. D. *Tests to investigate the efficiency of various coatings and coverings applied to the backs of painted panels with a view to reducing distortion following changes in atmospheric conditions.* Department of Scientific and Industrial Research, Forest Products Research Laboratory, Princes Risborough, England. 1950. Mimeographed.

(12) BUCK, Richard D. 'A note on the effect of age on the hygroscopic behaviour of wood.' *Studies in Conservation*, I (1952), pp. 39–45.

Bibliography

(13) Carità, R. 'Proposte per la parchettatura delle tavole' ('Proposals for the cradling of panels'). *Bollettino dell'Istituto Centrale del Restauro* (Rome), XVI (1953), pp. 173–188.

Improved methods for cradling using modern materials combined with modern knowledge of wood technology.

(14) Hermesdorf, P. F. J. M. 'Joining loose members of panel paintings.' *Studies in Conservation*, I (1954), pp. 87–91.

(15) Augusti, Selim. 'Traitement de conservation des peintures sur panneau' ('Conservation treatment of paintings on panel'). *Studies in Conservation*, I (1954), pp. 127–130.

(16) Brachert, Thomas. 'Zur Parkettierungsfrage' ('The question of cradling'). *Maltechnik*, LXI (1955), pp. 7–8.

Various methods of cradling are described.

(17) ICOM Commission for the Care of Paintings. 'The care of wood panels.' *Museum* (unesco, Paris), VIII (1955), pp. 139–194.

The most comprehensive survey so far of the problems and treatment of panel paintings. Illus. Bibliography.

(18) Carità, R. 'Proposte per la parchettatura delle tavole' ('Proposals for cradling of panels'). *Bollettino dell'Istituto Centrale del Restauro* (Rome), XXVII–XXVIII (1956), pp. 101–131.

A further attempt to evolve a safe and effective method of cradling.

(19) Straub, R. E. 'A modified apparatus for re-joining heavy panels.' *Studies in Conservation*, II (1956), pp. 192–194.

(20) Schmidt-Thomson, Kurt. 'Trennen einer Altartafel' ('The division of an altar panel'). *Maltechnik*, LXIII (1957), pp. 6–11.

An account of sawing through a wood panel painted on both sides.

(21) Wehlte, K. 'Planierung einer Bildtafel als Sonderfall' ('The flattening of a panel painting — an exceptional case'). *Maltechnik*, LXIV (1958), pp. 104–111.

(22) De Wild, A. Martin. 'Redwood, eine ausgezeichnete Holzart für Restaurierungen' ('Redwood, an excellent type of wood for restorations'). *Maltechnik*, LXV (1959), pp. 49–50.

1960

(23) Keyszelitz, R. 'Roste auf Holztafelbildern nach der "Wiener Methode"' ('The cradling of wood panel paintings according to the "Vienna method"'). *Maltechnik*, LXVI (1960), pp. 73–75.

(24) Schneider, Thomas.'Eine Methode der Bildübertragung' ('A method for the transfer of paintings'). *Maltechnik*, LXVI (1960), pp. 105–111.

A description of the transfer to canvas of fragments of a bomb-damaged panel painting.

(25) Buck, Richard D. 'The use of moisture barriers on panel paintings.' *Studies in Conservation*, VI (1961), pp. 9–20.

Bibliography

(26) BOLESLAWSKI, Jozef. 'Metrologia laboratoryjna w konsewacji zabytkow. Pomiary odksztalcen podobrazi drewnianych' ('Laboratory metrology in conservation. Measuring the deformation in wood panels'). *Ochrona Zabytkow* (Warsaw), XIV (1961), No. 3–4, pp. 93–101. In Polish, French summary

A method for making direct kinetic observations on warping and deformation.

(27) STEVENS, W. C. 'Rates of change in the dimensions and moisture contents of wooden panels resulting from changes in the ambient air conditions.' *Studies in Conservation*, VI (1961), pp. 21–25.

(28) BUCK, Richard D. 'Is cradling the answer?' *Studies in Conservation*, VII (1962), pp. 71–74.

(29) KOZLOWSKI, Rudolf. 'An apparatus for glueing split panels.' *Studies in Conservation*, VII (1962), pp. 135–140.

(30) KOZLOWSKI, Rudolf. 'A new cradle model.' *Studies in Conservation*, VII (1962), pp. 56–66.

(31) WOLTERS, Christian and KÜHN, Hermann. 'Behaviour of painted wood panels under strong illumination.' *Studies in Conservation*, VII (1962), pp. 1–9.

(32) *Recent advances in conservation*, edited by G. THOMSON. Butterworth, London, 1963. (Papers given at the I.I.C. Rome Conference, 1961).

Papers on panel treatment are: 'Some applications of mechanics to the treatment of panel paintings' by Richard D. BUCK; 'Treatment of warped wood panels by plastic deformation, moisture barriers and elastic support,' by Christian WOLTERS; 'The transfer of easel paintings,' by A. W. LUCAS; 'La conservation des peintures sur panneaux' ('The conservation of paintings on panel'), by G. URBANI.

(33) SCHEEL, Jan. 'Plexiglass-Parkettierung für abnorm-zerstörte Holztafeln' ('Plexiglass parquetry for abnormally disrupted wood panels'). *Maltechnik*, LXIX (1963) pp. 42–45.

(34) *Über die Erhaltung von Gemälden und Skulpturen* (On the preservation of paintings and sculptures), edited by Rolf E. STRAUB. Zürich and Stuttgart, 1963. 176 pp.

Contributions on treatment of panel supports are: 'Ein neues Verfahren zur Übertragung von Tafelmalereien bei teilweiser Beibehaltung des Bildträgers' ('A new process for the transfer of panel paintings with partial retention of the picture support') by Peter F. J. M. Hermesdorf; 'Ein Verfahren zur Übertragung italienischer Tafelbilder des 13. bis 15. Jahrhunderts' ('A method for transfer of Italian panel paintings of the 13th to 15th centuries'), the method of Augusto VERMEHREN, described by Edgar DENNINGER; 'Über die Erhaltung von Holztafelbildern' ('The preservation of wood panel paintings') by Rolf E. STRAUB.

(35) BOISSONAS, Pierre. 'Emploi du vacuum pour les tableaux sur bois' ('The use of vacuum for paintings on wood'). *Studies in Conservation*, IX (1964), pp. 43–49.

(36) BERGER, Gustav A. 'A vacuum envelope for treating panel paintings.' *Studies in Conservation*, X (1965), pp. 18–23.

A method for treating insecure paint on curved panels under vacuum in a plastic envelope.

(37) BRAMMER, Hans. 'Vacuum-Packung für Bildtafeln' ('A vacuum enclosure for panel paintings'). *Maltechnik*, LXXI (1965), pp. 102–104.

The application of the vacuum process (more often used for canvas paintings) for reattachment and impregnation of panel paintings.

(38) STRAUB, Rolf E. *Konservierung und Denkmalpflege*, I. *Tafelbild* (Conservation and restoration of works of art, I. Panel paintings). Verlag Berichthaus, Zurich, 1965. See also: *Section 22* (27), *Section 27* (10).

SECTION 11

Treatment of canvas supports

1930

(1) SCHMIDT-DEGENER, F. 'Wax relining of picture canvases.' *The Museums Journal*, London, XXXII (1932), pp. 86–87.

(2) GETTENS, R. J. and STOUT, G. L. 'The problem of lining adhesives for paintings.' *Technical Studies in the Field of the Fine Arts*, II (1933), pp. 81–104.

(3) WEHLTE, Kurt. 'Schutz der Bildrückseite' ('The protection of the backs of pictures'). *Kunst und Wirtschaft*, XIV (1933), pp. 78–89.

The advisability of putting a protective layer on the backs of canvas paintings.

(4) LYON, R. Arcadius. 'Comments on relining.' *Technical Studies in the Field of the Fine Arts*, II (1934), pp. 217–222.

(5) CURSITER, Stanley and PLENDERLEITH, H. J. 'The problem of lining adhesives for paintings — wax adhesives.' *Technical Studies in the Field of the Fine Arts*, III (1934), pp. 90–113.

(6) ROSEN, David. 'Treatment of the edges of canvas paintings.' *Technical Studies in the Field of the Fine Arts*, IV (1935), pp. 111–112.

(7) STOUT, G. L. 'An iron for relining.' *Technical Studies in the Field of the Fine Arts*, IV (1935), pp. 113–118.

(8) CURSITER, Stanley and DE WILD, A. Martin. 'Picture relining.' *Technical Studies in the Field of the Fine Arts*, V (1937), pp. 157–179.

(9) 'A note on picture relining.' *Ibid*, VI (1938), pp. 174–179.

(10) 'Picture relining with wax.' *Ibid*, VII (1938), pp. 80–87.

(11) 'Picture relining.' *Ibid*, VII (1939), pp. 191–195.

1950

(12) ROTH, James. 'Wax relining.' *Museum News* (Washington, D.C.), 1 November 1951, pp. 6–7.

Bibliography

(13) RUHEMANN, H. 'The impregnation and lining of paintings on a hot table.' *Studies in Conservation*, I (1953), pp. 73–76.

(14) STRAUB, R. E. and REES JONES, Stephen. 'Marouflage, relining and the treatment of cupping with atmospheric pressure.' *Studies in Conservation*, II (1955), pp. 55–63.

(15) DRINKWATER, G. Nevin. 'A new hot table for relining.' *Studies in Conservation*, III (1957), pp. 89–91.

(16) STRAUB, R. E. 'Das Heiztisch-Unterdruckverfahren zur Konservierung von Leinwandbildern' ('The vacuum hot-table process in the conservation of canvas paintings'). *Maltechnik*, LXIV (1958), pp. 70–77.

The apparatus and method used at the Schweizerisches Institut für Kunstwissenschaft, Zürich.

(17) DE WILD, A. Martin. 'A vacuum-relining apparatus for general use.' *Studies in Conservation*, IV (1959), pp. 73–77.

(18) MARIJNISSEN, Roger and SEGHERS, Jerome. 'Het verdoeken van grote schilderijen' ('The treatment of large paintings'). *Bulletin de l'Institut Royal du Patrimoine Artistique* (Brussels), II (1959), pp. 67–72 (French summary).

The repair of an exceptionally large early 19th century canvas painting.

(19) REES JONES, Stephen and HERMESDORF, P. F. J. M. 'The adhesive strength of wax-resin compounds.' *Studies in Conservation*, IV (1959), pp. 5–12.

1960

(20) ICOM Commission for the Care of Paintings: Fabric paint supports.' *Museum* (UNESCO, Paris), XIII (1960), pp. 134–171.

A comprehensive review, with bibliography.

(21) SLABCZYNSKI, Stefan. 'The large vacuum hot-table for wax relining of paintings in the Conservation Department of the Tate Gallery.' *Studies in Conservation*, V (1960), pp. 1–15.

(22) 'Some notes on vacuum hot-tables.' *Studies in Conservation*, V (1960), pp. 17–24.

With contributions by H. RUHEMANN, Alain G. BOISSANAS, Christian WOLTERS (Doerner Institute, Munich), Elizabeth PACKARD and Peter MICHAELS (Walters Art Gallery, Baltimore).

(23) BOISSONAS, Alain G. 'Relining with glass-fibre fabric.' *Studies in Conservation*, VI (1961), pp. 26–30.

(24) BRANDT, Walfried. 'Keilrahmen, abnorme Formen und Formate' ('Abnormal shapes and sizes in keyed stretchers'). *Maltechnik*, LXIX (1963), pp. 103–107.

A useful article on the construction and function of unusual (e.g. oval and baroque-shaped) keyed stretchers.

(25) DE WILD, A. Martin. 'Befestigungsmethoden von Malleinwand' ('Methods for fixing artist's canvas'). *Maltechnik*, LXIX (1963), pp. 97–102.

A review of methods for fixing canvas to stretchers, including a modern stapling tool.

(26) DE WILD, A. Martin. 'Wiederfestigung von Leinwand und Bildschicht' ('Reinforcement of canvas and paint layers'). *Maltechnik*, LXX (1964), pp. 97–111.

Bibliography

(27) BERGER, Gustav A. 'Relining outsize paintings.' *Studies in Conservation*, X (1965), pp. 140–146.

A method whereby canvas paintings too large to be relined on a hot table can be relined on the floor using a simple suction device.

(28) BRACHERT, Thomas. 'Probleme bei der Doublierung von Leinwandbildern' ('Problems in the relining of canvas pictures'). *Maltechnik*, LXXI (1965), pp. 80–81.

(29) LINARD, Henri. 'Amélioration dans certains cas du procédé de rentoilage à la cire-résine par l'emploi de "Someline" ' ('Use of "Someline" for wax-resin relining in certain cases'). *Studies in Conservation*, X (1965), pp. 24–26.

The use of a thin felted fabric composed of synthetic fibre in place of the usual woven relining canvas for paintings where the texture of the relining canvas might prove objectionable.

(30) STRAUB, Rolf E. 'Nachteile des Doublierens auf dem Vacuum-Heiztisch und Wege zu ihrer Behebung' ('Disadvantages of relining on the vacuum hot-table and ways of overcoming them'). *Maltechnik*, LXXI (1965), pp. 97–102. See also *Section 5 (24)*.

(31) GRANWEHR, O. and BRACHERT, T. 'Selbstgebauter Heiztisch' ('A home-made hot-table'). *Maltechnik*, LXXII (1966), pp. 43–46.

A hot table for relining constructed at the Schweizerisches Institut für Kunstwissenschaft, Zürich; useful details of materials, construction and costs.

SECTION 12

Infestation by insects and moulds

1930

(1) REES JONES, Stephen and RITCHIE, Patrick D. 'Radiographic detection of lyctris larvae in situ.' *Technical Studies in the Field of the Fine Arts*, V (1937), pp. 179–181.

Detection of wood-worm by X-rays.

1940

(2) GETTENS, R. J., PEASE, Murray and STOUT, G. L. 'The problem of mould-growth in paintings.' *Technical Studies in the Field of the Fine Arts*, IX (1941), pp. 127–144.

1950

(3) LIBERTI, Salvatore. 'Nuovi ritrovati nella disinfestazione delle opere d'arte' ('New discoveries in the disinfestation of works of art'). *Bollettino dell'Istituto Centrale del Restauro* (Rome), XVI (1953), pp. 155–175.

A comparison of methods and materials including the use of methyl bromide and compounds of chloro-naphthalene.

Bibliography

(4) MARCONI, B. 'La lutte contre les insectes attaquant le bois, à l'aide des rayons X, des ondes radio ultra-courtes et des ultra-sons' ('The war against insects attacking wood, using X-rays, ultra-short radio waves and ultrasonics'). *Ochrona Zabytkow* (Warsaw), VI (1954), pp. 218–223. In Polish with French summary.

(5) LIBERTI, Salvatore. 'Sull'uso di cloronaftaline a bassa clorurazione quali disinfestanti del legno' ('The use of chloronaphthalenes for wood disinfestation'). *Bollettino dell' Istituto Centrale del Restauro* (Rome), XXIII–XXIV (1955), p. 199.

(6) DENNINGER, Edgar. 'Verbesserte Holzwurmbekämpfung' ('Improved protection against woodworm'). *Maltechnik*, LXIII (1957), pp. 65–69.

(7) TONOLO, A. and GIACOBINI, C. 'Importanza dell umidità relativa per lo sviluppo di microorganismi nei dipinti su tela' ('The importance of relative humidity for the development of micro-organisms on canvas paintings'). *Bollettino dell'Istituto Centrale del Restauro* (Rome), XXXVI (1958), pp. 191–205.

1960

(8) WAHLS, A. R. 'Holzschädlinge und deren Bekämpfung' ('Wood pests and their control'). *Maltechnik*, LXXII (1966), pp. 18–23.

An account of the types of insect and fungal attack which occur on wood, particularly of panel paintings, and methods of prevention and extermination.

SECTION 13

Paint films: properties, defects, deterioration, etc.

1920

(1) EIBNER, Alexander. *Sprung und Rissbildung an trocknenden Ölfarbenaufstrichen und auf Ölbildern.* (The formation of cracks and fissures in drying oil paint layers and in oil paintings). Munich, 1920.

A classic treatment of the subject, not yet superseded. (H.R.).

(2) RENDERS, Émile. 'Cracks in Flemish Primitives.' *The Burlington Magazine*, LII (1928), pp. 59–65.

Interesting observations and theories, though not scientifically based, on the formation of craquelure in Flemish primitives.

1930

(3) HIERONMYI, Angelina. 'Uber Trübungen und Verdunkelungen von Gemälden' ('The obscuration and darkening of paintings'). *Technische Mitteilungen für Malerei*, XVIX (1933), pp. 35–37.

(4) EIBNER, Alexander. 'The yellowing of oil films and its prevention.' *Paint and Varnish Production Manager* (New York), XIII (1935), pp. 7–8, 10, 12–13.

Bibliography

(5) LAURIE, A. P. 'The yellowing of linseed oil.' *Technical Studies in the Field of the Fine Arts*, IV (1936), p. 145.

(6) LAURIE, A. P. 'The refractive index of a solid film of linseed oil : rise in refractive index with age.' *Proceedings of the Royal Society* (London), XLIX (1937), pp. 123–133.
The hopes based on this pioneer work were not fulfilled. (H.R.).

(7) STOUT, George L. 'Classes of simple paint structure.' *Technical Studies in the Field of the Fine Arts*, VI (1938), pp. 221–239.

(8) STOUT, G. L. and PEASE, M. 'A case of paint cleavage.' *Technical Studies in the Field of the Fine Arts*, VII (1938), pp. 33–45.
A fundamental work, showing that it is possible for a shrunken varnish film to pull off the paint beneath. (H.R.).

1950

(9) HESS, Manfred. *Paint film defects — their causes and cure.* 1st edn. London 1951, latest edition London 1965.
A review of paint defects primarily in the field of industrial finishings, but the classification and causes are useful in the study of pictures.

(10) FELLER, Robert L. 'Color change in oil paintings.' *Carnegie Magazine* (Pittsburgh, Pa.), XXVIII (1954), pp. 276–281, 285.
A useful survey of the changes in colour which occur in paintings other than those directly affecting the pigment.

(11) BRACHERT, T. 'Rissbildung an Gemälden' ('The formation of cracks in paintings'). *Maltechnik*, LXII (1956), pp. 105–112.
See also *Section 9* (5); *Section 27* (22), (30), (58), (63), (65), (73), (78), (83), (91), (98), (107).

SECTION 14

Cleaning (i.e. the operation of varnish removal), specifically

The following are the most important of the comparatively few publications exclusively devoted to the topic of varnish removal. Further information on the subject will be found in a number of the items in *Section 4, Works on, or containing sections on, restoration, post–1900*. Properties of picture varnishes are included in *Section 16*, below, *Picture varnishes and other surface coatings*. Of the scientific publications concerning solubility of varnish and oil films, the few listed in this section seem to the present writers to be most relevant to practical cleaning of pictures, but others are listed in *Section 27, Technical and scientific examination, general*.

1930

(1) VAN PUYVELDE. 'Le nettoyage des tableaux anciens' ('The cleaning of old pictures'). *Annuaire Général des Beaux-Arts de Belgique* (Brussels), 1933, pp. 19–30.

Bibliography

(2) LAURIE, A. P. 'Dévernissage des tableaux anciens et la suppression des repeints' ('The cleaning of old pictures and the suppression of repaints'). *Mouseion*, XXV–XXVI (1934), pp. 216–219.

(3) LAURIE, A. P. 'Restrainers and solvents used in cleaning old varnish from pictures.' *Technical Studies in the Field of the Fine Arts*, IV (1935), pp. 34–35.

(4) STOUT, G. L. 'A preliminary test of varnish solubility.' *Technical Studies in the Field of the Fine Arts*, IV (1936), pp. 146–161.

A pioneer paper attempting a realistic laboratory test of the cleaning process. (H.R.).

1950

(5) BRACHERT, Thomas. 'Zum Problem der Firnisabnahme' ('The problem of varnish removal'). *Maltechnik*, LXI (1955), pp. 67–71.

(6) CORRADINI, Giovanni. 'Reinigen von impressionistischen Bildern' ('The cleaning of Impressionist paintings'). *Maltechnik*, LXIII (1957), pp. 78–81.

An excellent summary. Acetone (diluted) without friction was preferred for cleaning to 'weaker' solvents requiring friction. (H.R.).

(7) MORA, Paolo and TORRACA, Giorgio. 'Solventi per la pulitura dei dipinti a tempera' ('Solvents for the cleaning of tempera paintings'). *Bollettino dell'Istituto Centrale del Restauro* (Rome), XXXI–XXXII (1957), pp. 171–173.

A discussion of the requirements of solvents for cleaning tempera paintings. The properties and uses of dimethylformamide and n-butylamine are considered for the purpose.

(8) RUHEMANN, Helmut. 'Firnisabnahme als Problem' ('The problem of varnish removal'). *Maltechnik*, LXIX (1963), pp. 47–48.

A summary of the position as the author saw it at that time in the light of recent technical research.

(9) STOLOW, Nathan. *Solvent action: fundamental researches and picture cleaning*. Lecture given to the seminar on resinous coatings at the Intermuseum Conservation Association, Oberlin, Ohio, April 1957, also to the Seminar on Conservation at the Brooklyn Museum, New York, Feb. 1958. Copies mimeographed by the National Gallery of Canada, Ottawa, 1957.

(For a paper on a related subject by the same author, see *Section 27* (69), below).

(10) FELLER, Robert L., JONES, Elizabeth H. and STOLOW, Nathan. *On picture varnishes and their solvents*. Reports presented to the seminar on resinous surface coatings sponsored by the Intermuseum Conservation Association, April, 1957. Published, Oberlin, Ohio, 1959.

For a review of this publication see *Section 16, Picture varnishes*, p. 442. (See also papers by the same authors, *Section 4*, p. 408 in *Recent Advances in Conservation*, edited G. Thomson, Butterworth, London, 1963.)

(11) *Über die Erhaltung von Gemälden und Skulpturen* (On the preservation of paintings and sculptures), edited by Rolf E. STRAUB. Zürich and Stuttgart, 1963. 176 pp.

Pages 49–57, 'Ein technischer Beitrag zum Problem der Firnisabnahme' ('A technical approach to varnish removal') by Stephen REES JONES. See also *Section 27* (48), (69), (70), (104).

Bibliography

Section 15

Retouching (Technique of retouching; for ethics and aesthetics of retouching see also *Section 7* above)

1910

(1) Bauer-Bolton, Victor. *Sollen fehlende Stellen bei Gemälden ergänzt werden?* (Should missing areas of paintings be made good?). Publ. Verlag der Technische Mitteilungen für Malerei, Munich, 1914.

The author argues acutely the impossibility of perfect reconstruction of missing parts in paintings and the undesirability of deceptive retouching.

He suggests close matching but leaving the retouchings at a slightly different (lower) level, so that they can be easily perceived by reflected light.

Bauer-Bolton denounces the complete lack of scientific approach and of rational teaching of restoration in his time. He advocates enthusiastically the Pettenkofer technique (see *Section 3* (No. 52)). He also advocates systematic recording by photography in order to put an end to the state of affairs where 'anybody can always proffer *ad libitum* any accusation or excuse'. On p. 39 he remarks: 'Good photographs of a retouched painting, taken before the retouching was done, are incontrovertible evidence against later additions. This settles for good the argument over making compensations discernible.' He also discusses the setting up of a central photographic archive, and of internationally agreed formats and codes to 'record the *status quo* of pictures' (the scheme to include its obligatory use in private collections). (H.R.).

1930

(2) Ruhemann, Helmut. 'Une méthode de restauration à la cire neutre' ('A method of restoration with neutral wax'). *Mouseion*, XVII–XVIII (1932), pp. 167–169.

A description of the method of retouching introduced by A. Klausner.

(3) Maurer, Robert. 'Ein neues Verfahren der Gemäldeerhaltung.' ('A new process for picture conservation'). *Technische Mitteilungen für Malerei*, LIII (1937), pp. 219–225, 231–235.

Some of the processes described in this article would now be regarded as old-fashioned, but there is an interesting and novel scheme for carrying out any retouchings needed on a picture not on the picture surface itself but on a thin transparent sheet of cellulose adhered to the picture surface with wax. In this way retouchings do not become an inherent part of the painting and may easily be removed if required.

(4) Susat, Alberto. 'Über das Restaurieren alter Gemälde' ('On the restoration of old paintings'). *Technische Mitteilungen für Malerei*, LIII (1937), pp. 93–95.

The author suggests certain guides in connection with inpainting of losses, particularly the use of neutral tones for large areas of loss.

1940

(5) Stout, G. L. 'Note: Treatment of blemished paintings.' *Technical Studies in the*

Bibliography

Field of the Fine Arts, X (1941), pp. 99–112.

Different methods of inpainting losses are compared.

1950

(6) PHILIPPOT, Albert and Paul. 'Le problème de l'intégration des lacunes dans la restauration des peintures' ('The problem of the integration of lacunae in the restoration of paintings'). *Bulletin de l'Institut Royal du Patrimoine Artistique* (Brussels), II (1954), pp. 5–19.

1960

(7) PHILIPPOT, Albert and Paul. 'Réflexions sur quelques problèmes estétiques et techniques de la retouche' ('Reflections on some aesthetic and technical problems of retouching'). *Bulletin de l'Institut Royal du Patrimoine Artistique* (Brussels), III (1960), pp. 163–172.

The above two articles contain descriptions of the method of retouching used in the Institut Royal du Patrimoine Artistique at Brussels. Retouchings carried out in egg tempera are given a thin rubbing with oil, instead of being varnished, and a 'fixative' the nature of which is not specified. The authors quote the De Mayerne Ms. to substantiate the claim that on top of oil paint there is generally an appreciable and visible layer of oil likely to cause yellowing (for my comment on this point see p. 399). In describing the process of cleaning (i.e. varnish removal) they speak of '*l'allègement* des vernis et enlèvement des repeints' ('the *reduction* of the varnish and the removal of repaints'). How, though, is it possible to remove repaints which lie under old varnish if the varnish is not completely removed but only reduced in thickness? A. Philippot's method of retouching is based on the confidence in the lastingness of his superbly matched integrations and the belief that they will never need to be removed. (H.R.).

(8) ALTHÖFER, Heinz. 'Die Retusche in der Gemälderestaurierung' ('Retouching in the restoration of paintings'). *Museumskunde* (Berlin), II (1962), pp. 73–78, and III (1962), pp. 144–170.

A comprehensive account, illustrated with numerous examples, of the history and technique of retouching, with a comparison of the various methods both from a technical and an aesthetic viewpoint.

(9) PHILIPPOT, Paul. 'Die Integration von Fehlstellen in der Gemälderestaurierung' ('The integration of losses in the restoration of paintings'). *Oesterreichische Zeitschrift für Kunst- und Denkmalpflege* (Vienna), XVI (1962), pp. 119–128.

(10) STRAUB, Rolf E. 'Retouching with synthetic resin paint.' *The Museums Journal* (London), LXII (1962), pp. 113–119.

A description of the use of a polycyclohexanone resin (MS2A) as a retouching medium is described (but see also *Ibid*, LXIII (1963), pp. 123–124, for an added note concerning the limitations of the material in this capacity).

(11) STRAUB, Rolf E. 'Retuschieren mit Kunstharzfarben' ('Retouching with synthetic resin paints'). *Maltechnik*, LXIX (1963), pp. 65–73.

Bibliography

SECTION 16

Picture varnishes and other surface coatings

1910

(1) HOLMES, C. J. 'Essay on mastic varnish.' *The Burlington Magazine*, Vol. XXXV (919, Part II), pp. 68–75.

The author explains that many critics of picture cleaning at this time are ignorant of the nature of varnish removal, or even of the fact that picture cleaning generally involves this process. He also lists reasons for cleaning, and describes the properties of mastic varnish.

1930

(2) BARRY, T. Hedley. *Natural varnish resins*. London, 1932.

Although not specifically relating to pictures or their restoration this book forms a good background to the history, use and properties of natural resins used in varnishes.

(3) BIGELOW, E. and GETTENS, R. J. 'The moisture permeability of protective coatings.' *Technical Studies in the Field of the Fine Arts*, I (1932), pp. 63–68.

Laboratory experiments to assess the protective quality of various surface coating films with regard to moisture.

(4) GETTENS, R. J. and BIGELOW, E. 'Moisture permeability of protective coatings.' *Technical Studies in the Field of the Fine Arts*, II (1933), pp. 15–25.

(5) TOCH, Maximilian. 'Dammar as a picture varnish.' *Technical Studies in the Field of the Fine Arts*, II (1934), pp. 149–152.

(6) ROSEN, David. 'A wax formula.' *Technical Studies in the Field of the Fine Arts*, III (1934), pp. 114–115.

Wax as a protective coating for the surface of pictures.

(7) GETTENS, Rutherford J. 'Polymerized vinyl acetate and related compounds in the restoration of works of art.' *Technical Studies in the Field of the Fine Arts*, IV (1935), pp. 15–27.

One of the earliest applications of a modern synthetic resin, including as a varnish, to the field of conservation.

(8) STOUT, George L. 'A preliminary test of varnish solubility.' *Technical Studies in the Field of the Fine Arts*, IV (1936), pp. 146–161.

(9) CROSS, H. F. and STOUT, G. L. 'Properties of surface films.' *Technical Studies in the Field of the Fine Arts*, V (1937), pp. 241–249.

Properties of natural and synthetic resin surface coatings.

(10) RAWLINS, F. I. G. 'The optical properties of some common varnishes.' *Technical Studies in the Field of the Fine Arts*, VI (1938), pp. 180–182.

1950

(11) MILLS, J. S. and WERNER, A. E. A. 'Paper chromatography of natural resins.' *Nature* (London), CLXIX (1952), p. 1064.

Bibliography

An account of the first fundamental study of the chemistry of the natural resins used for picture varnishes, and a key to their unsuitability for that purpose. See also other papers by J. S. Mills under *Section 27, Technical and Scientific Examination, general.*

(12) FELLER, Robert L. 'Infra-red analysis of dammar and mastic.' *Science*, Washington, D.C., CXX (1954), pp. 1069–1070.

(13) BROMMELLE, N. 'Bloom in varnished paintings.' *The Museums Journal*, London, LV (1956), pp. 263–266.

(14) THOMSON, Garry. 'Test for cross-linking of linear polymers.' *Nature*, London, CLXXVIII (1956), p. 807.

A report of a test which showed the unsuitability of some methacrylate polymers as picture varnishes because of decrease in solubility with age and exposure to light or heat.

(15) FELLER, R. L. 'Cross-linking of methacrylate polymers by ultra-violet radiation.' Papers presented at the New York meeting of the American Chemical Society, *Journal of the American Chemical Society, Division of Paint, Plastics and Printing Ink Chemistry*, XVII (1957), 465–470.

(16) THOMSON, Garry. 'Some picture varnishes.' *Studies in Conservation*, III (1957), pp. 64–79.

An assessment of the varnishes available up to this date.

(17) FELLER, R. L. 'Factors affecting the appearance of a picture varnish.' *Science* (Washington, D.C.), CXXV (1957), pp. 1143–1144.

(18) FELLER, R. L. 'Dammar and mastic varnishes — hardness, brittleness and change in weight upon drying.' *Studies in Conservation*, III (1958), pp. 162–174.

(19) STOLOW, Nathan. *Solvent action: fundamental researches and picture cleaning.* Lecture given to the seminar on resinous coatings at the Intermuseum Conservation Association, Oberlin, Ohio, April, 1957, also given to a Seminar on Conservation held at the Brooklyn Museum, New York, Feb. 1958. Copies mimeographed by the National Gallery of Canada, Ottawa. 13 pp.

(20) FELLER, R. L., JONES, Elizabeth H. and STOLOW, Nathan. *On picture varnishes and their solvents.* Reports presented to the seminar on resinous surface coatings sponsored by the Intermuseum Conservation Association, Oberlin, April, 1958. Published Oberlin, Ohio, 1959. 220 pp., tables and charts.

A model of a scientific publication, comprehensible by non-scientists, indispensable for restorers who want to keep abreast with developments in their field. From the point of view of the practising restorer Elizabeth Jones' contribution, 'The Removal of Varnish', deserves first place. She describes in detail her 'reforming' method. After removing the surface grime the varnish film is softened by spraying on the surface a mixture of 4 parts ethyl alcohol, 1 part diacetone alcohol and 1 part cellosolve acetate, for 2–4 seconds. After a period of 1 hour to 1 week the varnish is removed by rolling (see pp. 204–206 of the present book); this can now be done with a far weaker solvent than would have been effective before the spraying. The surprising experience that in no case was the actual paint surface even of resin-oil paintings softened or 'affected in any way by the reforming', has been confirmed and explained by specialist chemists in a thorough research using infra-red spectroscopy, radioactive ethyl alcohol and a Geiger counter. It was ascertained that the varnish film is swelled by the solvent which is absorbed by the varnish or evaporates before it can attack the paint film. 'The paint film beneath is exposed for a shorter time to a smaller concentration of solvent molecules. The surface coating can be removed with less risk of swelling the paint film beneath'. Miss Elizabeth Jones also gives a brief survey of the disadvantages of Prof. Pettenkofer's Regenerating method, a now obsolete predecessor of the Reforming method, for which, by the way, she does not claim priority. There is however no doubt that it was she who perfected and established this method in painstaking experiments and in 15 years of actual application on well over 1000 paintings of many types and periods. Some especially difficult and completely successful cases, e.g. paintings by Delacroix, I had the opportunity of examining myself.

Dr. Robert L. Feller's paper contains in a concise and comprehensible form valuable information on the compounds used in the making and dissolving of varnishes including useful practical advice and will greatly help the restorer to understand the chemical and physical fundamentals involved. Unfortunately, since the seminar was held, it has been discovered that 27H varnish becomes more insoluble with time (it 'cross-links', as the scientist says); he acknowledges this in his notes added to the appendix of the book here reviewed (pp. 200–212) and upon further research he comes to the following conclusions: He, Dr. Feller, would prefer that no picture varnish would proceed to a state of comparative insolubility (point A in his figure 3, after about 28 years), but, he continues, there was little cause for alarm since after ten years' hardening the n-butyl methacrylate films 27H though no longer soluble could still be removed safely, if only in a gel state.

The subject should be thoroughly considered and fully investigated. However, it is disappointing that 27H varnish can no longer be recommended for use on valuable paintings after it had been shown by Dr. Feller's thorough research to have considerable advantages over other varnishes.

In this context it is perhaps relevant to repeat that the pictures the contemporary cleaner handles are rarely 'virgin' films (still unleached) like those serving in the experiments, but have nearly all been cleaned (and possibly leached) already several times. However, even speaking of the theoretically 'virgin' films Stolow writes (p. 86): 'While the leaching action cannot be remedied, it is *possible* to minimize *as much as possible* [my italics] the mechanical action' and earlier: 'This swelling in itself does not produce a great danger to an oil painting surface provided mechanical action on the paint is absolutely minimized.' Still, the main point that reduces the results of these experiments to academic importance is that the overriding variable that makes efficient and safe varnish removal possible, even from oil-resin paintings, namely the fast evaporation of acetone (3 times faster than methyl alcohol and 4 times faster than ethyl alcohol) had not been taken into account at all in the immersion tests. If any tangible advance is to accrue from this admirably painstaking research the relative simultaneously operative value of the different variables (Stolow mentions 8 but there are probably more) must be assessed; but this can perhaps only be done with the collaboration of an experienced and scientifically trained picture restorer who could help to devise more realistic tests.

Of the parameter criterion, Stolow himself says that: 'acetone, diacetone alcohol, the branched alcohols, e.g. isopropyl and isobutyl alcohols, do not fit into the picture too well'. This disqualifies for the parameter criterion all but three of the most useful solvents. The rest are, according to my experience, either practically ineffective or not indispensable for picture cleaning. (H.R.).

Dr. Nathan Stolow's section: *Solvent Action: Some Fundamental Researches into the Picture Cleaning Problem* (pp. 60–91), contains much useful information concerning this problem, including reference to publications by Déon, Faraday, The Catalogue of the Cleaned Pictures Exhibition, National Gallery, London in 1947 and I. Graham's measuring of the swelling of oil or oil resin films. Pages 64–90 Stolow devotes to '*Leaching and Swelling of Virgin Films of Drying Oils*'.

This piece of research has proved beyond doubt that certain 'leachable matter' can be leached out by solvents commonly used in picture cleaning and Dr. Stolow together with Mr. Rees Jones have put varnish removal on a scientific plane by their research in drawing attention to the dangers of swelling and leaching, but it is regrettable that they did not warn the reader how far removed their forced laboratory experiments necessarily were from the actual conditions prevailing during varnish removal from paintings. As it is, the layman reader can be led to believe that in ordinary cleaning, as in the experiments, up to 28 per cent of an old paint film is leached out. I have even read in print the amazing assertion by a specialist scientist that in reality a greater loss of matter is to be expected than in the swelling and leaching experiments. In reality it is of course infinitely smaller, in fact probably too small to be measurable, because the contact of a 'strong' solvent with the actual paint is a matter of seconds, not 20–120 hours; the restorer deals with pigmented films (which even in Stolow's experiment reach no more than 3·5 per cent leaching after 120 hours of immersion in methyl alcohol), usually over 100 to 400 years old. (H.R.)

1960

(21) FELLER, Robert L. '*Characteristics of resin AW-2*' Bulletin of the American Group, I.I.C., III (1962), No. 1, pp. 9–10.

Characteristics, including the original German patent, of the synthetic resin AW-2 which is used as a picture varnish.

See also: *Section 17* (2), *Section 27* (53), (57), (60), (61), (64), (66), (94), (100), (105).

SECTION 17

Apparatus (miscellaneous and excluding that specifically for treatment of panel and canvas supports)

1930

(1) RUHEMANN, Helmut. 'Neuer Apparat zur Behandlung von Blasen an Gemälden.' ('A new apparatus for the treatment of blisters on paintings'). Berichte aus dem Restaurationsatelier, Gemäldegalerie, in *Berliner Museen, Berichte aus den Preussischen Kunstsammlungen* (Berlin), 51st year (1930), p. 147.

Bibliography

The same type of apparatus, with only minor modifications, is still in use.

1950

(2) WEHLTE, Kurt. 'Spritzgeräte für Maler und Restauratoren' ('Spraying apparatus for the painter and restorer'). *Maltechnik*, LXII (1956), pp. 97–105.

(3) WEIHS, Fritz. 'Ein neuer electrischer Heizspachtel' ('A new electrically heated spatula'). *Maltechnik*, LXII (1956), pp. 40–42.

(4) GETTENS, R. J. 'Examining tables in use at the Freer Gallery of Art.' *Studies in Conservation*, IV (1959), pp. 23–27.

(5) LANK, Herbert. 'A simple stereoscopic microscope stand for picture examination.' *Studies in Conservation*, IV (1959), pp. 152–154.

1960

(6) STRAUB, R. E. 'An apparatus for the surface examination of pictures.' *Studies in Conservation*, VI (1961), pp. 46–48.

(7) BRANDT, Walfried. 'Fotostaffelei für Gemäldeaufnahmen' ('A photographic easel for photography of paintings'). *Maltechnik*, LXVIII (1962), pp. 37–44.

The adaptation of an ordinary artist's easel for photography of paintings under fluorescent tubes, flash or ultra-violet illumination.

(8) KÜHN, Hermann. 'Eine Universalleuchte zur Gemäldeuntersuchung' ('An all-purpose lamp for examination of paintings'). *Museumskunde* (Berlin), III (1963), pp. 190 ff.

A lamp adaptable for visible, ultra-violet, sodium and infra-red illumination.

(9) BUCK, Richard D. 'Design for a binocular supporting arm.' *Bulletin of the American Group, I.I.C.*, V (1964), No. 1, p. 16.

(10) LEMMER, Geoffrey M. 'A supporting arm for low power microscopes.' *Bulletin of the American Group, I.I.C.*, VI (1966), No. 1.

(11) SCHMID, Klaus-Peter. 'Handauflage für Restauratoren und Maler' ('A hand-rest for the restorer and painter'). *Maltechnik*, LXXII (1966), pp. 71–75.

The author has designed a simple hand-rest for attachment to the easel as a substitute for a mahl-stick.

SECTION 18

Materials (other than varnishes, specifically) *used in restoration*

A comprehensive bibliography of literature on painting materials will appear in a second book by the present author now in preparation. The following is a short list of works of interest and use to the conservator of paintings :

Bibliography

1910

(1) CHURCH, Arthur H. *The chemistry of paints and paintings.* 4th edn. London, 1915.

Still a useful and informative book showing a considerable awareness of the fundamental problems of conservation. For review of chapters concerning restoration see *Section 3 (56)*.

1920

(2) DOERNER, Max. *The materials of the artist and their use in painting, with notes on the techniques of the old masters.* The original German edition, *Malmaterial und seine Behandlung im Bilde,* was published in Munich in 1922, the first English translation in 1935.

Helmut Ruhemann's critical review of this work appears in Appendix D, pp. 355–360.

1930

(3) MAYER, Ralph. *The artist's handbook of materials and techniques.* 1st edn. New York, 1938. The most recent English edition, considerably revised, Faber and Faber, London, 1965.

One of the best reference books on artists' materials at present in print. For discussion of the chapter specifically on restoration see *Section 4 (29)* of the Bibliography, p. 403.

(4) MORELL, R. S. *The scientific aspect of artists' and decorators' materials.* London, 1939.

1940

(5) GETTENS, Rutherford J. and STOUT, George L. *Painting materials, a short encyclopedia,* Van Nostrand, New York, 1942. Reprinted by Dover Publications, Inc., New York, 1966.

By far the most accurate and reliable source of information available on the subject of materials used as supports, grounds, pigments, media, adhesives, varnishes, solvents, also tools and equipment, in painting past and present. One of the few books on painting materials in which each of the present authors has failed to find any error of fact. Our gratitude for the recent reappearance of the book in print is only slightly tempered with regret that the authors have not undertaken a new and enlarged edition since some parts, particularly those dealing with media and varnishes, are of necessity out of date after 25 years of development of modern synthetic materials.

(6) HILER, Hilaire. *The painter's pocket guide. Methods and materials.* 2nd edn. revised and enlarged. Los Angeles, 1945. Suffers from certain inaccuracies and inadequacies. See also *Section 4 (25)*.

(7) TOCH, Maximilian. *Paint, paintings and restoration.* 2nd edn. New York, 1945.

For comments on the chapter on restoration see *Section 4* (18) of the Bibliography, p. 400.

1950

(8) WERNER, A. E. A. 'Plastics aid in conservation of paintings.' *British Plastics,* 1952, pp. 363–366.

Bibliography

Summary by a chemist of those plastics which could be of use in the conservation of paintings.

(9) BROMMELLE, N. S. and LUCAS, A. 'Failure of synthetic materials in picture conservation.' *The Museums Journal* (London), LXIII (1953), pp. 149–151.

The authors, practical picture restorers, point out the limitations of synthetic materials in picture restoration.

(10) GLUCK, H. 'The dilemma of the painter and conservator in the synthetic age.' *The Museums Journal* (London), LIV (1954), pp. 149–158.

An account of the personal experiences of a present-day painter who has found the products of the artists' colour merchants unsatisfactory in use.

(11) ALTHÖFER, H. 'The use of polyethylene glycols in the field of painting restoration.' *Studies in Conservation*, IV (1959), pp. 31–34.

The author suggests various applications for polyethylene glycols (sold under the trade-name of *Carbowax* in England) including its use as an ingredient in relining adhesives, putty and retouching media.

1960

(12) Three notes on the limitations of polyethylene glycols' contributed by M. HEY, M. ALTHÖFER and R. ORGAN. *Studies in Conservation*, V (1960), pp. 159–162.

The authors point out disadvantages likely to be encountered in the use of this material in conservation, particularly for paintings, despite its successful application to some archaeological materials.

(13) DENNINGER, F. 'Kunststoffdispersion in Malerei und Restaurierung' ('Plastic dispersions in painting and restoration'). *Maltechnik*, IV (1960), p. 97.

(14) *Synthetic materials used in the conservation of cultural property.* Compiled by R. FELLER, A. VAN SCHENDEL and G. THOMSON. Rome Centre Publication No. 5, Rome, 1963.

An invaluable guide to the classification, physical and chemical properties and sources of supply of modern synthetic materials used for surface coatings, media, adhesives etc. in conservation and restoration.

See also *Section 15* (10), (11); *Section 16* (7).

SECTION 19

Premises — studios, laboratories, workshops (planning, equipment, organization, etc.)

1930

(1) LAURIE, A. P. 'Un laboratoire pour l'examen des peintures.' *Mouseion*, XVII–XVIII (1932), pp. 119–122.

(2) RAWLINS, F. I. G. 'The physical laboratory at the National Gallery.' *Science Progress* (London), XXX (1935), pp. 236–242.

Bibliography

The setting-up of a physical laboratory at the National Gallery, London.

1940

(3) Marceau, Henri. 'Conservation and technical research.' *Philadelphia Museum Bulletin*, Vol. XXXV (1940), 13 pp.

A description of the premises and facilities for technical examination and conservation of pictures at the Philadelphia Museum of Art.

1950

(4) Buck, R. D. 'Intermuseum Laboratory.' *Allen Memorial Art Museum Bulletin* (Oberlin, Ohio), Fall, 1952, pp. 29–30.

Announcement of the opening of a laboratory at Oberlin, Ohio, to serve the conservation needs of a number of museums and galleries in the surrounding area. The aims and conditions of establishment are outlined. See also: 'An experiment in co-operative conservation.' *Studies in Conservation*, II (1956), pp. 101–109.

(5) Hours, Maedeleine. 'Le laboratoire du Musée du Louvre' ('The laboratory of the Louvre Museum'). *Cahiers Français d'information*, No. 198, 15 Feb., 1952. Published by La Documentation Française, 16, Rue Lord-Byron, Paris.

An account of the laboratory for scientific, and, particularly, photographic investigation set up at the Louvre Museum, Paris.

(6) Drinkwater, G. Nevin. 'A conservation room.' *The Museums Journal* (London), LVI (1956), pp. 218–220.

The establishment in a small provincial museum (the Shipley Art Gallery, Gateshead, Co. Durham, England) of a department for the technical examination and the restoration of paintings.

(7) Augusti, Selim. 'The conservation laboratory of the Museo e Gallerie Nazionale di Capodimonte, Naples.' *Studies in Conservation*, IV (1959), pp. 88–95.

Easel paintings are among the objects examined and treated.

1960

(8) Boustead, William D. 'The conservation department of the New South Wales Art Gallery, Australia.' *Studies in Conservation*, V (1960), pp. 121–131.

Particularly interesting with reference to the special conservation problems of a warm damp climate.

(9) Gettens, Rutherford J. 'European conservation laboratories.' *Museum News* (Washington, D.C.), XXXIX (1960–61), No. 4, pp. 23–27.

A useful review of the conservation departments of European museums and art galleries which the author visited in 1960. Illus.

(10) *International Inventory of the museum laboratories and restoration workshops*. Rome Centre Publication No. 1, Rome, 1960. (Published also in French).

A list of conservation laboratories, studios and workshops all over the world and for every type of object. Information is given about facilities, staff, apparatus, premises, etc., type of work carried out and research projects and aims. Of necessity this handbook is now considerably out of date.

(11) DEMUS, Otto. 'Die Werkstätten des Bundesdenkmalamtes' ('The workshops of the federal monuments agency'). *Oesterreichische Zeitschrift für Kunst und Denkmalpflege* (Vienna), XV (1961), p. 2.

Pictures are among the many works of art restored in this department of conservation.

(12) SCHIFF, Gert. 'Das Schweizerische Institut für Kunstwissenschaft, Zürich.' *Maltechnik*, LXVII (1961), pp. 81–86.

An account of this Institute, which includes facilities for technical examination, photography, restoration and research into materials and techniques of works of art including paintings.

(13) STRAUB, R. E. 'The laboratories of the Swiss Institute for Art Research.' *Studies in Conservation*, VI (1961), pp. 41–45.

(14) MÜHLETHALER, Bruno. 'The research laboratory of the Swiss National Museum at Zürich.' *Studies in Conservation*, VII (1962), pp. 35–42.

(15) BROMMELLE, N. S. 'Conservation studios.' *The Museums Journal* (London), LXIII (1963), pp. 74–79.

The requirements of conservation studios, including those for picture restoration. Contribution to a Study Group on Planning Museums and Art Galleries, Bristol City Art Gallery, 1962.

(16) AGRAWAL, O. P. 'The conservation laboratory of the National Museum, New Delhi.' *Studies in Conservation*, VIII (1963), pp. 99–105.

Paintings are among the objects examined and treated.

(17) STOLOW, Nathan. 'Conservation and scientific research at the National Gallery of Canada.' *Professional Public Service* (Ottawa), XLII (Feb. 1963), pp. 4–7.

The author includes a plan of the laboratories and studios, also details of equipment.

(18) 'L'Institut Royal du Patrimoine Artistique et son nouveau bâtiment.' *Bulletin de l'Institut Royal du Patrimoine Artistique* (Brussels), VII (1964), pp. 9–131.

A detailed account of the new premises of the Institute at Brussels, its building, equipment and organization; contributions by P. COREMANS, C. RIMANGRE, R. V. SNEYERS, L. CASSIMAN, A. de GRAVE and M. VANDENSTOCK.

(19) SLABCZYNSKI, Stefan. 'Establishing a laboratory for restoration of paintings.' *The Museums Journal* (London), LXIV (1964), pp. 36–49.

Advice on staff, accommodation, technical equipment, required for setting up a conservation department for a large art gallery.

(20) ROBERTSON, Clements L. 'A museum conservation laboratory.' *Museum News* (Washington, D.C.), XLIII (1965), No. 5, pp. 15–21.

An account of a new conservation department for paintings at the City Art Museum, St. Louis, U.S.A.

Bibliography

Section 20

Museology and conservation, general

1950

(1) Buck, R. D. 'The inspection of collections.' *Museum News* (Washington, D.C.), XXIX, No. 7 (October, 1951).

(2) Kirby, John Carroll. 'The care of a collection.' *Journal of the Walters Art Gallery, Baltimore*, Special Technical Issue, XV–XVI (1952–53), pp. 9–29.

An account of the conservation of the collection of pictures and art objects at the Walters Art Gallery, Baltimore.

(3) Constable, W. G. 'Curators and conservation.' *Studies in Conservation*, I (1954), pp. 97–102.

(4) Constable, W. G. 'Curatorial problems in relation to conservation.' *Bulletin of the Fogg Museum of Art* (Cambridge, Mass.), X (1956), pp. 151–155.

1960

(5) unesco (United Nations Education, Scientific and Cultural Organization). *The organization of museums—practical advice*. Paris, s 1960. 180 pp., illus. No. IX of a series 'Museums and Monuments.'

The sections concerning conservation are: Chapter VII, The museum laboratory, by Paul Coremans; Collections, their care and storage, by Hiroshi Daifuku; Museum architecture, by Bruno Molajoli.

(6) Keck, Caroline K., Block, Huntington T., Chapman, Joseph, Lawton, John B. and Stolow, Nathan. *A primer on museum security*. Published by the New York State Historical Association, Cooperstown, New York, 1966. 85 pp.

A useful general guide to maintaining safety in the museum or art gallery: Physical security (with regard to theft, fire, etc.); Insurance; Environment (humidity and temperature control); Light and its effects; Other security factors (e.g. dirt, cleaning, mould, vandalism; transport, packing, etc.) See also: *Section 4* (67).

Section 21

Air conditioning — regulation of temperature and relative humidity; control of dust and atmospheric pollution

1930

(1) Ricci, Corrado. 'Les agents atmosphériques et la conservation des oeuvres d'art' ('Atmospheric agents and the conservation of works of art'). *Mouseion*, XV (1932), pp. 8–13.

Bibliography

(2) COURTAULD INSTITUTE OF ART, London. *Some notes on atmospheric humidity in relation to works of art*. London, 1934.

(3) AHRENS, W. 'Contrôle et réglage de la température et de l'humidité dans les musées' ('Control and regulation of temperature and humidity in museums'). *Mouseion*, XXV–XXVI (1934), pp. 125–131.

Description of a pioneer scheme for air-conditioning the State museums of Berlin.

(4) COREMANS, P. 'Air conditioning in museums.' *The Museums Journal* (London), XXXVI (1936, pp. 341–345 [Translation from an article in the *Bulletin des Musées Royaux d'Art et d'Histoire (Brussels)*, VII (1935), (iii), No. 6, pp. 146–148].

(5) CURSITER, Stanley. 'Control of air in cases and frames.' *Technical Studies in the Field of the Fine Arts*, V (1936), pp. 109–116.

An early use of trays of certain salts placed in the base of a closed showcase or glazed frame to produce an atmosphere of chosen relative humidity.

(6) BECKET, H. E. 'Condensation on unglazed pictures.' *The Journal of the Institution of Heating and Ventilating Engineers* (London), V (1937), pp. 134–137.

The problem of the condensation which sometimes occurs on the surfaces of pictures hung on a cold exterior wall.

(7) RAWLINS, F. I. G. 'Atmospheric pollution, with special reference to the National Gallery.' *The Heating and Ventilating Engineer* (London), XI (1937), pp. 223–230.

1940

(8) RAWLINS, F. I. G. 'The control of temperature and humidity in relation to works of art.' *The Museums Journal* (London), XLI (1942), pp. 279–283.

(9) FLETCHER, Paul. 'The engineering aspect of the wartime storage of art treasures.' *Journal of the Institution of Heating and Ventilating Engineers* (London), XI (1943), pp. 186–190.

A survey of atmospheric conditioning of safe war-time storage places, including the slate quarries used to house some of the pictures from the National Gallery, London.

(10) RAWLINS, F. I. G. 'Some physical aspects of storage of works of art.' *Journal of the Society of Heating and Ventilating Engineers*, XI (1943), pp. 175–185.

A survey of storage conditions and hazards of storage, particularly during the second world war.

(11) RAWLINS, F. I. G. 'La conservation des tableaux dans les abris pendant la guerre. Quelques aspects scientifiques du problème' ('The conservation of pictures in shelters during the war. Some scientific aspects of the problem'). *Mouseion*, LV–LVI (1946), pp. 35–51.

Useful experience of desirable atmospheric conditions for pictures was gained during their storage in the 1939–45 war, particularly from the conditions in slate quarries in Wales.

(12) KROGH, A. 'The dust problem in museums and how to solve it.' *The Museums Journal* (London), XLVII (1949), pp. 183–188.

Methods of combating dust in museums where full air conditioning incorporating dust extraction is not possible.

Bibliography

1950

(13) KEELEY, T. R. and RAWLINS, F. I. G. 'Air conditioning at the National Gallery, London.' *Museum* (UNESCO, Paris), IV (1950), pp. 193–200.

An account of the installation of the first fully air-conditioned room in the National Gallery, London.

(14) STOUT, George L. 'Air conditioning in storage.' *Worcester Art Museum News Bulletin and Calendar* (Worcester, Mass.), XVII (1952) pp. 24–31.

(15) WERNER, A. E. A. 'Heating and ventilation.' *The Museums Journal* (London), LVII (1957), pp. 159–166.

Practical advice on heating and ventilation of museums and art galleries.

1960

(16) 'Climatology and conservation in museums,' compiled by H. J. PLENDERLEITH and P. PHILIPPOT, *Museum* (UNESCO, Paris), XIII (1960), pp. 201–289. Also reprinted by the Rome Centre as Works and Publications No. 3, 196.

A comprehensive and invaluable review with a good bibliography.

(17) BROMMELLE, N. S. 'Technical services — air conditioning and lighting from the point of view of conservation.' *The Museums Journal* (London), LXIII (1963), pp. 32–42.

Contribution to a study group on the planning of museums and art galleries, Bristol City Art Gallery, 1962.

(18) AMDUR, Elias J. 'Humidity control — isolated area plan.' *Museum News* (Washington, D.C.), XCIII (1964), pp. 58–60. Technical Supplement No. 4, Part II (for Part I, see below No. (19)).

Construction of a 'building within a building' to make it easier to maintain adequate indoor humidity in museums in cold climates.

(19) BUCK, Richard D. 'A specification for museum air conditioning.' *Museum News* (Washington D.C.), XCIII (1964), pp. 53–57. Technical Supplement No. 4, Part I (for Part II, see above No. (18)).

An admirable up-to-date guide to principles and practice.

(20) SACK, Susanne P. 'A case study of humidity control.' *Brooklyn Museum Annual* (Brooklyn, New York), V (1963–64), pp. 99–103.

The construction and maintenance of a sealed case with controlled atmosphere for the protection of a valuable panel painting during its exhibition on loan.

(21) THOMSON, Garry. 'Air pollution — a review for conservation chemists.' *Studies in Conservation*, X (1965), pp. 147–167.

The most comprehensive review so far, outlining the problem of atmospheric pollution and its deteriorating effects and suggesting possible remedies.

(22) PADFIELD, Tim. 'The control of relative humidity and air pollution in show cases and picture frames.' *Studies in Conservation*, XI (1966), pp. 8–27.

(23) STOLOW, Nathan. 'Fundamental case design for humidity-sensitive museum

collections.' *Museum News* (Washington, D.C.), Technical Supplement No. 11, XLIV (1966), No. 6, pp. 45–52.

A review of the history of the basic principles and application of enclosing an object in a case in a controlled environment. An example is shown of a humidity-controlled display case for an early 14th century Italian triptych on panel. See also : *Section 20 (6)*, *Section 22 (37)*.

Section 22

Lighting and deteriorating effects of light (types of fitting, level of illumination, colour rendering, damaging effect of light)

Since 1945 types of lighting have changed to such an extent and so much research has been done on all aspects of lighting both outside and within the field of conservation and museology, that it seems pointless, particularly in a book dealing primarily with restoration, to quote very early articles or books on the subject. The following are some of the relevant more recent works :

1945

(1) DATES, H. B., LOGAN, H. L. and KNUDSTRUP, A. J. C. 'Art gallery lighting report of the Committee on Art Gallery Lighting of the Illuminating Engineering Society.' Illuminating Engineering (Baltimore), XL (1945), pp. 11–36.

Now out of date, but interesting as one of the first post-war treatments of the subject. Bibliography. Illus. Tables.

1950

(2) LIBERTI, Salvatore. 'Le illuminazioni al neon dei musei e generalmente dei dipinti' ('Neon lights for museums and for paintings generally'). *Bollettino dell' Istituto Centrale del Restauro* (Rome), I (1950), pp. 27–28.

(3) COMMISSION INTERNATIONALE D'ÉCLAIRAGE. *The lighting of galleries and museums.* Part I by J. B. BICKERDIKE and W. A. ALLEN. Part II by E. RAWSON-BOTTOM.

Reports to the Stockholm meeting of the C.I.E. in 1951.

(4) GENARD, J. 'Extreme ultra-violet radiation from tubular fluorescent lamps and its effects on museum lighting.' *Museum* (UNESCO, Paris), V (1952), pp. 53–65. See also *The Museums Journal* (London), LII (1952), pp. 5–18.

Wavelength characteristics of various light sources are reviewed, including those of the (then) newly introduced fluorescent tubes.

(5) CARITÀ, Roberto. 'Nota sull'illuminazione artificiale delle opere d'arte' ('A note on artificial lighting of works of art'). *Bollettino d'Arte*, IV (1953), pp. 357–364.

(6) JUDD, D. B. *Radiation hazards of museum light sources.* National Bureau of Standards Report 2254, Washington, 1953.

Bibliography

(7) SANTINI, Manlio. 'Luce naturale e luce artificiale in relazione alle opere d'arte' ('Natural light and artificial light in relation to works of art'). *Bollettino dell'Istituto Centrale del Restauro* (Rome), XVI (1953), pp. 189–203.

Advantages and disadvantages of different types of fluorescent tubes.

(8) COOPER, B. S. 'Fluorescent lighting in museums.' *The Museums Journal* (London), LIII (1954), pp. 279–290.

(9) HARRISON, Lawrence S. *Report on the deteriorating effects of modern light sources.* Published by the Metropolitan Museum of Art, New York, 1954.

(10) INTERNATIONAL COUNCIL FOR MUSEUMS (ICOM Commission for Lighting of Museum Objects). *Utilisation des lampes fluorescentes dans les musées* ('The use of fluorescent lamps in museums'). Published by ICOM, Paris, 1954 in both French and English.

(11) BALDER, J. J. 'The discolouration of coloured objects under the influence of daylight, incandescent lamp light and fluorescent lamplight.' *De Museumdag* (Netherlandish Museums Association, Leiden). 1956, 48 pp., illus. In English.

A comparison of the fading and discolouring effects of various light sources.

(12) ROSSMAN, Ernst. 'Atelier Röhrenleuchte' ('Fluorescent-tube lighting for studios'). *Maltechnik*, LXII (1956), pp. 42–44.

Fluorescent tubes suitable for artists' or restorers' studios.

(13) SCOTT, H. P. 'Lighting and protection for an art museum.' *Electrical Construction and Maintenance* (New York), LV (1956), pp. 76–82.

A description of the lighting installation of the Francina Clark Art Institute, Williamstown, Mass.

(14) BAUCIK, G. and KAMMERER, H. 'Die Beleuchtung der Alten Pinakothek in München' ('The illumination in the Alte Pinakothek at Munich'). *Lichttechnik* (Berlin), IX (1957), pp. 547–550.

A description with technical details.

(15) DÉRIBÉRÉ, M. 'Lumière et couleur dans la présentation des objets' ('Light and colour in the presentation of objects'). *Couleurs* (Paris), IXX (1957), pp. 15–25.

Lighting requirements for effective viewing combined with good conservation.

(16) THOMSON, Garry. 'Visible and ultra-violet radiations.' *The Museums Journal* (London), LVII (1957), pp. 27–32.

A report on studies carried out under the former Museum Lighting Sub-committee of the National Illumination Committee; information on the proportion of ultra-violet and visible radiation in different types of light sources and the deteriorating effects of different wavelengths.

(17) RAWSON-BOTTOM, W. E. and COOPER, B. S. 'Museum lighting.' *The Museums Journal* (London), LVIII (1958), pp. 167–173.

A review article of types of lighting and effects of lighting.

(18) RAWSON-BOTTOM, W. E. and HARRIS, J. B. 'Artificial lighting as applied to museums and art galleries.' *Transactions of the Illuminating Engineering Society*, XXIII (1958), No. 1, pp. 6 ff.

Bibliography

A series of valuable articles on museum lighting, appearing in *Museum News* (Washington, D.C.) :

(19) McCandless, Stanley. 'Museum lighting.' Part 1, *Museum News*, XXXVII (1959), No. 1, pp. 8–11; Part 2 in XXXVII (1959), No. 2, pp. 8–11.

(20) Kelly, Richard. 'Museum lighting.' *Museum News*, XXXVII (1959), No. 3, pp. 16–19.

(21) Lusk, Carrol B. 'Museum lighting.' *Museum News*, XXXVIII (1959), No. 2, pp. 28–31.

(22) Kalff, Louis C. 'Museum lighting in Europe.' *Museum News*, XXXVIII (1959), No. 4, pp. 24–27 and No. 10, pp. 20–23.

1960

(23) Crawford, B. H. 'Colour rendition and museum lighting.' *Studies in Conservation*, V (1960), pp. 41–51.
Assessment of the appearance of colours of objects under different types of illumination.

(24) Brommelle, N. S. and Harris, J. B., a series of articles on 'Museum Lighting' :
Part 1. 'Colour rendering.' *Museums Journal* (London), LXI (1961), pp. 169–176.
Part 2. 'Artificial lighting.' *Ibid*, LXI (1961), pp. 259–267.
Part 3. 'Aspects of the effect of light on deterioration.' *Ibid*, LXI (1961), pp. 337–346.
Part 4. 'Viewing the object.' *Ibid*, LXII (1962), pp. 178–186.

(25) Crawford, B. H. and Palmer, D. A. 'Further investigations of colour-rendering and the classification of light sources.' *Studies in Conservation*, VI (1961), pp. 71–82.
Includes description of experiments with lighting of paintings.

(26) Denninger, Edgar. 'Leuchtstoffröhren in Atelier und Ausstellung' ('Fluorescent tube lighting in the studio and in display'). *Maltechnik*, LXVII (1961), pp. 3–6.

(27) Kollmann, F., Schneider, A. and Teichgraeber, R. 'Investigations on the heating-up, warping and drying of wooden picture panels illuminated with high intensities.' *Holz als Roh- und Werkstoff* (Berlin), IXX (1961), pp. 45–47.

(28) Kühn, Hermann. 'Verwendung von Ultraviolett-Lichtschutzlacken in Museum' ('The use of ultra-violet filter lacquers in the museum'). *Museumskunde* (1961), Part 1, pp. 22–30.

(29) Ruhemann, Helmut. 'Experiences with the artificial lighting of paintings.' *Studies in Conservation*, VI (1961), pp. 83–85.

(30) Thomson, Garry. 'A new look at colour rendering, level of illumination and protection from ultra-violet radiation in museum lighting.' *Studies in Conservation*, VI (1961), pp. 49–70. An excellent summary of the present position.

(31) Howard, Richard Foster. 'Museum lighting.' *Museum News* (Washington, D.C.), XL (1962), No. 7, pp. 22–27.

(32) 'Le problème de l'éclairage dans les musées' ('The problem of lighting in museums'). *Musées et collections publiques de France et de la Communauté*, XXVIII (July–Sept. 1961); See also *ICOM News*, XV (Feb. 1962), p. 30.

Bibliography

Proceedings of a two-day seminar held by the French Association des Conservateurs, May 1961.

(33) VASSAS-DUBUISSON, C. 'Lumière et conservation'). (*'Lighting and conservation'*). *Musées et collections publiques de France et de la Communauté*, Nouvelle Série XXXIII (Oct.–Dec. 1962).

(34) WOLTERS, Christian and KÜHN, Hermann. 'Behaviour of painted wood panels under strong illumination.' *Studies in Conservation*, VII (1962), pp. 1–9.

(35) FELLER, Robert L. 'Standards of exposure to light.' *Bulletin of the American Group*, *I.I.C.*, IV (1963), No. 1, pp. 10–12.

A discussion of the blue-wool scale of light-fastness measurement for dyestuffs and its application to the measurement of fading of fugitive organic pigments, such as alizarin, gamboge, quercitron lakes etc., used in the past in painting.

(36) FELLER, Robert L. 'The deteriorating effect of light on museum objects.' *Museum News* (Washington, D.C.). Technical Supplement to XLII (1964), No. 10, pp. i–viii.

A useful survey with a good bibliography.

(37) THOMSON, Garry. 'Impermanence; some chemical and physical aspects.' *The Museums Journal* (London), LXIV (1964), pp. 153–169.

(38) DOE, Brian. 'Notes on museum and art gallery lighting in the tropics.' *Studies in Conservation*, X (1965), pp. 64–71.

Useful information in this specialized field. See also: *Section 20 (6), Section 21 (17), Section 23 (8)*.

SECTION 23

Colour and conservation

1840

(1) GOETHE, J. W. von. *Zur Farbenlehre*, translated from the German by Charles Lock EASTLAKE as *Goethe's theory of colours*, London, 1840.

Although Goethe's theory of colour has been largely superseded by modern theories based on measurement of colour, this translation remains of interest. Eastlake, at that time a practising painter, but later to become first director of the National Gallery, London, supplies copious footnotes. Included in these are the results of some of his researches into the history of picture varnishes and his personal reactions to colour in old master paintings.

1900

(2) OSTWALD, Wilhelm. *Letters to a painter*. Boston, 1907. 162 pp.

An account by a colour theorist who was deeply involved in art, of the development of colour theory from Newton to his own time and its application to paintings.

Bibliography

1930

(3) RAWLINS, F. I. G. 'Studies in the colorimetry of painting.' *Technical Studies in the Field of the Fine Arts*, Part I in IV (1936), pp. 179–186; Part II in V (1937), pp. 150–156; Part III in IX (1941), pp. 207–220; 'A note in conclusion,' in X (1942), pp. 230–231.

A description of the author's work at the National Gallery, London, on measurement of colour using the Lovibond Tintometer. Included are examples of measurements of differences in colour between areas of paintings before and after removal of aged and discoloured varnishes.

(4) BARNES, Norman F. 'A spectrophotometric study of artists' pigments.' *Technical Studies in the Field of the Fine Arts*, VII (1939), pp. 120–138.

Useful for understanding the colour properties of pigments; spectrophotometric curves are given for all the usual pigments.

1940

(5) EVANS, Ralph M. *An introduction to color*. John Wiley and Sons, New York, 1948. 340 pp.

A useful background to modern colour theory. Also of special interest is Chapter XVIII, 'Paints and Pigments', and pp. 70–72 in which is given an explanation of the visual effect of varnish films upon colours beneath.

(6) RAWLINS, F. I. G. 'A "Tintometric" comparison of artists' pigments.' *Technical Studies in the Field of the Fine Arts*, IX (1940), pp. 3–10.

A quantitative measure of colour values of artists' pigments using the Lovibond Tintometer.

1950

(7) RUHEMANN, H. 'The Masters' methods and colour reproduction.' *The British and Colonial Printer* (London), CXLVIII (1951), pp. 542–543, 546.

An address to the Process Engravers Club, followed by discussion. An assessment of the possibilities and limitations of modern colour printing in reproducing paintings by old masters; the author also remarks on the effect which the presence of discoloured varnishes on pictures has had on their colour reproductions. Reprinted in Appendix D, pp. 348–354.

(8) FELLER, Robert L. 'Color change in oil paintings.' *Carnegie Magazine* (Pittsburgh, Pa.), XXVIII (1954), pp. 276–281, 285.

A useful survey of the changes in colour which occur in paintings other than those directly affecting the pigment.

(9) BROMMELLE, Norman. 'Colour and conservation.' *Studies in Conservation*, II (1955), pp. 76–85.

The first serious attempt to apply modern colour theory to the problem of conservation, particularly in the field of picture restoration.

Bibliography

(10) Santini, Manlio. 'Applicazione del metodo spettrofotometrico nelle determinazioni colorimetriche sui dipinti' ('Application of spectrophotometric method in colorimetric determinations on paintings'). *Bollettino dell' Istituto Centrale del Restauro* (Rome), XXIII–XXIV (1955), pp. 95–129.

Measurement of colours on paintings by means of a modern type of visual spectrophotometer, including measurement of differences of colour between areas before and after cleaning. Useful data; also provides a theoretical background to colour and vision.

1960

(11) Johnston, Ruth M. and Feller, Robert L. 'The use of differential spectral curve analysis in the study of museum objects.' *Dyestuffs* (Journal of the National Aniline Division, Allied Chemical and Dye Corporation, New York), XLIV (1963), No. 9, pp. 1–10.

Reflectance spectrophotometry as applied to works of art, particularly pictures. Interpretation of the results can give information concerning composition of pigments used and changes in colour which occur, for example in fading or with varnish removal.

Section 24

Packing and transport

1940

(1) Rosengrant, Robert G. 'Packing problems and procedure.' *Technical Studies in the Field of the Fine Arts*, X (1942), pp. 138–156.

(2) American Association of Museums. 'Packing and handling of art objects.' *Musem News* (Washington, D.C.), XXXVI (1948), No. 9, pp. 7–8.

(3) Sugden, Robert P. *Care and handling of art objects.* The Metropolitan Museum of Art, New York, 1946.

A handbook on the safeguarding of works of art: storage, packing, transportation, insurance.

1950

(4) Wolters, Christian (and others). 'Die Gemälde der Dresdener Galerie' ('The paintings of the Dresden Gallery'). *Kunstchronik* (Nürnberg), IX (1956), Heft 5, pp. 124–125.

A discussion of the hazards of transporting pictures centring round discussion of the movement of the Dresden collection.

(5) Buck, R. D. 'Packing paintings for shipment.' *Intermuseum Conservation Association Bulletin* (Oberlin, Ohio), IV (1958), 3 pp. Mimeographed.

(6) Toishi, K. 'Humidity control in a closed package.' *Studies in Conservation*, IV (1959), pp. 81–87.

Bibliography

1960

(7) BRJANTZEV, A. and GASHKOV, A. 'A new device for packing pictures.' *Soobshcheniya Gosudarstvennogo Ermitazha* (State Hermitage Bulletin, Leningrad), XVIII (1960), pp. 64–65.

A box containing a set of frames which can accommodate pictures of various shapes and sizes.

(8) STOLOW, Nathan. 'On the moving of works of art.' *Canadian Art* (Ottawa), LXX, Sept. 1960, pp. 289–290.

See also the same author's contribution to the I.I.C. Rome Conference of 1961, published in *Recent Advances in Conservation*, ed. by G. Thomson, Butterworth, London, 1963.

(9) HOURS, Madeleine. 'Rapport sommaire sur la construction et l'utilisation d'un container spécial destiné au transport de la Joconde' ('Report on the construction and use of a special container for transporting La Joconde'). *Bulletin du Laboratoire du Musée du Louvre* (Paris), VIII (1963), pp. 45–51.

Description of the packing case designed for transporting Leonardo da Vinci's *Mona Lisa* to America.

(10) LITTLE, David B. 'Safeguarding works of art: transportation, records and insurance.' *History News* (Nashville, Tenn.), XVIII (1963), Technical Leaflet 9.

(11) MICHAELS, Peter. 'Lender beware.' *Museum News* (Washington, D.C.), XLIII (1964), No. 1, pp. 11–12.

A survey of the hazards of transport, change of environment and exposure to light to which works of art on loan may be subjected.

(12) THOMSON, Garry. 'Relative humidity — variation with temperature in a case containing wood.' *Studies in Conservation*, IX (1964), pp. 153–169.

From theoretical and practical studies the author derives a useful simple equation for predicting changes of R. H. with variations in outside temperature for a closed case containing wood (e.g. a panel painting).

(13) FALL, Frieda Kay. 'New industrial packing materials: their possible uses for museums.' *Museum News* (Washington, D.C.), Technical Supplement No. 10, XLIV (1965), No. 4, pp. 47–52.

The properties and applications of materials such as polystyrene and polyurethane are discussed.

(14) STOLOW, Nathan. *Controlled environment for works of art in transit.* Rome Centre Publication No. VI, Butterworths, London, 1966.

Theoretical background and sound practical advice for packing and transport. See also: *Section 4* (67), (69); *Section 20* (6).

Bibliography

SECTION 25

Safety precautions and health hazards

1960

(1) Brachert, T. 'Verhütung von Gesundheitsschäden im Restaurieratelier' ('Prevention of injury to health in restoring studios'). *Maltechnik*, LXVIII (1962), pp. 65–68.
Toxicity of solvents and other materials used in restoration.

(2) Mallary, Robert. 'The air of art is poisoned.' *Art News* (New York), LXII (1963), No. 6, pp. 34–37, 60–61.
The author, a sculptor, describes his experiences of the toxicity of solvents and materials such as synthetic resins and describes safety measures in their use.
See also: *Section 16* (19) and *Appendix D*, pp. 326–327.

SECTION 26

Insurance

1960

(1) Block, Huntington T. 'Insurance in the conservation laboratory. Part I.' *Bulletin of the American Group — I.I.C.*, I (1961), No. 2, pp. 5–7.

(2) Quandt, Eleanor S. 'Insurance in the conservation laboratory. Part II.' *Ibid*, I (1961), No. 2, pp. 7–9.
The above two articles describe, of course, American practice and procedure in insurance matters.
See also: *Section 20* (6); *Section 24* (3) and *Appendix D*, p. 326.

B. TECHNICAL AND SCIENTIFIC EXAMINATION

Including all methods of physical and chemical investigation applied either to the picture itself or to its components.

SECTION 27

Technical and scientific examination, general and miscellaneous

1920

(1) Laurie, A. P. 'On the change of refractive index of linseed oil in the process of drying and its effect on the deterioration of oil paintings.' *Proceedings of the Royal Society* (London), CCII (1926), pp. 176–181.

Bibliography

(2) DE WILD, A. M. *The scientific examination of pictures.* G. Bell & Sons Ltd. London, 1929. 106 pp., illus.

Dr. de Wild, a restorer of paintings by inheritance and vocation, has taken the trouble to acquire a doctorate in chemistry. This book consists largely of his thesis which cuts new ground in the systematic identification of pigments present in paintings of different epochs. Thanks to the collaboration of the Dutch picture galleries he was able to examine microscopic samples from about 300 authentic paintings from 1430 to 1860. The results are arranged in a graph which shows at a glance in what periods the various pigments were in use. Microphotographs (105–120 X) document the identification of each pigment and the pictures from which the samples were taken are catalogued in detail.

Whenever stylistic and other technical characteristics do not suffice to date a doubtful picture properly, this table and the accurate methods of identification de Wild describes will offer a considerable additional aid.

In his brief chapter on The Restoration and Conservation of Paintings de Wild points out that the effect of Pettenkofer's regenerating method is only transitory and he continues : 'A lasting improvement of a varnish film can only be achieved by its complete removal and replacement by a new one.'

De Wild stresses the advantages of wax relining over glue relining. A concise description of the use of X-rays and ultra-violet rays in the examination of paintings and a few excellent illustrations of characteristic examples conclude the volume. (H.R.)

1930

(3) CELLERIER, J.-F. 'Les méthodes scientifiques en usage dans l'examen des peintures' ('Scientific methods in use in the examination of paintings'). *Mouseion*, XIII–XIV (1931), Nos. 1–2, pp. 3–21.

(4) EIBNER, A. 'L'examen microchimique des tableaux et décorations murales' (Microchemical examination of pictures and mural decorations'). *Mouseion*, XIII–XIV (1931), Nos. 1–2, pp. 70–93.

(5) GOULINAT, Jean Gabriel. 'L'apport des procédés scientifiques dans la restauration des peintures' ('The application of scientific methods in the restoration of paintings'). *Mouseion*, XV (1931), No. 3, pp. 47–54.

(6) GRAEFF, Walter. 'L'examen des peintures et les moyens optiques' ('The examination of paintings and optical means'). *Mouseion*, XIII–XIV (1931), Nos. 1–2, pp. 21–42.

(7) SCHEFFER, F. E. C. 'L'examen chimique des tableaux' ('The chemical examination of pictures'). *Mouseion*, XIII–XIV, (1931), Nos. 1–2, pp. 93–104.

(8) EIBNER, A. 'L'examen microchimique des agglutinants' ('The microchemical examination of binding materials'). *Mouseion*, XX (1932), No. 4, pp. 5–23.

The first real attempt to carry out a systematic examination of paint media.

(9) GETTENS, R. J. 'A microsectioner for paint films.' *Technical Studies in the Field of the Fine Arts*, I (1932), pp. 20–28.

(10) PLENDERLEITH, H. J. 'Notes on technique in the examination of panel paintings.' *Technical Studies in the Field of the Fine Arts*, I (1932), pp. 2–7.

(11) GETTENS, R. J. 'An equipment for the microchemical examination of pictures and

Bibliography

other works of art.' *Technical Studies in the Field of the Fine Arts*, II (1934), pp. 185–202.

(12) AUGUSTI, Selim. 'Metodo sistematico per il riconoscimento microchimico dei colori minerali' ('A systematic method for the microchemical identification of mineral pigments'). *Mikrochemie* (Vienna), XVII (1935), pp. 1–10 and 344–355.

(13) EIBNER, A. 'L'analyse microchimique des couleurs' ('Microchemical analysis of pigments'). *Mouseion*, XXIX–XXX (1935), Nos. 1–2, pp. 113–127.

A review of earlier work on the subject of pigment analysis is included.

(14) LAURIE, A. P. 'The microscopic examination of the surface of a picture.' *Technical Studies in the Field of the Fine Arts*, III (1935), pp. 198–199.

(15) DUPONT, Jacques. *Au laboratoire du Musée du Louvre: Jérome Bosch, le Retable de Saint-Antoine du Musée National de Lisbonne.* (At the laboratory of the Louvre Museum: Hieronymous Bosch, the Retable of St. Anthony from the National Museum, Lisbon.) Editions d'Histoire et d'Art, Paris, 1936.

(16) GETTENS, R. J. and STOUT, G. L. 'The stage microscope in the routine examination of homogeneous binding mediums.' *Technical Studies in the Field of the Fine Arts*, IV (1936), pp. 207–233.

(17) MANCIA, Renato. *L'esame scientifico delle opere d'arte ed il loro restauro* (The scientific examination of works of art and their restoration). 2 volumes. Published by Hoepli, Milan and Rome, 1936.

In connection with easel paintings (other types of objects are also dealt with): the setting up of a laboratory for scientific examination of works of art; physical and chemical examination of pigments; the use of ultra-violet, infra-red, monochromatic light and X-rays; identification of wood; an attempt to improve methods of cradling (incorporating aluminium strips).

(18) GETTENS, Rutherford J. 'The cross-sectioning of paint films.' *Technical Studies in the Field of the Fine Arts*, V (1937), pp. 18–22.

(19) LAURIE, A. P. 'The refractive index of a solid film of linseed oil — rise in refractive index with age.' *Proceedings of the Royal Society* (London), CLIX (1937), pp. 123–133.

(20) RAWLINS, F. I. G. 'The physics and chemistry of paintings.' *Journal of the Royal Society of Arts* (London), LXXXV (1936–37), pp. 933–968, 971–988.

Three Cantor Lectures given before the Royal Society of Arts, March, 1937.

(21) STOUT, George L. 'Classes of simple paint structure.' *Technical Studies in the Field of the Fine Arts*, VI (1938), pp. 221–240.

A useful categorization for paint films according to ratio of pigment to medium, pigment particle size, etc.

(22) STOUT, George L. 'One aspect of the so-called "mixed-technique".' *Technical Studies in the Field of the Fine Arts*, VII (1938), pp. 58–72.

Microscopical and chemical investigation of layers of tempera and oil paint in 15th and early 16th century paintings.

(23) BAIER, Ernst and MULLER-SKJOLD, F. 'Das polarisations-mikroskop als analytisches Hilfsmittel bei der Lösung maltechnischer Fragen' ('The polarizing microscope as analytical aid to the solution of problems of painting technique'). *Angewandte Chemie* (Berlin), LII (1939), pp. 533–535.

Bibliography

(24) Barnes, Norman F. 'A spectrophotometric study of artists' pigments.' *Technical Studies in the Field of the Fine Arts*, VII (1939), pp. 120–138.

Useful visual spectrophotometric curves for all the usual artists' pigments with tables of optical characteristics.

(25) Rawlins, F. I. G. 'The chemical physics of paintings.' *Science Progress* (London), XXXIII (1939), pp. 493–502.

(26) Rawlins, F. I. G. 'Evidence: its nature and place in the scientific examination of paintings.' *Technical Studies in the Field of the Fine Arts*, VIII (1939), pp. 75–82.

1940

(27) Rawlins, F. I. G. *From the National Gallery laboratory*. Printed for the Trustees of the National Gallery, London, 1940.

Examples of X-ray, infra-red photographs, photomicrographs and photomacrographs of pictures in the collection of the National Gallery, London.

(28) Buck, R. D. and Stout, G. L. 'Original and later paint in pictures.' *Technical Studies in the Field of the Fine Arts*, VIII (1940), pp. 123–150.

Methods of technical and scientific examination for distinguishing between original paint and later retouching or repaint.

(29) Plenderleith, H. J. 'Application of modern physics in the examination of paintings.' *Nature* (London), CXLVII (1941), pp. 165–166.

(30) Rawlins, F. I. G. 'The rheology of paintings.' *Technical Studies in the Field of the Fine Arts*, X (1941), pp. 59–72.

Application of the physical concepts of flow and deformation to the study of painting materials.

(31) Augusti, Selim. *Il contribuo della chimica e della fisica all'esame dei dipinti*. (The contribution of chemistry and physics to the examination of paintings). Florence, 1942, 8pp.

(32) Keck, Sheldon. 'The technical examination of paintings.' *Brooklyn Museum Journal* (Brooklyn, New York), 1942, pp. 68–82. Illus. by 36 photographs.

An excellent summary of the most useful methods of examination available at the time.

(33) Rawlins, F. I. G. 'Physics in painting.' *Report of Progress in Physics* (London), IX (1942–43), pp. 334–348.

(34) Bontinck, E. *Physique et peinture; Une introduction à l'étude des phénomènes physiques appliquées à la technique picturale*. (Physics and painting; an introduction to the study of physical phenomena applied to the pictorial technique). Brussels, 1943. Paris-Brussels, 1944.

(35) Rawlins, F. I. G. 'Science in the service of the fine arts.' *Endeavour* (London), II (1943), pp. 93–98.

(36) Packard, Elisabeth and Kirby, John C. 'The structure of some South German panel paintings.' *Journal of the Walters Art Gallery, Baltimore*, X (1947), pp. 90–97, 101.

(37) Rawlins, F. I. G. 'Scientific methods in the conservation of pictures.' *Endeavour* (London), VII (1948), pp. 104–110.

Bibliography

A review of the scientific evidence of the condition and structure of the ten cleaned pictures in the National Gallery, London, which were considered by the Weaver Committee of 1947.

AUGUSTI, Selim:

(38) 'Differenziazione e riconoscimento microchimico dei colori minerali' ('Microchemical differentiation and identification of mineral pigments), *Industria della Vernice* (Milan), No. 27 (July, 1949), 10 pp.

(39) 'Ricerca microchimica dei cationi per la identificazione dei colori minerali' ('Microchemical investigation of cations for the identification of mineral pigments'). *Ibid*, No. 29 (Sept., 1949), 11 pp.

(40) 'Ricerca microchimica degli anioni nei colori minerali prelevati dai dipinti' ('Microchemical investigation of anions in mineral pigments removed from paintings'). *Ibid*, No. 31 (Nov., 1949), 4 pp.

(41) HOURS, M. 'Nouveaux matériels et procédés au Laboratoire du Musée du Louvre' ('New materials and processes at the Laboratory of the Louvre Museum'). *Bollettino dell' Istituto Centrale del Restauro* (Rome), III–IV (1950), pp. 65–69.

(42) LEFÈVE, R. and SNEYERS, R. 'La microchemie des peintures anciennes; une nouvelle méthode de préparation des coupes' ('The microchemistry of old pictures; a new method for preparation of sections'). *Mededelingen van de Vlaamse Chemische Vereniging*, Brussels, XII (1950), pp. 99–101.

The preparation of transparent paint cross-sections for viewing by transmitted light.

(43) COREMANS, Paul. PHILIPPOT, A. and SNEYERS, R. *Van Eyck — l'Adoration de l'Agneau; éléments nouveaux intéressant l'histoire de l'art* (Van Eyck — the Adoration of the Lamb; new elements relating to the history of art). De Sikkel, Antwerp, 1951. 6 pp., 4 plates.

Chiefly concerned with the recognition of various later additions to the paint surface (see also under *Section 5*, Accounts of particular restorations).

(44) RAWLINS, F. I. G. 'The scientific examination of paintings.' *Journal of the Oil and Colour Chemists' Association* (London), XXXIV (1951), pp. 337–345.

(45) COREMANS, P., GETTENS, R. J. and THISSEN, J. 'La technique des "Primitifs" Flamands' ('The technique of the Flemish "Primitives" '). *Studies in Conservation*, I (1952–53), pp. 1–29.

An epoch-making piece of research showing that the medium of a typical Flemish primitive, a picture by D. Bouts, was based on drying oil. (H.R.).

(46) HOURS, Madeleine. 'Notes sur l'étude de la peinture de Léonard de Vinci au Laboratoire du Musée du Louvre' ('Notes on the study of the painting of Leonardo da Vinci in the laboratory of the Louvre Museum'). *Études d'Art* (Paris), Nos. 8, 9, 10, 1952), pp. 201–210.

A communication to the Congrès International du Val de Loire, July, 1952.

(47) WERNER, A. E. *Scientific examination of paintings*. Royal Institute of Chemistry, Lectures, Monographs, Reports, No. 4, London, 1952.

(48) GRAHAM, Ian. 'The effect of solvents on linoxyn films.' *Journal of the Oil and Colour Chemists' Association* (London), XXXVI (1953), pp. 500–506.

Bibliography

A preliminary report on an investigation, carried out at the National Gallery, London, of the processes that occur during the removal of varnish from pictures by means of solvents. Swelling of the oil film was measured by optical methods.

(49) HANSON, N. W. 'Some recent developments in the analysis of paints and painting materials.' *Official Digest, Federation of Paint and Varnish Production Clubs* (Philadelphia), No. 338 (1953), pp. 163–174.

Included are details of the analysis of bottles of media from J. M. W. Turner's paint boxes, particularly by means of infra-red absorption spectrophotometry. See below, No. (55), for further details.

(50) *Les Primitifs Flamands, III. Contributions à l'étude des Primitifs Flamands, 2. L'Agneau Mystique au Laboratoire.* De Sikkel, Antwerp, 1953.

The third of a series of volumes concerning the history, technique, examination and restoration of Van Eyck's polyptych. This volume deals with the technical examination, condition and treatment of the polyptych when work was being carried out on it at the Institut Royal du Patrimoine Artistique at Brussels. Profusely illustrated.

(51) BONES, R. A. 'The analysis of calcium sulphate grounds by an X-ray diffraction process.' *Studies in Conservation*, I (1954), pp. 174–189.

(52) COREMANS, Paul. 'La technique des "Primitifs Flamands",' III. *Studies in Conservation*, I (1954), pp. 145–161.

A summary of the findings of the technical examination of the Van Eyck polyptych 'The Adoration of the Mystic Lamb'. The medium of the paint layers has a basis of drying oil except in some areas of blue where aqueous layers are present to a limited extent. (See also above, No. (50)).

(53) FELLER, R. L. 'Infra-red analysis of dammar and mastic.' *Science* (American Association for the Advancement of Science, Washington, D.C.), CXX (1954), pp. 1069–1070.

(54) GETTENS, R. J. and MORSE, M. E. 'Calcium sulphate minerals in the grounds of Italian paintings.' *Studies in Conservation*, I (1954), pp. 174–189.

(55) HANSON, N. W. 'Some painting materials of J. M. W. Turner (English painter 1775–1851).' *Studies in Conservation*, I (1954), pp. 62–73.

An account of the chemical analysis, using modern analytical methods, of the contents, both pigments and media, of paint boxes of J. M. W. Turner. See also above, No. (49).

(56) MACEK, K. and HAMSIC, M. 'Paper chromatography — a new method for the characterization of binding media.' *Umeni* (Prague), II (1954), pp. 58–63.

The first application of chromatography to the problem of the identification of paint media in pictures, particularly protein media. A pioneer work.

(57) MILLS, J. S. and WERNER, A. E. A. 'Partition chromatography in the examination of natural resins.' *Journal of the Oil and Colour Chemists' Association* (London), XXXVII (1954), pp. 131–142.

Chromatographic methods introduced for examination of natural resins, of the type used for picture varnishes, in the laboratory of the National Gallery, London.

(58) PLESTERS, R. J. 'The preparation and study of paint cross-sections.' *The Museums Journal* (London), LIV (1954), pp. 97–101.

Bibliography

(59) RAWLINS, F. I. G. and WERNER, A. E. A. 'Some scientific investigations at the National Gallery, London.' *Endeavour* (London), XIII (1954), pp. 140–146.

Reproduced are paper chromatographs of natural resins, an optical method for studying the effect of solvents on linoxyn films, cross-sections of paint samples from pictures. Illustrated in colour.

(60) MILLS, J. S. and WERNER, A. E. A. 'The analysis of dammar.' *Paint* (London), XXV (1955), p. 307.

(61) MILLS, J. S. and WERNER, A. E. A. 'The chemistry of dammar resin.' *Journal of the Chemical Society* (London), September 1955, pp. 3132–3140.

(62) RUHEMANN, H. 'Technical analysis of an early painting by Botticelli.' *Studies in Conservation*, II (1955), pp. 17–40.

See pp. 103–116 of the present work.

(63) STRAUB, R. E. and REES JONES, S. 'Mikroskopische Querschnitte von Gemälden' ('Microscopical cross-sections from paintings'). *Maltechnik*, LXI (1955), pp. 119–125.

(64) MILLS, J. S. 'The constitution of the neutral tetracyclic triterpenes of dammar resin.' *Journal of the Chemical Society* (London), 1956, pp. 2196–2202.

Fundamental analysis and separation by chromatographic methods of the numerous chemical constituents of dammar resin.

(65) PLESTERS, Joyce. 'Cross-sections and chemical analysis of paint samples.' *Studies in Conservation*, XII (1956), pp. 110–157.

Numerous examples of microscopical studies of paint cross-sections and analysis of paint samples from pictures in the collection of the National Gallery, London, and elsewhere. Tables of analysis.

(66) THOMSON, Garry. 'Test for cross-linking of linear polymers.' *Nature* (London), CLXXVIII (1956), p. 807.

A chromatographic method for discovering whether polymeric materials such as certain acrylic resins used as picture varnishes, are likely to cross link and become less soluble.

(67) DELBOURGO, S. 'La lumière de sodium et ses applications au Laboratoire du Musée du Louvre' ('Sodium light and its application in the Laboratory of the Louvre Museum'). *Bulletin du Laboratoire du Musée du Louvre*, II (1957), pp. 41–47.

The use of sodium light to penetrate the surface of paintings more effectively than white light.

(68) HOURS, Madeleine. *À la découverte de la peinture par les méthodes physiques* (The discovery of painting by physical methods). Arts et Métiers Graphiques, Paris, 1957. 148 pp., 146 plates.

A description of optical and radiographic methods of studying pictures used at the laboratory of the Louvre museum; these include the use of raking light, sodium light, macro and micro-photography, spectroscopy, infra-red and ultra-violet radiation, X-radiography.

(69) STOLOW, N. 'The action of solvents on drying-oil films. Parts 1 and 2.' *Journal of the Oil and Colour Chemists' Association* (London), XL (1957), Part 1, pp. 377–402; Part 2, pp. 488–499.

Bibliography

The author's investigations at the Courtauld Institute of Art, University of London, concern the effect of solvents on specially prepared films of drying oils. The phenomena of swelling, leaching, density changes and diffusion of solvents were studied, together with the effect of ageing the oil film up to 117 weeks at a temperature of 32° C. A great deal of important information on the effect of solvents on oil films is assembled in this work. It must be pointed out, however, that the conditions of test are far-removed from conditions of cleaning an actual picture with solvent. In the experiments described, the comparatively young oil films were suspended in solvent for a considerable period in order to induce swelling and leaching for the purpose of study. As long ago as 1917, Katz (*Gesetze der Quellung, KolloidchemischeHefte*, IX (1919), pp. 1–6) drew attention to the danger of removal of a swollen paint film, but says that this risk can be avoided in cleaning old paintings by dissolving the varnish film rapidly and by appropriate handling. A similar warning was given by A. M. de Wild in 1929. (H.R.).

(70) Stolow, Nathan. 'The measurement of film thickness and of solvent action on supported films.' *Studies in Conservation*, III (1957), pp. 40–44.

Apparatus and method for the rapid determination of thickness of paint and varnish films, and for determining the rates of swelling and de-swelling of such films with the action of solvents.

(71) Thomson, Garry. 'A method for the measurement of solid film thicknesses in the 5 to 30 micron range.' *Journal of Scientific Instruments* (London), XXXIV (1957), p. 333.

An optical method applicable to measurement of thickness of paint and varnish films.

(72) Hey, M. 'The analysis of paint media by paper chromatography.' *Studies in Conservation*, III (1958), pp. 183–193.

A distinction between glue protein, egg protein and drying oil media effected by means of paper chromatography.

(73) Ruhemann, H. 'Criteria for distinguishing additions from original paint.' *Studies in Conservation*, III (1958), pp. 145–161.

See pp. 181–189 of the present work.

(74) Stolow, Nathan. '*Solvent action: fundamental researches and picture cleaning.*' Mimeographed by the National Gallery of Canada, Ottawa, 1958, 13 pp.

A lecture given to the Seminar on Resinous Coatings held at the Intermuseum Conservation Association, Oberlin Ohio, April 1957. Also given to a seminar on Conservation held at the Brooklyn Museum, New York, Feb. 1958.

(75) Sneyers, R. and Thissen, J. 'L'identification d'un surpeint sur une Assomption de la Vierge d'Albert Bouts' ('The identification of overpaint on an Assumption of the Virgin by Albert Bouts'). *Bulletin de l'Institut Royal du Patrimoine Artistique* (Brussels), IV (1958), pp. 146–148.

(76) Sneyers, R. and Thissen, J. 'La Justice d'Othon de Thierry Bouts. Examen de laboratoire' ('The Justice of Othon by Dieric Bouts. Examination in the laboratory'). *Bulletin de l'Institut Royal du Patrimoine Artistique*, Brussels, IV (1958), pp. 146–148.

(77) Boston Museum of Fine Arts Research Laboratory. *Application of science in examination of works of art*. Published by the Museum of Fine Arts, Boston, Mass., 1959.

Proceedings of a seminar held at the Museum of Fine Arts, September, 1958, 198 pp.

Bibliography

Papers relevant to the conservation of pictures comprise: 'Problems of setting up a museum laboratory' by Nathan Stolow; 'Examination of works of art embracing the various fields of science' by W. J. Young; 'Identification of pigments and inerts on paintings and other museum objects' by Rutherford J. Gettens; 'Identification and analysis of resins and spirit varnishes' by Robert L. Feller; 'Limitations of wood anatomy in the study of objects of art' by William L. Stern.

(78) COREMANS, Paul and THISSEN, Jean. 'L'introduction des lames minces dans l'examen des peintures' ('The introduction of thin sections to the examination of paintings'). *Bulletin de l'Institut Royal du Patrimoine Artistique*, II (1959), pp. 41–46.

The study of transparent cross-sections of samples of paint.

(79) FELLER, R. L., JONES, Elizabeth R. and STOLOW, Nathan. *On picture varnishes and their solvents*. Reports presented to the seminar on resinous surface coatings sponsored by the Intermuseum Conservation Association, Oberlin, April, 1958. Published Oberlin, Ohio, 1959. 220 pp., tables, charts.

For H.R.'s review, see *Section 16, Picture Varnishes* (20), pp. 443–445.

(80) MARETTE, Jacqueline. *La connaissance des primitifs par l'étude du bois, du XIIᵉ au XVIᵉ siècle* (The identification of primitives by the study of the wood, from the thirteenth to the sixteenth centuries). Picard, Paris, 1959. 383 pp., 41 plates.

An attempt to relate the identification of the type of wood of early panel pictures with the period, school and artist.

(81) RAWLINS, F. I. G. 'Scientific methods in the care of works of art.' *Journal of the Royal Society of Arts* (London), CVIII (1958–59), pp. 519–532.

A paper read at the Royal Society of Arts, March, 1960.

1960

(82) DELBOURGO, Suzanne and PETIT, Jean. 'Application de l'analyse microscopique et chimique à quelques tableaux de Poussin'). *Bulletin du Laboratoire du Musée du Louvre* (Paris), V (1960), pp. 40–54. Illustrated in colour.

(83) ELSKENS, Ivan. 'L'introduction des lames minces dans l'examen des peintures. Etude spectrophotométrique ('The introduction of thin sections to the examination of paintings. Spectrophotometric study'). *Bulletin de l'Institut Royal du Patrimoine Artistique* (Brussels), III (1960), pp. 20–34.

A combination of microscopy and spectrophotometry, enabling spectrophotometric analysis to be done on minute samples of paint; an important development.

(84) KÜHN, Hermann. 'Detection and identification of waxes, including Punic wax, by infra-red spectrography.' *Studies in Conservation*, V (1960), pp. 71–81.

The detection and identification of waxes in paint media, coatings, etc.

(85) COREMANS, Paul. 'La recherche scientifique et la restauration des tableaux' ('Scientific research and the restoration of pictures'). *Bulletin de l'Institut Royal du Patrimoine Artistique* (Brussels), IV (1961), pp. 109–116.

(86) KÜHN, Hermann. 'Safran und dessen Nachweis durch Infrarotspektrographie in Malerei und Kunsthandwerk' ('Saffron and its detection by infra-red spectrography in

Bibliography

paintings and applied arts'). *Leitz-Mitteilungen für Wissenschaft und Technik* (Wetzlar), II (1961), pp. 24–28.

Of special interest since saffron, being an organic pigment, is difficult to detect in paintings.

(87) STRAUB, R. E. 'An apparatus for the surface examination of paintings.' *Studies in Conservation*, VI (1961), pp. 46–48.

(88) HORNBLOWER, A. P. 'Archaeology application of the electron probe microanalyser.' *Archaeometry* (Oxford), V (1962), pp. 108–112.

One of the applications of the electron probe described is the identification of cobalt in individual pigment particles in a paint cross-section of the size usual for ordinary microscopical examination.

(89) JONES, P. L. 'Some observations on methods for identifying proteins in paint media.' *Studies in Conservation*, VII (1962), pp. 10–16.

An assessment of existing methods of identification is given and a description of a new immunological method utilizing the effect of protein in paint media on rabbit antiserum.

(90) DE SILVA, R. H. 'The problem of the binding medium particularly in wall paintings.' *Archaeometry* (Oxford), VI (1963), pp. 56–64.

Although the author's chief interest is in wall paintings, he gives a good summary of work on the analysis of binding media of all types of painting up to this date.

(91) EWALD, F. 'Studien zur Altersbestimmung von Oelgemälden durch Schmelzversuche an Farbschichten' ('Studies in determination of the age of oil paintings by investigation of the melting of samples of the paint layers'). *Fette, Seifen, Anstrichmittel* (Hamburg), LVI (1963), pp. 358–368.

A new possibility for assessing the age of paint by determination of melting point.

(92) JOHNSTON, Ruth M. and FELLER, Robert L. 'The use of differential spectral curve analysis in the study of museum objects.' *Dyestuffs* (Publ. by Allied Chemical, National Aniline Division, New York), XXXXIV (1963), No. 9, pp. 1–10.

Interesting applications of visual spectrophotometry to problems of paintings, their deterioration and their conservation.

(93) KLEBER, R. and TRICOT-MARCX, F. 'Essai d'identification d'une colle animale utilisée par Rubens' ('Identification of an animal glue used by Rubens'). *Bulletin de l'Institut Royal du Patrimoine Artistique* (Brussels), VI (1963), pp. 57062.

(94) KLEBER, R. and TRICOT-MARCX, F. 'Identification d'un vernis moderne recouvrant la Descente de Croix de Rubens' ('Identification of a modern varnish covering Rubens's *Descent from the Cross*'). *Bulletin de l'Institut Royal du Patrimoine Artistique* (Brussels), VI (1963), pp. 63–68.

(95) MASSCHELEIN-KLEINER, L. 'Perspectives de la chimie des liants picturaux' ('Perspectives of the chemistry of paint media'). *Bulletin de l'Institut Royal du Patrimoine Artistique* (Brussels), VI (1963), pp. 109–126.

(96) REES JONES, Stephen. 'Ein technischer Beitrag zum Problem der Firnisabnahme' ('A technical contribution to the problem of varnish removal'). In: *Über die Erhaltung von Gemälden und Skulpturen* (On the preservation of paintings and sculpture), edited by Rolf E. STRAUB. Zürich and Stuttgart, 1963, pp. 49–57. See above, *Section 4* (70).

Bibliography

Largely based on the results of the researches of N. Stolow.
See pp. 198–202.

(97) Strong, Roy C. 'Holbein's cartoon for the Barber-Surgeons Group rediscovered — a preliminary report.' *The Burlington Magazine*, CV (1963), pp. 4–14.

The lost cartoon of Holbein's portrait group had been assembled, stuck down on canvas and overpainted by a later hand. X-radiography revealed the pricked design, and microscopical cross-sections the presence of paper and drawing layers.

(98) Feller, R. L. and Matous, J. J. 'Critical pigment volume concentration and chalking in paints.' *Bulletin of the American Group—I.I.C*, V(1964), No 1, pp. 25–26.

Investigation of the phenomenon of 'chalking' which has considerable importance for the appearance and condition of paint, both in its commercial application and in pictures.

(99) Hours, Madeleine. *Les secrets des chefs d'oeuvre* (The secrets of masterpieces). Editions Robert Laffont, Paris, 1964. 224 pp., 8 colour plates.

Mainly concerned with investigation of works of art by physical methods such as infra-red, ultra-violet and X-rays, as carried out in the laboratory of the Louvre Museum, Paris.

(100) Keck, Sheldon and Feller, Robert L. 'Detection of an epoxy-resin coating on a seventeenth century painting.' *Studies in Conservation*, IX (1964), pp. 1–8.

The application of modern methods of analysis to the identification of a comparatively insoluble varnish coating.

(101) Kléber, Robert and Masschelein-Kleiner, Liliane. 'Contribution à l'analyse des composés résineux utilisées dans les oeuvres d'art' ('Contribution to the analysis of resinous compositions used in works of art'). *Bulletin de l'Institut Royal du Patrimoine Artistique* (Brussels, VII (1964), pp. 196–218.)

The principal methods described are those of infra-red spectrophotometry and thin-layer chromatography, both used in the identification of natural resins in varnishes, of media and of 'copper resinate' green colours.

(102) Thissen, Jean and Vynckier, Josef. 'Note de laboratoire sur les oeuvres de Juan de Flandes et de son école a Palencia et à Cervera' ('A note from the laboratory concerning the works of Juan de Flandes and his school at Palencia and Cervera'). *Bulletin de l'Institut Royal du Patrimoine Artistique* (Brussels), VII (1964), pp. 234–247.

An exhaustive investigation into the materials and technique, including photomicrographs of thin sections of wood of panels, canvas threads and cross-sections of paint.

(103) Houtman, J. P. W. and Turkstra, J. 'Neutron activation analysis of trace elements in white lead and the possible application for age determination of paintings.' Reactor Institute at Delft Report No. 133–64–05, September, 1964 (Paper No. SM–55/91 submitted at the IAEA Symposium on Radiochemical Methods of Analysis, Salzburg, Oct. 1964). Later published in *Radiochemical Methods of Analysis* (International Atomic Energy Agency, Vienna), I (1965), pp. 85–103. In English, with summaries in French, Russian and German.

Trace impurities in lead white taken from twenty-five paintings ranging in date from 1510 to 1909 were shown to vary according to age. This method of investigation, still very new, seems to have an important future.

Bibliography

(104) JONES, P. L. 'The leaching of linseed oil films in iso-propyl alcohol.' *Studies in Conservation*, X (1965), pp. 119–129.

(105) FELLER, Robert L. and BAILLIE, Catherine W. 'Studies of the effect of light on protective coatings using aluminium foil as a support: determination of ratio of chain breaking to cross-linking.' *Bulletin of the American Group, I.I.C.*, VI (1966), No. 1.

Investigation of the effects of exposure to light on synthetic resins which may be used as picture varnishes or otherwise in conservation.

(106) 'Identification of the material of paintings.' Series editor R. J. GETTENS. Introduction by Richard D. BUCK.
'I. Azurite and blue verditer' by Rutherford J. GETTENS and Elizabeth West FITZHUGH. *Studies in Conservation*, XI (1966), pp. 54–61.
'II. Ultramarine blue, natural and artificial,' by Joyce PLESTERS. *Ibid*, pp. 62–91.

The beginning of a series designed to form a handbook of the identification of painting materials.

(107) MILLS, John S. 'The gas chromatographic examination of paint media. Part I. Fatty acid composition and identification of dried oil films. *Studies in Conservation*, XI (1966), pp. 92–107.

See also: *Section 17* (4), (5), (6), (8), (9), (10).

SECTION 28
Photographic techniques, general

References in this section concern photographic techniques as an aid to restoration. It has been found more convenient to sepearate works on the application of infra-red, ultra-violet and X-rays into sections 29, 30 and 31 respectively. The use of photography in the study of painting techniques and in matters of authentication will be further considered in a second book by the same author now in preparation.

1930

(1) LAURIE, A. P. 'La microphotographie appliquée à l'étude de la technique de Rembrandt et de son école' ('Photomicrography applied to the study of the technique of Rembrandt and his school'). *Mouseion*, XV (1911), No. 3, pp. 5–8.

Mainly concerned with the study of brushwork by photomicrography, or, more correctly termed, photomacrography at c. 2–10 × magnification. But see p. 216 of present book.

(2) ROSEN, David and MARCEAU, Henri. 'A study in the use of photographs in the identification of paintings. *Technical Studies in the Field of the Fine Arts*, VI (1937), pp. 75–105.

1950

(3) 'Le contrôle photographique de la restauration au laboratoire du Musée du

Bibliography

Louvre' ('Photographic recording of restoration at the laboratory of the Louvre Museum'). *Museum* (UNESCO, Paris), III (1950), pp. 328–333.

(4) DÉRIBÉRÉ, M., PORCHEZ, J. and TENDRON, G. *La photographie scientifique dans l'identification et l'expertise* (Scientific photography in identification and expertise). Paris, 1951.

(5) RAWLINS, F. I. G. 'Densitometry of photographic films and plates.' *Studies in Conservation*, I (1954), p. 131.
    Includes the application of densitometry to X-radiographs of paintings.

(6) DELBOURGO, S. 'La macro- et la micro-photographie en couleurs au Laboratoire du Musée du Louvre' (Colour macro- and microphotography at the Laboratory of the Louvre Museum'). *Bulletin du Laboratoire du Musée du Louvre*, I (1956), pp. 13–15.

(7) HOURS, M. and DÉRIBÉRÉ, M. 'Projet d'unification dans les appellations de photographies scientifiques des oeuvres d'art' ('A project for the standardization of nomenclature for scientific photography of works of art'). *Bulletin du Laboratoire du Musée du Louvre*, I (1956), pp. 67–68.

(8) NICKEL, H. 'Fotografie als Hilfswissenschaft der kunsthistorischen und archäologischen Disziplinen' ('Photography as a scientific aid to art-historical and archaeological disciplines'). *Kunstchronik* (Nürnberg), XI (1958), Part 2, pp. 41–42.
    Summary of a symposium at the Art Historical Institute and Archaeological Seminary at Martin Luther University, Halle-Wittenberg.

1960

(9) LOOSE, Louis. 'La macrophotographie stéréoscopique' ('Stereoscopic photomacrography'). *Bulletin de l'Institut Royal du Patrimoine Artistique* (Brussels), IV (1961), pp. 44–56.

(10) GIGER, Silvia. 'Reducing scattered light in the photomicrography of opaque cross-sections.' *Studies in Conservation*, VII (1962), pp. 43–47.
    Improving techniques for colour photomicrography of paint sections.

(11) VERSTEEGEN, Roger. 'La lumière réfléchie appliquée à la photographie des objets de musée' ('Reflected light applied to the photography of museum objects'). *Bulletin de l'Institut Royal du Patrimoine Artistique* (Brussels), VII (1964), pp. 219–228.
    Apparatus and technique useful, among other things, for revealing the surface texture of paintings.
    See also: *Section 17* (7), (8).

SECTION 29

Application of infra-red radiation

1930

(1) TOCH, Maximilian. 'Photography of pigments by infra-red rays only.' *American Photographer* (Brunswick, New York), XXVI (1932), pp. 432–434.

Bibliography

(2) RAWLING, S. O. *Infra-red photography*. Blackie & Son Ltd., London, 1933, 57 pp.

(3) LYON, R. Arcadius. 'Infra-red radiations and examination of paintings.' *Technical Studies in the Field of the Fine Arts*, II (1934), pp. 203–212.

(4) MÜLLER-SKJOLD, F. and SCHMITT, H. 'Zur Anwendung der Infrarot-photographie in der Maltechnik' ('The use of infra-red photography in painting technique'). *Zeitschrift für angewandte Chemie* (Berlin), XLIX (1936), pp. 537–640.

(5) COREMANS, P. 'Les rayons infra-rouges' ('Infra-red rays'). *Bulletin des Musées Royaux d'Art et d'Histoire* (Brussels), 1938, No. 6 (July–August), pp. 87–91.

(6) FARNSWORTH, Maria. 'Infra-red absorption of paint materials.' *Technical Studies in the Field of the Fine Arts*, VII (1938), pp. 88–98.

(7) RAWLINS, F. I. G. 'A novel infra-red camera for art gallery work.' *The Museums Journal* (London), XXXVIII (1938), pp. 186–188.

1940

(8) KECK, Sheldon. 'A use of infra-red photography in the study of technique.' *Technical Studies in the Field of the Fine Arts*, IX (1941), pp. 145–152.

(9) DÉRIBÉRÉ, Maurice. *Les applications pratiques des rayons infra-rouges* (The practical applications of infra-red rays). Published Dunod, Paris, 1943. 222pp., illus.

(10) PEASE, Murray. 'New light on an old signature.' *Bulletin of the Metropolitan Museum of Art* (New York), IV (1945), pp. 1–4.
    Traces of an earlier signature revealed by infra-red.

(11) CLARK, Walter. *Photography by infra-red*. 2nd edn. New York, 1946. 472 pp., illus.
    The principles, practice and application are treated, including a section on infra-red photography of pictures and documents.

(12) MOURA, Abel. 'Os raios infra-vermelhos e ultra-violetas aplicados no exame das pinturas' ('Infra-red and ultra-violet rays applied to the examination of paintings'). *Cadernos do Centro de Estudos de Arte e Museologia*, Instituto para a alta Cultura, Lisbon, IV (1946), 9 pp., illus.

1950

(13) EASTMAN KODAK Co. *Infra-red and ultra-violet photography*. 4th edition, Rochester, N.Y., 1951, 40 pp., illus., tables.

(14) MOSS, A. A. *The application of X-rays, gamma rays, ultra-violet and infra-red rays to the study of antiquities*. Handbook for Museum Curators, Part B, Section 4. Published by the Museums Association, London, 1954.
    Although not specifically dealing with pictures, this booklet provides a useful, simple but accurate introduction to the theory and practice of special radiations to the study of works of art and antiquities.

(15) WEHLTE, K. 'Gemäldeuntersuchung im infra-rot' ('Examination of pictures by infra-red'). *Maltechnik*, LXI (1955), pp. 52–56.

Bibliography

Useful data on infra-red filters.

(16) Hours, Madeleine. 'Amélioration des procédés d'utilisation de la photographie infra-rouge grâce à un nouvel écran phosphorographique' ('Improvement of the method of use of infra-red photography by means of a new phosphorescent screen'). *Bulletin du Laboratoire du Musée du Louvre*, I (1956), pp. 16–17.

(17) Loose, Louis. 'Nouveau procédé de tirage infra-rouge par masquage' ('A new process for taking infra-red photographs by means of masking'). *Bulletin de l'Institut Royal du Patrimoine Artistique* (Brussels), I (1958), pp. 85–93.

1960

(18) Nickel, H. L. 'Infrarot-Kontrastaufnahme von Gemälden' ('Infra-red contrast photography of paintings'). *Wissenschaftliche Zeitschrift der Martin-Luther-Universität, Halle-Wittenberg, Gesellschafts- und Sprachwissenschaftliche Reihe*, IX (1960), pp. 421–424.

(19) Bridgman, F. and Gibson, H. L. 'Infra-red luminescence.' *Studies in Conservation*, VIII (1963), pp. 77–83.

A method of photography which utilizes the property of certain pigments and other materials of emitting infra-red radiation when illuminated by a blue-green light-source.

Section 30
Application of ultra-violet radiation

1920

(1) Laurie, A. P. 'Examination of pictures by ultra-violet and X-rays.' *The Museums Journal* (London), (1929), pp. 246–247.

1930

(2) Dodds, L. V. 'Examination of documents and paintings.' *Art and Archaeology Journal* (New York), (1930), pp. 31–35, 52.

(3) Rorimer, James J. *Ultra-violet rays and their use in the examination of works of art.* Published by the Metropolitan Museum of Art, New York, 1931. 61 pp., illus.

Still the most extensive work yet published on the subject. Useful tables.

(4) Eibner, A. 'Les rayons ultra-violets appliqués à l'examen des couleurs et des agglutinants' ('Ultra-violet rays applied to the examination of pigments and media'). *Mouseion*, XXI–XXII (1933), pp. 32–69.

An interesting pioneer article on the application of U.V. fluorescence analysis to painting materials.

(5) Lyon, R. Arcadius. 'Ultra-violet rays as aids to restorers.' *Technical Studies in the Field of the Fine Arts*, II (1934), pp. 153–157.

Bibliography

1940

(6) DÉRIBÉRÉ, Maurice. *Les applications pratiques des rayons ultra-violets.* Published Dunod, Paris, 1947. 247 pp., 129 illus.

1950

(7) EASTMAN KODAK Co. *Infra-red and ultra-violet photography.* 4th edition, Rochester, N. Y., 1951. 40 pp., illus., tables.

(8) Moss, A. A. *The application of X-rays, gamma rays, ultra-violet and infra-red rays to the study of antiquities.* Handbook for Museum Curators, Part B, Section 4. Published by the Museums Association, London, 1954. See above, *Section 29* (14).

(9) WEHLTE, G. 'Fluoreszenz-Untersuchungen von Gemälden' ('Researches into the fluorescence of paintings'). *Maltechnik*, LXIII (1957), pp. 34–40.

SECTION 31
Application of X-radiography

As will be seen from the article by Charles F. Bridgman (see No. (43) below), X-radiography of paintings began almost with the discovery of X-rays. As a result there is a considerable volume of literature on the application of radiography to paintings. It has been impossible for reasons of space to quote in this section all the numerous articles in periodicals which illustrate the application of X-rays to the study of paintings. The choice has therefore been concentrated mainly on those books and articles which either describe the method of radiography of pictures or its use as a diagnostic tool for assessing the condition of paintings. The use of radiography for the purpose of stylistic diagnosis and in the investigation of the techniques and materials of the old masters and the detection of forgeries will be treated in detail in a second book by the present author, now in preparation.

1930

(1) BURROUGHS, Alan. 'Notes on the principles and process of X-ray examination of paintings.' *The Smithsonian Institution Report for 1927* (Washington, D.C.), pp. 529–533.

1930

(2) BAUER, Victor and RINNEBACH, Helmuth. 'L'examen des peintures aux rayons X, son importance et ses limites' ('The examination of paintings with X-rays, its importance and its limitations'). *Mouseion*, XII–XIV (1930), pp. 42–69.

(3) HAEBERLEIN, F. 'Zur Diagnostik von Kunstwerken mit Hilfe vön röntgenograph-

Bibliography

ischen Untersuchungsmethoden' ('The diagnosis of works of art with the aid of radiographic methods of investigation'). *Technische Mitteilungen für Malerei*, XII (June, 1931), pp. 137–138.

(4) WILDE, Johannes. 'L'examen des tableaux à l'Institut Holzknecht de Vienne' ('The examination of pictures at the Holzknecht Institute, Vienna'). *Mouseion*, XVI.(1932), pp. 69–80.

(5) WEHLTE, Kurt. 'Aus der Praxis der maltechnischen Röntgenographie' ('The practice of radiography of paintings'). *Technische Mitteilungen für Malerei*, XLVIII (1932), pp.69–80.

(6) WEHLTE, Kurt. 'Gemäldeuntersuchungen mit Röntgenstrahlen' ('Investigation of paintings with X-rays'). *Verhandlung der Deutschen Röntgen-Gesellschaft*, XXV (1932), pp. 12–18.

An early use of the X-ray source placed beneath a table on which the picture is laid. Illustrated.

(7) PETERTIL, E. 'La question des détériorations des couleurs par les rayons X' ('The question of the deterioration of colours by X-rays'). *Mouseion*, XXI–XXII (1933), pp. 27–31.

(8) PUYVELDE, Leo Van. 'L'application de la radiographie sur tableaux' ('The application of radiography to pictures'). *Journal de Radiologie* (Brussels), XVII (1933), pp. 83–90.

(9) WEHLTE, Kurt. 'Die Maltechnische Röntgenographie im Prozess um die Van Gogh Fälschungen' ('The radiography of paintings in the trial of the Van Gogh forgeries'). *Kunst und Wirtschaft* (Munich), XIV (1933), pp. 7–12.

(10) GÖTZKY, S. and GÜNTHER, P. 'Zur Frage der Schädigung von Gemälden durch Röntgenstrahlen' ('The question of damage to paintings by X-rays'). *Angewandte Chemie* (Weinheim, Germany), XLVII (1934), pp. 343–345.

(11) GÜNTHER, P. 'Zur Frage der Röntgenstrahlenwirkung auf Gemälde' ('The question of the effect of X-rays on paintings'). *Technische Mitteilungen für Malerei*, LII (1936), p. 42.

(12) MÜLLER-SKJOLD, F. 'Zur Frage der Schädigung von Gemälden durch Röntgenstrahlen' ('The question of damage to paintings by X-rays'). *Angewandte Chemie* (Weinheim, Germany), IL (1936), pp. 161–162.

(13) RINNEBACH, H. 'Zur Frage der Schädigung von Gemälden durch Röntgenstrahlen' ('The question of damage to pictures by X-rays'). *Technische Mitteilungen für Malerei*, LII (1936), pp. 55–60.

(14) WEHLTE, Kurt. 'Untersuchungsergebnisse über die Frage von Röntgenschäden an Gemälden und ihre praktische Bedeutung' ('Results of research on the question of X-ray damage to pictures and their practical significance'). *Technische Mitteilungen für Malerei*, LII (1936), pp. 175–178.

(15) WIEGEL, Albert. 'Die Geröntgeten Rembrandtgemälde der Staatlichen Gemäldegalerie Kassel' ('The X-radiography of pictures by Rembrandt at the State Gallery, Kassel'). *Technische Mitteilungen für Malerei*, LII (1936), pp. 3–6 and 112–113.

Bibliography

Experiments on possible harmful effects of X-rays.

The above six references are all concerned with a matter much discussed in the 1930s, the possibility of damage to pictures by X-rays. Experiments carried out at that time appear to show that the dosage of radiation received by a picture in the course of ordinary examination by X-radiography does not have any detectable damaging effect on it.

(16) Pouncey, Philip. 'Ercole Grandi's masterpiece.' *The Burlington Magazine*, LXX (1937, Part I), pp. 160–169.

X-radiography revealed that the altarpiece in the National Gallery, London, previously attributed to Ercole Grandi, is the work of two separate masters, the picture commenced probably by Gian Francesco de' Maineri, whose style can be recognized from the radiographs, and completed by Lorenzo Costa. It is an illustration of the use of radiography in elucidating a complex situation of which a restorer contemplating treatment of the picture would need to be aware.

(17) Rawlins, F. I. G. 'Physical factors in X-ray photography.' *Technical Studies in the Field of the Fine Arts*, VII (1937), pp. 74–79.

(18) Wolters, Christian. *Die Bedeutung der Gemäldedurchleuchtung mit Röntgenstrahlen für die Kunstgeschichte* (X-ray examination of paintings and its significance for the history of art). Frankfurt-am-Main, 1938. 138 pp., illus.

See below under Burroughs, A. (No. (19)) for critical review.

(19) Burroughs, Alan. *Art criticism from a laboratory*. Boston, 1938. 277 pp., illus.

The above two books dealing with the use of X-rays in the examination of paintings both appeared in 1938 – a characteristic instance of two authors in different parts of the world simultaneously getting hold of a topic which is 'in the air'. The month of publication is mentioned in neither case, so it is not possible to say which of the two books is earlier. However, they only partly cover the same ground. Both authors have great experience in the interpretation of X-ray photographs of paintings by old masters and explain the application of the comparatively new method (although a limited amount of X-ray examination of paint and paintings had been done as far back as the end of the 19th century and even by Röntgen himself, the discoverer of X-rays). Both authors give examples of how X-radiographs reveal details of the painter's technique which are not visible in ordinary light (unfortunately the photographic plates published do not always show clearly the points mentioned in the text) and they apply these discoveries to style criticism.

Wolters, with a broad yet acute understanding of Renaissance painting techniques, clearly distinguishes between three main ways of creating light and form and of building up a painting, and draws well-documented and precise conclusions regarding style from his technical findings. A brilliant example is the revelation of the feathery touch of the Hausbuch Master (so unmistakable in his drawings) below the smooth surface of his paintings. Another example is the contrast made between the portrait painter's naturalistic petty details with the *Idealform*, for instance in the works of Dürer. Equally well-founded are his comparative analyses of X-radiographs of original masters and eclectic works. His discussion of *pentimenti* is also valuable.

By comparison Burroughs' approach is more speculative and more in the conventional art historical tradition, also, in my view, a little over self-confident.

Bibliography

It is a pity that both authors, not themselves being painters or paint technicians, felt obliged to take over wholesale Doerner's unproven theories of 'Mischtechnik' and his surmise that 'a thinly tinted grisaille' was the general practice of most old masters in commencing their works.

Unfortunately Wolters' important pioneer work has never been published outside Germany and so is known to comparatively few readers. It would be a rewarding though difficult task to translate into equivalent English Wolters' distinguished German style.

(H.R.)

(20) RAWLINS, F. I. G. 'Physical factors in X-ray photography.' *Technical Studies in the Field of the Fine Arts*, VII (1937), pp. 74–79.

(21) RAWLINS, F. I. G. 'X-rays in the study of pictures.' *The British Journal of Radiology*, XII (1939), pp. 239–245.

Useful physical data.

1940

(22) ELLIOT, William J. 'The use of Roentgen rays in the scientific examination of paintings.' *American Journal of Roentgenology, Radium Therapy and Nuclear Medicine* (Springfield, Ill.), L (1943), pp. 779–790.

A description of the technique of X-radiography used at the time at the Worcester Art Museum (Mass.). (An interesting side-light of this article is the diagnosis by the author, a physician, of the ailments which various sitters for portraits described must have suffered from).

(23) PEASE, Murray. 'A note on the radiography of paintings.' *Bulletin of the Metropolitan Museum of Art* (New York), IV (1945–46), pp. 136–139.

A method is described of rotating film and picture in order to eliminate from the X-radiograph the image of obstructions, such as cradles applied to the back of the panel support.

(24) MARCONI, Bohdan. 'Roentgenografia Obrázow; Nowe Polskie urzadzenia i Metody' ('New Polish methods and devices for the X-raying of pictures'). *Ochrona Zabytków* (Warsaw), II (1949), pp. 25–30. French summary.

Included is a description of pioneer work on stereo X-radiography.

1950

(25) HOURS, Madeleine. 'La radiographie des tableaux de Léonard de Vinci' ('Radiography of pictures by Leonardo da Vinci'). *Revue des Arts* (Paris), No. 4 (1952), pp. 227–236.

The results of X-ray examinations of paintings by Leonardo carried out on the occasion of the exhibition 'Hommage à Léonard de Vinci.'

(26) PETRYN, Andrew. 'A note on X-rays and the visual pattern of the cradle.' *Journal of the Walters Art Gallery, Baltimore, Special Technical Issue*, XV–XVI (1952–53), pp. 46–47.

Diminution of the effect of the cradle was obtained by arranging the X-ray beam to

Bibliography

strike the surface of the picture at about 20° from the horizontal instead of perpendicularly.

(27) VERMEHREN, August. 'Sulle possibilità stereo-strato-radiografiche di un nuovo tipo di apparechio a raggi X in dotazione presso l'Istituto Centrale del Restauro in Roma' ('The possibility of stereo-strato-radiography with a new type of X-ray apparatus at the Istituto del Restauro in Roma.' *Bollettino dell'Istituto Centrale del Restauro*, XI–XII (1952), pp. 121–133.

(28) RAWLINS, F. I. G. 'Soft X-rays in the examination of paintings.' *Studies in Conservation*, I (1954), pp. 132–135.

The application of low voltage X-rays (about 6–12 K.V.) in the examination of thinly painted pictures.

(29) NORDENFALK, Carl. 'The new X-rays of Rembrandt's Claudius Civilis.' *Konsthistorisk Tidskrift* (Stockholm), XXV (1956), p. 30.

The use of extra large-size X-ray film to cover a very large picture without too many joins in the composite X-radiograph.

(30) RICHARDS, Albert G. 'A method for radiographing the topography of oil paintings.' *Studies in Conservation*, II (1956), pp. 189–191.

Radiographic study of the surface of paintings.

(31) VAN SCHENDEL, Arthur. 'Notes on the support of Rembrandt's *Claudius Civilis*.' *Konsthistorisk Tidskrift* (Stockholm), XXV (1956), pp. 38–42.

Application of X-radiography to the study of different types of canvas support.

(32) BRIDGMAN, C. F., KECK, S. and SHERWOOD, H. F. 'The radiography of panel paintings by electron emission.' *Studies in Conservation*, III (1958), pp. 175–182.

A method which can be used to obtain a radiographic image of the paint film of pictures, such as those on metal supports, which it is not possible to examine by ordinary X-radiography.

(33) CONRAN, G. L. and REES JONES, S. 'X-rays at Kenwood.' *The Museums Journal* (London), LVII (1958), pp. 237–231.

X-radiography of pictures in the collection of the Iveagh Bequest, Kenwood House, London; of technical interest for the use of a portable X-ray set operating at around 100 K.V.

(34) VAN SCHENDEL, A. 'The ghosts of the Staelmeisters.' *Museums Journal* (London), LVII (1958), pp. 234–236.

X-radiographs of Rembrandt's famous portrait group showed pentimenti and an unusual type of canvas. Extra-long strips of film and simultaneous exposure of several of such strips were used in order to avoid accidental differences in density of the developed and printed X-ray films.

(35) VERHAEGEN, Nicole. 'Revers de volets peints révélés par radiographie' ('The reverse of painted shutters revealed by radiography'). *Bulletin de l'Institut Royal du Patrimoine Artistique* (Brussels), I (1958), pp. 96–102.

The wings of a triptych, the *Adoration of the Magi* by Jean Provost, were shown to have earlier compositions beneath their visible paintings.

Bibliography

1960

(36) Hours, Madeleine. 'Nicolas Poussin: étude radiographique au Laboratoire du Musée du Louvre' ('Nicholas Poussin: radiographic study at the Laboratory of the Louvre Museum'). *Bulletin du Laboratoire du Musée du Louvre*, V (1960), pp. 3–39.

A study of radiographs taken of the pictures by Poussin in the Louvre collection on the occasion of the Poussin exhibition held at the Louvre in 1960. Interesting from both a technical and an art historical standpoint.

(37) Rees Jones, S. 'Notes on radiographs of five paintings by Poussin.' *The Burlington Magazine*, CII (1960), pp. 304–308.

An example of interpretation of radiographs on a scientific basis.

(38) Loose, Louis. 'La stéréoradiographie' ('Stereo-radiography'). *Studies in Conservation*, V (1960), pp. 85–88. English summary.

3-dimensional X-radiographs of objects of art including paintings.

(39) Kozlowski, Rudolf. 'La microstéréoradiographie' ('Microstereoradiography'). *Studies in Conservation*, V (1960), pp. 89–101. English summary.

(40) Bridgman, C. and Keck, S. 'The radiography of paintings.' *Medical Radiography and Photography* (Rochester, U.S.A.), XXXVII (1960), No. 3, pp. 62–70.

(41) Wehlte, Kurt. 'Röntgenographische Aufnahmetechnik von Gemälden' ('The technique of taking X-radiographs of paintings'). *Maltechnik*, LXVIII (1962), pp. 45–51.

(42) Horner, Helmut. 'Röntgenuntersuchung von Gemälden' ('X-ray investigation of paintings'). *Forschung und Fertigung* (Berlin), II (1963), pp. 6–11.

Useful data on the radiography of paintings.

(43) Bridgman, Charles F. 'The amazing patent on the radiography of paintings.' *Studies in Conservation*, IX (1964), pp. 135–139.

A most interesting account of the early history of the application of X-rays to the examination of paintings, an application dating back almost to the discovery of X-rays by Roentgen.

(44) Loose, Louis. 'La stratiradiographie et le tirage cathodique — une amélioration de la technique radiographique' ('Strati-radiography — an improvement in radiographic technique'). *Bulletin de l'Institut Royal du Patrimoine Artistique* (Brussels), VII (1964), pp. 172–186.

(45) Ruggles, Mervyn. 'An illuminator for viewing composite X-ray films.' *Studies in Conservation*, IX (1964), pp. 23–28.

(46) Bridgman, C., Michaels, P. and Sherwood, H. F. 'Radiography of a painting on copper by electron emission.' *Studies in Conservation*, X (1965), pp. 1–7.

By this means it is possible to obtain a radiograph of the paint film of a picture on a metal support, which would be impossible with ordinary X-ray photography.

(47) Meier-Siem, M. 'Die Röntgenuntersuchung von Gemälden' ('X-ray investigation of pictures'). *Röntgen-Blätter* (Offenburg, Wuppertal), XVIII (1965), pp. 406–419.

The technique of radiography of paintings, together with examples of X-rays of pictures by Rembrandt and the author's interpretation of them.

Index

Index

Index

Black and alizarin orange, for transparent deep brown, 247, 250

'Black oils' (Maroger), 404 (35)

'Black soap' for cleaning, 377, 378, 380

Blanching (see Pl. 66), possible causes of, 186, 197; indicating overpainting, 179; on a Michelangelo, 316

Bleaching: of prints, drawings, 410; of mould spots, 410

Blisters, 151, Pls. 39, 41; on Bellini's 'Virgin and Child', 152; laying and pricking, 21, 149, 385, 396, 397; new apparatus for treating, 445 (1); treating with size, 186; on wood paintings, 431 (2); blistering by fire, 412

Bloch, Martin: in south of France with H.R., 32; painting with Misch-Weiss, 360

Block, H. T., 451, 461

Blockx, J., 393

Bloom, blooming phenomenon, 317, 390, 443 (13); an 1808 mention of, 383 (21); final wax coating reducing risk of, 319 n; of older varnishes, 359; removal of, 403 (29)

Blues: 'blue distance' as Renaissance discovery, 238; 'blue shadows' as Impressionist discovery, 238; ten different blues in Botticelli's 'Adoration of the Kings', 105; azurite, 248, 249, 316, 472 (106); blue bice as copper pigment, 248; blue verditer, ultramarine, etc., 472 (106), *and see* Cobalt, Cerulean, Indigo, Lapis lazuli, Prussian blue, Ultramarine, etc., as separate entries; 'blue starch' for cleaning, 377 (Sanderson); blue-wool scale for measuring light-fastness, 457 (34)

'Blurring of images' fallacy, 229, 231

Blunt, A., 419

von Bode, Dr. W., 41, 42

Böhm, F., transfer method of (panel paintings), 162

Boissonnas, A. G., 408, 435

Boissonnas, P., 433

Boleslawski, J., 433

Bollettino d'Arte, Rome, 371

Bollettino dell' Istituto Centrale del Restauro, Rome, 288, 370; some accounts of particular restorations in, 413

Bologna, rate of cleaning at, 213

Bones, R. A., 466

Bonifazio, Giorgione's 'Adoration of the Magi' attributed to, before its cleaning, 238

Bonnard paintings: size paintings on cardboard, risk of using wax on, 154; some deliberately left unvarnished, 269; special advice to etchers of, 352-3

Bontinck, E., 464

Borelli-Vlad, L., 373

Borghese Gallery, a restoration at described, 413 (5)

Borghini, 'Il Riposo', *see* Procacci, U., 374

Bosch, Hieronymus: early abandons 'smooth handling', 352; half-tones of, 352

Boston, Isabella Stewart Gardner Museum, 55, 80, 256 n, 274; Museum of Fine Arts: (Sir) Philip Hendy at, 22, 43; research laboratories at, since 1930, 54, 468

Bottari, Giovanni, *Raccolta di Lettere*, 245 n; *see* Procacci, U., 374

Botticelli, 'The Adoration of the Kings', Pls. 25-8; technical analysis of, 103-16; changes to work, since leaving master's workshop, 110, 113, 114; colour layers in, 113-14; egg tempera characteristics shown (e.g. early craquelure), 113; foam craters in, 113, 115; fourteen elements seen in small hole, 110; green underpainting of flesh, 113, 115; macrophotograph of detail, 110, 111; medium, nature of tempera, investigated, 113, 115; monochrome form stage, 113; monochrome undermodelling of Renaissance painters, 114, 116; orange varnish stain in cracks, 115; panchromatic detail (*under 20 heads*), 106; pentimenti, major and minor, 109, 114; red paint, cross-section of, 105 (Diag. 4); X-ray photograph of, 31 details, 108-9

Boustead, W. D., 409, 449

Bouts, Dierk, technique of, *see* Coremans, 57

Bouvier, P. L., 50, 383, 384

'Boxing' pictures against deterioration, 102

Brachert, T., 406, 432, 436, 438, 439, 461

Bradley, Morton C., *The Treatment of Pictures*, 162 n, 198 n, 234 n, 270 n, 361, 421; on desirability of complete cleaning, for technical reasons, 80 n; M. Bradley Jr., and Reforming method, 204

Bragg, Sir William, F.R.S., 134

Brammer, H., 434

Branched alcohols, *see* Alcohols, Isopropyl and Isobutyl

Brandi, Professor Cesare, 80, 86, 97, 359, 405, 415, 424, 426, 427; and rigattino technique, 258; 'Il fondamento teorico del restauro', 72 n; 'Il Restauro secondo l'Istanza Estetica', 86, 86 n; 'Il restauro e l'interpretazione dell'opera d'arte', 258 n; 'The Restoration of the "Pietà" of Sebastiano del Piombo', 80, 86, 228, 228 n

Brandt, W., 435

Bredius, A. B., 372

Brick and water cleaning (early malpractice), 382 (19)

Bridgman, C. F., 475, 476, 480, 481; and Gibson, H. L., on infra-red luminescence, 127

Bristol Art Gallery: art history students at School of Art, 77; study group, 450 (15)

British and Colonial Printer, The, 141 n

British Journal of Aesthetics, 232 n

British Museum, science laboratories of 1921, 54

British Restorers Association, 23

Brittleness in oil paintings, 101, 102

Brjantzev, A., 460

Index

Index

Index

Index

Index

Index

Index

Index

Index

Index

Index

Index

Index

Index

Index

Index

Index